Mozart

A Musical Biography

KONRAD KÜSTER

Translated by Mary Whittall

CLARENDON PRESS · OXFORD

1996

Oxford University Press, Walton Street, Oxford OX2 6DP

Oxford New York
Athens Auckland Bangkok Bombay
Calcutta Cape Town Dar es Salaam Delhi
Florence Hong Kong Istanbul Karachi
Kuala Lumpur Madras Madrid Melbourne
Mexico City Nairobi Paris Singapore
Taipei Tokyo Toronto
and associated companies in
Berlin Ibadan

Oxford is a trade mark of Oxford University Press

Published in the United States
by Oxford University Press Inc., New York

First published in German © Deutsche Verlags-Anstalt GmbH Stuttgart 1990

English translation © Oxford University Press 1996

British Library Cataloguing in Publication Data
Data available

Library of Congress Cataloging in Publication Data
Küster, Konrad.
[Mozart. English]
Mozart: a musical biography / Konrad Küster;
translated by Mary Whittall.
p. cm.
Originally published: Stuttgart: Deutsche Verlags-Anstalt, 1990.
Includes bibliographical references and index.
1. Mozart, Wolfgang Amadeus, 1756–1791—Criticism and
interpretation. I. Whittall, Mary. II. Title.
ML410.M9K9813 1996 780'.92—dc20 [B] 95-35042
ISBN 0–19–816339–8

1 3 5 7 9 10 8 6 4 2

Typeset by Best-set Typesetter Ltd., Hong Kong
Printed in Great Britain
on acid-free paper by
Biddles Ltd., Guildford and King's Lynn

Acknowledgements

I would like to express my gratitude first and foremost to Wolfgang Plath and Wolfgang Rehm, the editors of the Neue Mozart-Ausgabe in Augsburg and Salzburg, for help in several different forms; further, to Alan Tyson for guidance in several significant matters of detail, to Peter Branscombe and Cliff Eisen for a series of valuable suggestions for improvements, and to Bruce Cooper Clarke for a stimulating exchange of ideas. I must also thank the libraries whose resources I was able to use, and Mary Whittall—not for her labours as translator alone but also for the points she raised in the role of general reader.

KONRAD KÜSTER

Grafenhausen, May 1994

Acknowledgement is made for permission to reproduce material from the following sources:

Augsburg, Mozart-Gedenkstätte: Pls. 3, 5, 7
Berlin, Staatsbibliothek Preussischer Kulturbesitz, Musikabteilung: Pl. 4
New York, Pierpont Morgan Library: front and rear endpapers
Salzburg, Internationale Stiftung Mozarteum: Pl. 1
Vienna, Historisches Museum der Stadt Wien: Pl. 12
Vienna, Österreichische Nationalbibliothek, Musiksammlung: Pl. 15 (Mus. Hs. 17.561, fo. 87r.)
Vienna, Stadtbibliothek: Pl. 14
Private collection: Pl. 6
Bie, O., *Die Oper* (Berlin, 1913): Pl. 8
Bory, R., *Wolfgang Amadeus Mozart* (Geneva, 1948): Pl. 2
Hutchings, A., *Mozart, der Musiker* (Baarn, 1976): Pl. 9
Kunze, S., *Mozarts Opern* (Stuttgart, 1984): Pl. 10
Stefan, P., *Don Giovanni* (Vienna, Leipzig, Zurich, 1938): Pl. 11
Wagner, M., *Mozart, Sinfonie C-Dur KV 551* (Mainz, 1979): Pl. 13

Reproduction material for the plates from sources in Augsburg, New York, Salzburg, and Vienna was made available by Bärenreiter-Verlag, Kassel.

Acknowledgements

The music examples are based on the Neue Mozart-Ausgabe (Bärenreiter-Verlag, Kassel); the music examples from *Così fan tutte* are based on the study score published by Eulenburg.

This translation is based on the text of the second German edition (1991), which was further revised by the author.

Preface

'The music is by the celebrated Herr Mozart'

Such were the words that first acquainted audiences in Donaueschingen—then the chief city of the principality of Fürstenberg—with the identity of the composer of *Le nozze di Figaro*.[1] That was in 1787; today, it is highly unlikely that a statement to that effect on a poster advertising a performance of the work would cause anyone to raise an eyebrow. Yet in Mozart's day the suggestion that it would still be played two centuries later would have provoked surprise: pieces of music were expected to go out of fashion like other artefacts. Even when the great biography of Mozart by his widow's second husband, Georg Nikolaus Nissen, appeared in 1828, the year of Schubert's death, it was prefaced by the admonition: 'If there is any other whose music grows not old after forty years, but still gives ever-increasing delight, he, and he alone, may dispute Mozart's pre-eminence.'[2] Now, more than five times forty years have passed since Mozart's death in 1791.

Today we often encounter Mozart while still children, sometimes in the form of stories about the child prodigy, exhibiting biographical fancifulness and the 'Aaah!' factor to some degree or another, sometimes when we start to learn the piano and pieces with single-figure Köchel numbers are placed before the 'young player' as salutations from 'the young Mozart'. He is one of that select band of composers who occupy an unconditional leading position in the concert-hall, the opera-house, the record shops, and the broadcasting studios, one of the happy few whose work unites music-lovers of all complexions, not just the fans of so-called 'classical' music but also those who stumble on him by chance, perhaps on the sound-track of award-winning films like *Out of Africa* (the Clarinet Concerto) or *Amadeus* (the early G minor Symphony). There is no knowing when one will meet Mozart; he is everywhere.

Mozart's music is also one of the focal centres of musical scholarship, an area in which substantial new discoveries have been made since the 200th

---

[1] On Donaueschingen, see K. Küster in *Baden und Württemberg im Zeitalter Napoleons* (exhibition catalogue; Stuttgart, 1987), i/2, 896 (item 1473).

[2] Nissen, *Biographie*, 1.

PL. I. Mozart at the keyboard with his sister and father, winter 1780–1. Oil painting by Johann Nepomuk della Croce. A portrait of Mozart's mother (died 1778) hangs on the wall.

anniversary of his birth in 1956. At the heart of this work lie the revelations in the new standard edition of his works, the Neue Mozart-Ausgabe. This started production in 1954 and the last of the volumes containing the music itself appeared in 1991. The meticulous study of the sources also laid firm foundations for new work on matters of interpretation: the deeper the delving into the sources, the more new and fascinating secrets have been brought to light (notably in the most recent Mozart centenary year, 1991). The study of the music has been underpinned by archival research; a new edition of all the surviving letters of the Mozart family and a collection of the available documents about the composer's life are helping to improve the links between biographical and musicological approaches. At the same time the Neue Mozart-Ausgabe provides an utterly reliable basis for inter-pretation and analysis of the works. Thus the circle is completed: the ubiquity of Mozart's music is due as much to the discoveries made by scholars as to the modern media, especially recordings, which in turn have had a lasting effect on what is now expected of biographers. It is no longer acceptable for biographies of musicians to spotlight the events of their lives alone: the works must receive more detailed attention than hitherto. The fact that even pieces which once languished in the remoter corners of Köchel's catalogue are now available for home listening to every collector of cassettes and CDs makes it imperative that the music should be regarded as one of the 'sources' of a biography of Mozart. The prime objective of this book is therefore to produce a 'musical biography' in which Mozart's works occupy the foreground, and to follow the course of the composer's life by the light of selected compositions. The approach is different from that of a 'pure' biography, which rounds out the stations of a life while casting only an occasional glance at individual works. This biography is concerned primarily with the work and the place its creation takes in the life—the artistic development which cannot be separated from the life. It may be a stonier path than that followed by traditional biographical writing, but a composer as popular as Mozart positively challenges the writer to take it.

Listening habits have changed since Mozart's time. It is not simply that we are accustomed to a greater volume of sound than his contemporaries were, nor can it be said that we have a worse relationship to music than they did, for they can scarcely have had the opportunities to hear so much music—and such a wide variety—as we do. But the fact that we have learnt to hear, understand, and value music written since 1800 gets in the way of our comprehension of things that Mozart's contemporaries appreciated as veiled but nevertheless unambiguous utterances by a composer; the sense of music that we perceive as merely 'beautiful' has to be explained to us, like the point of a joke in a foreign language. To be sure, we cannot re-create the listening habits of the people of a past age, but some penetration of the 'secrets' of their music is still possible.

Every biographer is forced to go more deeply into some periods in his subject's life than others, and that remains the case when one approaches Mozart via his music. Some of his best-loved works can therefore be mentioned only in passing; others may look relatively unimportant to a reader skimming the index, but as a rule they will be found either to provide a vantage-point from which to consider some biographical landmark or musically significant detail, or to allow a connection to be made with a person whom it was important for Mozart to meet. On the other hand, one problem is special to this particular subject: the Mozart who occupies such an unassailable position in the mind of posterity is not represented by works from every creative period of his life; that particular image is based on isolated compositions produced by the child prodigy, a selection of the works written by the young man in his Salzburg period, and finally a dense succession of works from the ten years in Vienna. These three groups are irregularly distributed in the life, but the biographer must also attend to those periods in which Mozart composed practically nothing really 'famous'. This unique circumstance deserves a chapter to itself, but the centre of attention inevitably lies among the later works.

Individual compositions by Mozart have had entire books written about them, notably the seven great operas. This is not only because of their length and substance but also on account of their many facets and the allusions which may escape modern audiences, even when a work is being sung in its original language to listeners who understand the Italian or German text. The problems increase when it is given in a 'singing' version in another language, for in the latter the exact sense is sacrificed all too often to the overriding imperative to match the number of syllables to the number of notes. There are producers, furthermore, who miss the opportunity to work Mozart's musical 'stage directions'—as well as those of the librettist—into their versions. The operas cannot be considered in depth in this book, but attention is focused on certain especially significant details: passages where Mozart played an active role in the dramatic conception, going beyond the librettist's ideas. The associations within each opera can thus be seen in a completely new light; where the text is quoted, the translation given here follows the original closely, rather than using a 'singing' version.

An anonymous poem entitled *Mozart's Tod*, which dates from shortly after 1800, describes how the sounds from Mozart's lyre mount from the banks of the Danube and reach the heavens, where they move Zeus to send Hermes to earth to raise the mortal to Olympus; the messenger wings his way earthwards, then hurries back to report that the composer is no mere mortal but a god—'Er ist ein Gott...'.[3] Such convictions about Mozart have been a prominent feature over the years in discussion of both his life and his work. The words 'Er ist ein Gott' contrast strikingly with the words used by Sarastro in *Die Zauberflöte* to overcome the priests' objections to Tamino's royal rank: 'Er ist Mensch'—'He is a man'. Do we not in fact rank Mozart's work even higher if we view it as an artist's fascinating play with the possibilities of his art? Some of the things in

---

[3] Nissen, *Biographie*, Anhang, 196.

Mozart's music that we are accustomed to admire as 'divine' seem to be so precisely calculated and so coolly thought out that genius manifests itself more cogently in the intention than in the element of happy chance. It is from the standpoint provided by this biographical principle that the forty snapshots are taken, in which this book will attempt to approach Mozart's career as mortal man and as musician.

Contents

Contents

Contents

List of Plates

Author's Note

Ludwig Ritter von Köchel (1800–77) planned his *Verzeichnis sämtlicher Tonwerke W. A. Mozart's* as a complete chronological list. Since the publication of the first edition of his catalogue in 1862 works that were lost have been rediscovered, while others have been found to be unauthentic and have been struck off the register; furthermore, later research has invalidated some of Köchel's dating. Although Köchel's original numbering has therefore become out of date, incomplete, and in places unreliable, his numbers were so widely accepted that it would have been ill advised to replace them by an entirely new enumeration, and the traditional numbers remained in use. Nevertheless, the catalogue needed to be brought, and kept, up to date without losing its chronological basis. The last revision of Köchel's original numbering was introduced by the editors of the sixth edition (1964), itself now in need of revision. The revised numbers are rarely encountered in general use (and then usually in parentheses after the traditional numbers). In the present volume they are shown, where necessary, with the prefix K⁶.

Abbreviations

ISM   Internationale Stiftung Mozarteum

MDB   O. E. Deutsch (ed.), *Mozart: Die Dokumente seines Lebens* (German and English editions)

MJb   *Mozart-Jahrbuch*

NMA   Neue Mozart-Ausgabe

Full details of other books and articles cited in notes exclusively in short form are given in the Select Bibliography, pp. 393–5.

1

The Minuet as a Teaching Medium: Mozart's Earliest Compositions (to c.1763)

In the first weeks of 1756 Leopold Mozart, then a 36-year-old chamber musician in the service of the Prince-Archbishop of Salzburg, was busy with the final pre-publication stages of a book which assured his place in the history of music. Before the year was out his *Versuch einer gründlichen Violinschule* was published in his home town of Augsburg by Johann Jacob Lotter, a Protestant whose business came mainly from the publishing of Catholic church music. Following the treatises on flute-playing by Johann Joachim Quantz, the virtuoso and teacher of Frederick the Great (1752), and on keyboard-playing by Carl Philipp Emanuel Bach, harpsichordist to the Prussian court and son of the great Johann Sebastian (1753), Leopold Mozart's book on the violin was the third in a few years to rank as a significant study of an individual instrument and, in the widest sense, of its potential for integration into musical life.

Much of Leopold Mozart's time in the early part of 1756, therefore, was spent in correspondence with Lotter about the preparation of his book, dealing with such questions as layout and the correction of printers' errors. It is perhaps not very surprising that—apart from the entry in the baptismal register of Salzburg Cathedral—the earliest mention of his new-born son comes in a letter to Lotter:

I have news, by the way, that on 27 January, at eight in the evening, my wife was safely delivered of a boy, though the afterbirth had to be removed and she was amazingly weak afterwards. But now, thank God, child and mother are both well. She commends herself to you both. The boy is called Joannes Chrisostomos, Wolfgang, Gottlieb. (9 February 1756)

The baby was baptized in the cathedral on 28 January. The first element of his name comes from his being born on the feast-day of St John Chrysostom. Instead of 'Gottlieb' the baptismal register gives the Greek form of the name, 'Theophilus', after the child's godfather, the merchant

Johann Theophil Pergmayr, who sometimes used the Latinate alternative 'Amadeus', much as his godson later signed himself 'Amadeo' or 'Amadè'.

Work on the *Violinschule* was only one of many tasks that kept Leopold Mozart busy around the time of his son's birth. He complained in another letter to Lotter:

I can tell you, I've so much to do that sometimes I don't know if I'm on my head or my heels, not because of over-much composition but because of over-many scholars and the operas at the court. And as you know yourself, when a man's wife is lying in, there is always some visitor or another to steal his time. These things eat up money and time. (12 February 1756)

His grumble about his 'scholars'—pupils—is more likely to reflect on them as individuals than to indicate a dislike of teaching in itself, for Leopold Mozart was without doubt a passionate pedagogue. That much was still evident two years before his death, when he was looking after a grandchild, the son of his daughter Nannerl. The child was scarcely 3 months old when Leopold Mozart wrote:

I cannot look at the child's right hand without emotion. The most skilled clavier-player cannot place his hand upon the keyboard as beautifully as he constantly holds his; whenever he is not moving his fingers about, they stay in the playing position, with his hand curved, and when he is asleep he lets his little hand lie as if the fingers really rested on the keys, with the best possible proportion in the spread and curve of the fingers. In short, it is the most beautiful thing you ever saw! I am often really sad when I see it, and wish he were but 3 years old, or more, for I am certain he would be able to play at once quite naturally. (11 November 1785)

There is no reason to suppose he had felt any differently about his children.

'Joannes Chrysostomus Wolfgangus Theophilus' was the seventh and last child of his parents. Of the earlier children, only Maria Anna, born in 1751 and called Nannerl, had survived. (One of the two boys who had died in infancy had, incidentally, also been given the name Amadeus.) Nannerl, four and a half years the elder, became her father's pupil first; it was for her that Leopold in 1759 compiled the 'Nannerl-Notenbuch' (Nannerl's Music Book), from which her brother began to study as early as 1760. Mozart was then 4 years old. (Nannerl's son may have begun keyboard tuition at a slightly earlier age; there were clearly parallels.) At first Mozart learnt the pieces from Nannerl's Music Book by ear, before he could read the notation. This makes it one of the most important documents for any biographer, because it gives an invaluable and profound insight into the progress of Mozart's early music lessons. After the first eight minuets his

father notes summarily: 'The preceding eight minuets were learnt by
Wolfgangerl at the age of 4', and there are similar remarks against two
later works. Finally we find this against a scherzo by Georg Christoph
Wagenseil, composer at the court of Vienna: 'Wolfgangerl learnt this piece
on 24 January 1761, three days before his fifth birthday, between 9 and
9.30 at night.' Two days later he mastered a minuet and a trio at the
same evening hour; as Nannerl Mozart told Friedrich Schlichtegroll, her
brother's biographer, in the second of the memoirs she wrote for him in
the spring and summer of 1792: 'From his early childhood onwards, he
liked best to play and compose at night and in the early morning. When
he sat down at the keyboard at nine in the evening, he could not be
persuaded to leave it before midnight. I believe he would have played all
night long.'

Only a short time later Mozart began to compose. It is easy to see how
he did it: his very earliest works survive only in his father's handwriting, for
he himself had not yet learnt to write music. He must have improvised at
the keyboard, therefore, and Leopold Mozart wrote down what he heard.
Even in the role of amanuensis, it would not have been right for the father
to be completely uncritical of the 5-year-old's creations, and so, as time
went on, Leopold Mozart must have introduced improvements here and
there in order to teach the child something as he composed.

Leopold Mozart probably wrote all these compositions down in
Nannerl's Music Book.[1] A number of pages, notably the most 'valuable',
were torn out of it at some later date and dispersed to the four winds, but
the surviving separate sheets can be proved beyond doubt to have come
originally from the album. Thus it is that Mozart's earliest surviving
composition is not K. 1: one of the most sensational of the finds that made
the revision of Köchel's catalogue necessary[2] was undoubtedly that of the
four keyboard pieces by Mozart, from Nannerl's Music Book, that came to
light in the Mozart bicentenary year of 1956.[3] Their existence had previously been completely unknown, but it was established that they must have
been written earlier than the accredited K. 1 (which had in the mean time
been recognized to consist of two separate minuets rather than a minuet
and trio). They were given the numbers 1*a–d* in the sixth edition of
Köchel, and the old K. 1 pieces duly appeared in the revised numbering as
1*e–f*. Mozart's earliest surviving work—and it must be one of the very first

---

[1] On all questions of the chronology of Mozart's works, see W. Plath in NMA IX/27,
vol. i, pp. xviii–xxi, and Tyson, *Mozart*, 61–72.

[2] See Author's Note, p. xvii. [3] Dent and Valentin, *Der früheste Mozart*.

he composed—is thus an Andante for keyboard. It is ten bars long, and after a mere four bars the tempo switches from 3/4 to 2/4. The first section really consists of only two bars of music, but each of them is repeated immediately. The music of the second section comprises a motivically somewhat amorphous cadential figure which is also repeated. Matters are not helped by some elementary technical mistakes. The twelve-bar Allegro, K^6 1*b*, in 2/4 time like the second part of the Andante, covers roughly similar musical ground. Leopold Mozart captioned the two pieces: 'Wolfgangerl's compositions in the first three months after his fifth birthday'.

The sequence of dates by which Mozart's musical development can be followed continues without a break in these two pieces: three days before his fifth birthday his father noted merely that he had learnt to play a piece, then within the next three months he learnt to compose music as well. These earliest pieces are not 'great music' in the strict sense of the term, of course, but there could hardly be a more shining testimony to what composing prodigies can achieve by the light of their unaided gifts and how much they still have to learn. A poet of genius, born in the age of Mozart, had to learn what a hexameter is, how to write alternating rhyme, and how to distinguish an iamb from a trochee; similarly his gifts alone could not tell the 5-year-old Mozart how to write ten bars of music without changing the time signature, or that consecutive (and hidden) fifths are normally frowned on, or how to give a short piece inner unity by means of tonality and thematic development. These are things that can be learnt, however, and a passionate pedagogue like Leopold Mozart knows how to space out the instruction so that lessons encourage gifts and help them to develop. The pedagogic passion was wedded to an archivist's meticulousness. It is scarcely conceivable that he would have thrown away one of his son's pieces because it was musically worthless; he also dated each work precisely. Thanks to this aspect of Leopold Mozart's character it is also possible to reconstruct, to a considerable extent, Mozart's progress as a composition pupil. What, then, did he learn in the period in which his earliest pieces were written?

The Andante, K^6 1*a*, in which the time signatures were of course contributed by Leopold Mozart, remains the only piece with that idio-syncratic, unmotivated change of tempo, for which the most obvious explanation is that Mozart had not yet learnt how to distribute the stresses within longer stretches of music. He already knew that small musical elements, such as those in the first section of his piece, can be repeated, and that in the second section the fingers are allowed to move more freely within the bounds of the cadential formulas that they have already explored in learning to play. The composition of K⁶ 1*b* shows no advances on that, but in the mean time experience has shown Mozart that it is unnecessary to change the tempo in a twelve-bar piece.

There are no compositions dating from the spring and summer of 1761. This does not necessarily mean that Mozart did not compose during that time, but it may reflect his 'compositional' practice. Mozart's earliest works are preserved only if his father wrote them down; it is possible, therefore, that the child continued to improvise as often as before, but without Leopold Mozart recording the results—perhaps because he regarded them as merely work in progress.[4] The next two pieces, an Allegro and a Minuet (both in F major, K⁶ 1*c–d*), date from December 1761. They show few of the uncertainties of the two previous compositions. In the ten months separating the two pairs of pieces Mozart has learnt some of the functions of a double bar with repetition marks in the middle of a piece—a fundamental characteristic of dance music. It can separate a thematically primary musical unit from a following, subordinate one, after which the first can return to round off the movement (K⁶ 1*c*, 11 December 1761); and it can mark the arrival at a new key (the dominant) which it is later possible to leave. In order to do that the initial key must first be presented at sufficient length and then modulated convincingly, and the second part must find the way back to the tonic, using new material of its own (K⁶ 1*d*, 16 December 1761).

Mozart does not lose his grasp on what he has learnt: in the next two pieces (K. 2 and 3, January/March 1762) he actually combines the two elements. Now, before the double bar, he has not only the 'subject', which will return at the end, but also a discrete modulation, which he will of course have to deny himself at the end. But what is far more important is the fact that Mozart learns in these pieces how to develop musical motifs. Hitherto repetition and contrast were the only means he knew of establishing a relationship between small musical elements, but now he can be seen learning the meaning of sequence. He does it at the keyboard, not on paper—that is, he plays a little musical phrase, then repeats it a tone lower without any other alteration (in K. 4 he will repeat it a tone higher as well). To do it he only needs to move his hands the space of one key, and

---

[4] See K. Küster, 'Mozarts elementarer Kompositionsunterricht', *Üben and Musizieren*, 8/6 (1991), 11–18.

they can go on following broadly the same motoric pattern as before. By May 1762 (Minuet, K. 4), now 6 years old, Mozart has learnt the use of moving the hands the distance of a fifth: it enables the 'modulation' segment from before the double bar to return at the end of the piece, transposed from the dominant to the tonic. All of this demonstrates a phenomenal musical memory: for the refinement of this latest minuet in particular, the 6-year-old composer needed to remember exactly what he had improvised in the middle of the piece in order to be able to reproduce it a fifth lower at the end.

He still had some way to go before he was ready to compose the two minuets which were known for so long as K. 1 (see Pl. 2). He wrote them out himself, in a confident albeit childish hand, and in learning to write music he had apparently also found out how to vary sequential passages so that there is more to the process than the purely mechanical change in the position of the hands. Apart from these additions to his fund of technical knowledge, the two pieces remain within the range of what he had previously learnt: bars 1–4 of the first minuet call for parallel transposition

Pl. 2. 'Minuet and Trio, K. 1' (now two minuets, K[6] 1e and 1f). Autograph manuscript of Mozart, aged 7 or 8.

of the hands, the first half of the piece modulates from the tonic (G major) to the dominant (D major), the conclusion of the second part recycles that of the first part (although it enjoys the new freedom acquired with the composer's ability to write). Above all, however, something more than the mere transposition of the hands lay behind the first four bars of the second minuet.

When had Mozart learnt to notate music, and where did these two minuets come in the process? The answer is not easy to find, because he did not date the first compositions he wrote out in his own hand as conscientiously as his father did the dictated pieces. Possibly the two procedures ran simultaneously for a time, so that even the dates recorded by the father cannot be assumed with complete certainty to indicate that the son could not already write music by then. It is conceivable at all events that Mozart went on dictating compositions to his father even after writing the K. 1 minuets. A concrete example seems to be a minuet in C major, which was probably composed in the autumn of 1763 (Minuet 1 of K. 6, keyboard version) and is in every respect at exactly the same stylistic level as the two K. 1 minuets. All three pieces are only sixteen bars long (unlike any of the minuets composed under Leopold Mozart's direct supervision, but like many of those included for keyboard practice in Nannerl's Music Book, and like some of those that Mozart wrote down without help from 1764 onwards), and in its sequential technique the C major minuet goes as far beyond mere transposition of the hands as the second of K. 1. Yet the C major minuet is one of the pieces written down in Nannerl's Music Book by Leopold Mozart. Did his son perhaps write an earlier, lost, draft version?

Stylistically there is nothing in the comparison to oppose giving the two minuets which bear the symbolic burden of the K. 1 number the date of 1763 also, with the proviso that they are more likely to have been written in the summer or autumn than in the spring. At the same time they are clearly neither Mozart's first compositions nor his earliest musical autographs. The ease of writing which a quill pen offered the child will not have been enough to free him at a stroke from the simpler techniques he had learnt first, and it may well be that even Mozart came only gradually to recognize the freedom conferred on him by the ability to write. One thing is reasonably certain: Mozart's first experiments in writing down his own music were made in Salzburg (see Chapter 2).

Leopold Mozart set a high value on laying solid foundations, and the course of the education he gave his children in practice is consistent with what he preached in his treatise on the violin. He warned against the example of people

who, hardly at ease with time, get straightaway to work on concertos and solos, in order (in their foolish opinion) to force themselves straight into the company of virtuosi. Many succeed so far that they play off with uncommon dexterity the most difficult passages in various concertos or solos which they have practised with great industry. These they know by heart. But should they have to perform only a couple of minuets melodically according to the instructions of the composer, they are unable to do so.[5]

Six of the nine keyboard pieces, K⁶ 1*b*–*f* and K. 2–5, are minuets. A tenth piece from this group of very early compositions is the Andante, K⁶ 1*a*, with its change of tempo; the three remaining pieces are in 2/4 time, from which it becomes clear that Leopold Mozart took steps to inhibit an excessive preference for triple motion. He wanted to instil in his son an instinct for time, both in the sense of recognizing the stresses in a musical phrase and the proper place for ornamentation and in that of constructing line and melody. The principles which he set out in his *Violinschule*, where they served primarily the edification of performing musicians, continued to guide him in teaching his son composition—for a piece of music must in itself bear witness to that instinct for time. His thoroughness will not have done his son's talent any harm.

Leopold Mozart was thrilled by his children's exceptional gifts. He saw no reason to hide them from the world, especially as he could hope for some financial gain if the children displayed their gifts to other people. As early as January 1762 he took the pair to Munich, where they played before the Elector of Bavaria, Maximilian III Joseph, and on 18 September of the same year, having scarcely been further than Augsburg and Salzburg in his life, he set off with them and his wife for Vienna. The first major stopping-place was the archiepiscopal seat of Passau; from there they continued their journey on the Danube. 'My children, by the way, arouse universal admiration, especially the boy', he wrote to his landlord in Salzburg, Lorenz Hagenauer, when they were still in Linz (3 October 1762). After their return to Salzburg he wrote briefly about the trip to his publisher, Lotter:

It will suffice if I tell you that on the eighth day after our arrival in Vienna we were summoned to Schönbrunn, where we were with the Emperor and Empress

---

[5] L. Mozart, *Versuch einer gründlichen Violinschule* (Augsburg, 1756), ch. 12, §2, 252; tr. E. Knocker (London, 1956), 215.

[Francis I and Maria Theresia] from three after dinner until six in the evening. Both my children had been given clothes, brought to our lodgings by the Keeper of the Privy Purse, and the Empress gave them 100 ducats. In addition, we were invited to all the greatest ministers' houses, and honoured with beautiful presents. We also spent thirteen days in Pressburg [Bratislava], where I bought a good travelling carriage, so that we could travel home in greater comfort in the cold weather. (17 January 1763)

2

'Over the Maxglan brook': The First Violin Sonata, the First Symphony, the First Aria

As well as visiting 'the greatest ministers' houses' in Vienna, Leopold Mozart also made contact with a number of foreign ambassadors. One such meeting shaped the entire family's destiny. 'I promised the French ambassador in Vienna to go to Paris as soon as it can be arranged. As soon as the swallows are here we shall be off' (17 February 1763). The Mozarts left Salzburg on 9 June 1763, and did not return for another three and a half years.

The journey bore its first fruit at the very first stop, in Wasserburg am Inn, and as a consequence of the hazards of travel in those days. The family was forced to wait there because a wheel on their carriage had broken. Leopold Mozart wrote to Lorenz Hagenauer: 'The latest news is that we went to see the organ, to pass the time, and I explained the pedals to Wolfgang. He had to try it for himself there and then, pushed the stool away, and improvised standing up, treading the pedals as if he had been doing it for months' (11 June 1763).

The letters contain information about almost every place the Mozarts stopped at, about the exertions and discomfort they suffered, and, naturally, about musical activities. Leopold Mozart had until then been no more than a middle-ranking musician at an archiepiscopal court that was perhaps not even in the first rank in the late eighteenth century. Suddenly he found himself in the big world, and he rose to the challenges it offered with an aplomb that compels respect. It is not simply that he related the new experiences to what he already knew from Salzburg; in the planning and execution of each stage of the journey, and in the estimate he made afterwards of its value, he developed a virtuosic skill that was almost unparalleled for his time and situation.

His watchword would serve a modern politician or road-manager equally well; 'One must constantly be putting one's hand in one's purse, and keep hold of one's five wits, and always have a plan in view for months ahead—but a plan that one can alter at a moment's notice if circumstances change' (22 February 1764). The plan he kept in view included the long-term benefits that he looked forward to reaping from the journey; whoever he met, he wanted to be able to approach them again, at a future date. The principle proved its worth in 1777–8, when he compiled a list of useful names and addresses for his son to take on his second journey to Paris. It included not only musicians and potential noble patrons but also the names of the inns where the family had lodged. He kept careful notes from the start of their journey in 1763, beginning with 'Wasserburg: Choirmaster Diez' and 'Golden Star Inn', for 10 June. Their stay in Koblenz in the autumn produced a typical cluster of people worth cultivating:

Baron von Walderdorff. B. v. Boos, Music Intendant and Imperial Marshal. French Ambassador. Baron v. Kerpen, chef de noblesse, privy counsellor, his wife, daughters large and small. Numerous sons, all musicians etc., namely: Franz, violino, eldest son and heir; Anselmus, very good violoncello, canon of Speyer and Trier; Wilhelm, violino, sub-lieutenant with the Imperial Teutschmeister Regiment; Carl, harpsichord, ensign under Colloredo; Fräul. Charlotte, harpsichord and sings, in a convent at Neiss [Neuss] near Cologne; Louis, violoncello and keyboard, canon of Speyer and Würzburg; Hugo, violino and harpsichord NB an especially good subject, is canon of Mainz . . .

But plenty of space was found for descriptions of the sights as well, for example in Brussels, which the family reached in October 1763:

At the Hôtel d'Angleterre. The big church, where the most beautiful paintings by Rubens and others are to be seen. NB in the chapel, Christ giving Peter the keys. The big Carmelite church where, besides the most beautiful paintings, the extraordinary pulpit carved from one large tree. The little Carmelite church, next door to the palace of the Duc d'Arenberg. Mechanic who made two figures which play the flute and two birds which sing.

And so they came to Paris, on 18 November 1763. Leopold Mozart saved up full description of that modern metropolis until after his return to Salzburg and confined himself for the time being to brief remarks. He told Lorenz Hagenauer: 'All I will say is that Paris is an open city, without gates, and it looks exactly like any village as you first enter. But that changes very quickly' (8 December 1763). Yet even this great city held no terrors for the vice-Kapellmeister turned travel courier. He found lodgings for himself and his family with the Bavarian ambassador, whose father-in-law was the Archbishop of Salzburg's Chief Chamberlain, Georg Anton

Felix von Arco. Friedrich Melchior von Grimm, secretary to the Duke of Orleans, wrote about the Mozart children in the *Correspondance littéraire* two weeks after their arrival, and Louis Carrogis de Carmontelle painted them with their father in watercolours (see Pl. 3). Numerous copies of the painting have survived, so it appears to have circulated as widely as Grimm's article; at all events, Leopold Mozart wrote to Hagenauer:

M. de Mechel, a copper-engraver, is working hand over fist to engrave our portraits, which have been painted very well indeed by an amateur, M. de Carmontel. Wolfgang is at the keyboard, I am standing behind his chair, playing the violin, and Nannerl is leaning on the clavecin with one arm, and holding music in her other hand, as if she is singing.   (1 April 1764)

The Mozarts had evidently met Christian von Mechel as soon as they reached Paris: after their hosts and members of their staff, and the composer Johann Gottfried Eckard, from Augsburg, his is the first name Leopold Mozart made a note of for his Paris recollections.

The circles at which Leopold Mozart's diplomacy was aimed included Baron von Grimm. The letter to Hagenauer quoted above pays tribute to him:

I must also tell you about this M. Grimm, my great friend, to whom I owe everything here. He is . . . a great philanthropist. My other letters and recommendations were all worthless . . . M. Grimm, to whom I brought a letter from a merchant's wife in Frankfurt, has done everything for us, on his own. He arranged our visit to the court; he took care of our first concert, and he paid me 80 louis d'or on his own account alone, which means that he bought 320 tickets, and then he paid for the lighting as well, which consumed more than sixty wax candles. This same Grimm obtained permission for the concert, and now he will take care of the second, for which more than 100 tickets have already been issued. See what a man of good sense and a kind heart can accomplish! He comes from Regensburg, but has been in Paris for more than fifteen years and knows how to set things up on the right footing, and as a result they turn out exactly as he wants them to. (1 April 1764)

Grimm also had a hand in the appearance of some of Mozart's works in print in the spring of 1764. These first published works comprised two pairs of sonatas for violin and keyboard, one pair (K. 6 and 7) dedicated to Princess Louise-Marie-Thérèse de Bourbon, the king's second daughter, and the other (K. 8 and 9) to Mme de Tessé. The latter, a lady-in-waiting at the court, had already made Mozart a present of a gold snuffbox in

L.C. De Carmontelle del.   Delafosse Sculp 1764.

LEOPOLD MOZART, Pere de MARIANNE MOZART, Virtuose âgée de onze ans
et de J.G.WOLFGANG MOZART, Compositeur et Maitre de Musique
âgé de sept ans.

Pl. 3. Leopold Mozart with his son and daughter, Paris, 1763. Engraving by Jean-Baptiste Delafosse (and Christian Mechel?) after Louis Carrogis de Carmontelle, 1764.

December 1763. Now that 'four sonatas by M. Wolfgang Mozart are at the engravers,' wrote his father,

Just imagine the furore, when it states on the title-page of these sonatas that they are the work of a 7-year-old child, and when the incredulous are invited to put it to the test, as has already happened, he asks someone to write down a minuet or something of the sort, and then immediately—without touching the keyboard— writes the bass beneath it and, if desired, the second violin part as well. (1 February 1764)

Mozart, now just 8 years old, had evidently acquired a certain proficiency and fluency in musical notation. His early autographs rarely bear an exact date, as mentioned earlier (the first to do so is the Kyrie, K. 33, of 12 June 1766, when the Mozarts were already on the way home to Salzburg). Leopold Mozart had probably foreseen, however, that the only conclusive proof of his son's compositional abilities would be the fact that the boy could write his music down himself. The tests he refers to in the letter of 1 February 1764 show that he was right. Could Mozart, then, already notate music before the family left Salzburg on 9 June 1763?[1]

Possibly the need for it was brought home to Leopold Mozart during the first visit to Vienna in 1762. There is evidence that the little Mozart could already at least read music by then—a year, that is, before the family set off on their tour of western Europe—in the second of the reminiscences written down by Nannerl Mozart in 1792:

In 1762 [probably October], when he played at the age of 6 for Emperor Francis, he sat down at the keyboard and said to the Emperor, who stood beside him, 'Is Herr Wagenseil here? He ought to stand there, he knows what to do.' So the Emperor let Wagenseil take his place beside the clavier. Then the boy said to Wagenseil, 'I'm playing a concerto by you, you must turn the pages for me.'

If that request to turn the pages was meant seriously, and was more than bluff on the boy's part, trying to give the impression he knew more than he really did, then it proves he could read music by then (he was still not 7).

A claim that Mozart could also write music by the summer of the following year, before the family left for Paris, is contained in another reminiscence dating from 1792—although a layer of legend must be suspected to embrace the kernel of truth. Johann Andreas Schachtner, trumpeter at the Salzburg court, wrote to Mozart's sister:

[1] See W. Plath in NMA IX/27, vol. i, pp. xx f.

Once I went home with your father after Thursday service, and we found the 4-year-old Wolfgangerl busy with his pen:

Papa: What are you writing?

Wolfg.: A clavier concerto, the first part is almost finished.

Papa: Let's see.

Wolfg.: It's not finished yet.

Papa: Let's see, it's bound to be something fine.

His father took it from him and showed me a smeary sheet of notes, most of which were written over ink-blots which he had rubbed out. (NB: Little Wolfgangerl, knowing no better, thrust the pen to the very bottom of the inkpot each time, and so, every time he reached the paper with it, a blot of ink dropped off, but he was not put out in the least: he wiped it away with the flat of his hand, and wrote on.)

At first we laughed at this apparent galimatias, but then his father began to attend to the most important thing, the notes and music; he stared at the sheet for a long time, and then two tears, tears of admiration and joy, fell from his eyes. 'Look, Herr Schachtner,' he said, 'look how correctly and properly it is all written, only it's of no use, because it is so extraordinarily difficult that no one could play it.' Wolfgangerl said: 'That's why it's a concerto, the player must practise until he gets it right, look, this is how it goes.' Then he played it, and managed to get just enough out of it for us to see what he intended. At that age he had the notion that playing a concerto and working miracles were one and the same thing. (24 April 1792)

Mozart was just 4 years old when he first began to play the piano; at 5 he began to compose music, and he was $6\frac{1}{2}$ and more at the time of the first journey to Vienna, when it appears he had already learnt to read music. (He must by then have had a 'notion', moreover, of what 'playing a concerto' meant, if he played one by Wagenseil—not necessarily a difficult one—while he was there; although if he did believe it was the same thing as 'working miracles' he was not of the same mind as his father, to judge by the latter's verdict on some virtuos.) If we can believe Schachtner, Mozart's earliest surviving autographs must date from before 9 June 1763; there is no reason to doubt that incidents such as those witnessed by Schachtner made a profound impression, even on an outsider, and therefore we need not doubt, either, that they happened in Salzburg. The only thing is that Mozart was then not 4 but probably somewhere near his seventh birthday. It is not very likely that the incident described above took place immediately before the departure for Paris, in view of the success of that journey. Mozart had already had some practice at writing by the middle part of the year, and at mastering the tricky business of how far to dip a pen into an inkpot, for there is no sign of blots such as Schachtner describes on the manuscript of the K. 1 minuets; as there is nothing in their musical material to contradict a dating in October 1763, at the latest, they may indeed have been composed during that year. As those two pieces show, new compositions from then onwards were written down in Nannerl's Music Book by Mozart himself as well as his father. It is possible, however, as already suggested, that Mozart also continued to dictate new pieces to his father for a while. At all events, some of the keyboard pieces which were recycled (with the addition of a violin part) in the four violin sonatas published in the spring of 1764 were entered in Nannerl's Music Book in the hand of Leopold Mozart. (Indeed, they may all have been but they do not all survive in that form.)

Leopold Mozart thus found himself increasingly often demoted to a copyist, though that allowed him as much scope as before to oversee his son's progress (as his corrections to Mozart's autographs demonstrate[2]). From that time on he wrote out instrumental parts, or made fair copies of full scores; he justified the first by reference to the expense of employing a professional copyist from outside the family; the second is proved by, for example, the form in which the aria 'Va dal furor portata', K. 21, survived (that is, in two full scores in Leopold Mozart's handwriting, which were clearly made at some distance from both the time and the place of composition). It is no easier to determine precisely when Leopold Mozart 'declined' into being a copyist than the moment when Mozart began to write; it is likely never to be known for certain whether the compositions by Mozart which his father wrote down in Nannerl's Music Book during the family's stay in Brussels in October 1763 were still taken at dictation or were copied (with corrections) from draft manuscripts. Leopold Mozart certainly did his best to encourage progress by giving his son a book of music manuscript paper in mid-1764, when they were in London, so that the child had somewhere to write down his sketches for himself whenever he pleased.

London was almost within their grasp after five months in Paris, when Leopold Mozart wrote with undisguised satisfaction: 'Now we have made the acquaintance of all the ambassadors of foreign powers here. The English ambassador, Milord Bedford, and his son are very well disposed to us, and the Russian, Prince Galitzin, loves us like his own children' (1 April 1764). Ten days later Paris lay behind them and they were on the way to London. A few weeks later Leopold Mozart confessed to

---

[2] Cf. e.g. Allroggen, 'Mozarts erste Symphonien', 400–3.

Hagenauer, whose wife had enquired about their plans: 'At the time of my departure from Salzburg I was only half resolved to go to London. But as everybody, even in Paris, urged us to go there, I made up my mind to do so . . . But we will not go to Holland, that I can assure her' (28 May 1764). In fact they did go to Holland later; perhaps we may deduce from that how firm Leopold Mozart's half-resolution to go to London was from the first.

But before reaching London they had to face another new experience: the open sea. Nannerl Mozart, like her father, kept a travel diary (although she evidently capitulated before the task of keeping a systematic record of her days in Paris). Now she wrote, succinctly but eloquently: 'In Calais I saw how the sea runs away and waxes again'. There was more to the experience than the observation of the movement of the tide, alas, as Leopold reported when they got to London: 'God be praised, we have come safely over the Maxglan brook, although we did not manage it without (pardon me) spewing. I was the hardest hit. Still, it saved us the expense of emetic medicines, and we are, thank God, all well' (25 April 1764)—well enough to compare the Channel crossing with the passage over what was probably the first watercourse they had encountered on leaving Salzburg, a stream at Maxglan, the place from which Salzburg Airport takes its name today.

London, too, was conquered at the double. 'We were already at court on the fifth day after our arrival', Leopold Mozart wrote on 28 May. There they met not only King George and Queen Charlotte but also Johann Christian Bach, the Queen's music master and the youngest son of Johann Sebastian Bach. The meeting laid the foundations of Mozart's lifelong admiration of the older composer, while Bach in turn was clearly fascinated by the abstruse musical games the 8-year-old was already capable of playing. Mozart's sister recalled a scene: 'Herr Johann Christian Bach, the Queen's music teacher, stood the son between his legs, the former played a few bars, then the latter continued, and in that way they played a whole sonata. Someone not seeing it would have thought that it was played by only one person.' (April[?] 1792) (Admittedly that particular game was probably not invented by Johann Christian Bach but by his brother and sometime teacher Carl Philipp Emanuel, who composed a symphony with his pupil Ferdinand Philipp Joseph, Prince Lobkowitz by the same method.[3]) The triumphal progress continued: the name of Mozart appeared in the London newspapers for the first time on 9 May, announcing a

---

[3] H. Miesner, 'Philipp Emanuels musikalischer Nachlaß', *Bach-Jahrbuch* 1939, 86.

concert eight days later in which 'Master Mozart' was to take part, and at the beginning of June an entire concert was given 'for the Benefit of Miss MOZART of Eleven [actually thirteen] and Master MOZART of Seven [eight] Years of Age, Prodigies of Nature', in which both performed; Mozart had been unwell in the latter part of May. Leopold Mozart summed up his son's development as follows: 'In a word, what he knew when we left Salzburg was a mere shadow of what he knows now' (28 May 1764).

Mozart had the time to digest and absorb his experiences—a worryingly long time, for his father was suddenly rendered incapable for about four weeks of doing all the things that he had been doing so expertly until then. Nannerl Mozart recalled:

In London, where our father was dangerously ill, we were not allowed to touch the piano, and so, in order to occupy himself, he composed his first symphony with all the instruments—trumpets and kettledrums—and I had to copy it out for him, from his copy. While he was composing and I was copying it, he said to me: 'Remind me to give the horn something to do!' (24 November 1799)

It looks as if her memory failed her in the matter of the instrumentation: the earliest work in which Mozart included a part for trumpet is the Recitative and Aria 'Or che il dover . . . Tali e cotanti sono', K. 36, composed for a performance on 21 December 1766, immediately after the family's return to Salzburg, while the first symphony with trumpets is K. 45, composed in Vienna early in 1768. The trumpeter Andre Schachtner knew from his own experience that 'until he was almost 9, he [Mozart] had an uncontrollable fear of the trumpet', at least 'when it was played alone, without other instruments' (24 April 1792). There was a gap in Schachtner's acquaintance with Mozart, of course, lasting from his eighth year to the eve of his eleventh birthday, and he cannot be trusted to have got the ages right. Leopold Mozart described another comparable instance of his son's being stricken with 'uncontrollable fear': 'I will describe the Tower [of London] to you when we are home again, and also tell you of how badly the roaring of the lions there frightened our Master Wolfgang' (19 March 1765). The fact that Mozart, shortly before his encounter with the lions, had written a symphony (K. 19) in the typical 'trumpet key' of D major, without including trumpets in the scoring, indicates that the trumpet still lay outside his compositional scope, even if it was not to be 'played alone, without other instruments'. All in all, it seems improbable that Mozart wrote a symphony with 'trumpets and kettledrums' during that visit to London.

On the other hand the autograph of a symphony has survived, from the time of the London stay of 1764, which could be the work the composer's sister refers to: it is the E flat major Symphony, K. 16. Leopold Mozart made some corrections to it, but he was probably not present when it was first written down, for it is only too easy to see that the quill pen used was badly cut[4] (however, there is no copy in the hand of Nannerl Mozart). The symphony certainly gives the horns something to do: in the second movement, above the tremolo triplet motion of the violins and the 2/4-like ostinato rhythm in the bass, they introduce a contrast to the predominant C minor atmosphere in the form of that distinctive theme in the major which runs like a thread through the whole of Mozart's *œuvre*, up to the finale of the 'Jupiter' Symphony (where we will consider it more closely). There is nothing here that does not conform with Nannerl Mozart's memoir, including the reference to the horn. Taken at face value, it is true, Mozart's remark to his sister could be interpreted to mean that he regarded writing for the instrument as one more task, even a chore, that still remained to be done; but it might have a more esoteric significance, indicating that he had already formed a plan to give something striking to the horn, but that for the moment he wanted neither to reveal it nor, indeed, to forget it.

Once Mozart had written his first symphony, others followed fast, and a concert took place in London in February 1765 at which all the symphonies performed were by him. The Op. 3 symphonies by Johann Christian Bach, which appeared in print in 1765 (and must therefore have already existed in manuscript in 1764), were probably a major model in some stylistic respects. A specific structural pattern, clearly recognizable in the allegro movements and already discernible in earlier compositions (in the Paris Violin Sonata, K. 7, for example), is an equally important feature;[5] unlike Haydn in many of his works, or—later—Beethoven, Mozart shaped the expositions of these early works as a succession of relatively small musical units rather than as an organic thematic development. Accordingly he began the E flat major Symphony, K. 16, with a short 'first subject', opened by a fanfare marked *f* and concluded by an extended *pp* cadence. This subject is heard twice, and then followed by a completely new musical figure: with an E flat pounding in quavers in the bass, Mozart stays with the home key for some time until it is suddenly (almost impercept-

---

[4] Allroggen, 'Mozarts erste Symphonien', 403.
[5] W. Burde, *Studien zu Mozarts Klaviersonaten: Formungsprinzipien und Formtypen* (Giebing, 1969), 58–61.

ibly) abandoned, and the dominant is emphatically asserted in its place by an imperfect cadential figure—again using new motivic material. The second subject in the dominant follows, a figure played *p* without wind support; this resolves into a sequence of two strongly cadential elements, which are dynamically and motivically independent and are repeated in the pattern AABB; these are followed in turn by an epilogue which offers an alternation of *p* and *f* and an affirmation of the dominant.[6]

As a motivic structure this is extraordinarily open to variation in detail but it is also concise, and with it Mozart discovered a formal principle that served him fruitfully all his life—not in the symphony alone but also at times in the aria (with appropriate harmonic variations), and especially in the concerto; with both these genres he used it in the orchestral introductions. It is altogether improbable that any symphony written in this first phase of Mozart's career would follow a fundamentally different principle. An attempt was made to ascribe to Mozart a symphony discovered in Odense in Denmark in 1982; it had previously been known as K[6] 16a, purely on the basis of a thematic quotation. Its motivic relationships turned out, however, to be based on totally different and not very well defined principles, and Mozart can be virtually ruled out as its composer. There were, in any case, substantial doubts about its provenance.[7]

Further sections of the first movements of the early symphonies also reveal a clear structural principle. The exposition is followed by a development section in which motivic elements from the first part of the exposition are elaborated; they are given more room now and the working of the 'first subject' is clearly separated from that of the 'continuation' (as is that of the 'modulation' in its turn). This process sheds light from another angle on the manner of articulation that has already been observed in the exposition. The recapitulation, finally, includes only those elements of the exposition which are not contained in the development; by these means the early-classical device of the 'shortened recapitulation' is given a special meaning (in K[6] 19a as well as in K. 16, though not in K. 19, the third of the London symphonies).

[6] 'First subject', b. 1; new figure in tonic, b. 23; imperfect cadence in dominant, up-beat to b. 29; 2nd subject, b. 31; cadential preparation, b. 35; 1st cadence, twice, bs. 37/41; 2nd cadence, twice, bs. 45/49; epilogue, twice, up-beat to bs. 54/56; affirmation of dominant, b. 57.

[7] See G. Allroggen in NMA IV/11, vol. i, p. viii, and W. Plath, 'Die Überlieferung von KV 16a', in J. P. Larsen and K. Wedin (eds.), *Die Sinfonie KV 16a 'del Sigr. Mozart'* (Odense, 1987), 45–9.

Mozart started a voyage in yet another direction during the stay in London. 'His head is always full of an opera now, which he wants to do in Salzburg with none but young performers', Leopold Mozart had reported to Salzburg as early as 28 May 1764. No opera was composed, but father and son took certain essential steps towards the operas that were composed later. Mozart had singing lessons from the castrato Giovanni Manzuoli (who sang the title-role in the first performance of *Ascanio in Alba*, in Milan in 1771). Furthermore, he wrote his first Italian operatic aria, 'Va, dal furor portata', K. 21, on a text from Pietro Metastasio's *Ezio*; a pasticcio version of *Ezio* was presented in London in the 1764–5 season, and Mozart's aria was probably first heard in 1765 in the context of one of the performances.

Leopold Mozart made the family's stay in London last as long as possible; in particular, he made as much as he could, in financial as well as other terms, of the opportunities to perform during the winter season of 1764–5. 'I am now here, where no one from the court in Salzburg has dared to venture before me, and none perhaps will ever venture in future', he wrote (13 September 1764). On 1 August 1765 he and his family crossed back over the English Channel, enjoying 'such a favourble wind that they made the crossing to Calais in three and a half hours' (Nannerl Mozart, April[?] 1792). From there they went to Holland, where they stayed until the end of April 1766, and then set off for home, via Paris and Geneva. They arrived back in Salzburg on 29 November 1766, three and a half years after leaving the city, the richer by a store of incomparable experiences. The father had accomplished something quite uncommon for a man of his professional standing, and accumulated wide experience in international diplomacy. Nannerl at 15 and her brother at all but 11 had been on such a journey (with all its accompanying impressions) as to set them wholly apart from other children of the same age. As Leopold Mozart had already written from London, his son had earned respect as a musician—and surely not solely on account of his age. He had been composing music for almost six years, of which he had spent only two at home in Salzburg; as a consequence his sister could say of his education, at least as a keyboard-player: 'I know of no practice at the clavier, when once he had reached the age of 7, because he always had to improvise for audiences, and give concerts, and read at sight, and that was all the practice he had' (from the later 1792 memoir). Yet keyboard music lost its previously unchallenged central position in Mozart's composing during this journey. After London, vocal music (particularly arias) and symphonies created a new focus for his attention. The development reached a temporary peak in the spring of 1767, when he composed his contribution to the sacred Singspiel *Die Schuldigkeit des ersten Gebots*, K. 35 (the second and third parts, by Michael Haydn and the Salzburg court organist Anton Cajetan Adlgasser, have not survived), and the Latin comedy *Apollo et Hyacinthus*, K. 38.

Salzburg could not hold the Mozarts for long. They set off again on 11 September 1767, this time for Vienna, almost exactly five years to the day from their first journey there. Much had happened since then and the imperial capital was to enjoy a share in all the changes.

3

From Opera to Concerto: *Exsultate, jubilate*, K. 165 (1773)

Contrary to their expectation, the Mozarts did not stay long in Vienna in 1767: an outbreak of smallpox drove them to Moravia at the end of October. In spite of their flight, both children contracted the illness, and it was January before the family went back to the imperial capital. They did not return to Salzburg for another twelve months. Clearly Leopold Mozart had no intention of beating a retreat without first putting paid to the rumours that were circulating in Viennese musical circles to his son's discredit, such as: 'that it could not possibly be true; that it was all done with mirrors, a charade; that it was set up in advance and he was given music to play which he already knew; that it was ridiculous to believe that he could compose, etc., etc.'. He wanted his son's musical abilities to have their due recognition and he found an ally in the Emperor himself, Joseph II, 'who twice asked Wolfgangerl if he has any desire to compose an opera and direct it himself' (30 January–3 February 1768). It was indeed during this year in Vienna that Mozart wrote his first *opera buffa*, *La finta semplice*, K. 51, on a text by Carlo Goldoni. It was not performed at the time, however, and the tongues went on wagging. Some people said that 'the music was not worth a fig; others that it did not fit the words, or went against the metre, because the boy did not command the Italian language well enough' (30 July 1768). Not even the praise of 'Father Hasse', who had dominated the operatic scene for decades, or that of Pietro Metastasio, whose librettos shaped operatic style for half a century, could make the envious fall silent, and *La finta semplice* was not performed until 1 May 1769—in Salzburg. But Leopold Mozart was hatching another plan, to which he first alluded in the earlier letter to Lorenz Hagenauer: 'What do you think? Is not the cachet of having composed an opera for the Viennese theatre the best way to gain a reputation not only in Germany but also in Italy?'

Leopold Mozart had already toyed with the idea of travelling to Italy in the summer of 1766, when the family reached Lyons on their way from Paris, but he had elected to go home to Salzburg instead. By early

May 1768, however, the idea had crystallized into an imperative intention to go to Italy at the earliest possible opportunity, now that he had had 'every encouragement from the Emperor himself to travel to Florence, all the Imperial States, and Naples' (11 May 1768), and especially while he himself, having reached the age of 48, still felt up to it, and his son was still young enough to arouse public interest on that account alone.

Leopold Mozart was 50, and his son almost 14, when at last they set off for Italy on 13 December 1769. Two months later he did not admit to very high hopes: 'Not much will come of Italy; the only comfort is that there is quite a lot of curiosity and understanding, and the Italians appreciate what Wolfgang can do' (17 February 1770). It is easy to see that in the end the journey exceeded expectations, even if Leopold Mozart deliberately understated the case when he made such remarks. They were away for almost exactly the same length of time as they had spent on the journey to Vienna and Moravia, and when Salzburg received the travellers again on 28 March 1771 young Wolfgang had been made a knight of the Order of the Golden Spur by the Pope (5 July 1770); thenceforth he could have called himself 'Ritter von . . .' like Gluck. He had been received into the illustrious Accademia Filarmonica in Bologna (9 October 1770) and appointed honorary maestro di cappella of the Accademia Filarmonica in Verona. He had written his first string quartet, K. 80, on 15 March 1770, in an inn in Lodi, and composed his first *opera seria, Mitridate, re di Ponto*, K. 87, for Milan. Father and son had measured the length of Italy as far as Naples, and its breadth from Turin to Venice; they had given concerts, and gained new musical impressions from attending the concerts of others, in countless towns and cities; finally, Mozart had in his pocket a contract from Milan for a second opera, and another from Padua to compose the oratorio *La Betulia liberata*, K. 118, on a text by Metastasio (it is not certain that it was ever performed in Padua, however).

The contract for a second opera for Milan, at least, made a second visit to Italy a concrete possibility. Like *Mitridate,* the new opera was earmarked for the carnival, and thus to be the chief work in the principal opera season, which usually began on 26 December. *Mitridate* was the carnival opera of the 1770–1 season, and *Lucio Silla* was to be that of 1772–3. The two operas were written on the same terms; Mozart was required to deliver the recitatives within the month of October, then to travel to Milan to compose the arias there in November;[1] thus he was already scheduled to leave Salzburg in the autumn of 1772.

In the end that turned out to be his third visit to Italy, for scarcely had he arrived back from the first when a commission from Vienna arrived in Salzburg, from Empress Maria Theresia, ordering a work for the wedding of her son Archduke Ferdinand. This was due to take place in Milan in October 1771, so father and son set off across the Brenner Pass again in August (as they were to do fourteen months later for the Milan première of *Lucio Silla*). Mozart's serenata teatrale *Ascanio in Alba*, K. 111, was the great success of the festivities, completely overshadowing the official wedding opera, Hasse's *Ruggiero*.

Of the three and a quarter years between the start of the first journey to Italy and the return from the third, Mozart spent only thirteen months in Salzburg; counting from the start of his first journey of all (to Munich in 1762), at any given time he had been at home for only half the total time he had been away. The circumstances that had enabled the Mozarts to travel so much were abruptly changed as the father and son arrived home from their success with *Ascanio* in Milan. On 16 December 1771, the day after their return, the Prince-Archbishop of Salzburg, Sigismund Christoph von Schrattenbach, died. The new Archbishop, Hieronymus Colloredo, elected on 14 March 1772, does not seem to have been ready to grant the Mozarts, both of them court musicians in his employment, the same generous leave of absence as his predecessor had done. During the following winter, the terms of the contract for *Lucio Silla* had to be honoured, but Leopold Mozart seems to have foreseen the way the situation in Salzburg would develop and to have pulled out all the stops in the effort to delay their return from Milan. He claimed to be ill and unable to travel, but in reality he was doing his best to find a post for his son in Italy, in the service of Grand Duke Leopold of Tuscany, later Emperor Leopold II. Only when all hopes had been dashed did he set off back to Salzburg.

During the weeks the Mozarts spent trying to prolong their stay in Italy, after the première of *Lucio Silla*, Mozart composed *Exsultate, jubilate*, his virtuoso work for solo soprano and lavish orchestral accompaniment, consisting of two arias linked by a recitative and concluding with an 'Alleluia'. Italian opera had become an important area of Mozart's activity since the commission to write *La finta semplice*, and Italian operatic style is one of the

---

[1] For the *Mitridate* contract (24 Mar. 1770), see Bauer and Deutsch (eds.), *Mozart: Briefe*, i; for the *Lucio Silla* contract, see Deutsch, *MDB*, under 4 Mar. 1771.

central factors of his early *œuvre*. But the works themselves are not widely known nowadays, principally because they pay homage to operatic ideals which are different from those we now expect from a musico-dramatic work, especially since the developments that took place during the nineteenth century. As a result we encounter Mozart's early vocal style only relatively rarely: when we do it is rather more likely than not to be represented by *Exsultate, jubilate*, the only one of those 'Italian' vocal works (albeit with a text in Latin) that can claim to be well known.

Mozart called it a motet, although that is a term more readily associated with sacred choral music of the Renaissance on the one hand and the Protestant cantoral tradition on the other, and suggests a work sung a cappella rather than one with an independent orchestral contribution. Mozart was alluding, however, to a usage the modern world has forgotten. A justification for using the term 'motet' of a Catholic sacred composition of the kind Mozart wrote is to be found in the pages of Johann Joachim Quantz's treatise on the flute (published in 1752 and already mentioned above, in the first paragraph of Chapter 1): 'In Italy this name is applied at present time to a sacred Latin solo cantata that consists of two arias and two recitatives and closes with an Alleluia, and is sung by one of the best singers during the Mass after the Credo'. With all types of sacred music, of course, 'each piece must accord with its purpose and with its words, so that a Requiem or Miserere does not resemble the Te Deum or a composition for Easter, the Kyrie resemble the Gloria in the Mass, or a motet a gay opera aria', but, Quantz conceded, 'in general the introduction of more liveliness is permitted in the church music of the Catholics than in that of the Protestants'.[2]

It was permissible, therefore, for the first movement, at least, of Mozart's motet to resemble 'a gay opera aria', which it does in both 'liveliness' and virtuosity—although the text does not really justify it. The second aria would not be wholly out of place in an opera, either, although it is a passionate invocation of the Virgin Mary ('Crown of Virgins, give us peace, relieve the passions under which the heart sighs'); it is possible to imagine a situation in an opera in which a lyrical aria of this kind would be appropriate. Mozart did not compose the second recitative which would normally follow the second aria, according to Quantz, and allowed the conclusion of the A major aria to lead straight into the F major 'Alleluia', which is shorter than the first movement but its equal in virtuosity.

[2] J. J. Quantz, *Versuch einer Anweisung die Flöte traversiere zu spielen* (Berlin, 1752; repr. Leipzig, 1983), xviii, §19, p. 288; tr. E. R. Reilly (London, 1956), 305–6.

The terms in which the Protestant Quantz described the modern Catholic motet of his time as a 'sacred Latin solo cantata' bring to mind a work which is almost half a century older than *Exsultate, jubilate* and has a text in German, but is strikingly similar in structure to Mozart's work and thus demonstrates the breadth of the tradition on which Mozart was able to build: Johann Sebastian Bach's solo cantata for soprano *Jauchzet Gott in allen Landen*. That too is a highly virtuoso composition, it too begins with the sequence aria–recitative–aria, in it too the penultimate movement leads without a break into an 'Alleluia' (although here the penultimate movement is a chorale arrangement, which makes Bach's cantata one movement longer than Mozart's motet). As a rule, the heading Bach gave his church cantatas was 'Concerto', but for this work he used the term 'Cantata', which he tended otherwise to use of his secular vocal music. Thus even terminologically the work illustrates what Quantz meant by his phrase 'sacred solo cantata'; the German text and the inclusion of the 'Protestant' chorale arrangement are the only features in which it differs from Mozart's idea of a 'motet'.

The virtuosity, if nothing else, shows that *Exsultate, jubilate* was destined for 'one of the best singers': it was written for the castrato Venanzio Rauzzini, for whom Mozart also composed the role of the primo uomo in *Lucio Silla* (that of Cecilio, not Sulla, the dictator of Rome, whose name gives the work its title). Leopold Mozart had praised Rauzzini in extravagant terms even before the opera's première: 'he sings it like an angel', he wrote (28 November 1772) of the castrato's rendition of the first aria when that was all that Mozart had written of the part. Rauzzini contributed, therefore, to the opera's success; it had already had seventeen performances by mid-January, when the management decided to defer the production of the second carnival opera by another week, although it had been scheduled to open four weeks after *Lucio Silla* to stimulate the box-office.[3] Clearly the fruitful collaboration of composer and singer was continued in *Exsultate, jubilate*.

Mozart could count among the gains of his first Italian journey the encouragement it gave him to try his hand at other forms of chamber music: the string quartet he wrote in Lodi is crucially significant, when we think of the importance that medium was to have in his later *œuvre*. The effect of the third visit to Italy was more immediate, for it clearly gave him the decisive impulse to take up the instrumental concerto, in which, along

---

[3] See document dated 16 Jan. 1773, in Bauer and Deutsch (eds.), *Mozart: Briefe*, i.

with opera, he enjoyed his 'most signal triumphs', as Charles Rosen has observed.[4] *Lucio Silla* is the seventh work by Mozart in the category of opera (if the dramatic serenatas are included); ten more reached the stage during his lifetime. He had turned his attention to the concerto before this, in fact, but only cursorily. True, there is Schachtner's anecdote about his early skirmish with the inkpot (but it is unclear what the word 'concerto' means in that context), and there is Leopold Mozart's mention of a trumpet concerto composed in Vienna in November 1768 (K. 47c, lost) and finally there are the seven concertos Mozart 'composed' up to 1772 at the latest, by orchestrating sonata movements by other composers while altering very little in their musical substance. Surprisingly, therefore, although Mozart is acknowledged as one of the greatest composers of concertos in the history of music, seventeen years (almost half his life) passed before he made any wholly original contribution to the genre. Might the reason be that until 1773 he had not found a form in which to develop his own style within the framework of the relationship of instrumental solos and tuttis? It is a plausible hypothesis, because the techniques he used in his arrangements of other composers' sonata movements led to results that were different formally from his later, original concertos.[5] Even so, Mozart had had plenty of practice at juxtaposing solos and tuttis in his operas by then; it is also surprising that—unlike the experience of many of his contemporaries—his vocal style had such direct formal effects on the instrumental concerto.

It is certainly true that the traditional da capo aria was not well suited to be the springboard for the leap from operatic aria to full-blown concerto movement; in its basic form it consists of a main section presented at the outset, a contrasting middle section, and a repeat of the first section. Since it is both the beginning and the conclusion of the aria the first section can encompass only a very limited tonal development, for it must both begin and end in the home key. That means that a da capo aria contains at least four extended, well-defined passages in the home key (the beginning and the end of the main section when it is first presented and when it returns unchanged after the middle section). A concerto movement of Mozart's day takes a quite different course: it is already approaching the end when the home key resumes a leading position for the first time since the start of the movement. In the mean time, traditionally, the orchestral tutti has presented the same material several times in different keys in ritornello

---

[4] Rosen, *The Classical Style*, 185.   [5] Küster, *Formale Aspekte*, 219–24.

sections, which may be shortened or varied, and which alternate with modulating passages where the soloist displays the range of his virtuosity. The steps whereby aria form and the concerto movement drew closer to one another are not altogether cut and dried, because the evolution progressed on several levels and did not always take a course straight enough to allow the construction of a single historical model. Mozart and his contemporaries obviously took the dramatic possibilities of da capo form as their starting-point. In effect a da capo ('from the beginning') aria brings the action of an opera to a temporary halt, because exactly the same thing must be said at the end as was said at the beginning. Manifold ingenious devices were developed to overcome this yawning caesura of several minutes' duration and to reduce da capo sections to dramatically practical proportions, while not abandoning the form as such, for it was an important conduit of both musical and vocal style. Diminishing the force of this authentic da capo (which incidentally gave the virtuoso singer the chance to ravish the ear with ornamentation) posed a threat to the element of contrast in the middle section, however; nobody wanted to surrender the established methods of transforming the music there (moving from the major to the minor mode, for example). Concerning the final stage in the evolutionary process, the Mozart scholar Hermann Abert concluded that the old middle section of aria form had been superseded 'by the placing of the second quatrain of the text as early as the second half of the main section, where it is equipped with the harmonic traits of the erstwhile middle section: the first part is then usually repeated with variations'.[6] In that respect this 'new' aria form is fundamentally similar to one that had already been used by Bach in his time, but it also draws close to the principles of sonata form in being able to embrace such procedures as exposition, development and recapitulation (which could also be accommodated in the traditional pattern of concerto-movement form).

However, Mozart went even further to bring aria form and the concerto movement closer together. There was no question, for him, but that the orchestral introduction of a concerto movement or an aria could follow much the same pattern as the exposition of a symphony (such as he developed in his London symphony, K. 16, but without the modulation, of course). The same principle can be observed in the tuttis of the seven concertos in which he arranged sonata movements by other composers. But an even more decisive factor was the need, in composing arias, to take

[6] Abert, *Mozart*, i. 196.

the singer's lungs into account, and to allow reasonable rests at places that made sense musically. These are positioned similarly in aria after aria and follow the course of the modulation. From the outcome of the evolution, which can already be discerned in *Exsultate, jubilate*, the following model can be derived: in order to move from the tonic to the dominant, and allow the latter to usurp the former's tonal hegemony temporarily, the soloist first presents the main theme in the tonic; with the introduction of new thematic material, the soloist abandons the tonic and finishes a second section on the (not yet fully stabilized) dominant, and only in a third section does the dominant become firmly enough established for Mozart to cadence within it, too (sometimes, as in the two arias of *Exsultate, jubilate*, the dominant of the dominant is introduced, without destabilizing the dominant). The second subject of the orchestral introduction follows and the first section of the aria reaches its conclusion by way of a series of virtuoso cadential flourishes. There are brief orchestral interjections at the joins between the separate sections, and the soloist has time to catch his breath. One of the consequences of this is that the second subject is normally presented by the orchestra; once his breathing-space has been 'covered' by that means, the soloist is able to stand up to the orchestra again with, usually, an independent melodic line.

It was this pattern of tonal progression, including its instrumental 'punctuation', that Mozart transferred to the concerto movement. There, as in an aria, a second section can be a kind of development, but in an aria (as a continuation within the framework of a genuine da capo aria) it can also be a varied repeat, the usual second half of a main section (cf. the first aria of *Exsultate, jubilate*). It made no difference whether the movement was fast or slow—Mozart cast the motet's second aria in the form closest to that of a concerto movement, on which he had already based the form of almost all the arias in *Ascanio in Alba* in 1771 (but only one in *Lucio Silla*).

It looks as if Mozart suddenly realized, early in 1773, that this form had a universal application: not only the outward similarities of aria and concerto movement, but also the concerto potential of the orchestral 'punctuation system'. The moment he was back in Salzburg he worte his B flat major Violin Concerto, K. 207—which has only recently been recognized as his first concerto, after it was discovered that the date he gave it, '1773', had been subsequently altered for reasons unknown to '1775'; previously the D major Piano Concerto, K. 175, composed in December 1773, was thought to be his first. *Exsultate, jubilate* is thus the last vocal work Mozart composed before the fruitful separation of aria form from the world of opera and its introduction into the world of the concerto.

Eventually aria form and concerto form parted company again; above all, in later arias, Mozart stopped giving the introduction an expansive sonata-like symphonic form, and thus dropped the bi-thematic principle; and as he turned increasingly to *opera buffa*, where action is all-important, he found that it demanded a different style of aria. The evolution of both genres thenceforth followed courses determined by their individual natures.

4

'Three-quarters of an hour at the most': The Masses of 1774–1777

On 4 September 1776 Mozart sent the offertory *Misericordias Domini*, K. 222, which he had composed the previous year, to Padre Giambattista Martini in Bologna. The Mozarts had met the renowned music theorist six years earlier, on their first visit to Italy, when he had been instrumental in securing Mozart's election to the Bologna Accademia Filarmonica, and now Mozart wanted to show him the progress he had made as a composer in the mean time. It is probably truer to say that Mozart was obeying instructions to show Padre Martini his progress, for the initiative came essentially from Leopold Mozart, who also wrote the text of the accompanying letter, which is in Italian but seems to have been conceived in German. The intervening six years had been eventful ones: among other things, Mozart had composed his three operas for Italy (*Mitridate, Ascanio*, and *Lucio Silla*) as well as two for German courts (*La finta giardiniera* for Munich and *Il re pastore* for Salzburg). Leopold Mozart had written to Padre Martini about *Mitridate*, but then the connection had fallen dormant. The Mozarts made the opportunity to write about their current circumstances and to depict themselves in a good light: 'My father is maestro di cappella at the cathedral and this gives me the opportunity to write as much church music as I please', Leopold wrote in his son's name, while he reported of himself: 'He has served the court for thirty-six years now and as he knows that the Archbishop cannot and will not endure the sight of elderly folk he puts little of his energies into performance, and has taken up the literature of the art as his favourite study' (4 September 1776).[1]

Leopold Mozart suppressed here the 'vice' that preceded his title of Kapellmeister. His statement that he had been in the service of the archbishops of Salzburg for thirty-six years is interesting inasmuch as 1743, rather than 1740, is usually regarded as the year of his first appointment. He

---

[1] Excerpts from the letter of 4 Sept. 1776 to Padre Martini are based on the German version published in Nissen, *Biographie*.

was expelled from Salzburg University, and entered the service of Count Thurn-Valsassina, in 1740: perhaps he had some casual contact with the musicians of the Archbishop's court even then. Be that as it may, he represented himself as one who was no longer solely an executant musician or the impresario and teacher of his son (now 20 years old) but thought of himself—especially when writing to Padre Martini—as primarily a researcher in the theory of music.

The letter's signatory, 'Wolfgango Amadeo Mozart', for his part, could report that he now composed chamber music (divertimentos, symphonies, and concertos) and church music (church sonatas as well as vocal pieces). The conditions for his development as a composer had—outwardly, at least—improved greatly since his first journey to Italy. Then, he had been an unpaid third concert-master, but he was promoted to paid second concert-master on 21 August 1772, with an annual salary of 150 gulden. The promotion was, however, a by-product of the reorganization of music in Salzburg in the wake of the election of Hieronymus, Count Colloredo as Prince-Archbishop earlier that year, in succession to Count Schrattenbach; Colloredo was plainly not inclined to continue keeping a vice-Kapellmeister and an adolescent concert-master in his establishment when they spent less time at the court than they did travelling around Europe. The consequence, for Mozart, was a complete transformation of the life he had known: he was required suddenly to be 'settled'. The year 1772 was also a turning-point both in his creative life and in the musical life of Salzburg as a whole, as a younger generation of composers came to the fore at the court in the persons of Mozart himself and Michael Haydn (born 1737), the younger brother of Joseph Haydn. The *Litaniae de venerabili altaris sacramento*, K. 125, and the *Regina coeli*, K. 127, composed in the spring of 1772, may be viewed in this context. Leopold Mozart and the court organist, Anton Cajetan Adlgasser, respectively twenty and ten years older than Michael Haydn, gave up the greater part of their composing activities.[2]

Schrattenbach had been a prince of the Baroque era, but Colloredo was a man of the Enlightenment. The difference, and the effect it had on the conduct of church services and on church music, can be likened to the decline of the South German and Austrian Baroque and the emergence of early Classicism in architecture. Musicians at the court of Salzburg may have hoped in the early months of 1772, before Colloredo's election, that

[2] Schmid, *Mozart und die Salzburger Tradition*, 1.

the musical pomp favoured by Schrattenbach would be carried over into the episcopacy of the next Prince-Archbishop, but if so they were doomed to disappointment. The injunctions issued by Pope Benedict XIV in 1749 in the encyclical 'Annus qui', calling among other things for restraint in church music for the good of the liturgy itself, had hitherto been ignored in Salzburg, but now Colloredo put them into practice. The Mozarts will have noticed the effects by the end of 1772, along with the stricter regulation of the court, but in any case Colloredo's bad name reached Salzburg before he did. Some slandered him (in whispers): 'Women, wine, and night / Have made His Highness's might', while others were blunter: 'The scourge of God is upon us now'.[3] From that time forwards, at all events, all references in the Mozarts' letters to matters that were in any sense politically ticklish were written in code; individual letters of the alphabet were substituted for others according to a pre-arranged system, so that the affected words could be read by initiates but did not immediately catch the censor's eye.

The effect of Colloredo's liturgical measures was felt only gradually. It was not until 1782 for example, after ten years in Salzburg, that he published a pastoral letter directing that German should replace Latin as the language for hymns, above all in the smaller churches. His earliest regulations concerned music in his own cathedral, and in particular the masses which he himself celebrated; presumably he believed in leading from the front. The Mozarts described the effects of the reforms in their letter to Padre Martini:

Our church music is very different from that of Italy, all the more so because a mass with Kyrie, Gloria, Credo, epistle sonata, and Agnus Dei may not last longer than three-quarters of an hour at the most, even on the most important feast-days when His Highness himself reads the service. This kind of composition requires special study, and yet it must be a mass with all the instruments—even military trumpets!

This statement has been interpreted as evidence that Colloredo 'simply forbade' his composers to write fugues (and possibly extended the ban to vocal solos).[4] Walter Senn has demonstrated convincingly, however, that there was no question of a ban of such severity.[5] It is true that if limits were placed on the length of time a mass might last the obvious places at which to wield the scissors were those where very little text was elaborated at great musical length: that is, the fugues in choral movements and the more

---

[3] Quoted by J. H. Lederer in NMA II/5, vol. vi, p. ix.   [4] Abert, *Mozart*, i. 253.
[5] In NMA I/1/1, ii and iii, prefaces.

extensive solo arias. It is not hard to perceive the practical goal that Colloredo was pursuing with his restriction on the duration of masses: he wanted the music cut back and made to serve the liturgy, instead of being allowed to grow luxuriantly at the expense of worship; the delivery of the words was to be enhanced by music, the better to fulfil their liturgical function, but they were not to be embellished to the point where they served merely as an excuse for an indulgent display of musical skills. From that point of view, the limit of three-quarters of an hour was altogether reasonable; the six sections of the Ordinary of the mass, which are the same in every service (Kyrie, Glori, Credo, Sanctus, Benedictus, and Agnus Dei), plus the church sonata and the Offertory, which is part of the Proper of the mass and therefore different each Sunday or feast-day, can be sung on those terms within that length of time.

Colloredo's reform did not lead to new musical forms but to a re-evaluation of existing ones. The missa solemnis became a rare phenomenon, for its ceremonial character demands textual repetition and the obvious way to enhance its 'solemnity' is to allow the more spacious forms—solo arias and choral fugues—to expand freely, and to subdivide the six sections of the Ordinary (above all the Gloria and Credo with their relatively long texts), thereby increasing the number of musical movements. The preference for solo aria and fugue is illustrated by, for example, the Gloria of the 'Dominicus' Mass, K. 66, which Mozart had composed in 1769 (during Schrattenbach's episcopacy, that is) for the first mass celebrated by Dominicus Hagenauer, the son of the Mozarts' landlord, who entered the priesthood. The Gloria opens with fifteen bars for chorus; there follow two solo movements of approximately equal length (the seventy-seven-bar 'Laudamus te' for soprano and the seventy-six-bar 'Domine Deus' for tenor), separated by the choir's 'Gratias agimus', which is only eleven bars long. 'Qui tollis' is also choral, and at twenty-nine bars it is the longest choral movement so far in the Gloria, but the reason for that is the length of the text rather than any musical factor. The longest of the solo arias (the 101-bar 'Quoniam', for soprano) leads up to the finale, the choral fugue 'Cum Sancto Spiritu', which is much longer, at 111 bars, than the other choral movements put together, and longer even than the preceding soprano aria. The total number of bars in this Gloria is thus 420, of which the three solo movements claim 254, and the first three choruses 55, but the 111 bars of the closing fugue treble the choral total. We should beware of overvaluing a numerical breakdown like this, but it does reflect the musical facts. The only other Gloria Mozart wrote that matches the ceremonial character of K. 66 is the monumental one in his C minor Mass, K. 427, of 1783; with the text divided almost exactly as it is in the 'Dominicus' Mass, there are three solo movements totalling 413 bars, and four choral movements, of which the closing fugue is 190 bars long and the other three amount to 134 bars altogether.

The 'three-quarters of an hour' rule made such expansiveness impossible. The first thing that had to go was the subdivision of sections of the mass, while the length of fugal finales—'Cum Sancto Spiritu' at the end of the Gloria, 'Et vitam venturi saeculi' at the end of the Credo—became dependent on how elaborately the preceding portions of the text had been set. Altogether, the desired extent of a mass setting came to approach that of the missa brevis, in which the text is delivered without expansive repetitions, especially in those sections that have longer texts. But even in the missa brevis, how the text is set without repetition remains relatively open.

The ceremonial character of the mass was changed not only by the treatment of the text, however, but also by means of orchestration. The Archbishop's request for 'a mass with all the instruments—even military trumpets' clearly referred to high masses on the most important feasts in the church calendar, especially those days when the Archbishop himself would officiate. For an 'authentic' missa brevis, on the other hand, the 'church trio' (two violins and continuo) with organ sufficed; these were the normal instrumental forces used on ordinary Sundays and minor feasts—when, too, the mass took the form of the missa brevis. On major feast-days, on the other hand, the church trio was joined by a large complement of wind instruments. Clearly, the trombones that might be called upon to support choral singing were always regarded as separate from the other instrumental elements.

The end evidently pursued by Colloredo, a mass that was a missa brevis in form and a missa solemnis in instrumentation, was in fact already customary in Salzburg before his accession; the only new thing was his wish to have this 'missa brevis et solemnis' at high masses when he himself was the celebrant. Even so, substantially longer settings of the mass continued to be sung in Salzburg Cathedral. On All Saints' Day 1777, when the Archbishop was away from Salzburg, although it was a major feast of the kind when he might be expected to celebrate mass in his own cathedral, the music lasted one and a half hours. Clearly there was no general ban on fugues, at all events, but only a restriction on duration, and that affected only masses celebrated by the Archbishop himself, and applied as much to solo movements as to fugues. If Colloredo had forbidden his musicians to write fugues, the Mozarts would probably have found a way of saying so in unexceptionable but unmistakable terms in their letter to the arch-contrapuntist Padre Martini, of all people. It was still permitted, as before, to write fugal settings for the finales of the Gloria and the Credo, and for the 'Dona nobis pacem' at the end of the Agnus Dei, only it now meant cuts in other sections of the mass.

One particularly effective means of achieving brevity is 'polytextualism', when different texts are sung simultaneously by two or more vocal parts. A single bar in Joseph Haydn's early Missa Brevis in F (Hob. XXII: 1) suffices for the following text: 'Quoniam tu solus sanctus' (soprano), 'tu solus Dominus' (tenor), 'tu solus altissimus' (alto), 'Jesu Christe' (bass). The entire text is there—even if it is not really entirely audible. In Mozart, on the other hand, polytextual structures always retain a soloistic element, and the voices always start consecutively, so that listeners can at least keep track of how the text is divided between the singers. Thus a text can be followed in its correct order in the Gloria of the 'Organ solo' Mass, K. 259, for example, if the words are read in the order in which the voices (all solo) enter: soprano, then tenor, lastly bass.

Soprano: Domine Deus, Rex caele-stis, De-us Pa-ter o-mni-po-tens.

| | | |

Tenor: Do-mi-ne Fi-li uni-ge-ni-te.

| | |

Bass: Je-su   Chri-ste.

'Brevis' (short) and 'solemnis' (solemn) are not mutually exclusive terms, and so there is not as clear a generic distinction as posterity might like. Even in the eighteenth century, in borderline cases, people did not insist on assigning masses to one category or the other, and so both terms might be used of the same composition at different times. For example, when the need arose it was possible to turn Mozart's Missa Brevis, K. 192, into a 'missa brevis et solemnis' by adding trumpets. If instrumentation is the criterion, only three of the masses of 1773–7 were actually composed as missae breves (with an accompaniment, that is, of church trio and organ): K. 192, 194, and 275. If the nature of the text is also taken into account, K. 220 (the 'Spatzenmesse'), K. 258, and the 'Organ solo' Mass, K. 259, must be counted as 'missae breves et solemnes'.[6] By the same token, the

[6] On this topic in general, see W. Senn, 'Beiträge zur Mozartforschung', *Acta musicologica*, 48 (1976), 205–27, esp. 208.

remainder—the 'Trinitatis' Mass, K. 167, the 'Credo' Mass, K. 257, and the 'Missa longa', K. 262—are 'missae solemnes', but in none of them are the sections of the mass subdivided as they are in the 'Dominicus' Mass or the C minor Mass, and none of them is as long as either of those. There are some short slow sections in the Glorias and Credos, but most of them do not amount to fully fledged separate movements and remain integral parts of the greater whole.

The Mozarts' reference to the time limit imposed on the mass, in their joint letter to Padre Martini, draws attention to an aspect that is at least relatively and approximately concrete: the total number of bars in individual movements. But even the lengths that can be calculated on this basis show that the limits remain imprecise. The Credo of the so-called Missa Solemnis, K. 337, for example, is shorter (176 bars) than that of K. 194 (183 bars), although the latter is unmistakably a missa brevis. Mozart compensates for this disproportion between 'brevis' and 'solemnis' in K. 337 as a whole with intensive solos in the conclusion of the Gloria and in the Agnus Dei, and with a fugue in the Benedictus—the very means that Colloredo is supposed to have forbidden. Even so, K. 337 remains shorter overall than another, earlier missa brevis, K. 192. There is a more drastic example yet: the first mass by Mozart to exemplify the type 'missa brevis et solemnis' is the 'Spatzenmesse' (Sparrow Mass), K. 220 (which takes its name from the violin figure resembling a sparrow's call, heard in the Sanctus just before 'Pleni sunt coeli'). It is the second shortest of all Mozart's masses and its total number of bars is only two-thirds of that of K. 192, the longest missa brevis.

As the Mozarts said, 'this kind of composition requires special study': setting a lot of text in a small musical space, and producing something of high artistic quality, was possibly even more demanding than pouring the same text into the unlimited expanse of a 'missa solemnis'—which can hardly avoid being impressive between the crowning glory of Gloria, Credo, and Agnus Dei, each with a fugue, on the one hand, and the unworldly rapture of a solo setting of 'Et incarnatus est' and Benedictus on the other. A missa brevis could be so brief as to render artistic considerations virtually irrelevant, but that was not its definitive trait. The delivery of the text, even in a missa brevis, allowed a breadth which could be equalled by that of the 'missa brevis et solemnis' which Colloredo evidently favoured. In that case, we may ask why the Mozarts spoke of a 'special study': if the boundary between 'brevis' and 'brevis et solemnis' was so fluid, a composer attempting the latter was not entering virgin territory.

Was 'solemnis' the word in Mozart's mind as he set to work on an archiepiscopal high mass? In that case he might have had a problem with the brevity required. Or did he feel challenged to produce something special, which would justify adding the epithet 'et solemnis' to a short mass? In that case he might have found that the crucial problem was the compression of the ceremonial aspect (as represented in the style and the instrumental accompaniment, rather than in the word-setting). The former is not very likely, for Leopold Mozart, at least, with over thirty years' experience as a cathedral musician, must have been long familiar with the character of a 'missa brevis et solemnis'. What was new was the Archbishop's choice of the genre for masses celebrated by himself: new not only as a matter of liturgical practice but also as an artistic challenge to the composers, who undoubtedly found it a severe restraint. This explains the notable distrust, at least, with which the Mozarts greeted the Prince-Archbishop's wish; they may also have slightly exaggerated their view of the situation for Padre Martini's benefit. At all events, Mozart's masses of this period—beginning with the 'Spatzenmesse', which was the first to conform to the new restraints—do not show Mozart in open rebellion against the Archbishop's wishes.

5

Mastering the Concerto: The Violin Concertos of 1775

Nearly three months had passed since the première of *Lucio Silla* when Mozart arrived home in Salzburg on 13 March 1773 from what turned out to be his last visit to Italy. Barely a month later he had finished his first instrumental concerto.[1] It looks as if he decided to survey the whole field, for this first concerto (for violin, in B flat major, K. 207) was followed over the next fourteen months by a keyboard concerto (in D major, K. 175), one for several solo instruments (Concertone for two solo violins, with additional solo contributions from oboe and, in the last movement, obbligato cello; C major, K. 190), and one for woodwind (bassoon, in B flat major, K. 191). Of the complete range of instruments for which Mozart was eventually to write a concerto, brass is the only category he did not touch at this time (the lost trumpet concerto, K. 47c, was written several years earlier, while the horn concertos date from after the move to Vienna in 1781). Later he was to write concertos for other woodwind—flute, oboe, and clarinet—and expand the potential of the concerto for two or more instruments. Nevertheless, in that fourteen-month period he mapped out the entire spectrum of fundamental choices of instrumental soloists; this exploratory phase culminated with his finishing the Concertone and the Bassoon Concerto only five days apart (31 May and 4 June 1774).

The year 1775 is one of the few in which Mozart finished two operas (*La finta giardiniera* and *Il re pastore*); otherwise it is dominated by the four violin concertos: K. 211 (in D major), K. 216 (in G major), K. 218 (again in D major), and K. 219 (in A major). Such intense concentration on the procedures and techniques of one musical medium always meant, in Mozart's case, that he not only applied them in individual compositions but also developed further his ideas as a whole about the genre to which the pieces belonged. So, having surveyed the terrain of the instrumental concerto so comprehensively, what advances did Mozart make in these four compositions?

[1] C. H. Mahling in NMA V/14, vol. i, p. xi.

As we have already seen with reference to *Exsultate, jubilate* (Chapter 3), Mozart had discovered the elements of concerto form in vocal music. He had used the form which he derived from the motet in the outer movements of his first two concertos (it was thus 'the' virtuoso concerto form for him at that stage; it also occurs in middle movements[2]). But other possible forms (notably rondo) present themselves in the finales of concertos composed from 1774 onwards, and later Mozart even wrote rondos to replace the original finales of the two concertos of 1773 (the Rondo, K. 382, for the Piano Concerto, K. 175; probably the Rondo, K. 269, for the Violin Concerto, K. 207). It is true that these rondo forms, as well as the structures of some middle movements, are specially tailored to the circumstances of a concerto, that is, they exploit the tutti–solo contrast, but even in music without that special relationship (symphony, sonata, quartet, etc.) rondos may occur in a form which is at least comparable. Only the first-movement form, Mozart's concerto form as such, is inconceivable in a context where there is no soloist.

Thus in his concertos of 1773–4 Mozart adapted a form which had originated in the musical language of opera to the uses of purely instrumental music. The experiments in which he developed the form in the violin concertos of 1775 can be followed step by step,[3] especially if we take the Serenade, K. 204, into consideration as an intermediate step between the D major Concerto, K. 211 (14 June 1775), and the G major Concerto, K. 216 (12 September 1775), for the Serenade was finished on 5 August 1775 and contains a comparable allegro movement for solo violin and orchestra.

In the 'concerto-form' aria, the orchestra first plays a 'prelude' and then the soloist sings the 'first subject' from that opening tutti—sometimes with a free, virtuosic conclusion. After a tutti interjection, the singer takes the lead in the process of modulation, progressing in a first stage from the tonic to the dominant; a second stage serves to stabilize the dominant so that the second subject from the opening tutti, now also in the dominant, can follow. The soloist's free-ranging melodic lines thread through the first of these two segments; the second provides a platform for intensive virtuosic elaboration. This is the model followed by the D major Violin Concerto, K. 211, but the Allegro of the Serenade, K. 204, contains the first signs of a new technique: here, both modulatory segments begin with a 'melodic'

---

[2] On concerto form in the slow movements of Mozart's concertos in general, see K. Weising, *Die Sonatenform in den langsamen Konzertsätzen Mozarts* (Hamburg, 1970).

[3] See Küster, *Formale Aspekte.*

feature; the first is completely dominated by it, but the second moves on to the customary virtuoso display. It is not hard to guess what happens next, in the G major concerto: both segments begin 'melodically' and then take off into virtuosity.

That is the most striking formal change to affect Mozart's concerto composition in 1775. In the G major Concerto it creates an unmistakable impression that he now had a significantly longer breath. But it is not the only thing with which he experimented that year, nor had he yet reached the end of a large-scale evolution.

The first of the two D major concertos shows Mozart already refining his technique for starting a recapitulation: from now onwards it is only very exceptionally that statements of the first subject occur twice, directly one after another, at this point in a concerto (once as a tutti, once as a solo, as is the case in most concertos of the preceding era): a single statement becomes the rule. In the G major Concerto, additionally, Mozart gives the solo part its own motivic material at the beginning of the development section; on the other hand, in the D major Concerto, K. 218 (finished only four weeks later), he brackets this solo entry to the tutti just preceding it, inasmuch as he has the soloist repeat the melody with which the tutti ended; thus, all of a sudden, the strict ordering of the movement in discrete solo and tutti sections is disrupted. (Mozart took this manœuvre to its ultimate height eighteen months later, in the 'Jeunehomme' Piano Concerto in E flat major, K. 271, in which the soloist introduces himself in the first few bars of what sets off as the opening tutti.) A third point affects the presentation of the second subject. In the G major Concerto, as in the early arias, it is still the orchestra that presents it during the solo exposition: the oboes play it first, and only after that does the soloist take it up. In the second D major Concerto, however, the soloist joins in with the orchestra when the second subject first makes an appearance, and in the A major Concerto Mozart even dispenses with the caesura which still serves in K. 218 to separate the theme from what goes before it. This makes the second subject part of an uninterrupted solo line (at most, the soloist may think fit to mark it with a minimal caesura), and none of its melodic material originates with any other instrument. By this process the second subject, which was left to the orchestra in Mozart's earlier concertos and arias, suddenly becomes the preserve of the soloist alone.

The techniques for modulating and stabilizing the dominant in the solo exposition, for letting the soloist take over the second subject, for bracketing together the tutti which concludes the exposition and the solo start of the development, and for beginning the recapitulation became staple structural features of all Mozart's later concertos—although he did not always use all of them, and he continued to develop them further. One outcome of the new motivic construction in the solo exposition was that the 'breathing-spaces' bequeathed to the instrumental concerto by the vocal aria ceased to be redundant and took on a role in the punctuation of the revised form. It was not only modulation and stabilization that could now be treated as separate processes, but also melodic statement and virtuosic elaboration. After developing this system in a series of violin concertos, Mozart lost no time in composing two piano concertos in accordance with the new framework: the completion of the A major Violin Concerto, K. 219, on 20 December 1775 was followed by the composition of the piano concertos in B flat major and C major (K. 238 and K. 246) in January and April 1776.

It is only in tracing the development of underlying features like these that a continuous line can be drawn from the first to the last of the 1775 violin concertos; even their first movements contain specific constructions that give each concerto its own individual technical (as well as melodic) identity, especially the three composed in the autumn of 1775 (K. 216, 218, 219). The opening theme of the G major Concerto anticipates, in miniature, the form of the entire opening tutti: the music begins loudly (*f*) and in the fifth bar, after a fermata, starts a response to what has just been said, but does not finish it; a high c''' on the first violins remains in isolation, while the theme's closing cadence (*p*) is swallowed up in the entry (*f*) of the next element of the ritornello. In the larger expanse of the opening tutti as a whole, too, Mozart introduces a loud 'closing' cadence correspondingly early, long before the tutti is over: we have heard only two-thirds of it, and the remaining third is all played *p*, which does not allow the orchestra to come to a fitting conclusion. As a result the soloist's entry is like a deliverance.

A distinctive detail like that is not one that can be reproduced routinely in other works. The only other work in which the first movement has a similar quiet, inconclusive cadence is the Sinfonia Concertante for violin and viola composed four years later, and it has another thing in common with the G major Violin Concerto: in order to give the movement an effective, loud ending, Mozart brings back the melodic element with which the orchestral tutti bridged the 'breathing-space' between the soloist's presentation of the first subject and the modulation segment. These are the only two works in which Mozart reuses in the closing tutti material he has introduced in a solo (here, the solo exposition). There will be occasion to refer to this again: does it mean that the Sinfonia Concertante was actually influenced by the G major Concerto—perhaps prompted by a performance in the interim?

The A major Concerto, K. 219, similarly has its unique aspect. Mozart begins the piece with a single chord, *f*, and then unfolds a line in the first violins which rises in quavers, *p*, until it reaches the next loud chord. (A rather similar rising line is found in Vivaldi's Violin Concerto, Op. 6 No. 4,[4] but the consequences are different there.) As a matter of compositional form, we can expect that such a 'first subject' will be heard again at the start of the solo exposition, which is due next—yet it does not seem a very promising one. The theme engages the listeners' interest, of course, but it is not one that will allow the soloist to present himself at his best. Mozart's solution is twofold. Firstly, he has the soloist enter not with the orchestral first subject but with material of his own, with which he interrupts the allegro aperto; this material consists of six adagio bars, at the end of which the soloist is supposed to improvise something approximately comparable to the solo cadenza at the end of the movement (unfortunately soloists rarely recognize this opportunity). After that the allegro aperto returns, along with the quiet rising line of the first subject—but only in the orchestra; it serves the soloist as the base above which he unfolds a completely free melodic line which renders the 'theme' almost inaudible. If Mozart spied out the possibilities of allowing an opening tutti to end quietly in the G major Concerto, in the A major Concerto he comes within a hand's breadth of beginning it quietly. Scanning the passage as a whole shows how quickly he came up against limitations: a soloist, especially a violinist, cannot make an effective quiet entry against an orchestra. All the Salzburg concertos begin with a forte (although it is only a single chord in the case of the A major Concerto), and it was only in the Vienna keyboard concertos that Mozart discovered how to let not only the orchestra but also the soloist begin quietly; in this he was undoubtedly helped by the fact that a solo pianist can enter completely alone, so that the question of volume becomes less significant. But the path was a stony one: all Mozart's attempts to reach the goal during his last years in Salzburg remained fragments.

Thus Mozart explored different possibilities in each of these concertos (the D major, K. 218, is the only concerto in which he omitted the

---

[4] A. Schering, *Geschichte des Instrumentalkonzerts bis auf die Gegenwart*, 3rd edn. (Leipzig, 1927; repr. Hildesheim, 1988), 91.

recapitulation of the first subject), and in doing so introduced lasting changes in the evolution of the standard form. It became more integrated, more fully planned than in an equally fascinating but on the whole perhaps more tentative work like the B flat major Concerto, K. 207, composed in the spring of 1773 as the first in the Salzburg series of concertos.

Changes of comparable significance can be observed in the finales of these concertos. In all four of those composed in 1775 the last movement is a rondo, the classic form produced by the alternation of a refrain (which recurs several times during the course of a work, is always in the home key, and may or may not be cut short at its end) and a series of motivically independent episodes. If A represents the rondo refrain, and other letters the episodes, these four finales all have the basic layout ABACADA. But Mozart was clearly not content with that, and wanted to compose finales sufficiently substantial to stand up to the weight of his first (and second) movements. Even in the first of these concertos, the D major, K. 211, he varies the form: instead of having the refrain follow immediately after the third episode, he first brings back the opening themes of the earlier episodes: C, then B. The refrain's last return is thus delayed, and when it comes it is expanded by motivic cells from the soloist's material.

The composer goes further in the other three concertos of this group. He does away with the third episode (D) and replaces it with a piece of folk-like music. In the G major Concerto the Rondo is an Allegro in fast triple time; it is suddenly interrupted by a G minor andante in common time, which switches without warning into a lively, lilting melody in the major (more of this below); and as suddenly as the interruption intervened, it is over again, and the 3/8 tempo is restored.

For the corresponding spot in the D major Concerto, Mozart chose two musette themes. The characteristic of the musette, a member of the bagpipe family, is the combination of a pipe on which a melody can be played with other pipes which emit a single sustained note (they have no holes for fingering). The first of these tunes begins by denying its musette nature, but when it returns towards the end of the section the solo violin establishes its 'provenance' by playing a sustained a'' which was not there first time round. The second bagpipe theme comes between the two appearances of the first, and in this the soloist plays both the melody and the 'drone' harmony.

Finally, the A major Concerto has an 'alla turca' section, with a tune from Hungarian folk-music which had absorbed elements of Turkish music (the generic term is 'törökös'). Mozart may have learnt it from Michael

Haydn, who served the Bishop of Grosswardein, then in Hungary (Nagyvárad; now Oradea in Romania), before coming to Salzburg. (Even so, Mozart knew the tune by 1772, when he used it in sketches for a ballet, *Le gelosie di serraglio*, K⁶ 135a.[5]) Here once more the 'folk-music' section is in two contrasting parts: the second is characterized by sforzandos which make a strong contrast to the soloist's smooth, minor-mode line in the preceding part. The vehemence of the forte chords owes much to the double basses, which Mozart tells to play 'coll'arco al roverscio'—with bows reversed, or 'col legno' in modern musical Italian.

These 'foreign bodies' in the rondo context give the finales of these concertos a special charm, but they also make it necessary to expand the closing section: simple reiteration of the refrain would be an anticlimax, and so in all three Mozart brings back and elaborates elements from the first episode. The development which can be observed taking place during the finales of these concertos reaches its conclusion in the A major Concerto, however, Later, in the rondo finales of the keyboard concertos, Mozart struck out along new paths, as also in the Rondo, K. 269, mentioned earlier in this chapter, which is believed to have been written to replace the original finale of the B flat major Violin Concerto of 1773.

Mozart must have composed a new movement for the A major Concerto as well, not because of his own second thoughts but to satisfy Antonio Brunetti, first violin in the Salzburg court orchestra. In one of his letters to his son Leopold Mozart mentioned the 'Adagio for Brunetti, the other being too studied for his liking' (9 October 1777). This was almost certainly the E major Adagio for violin and orchestra, K. 261, which greatly resembles the original concerto movement in the shaping of the lines; there are a number of places (notably at cadential caesuras, for obvious reasons) which are approached, negotiated, and moved on from in so similar a way that it would be possible to switch from one movement to the other without the least disruption;[6] in other places the motivic material of the later seems to have been borrowed from the earlier (above all in the 'sighs'). It cannot therefore have been that aspect of the original slow movement which displeased Brunetti. Its formal layout is particularly complex, however: the relatively expansive orchestral prelude (22 bars, in 2/4 time, compared with only 4 in 4/4 in K. 261) provides an exceptionally large amount of the soloist's motivic material: virtually every cell (except bars 3–8 and 20–2) is included, in a new order, in the soloist's part. As a

[5] B. Szabolsci, 'Exoticisms in Mozart', *Music and Letters*, 37 (1956), 323–32, esp. 328.

[6] e.g. from b. 28 of K. 219/2 to b. 10 of K. 261, or from bs. 68–9 to bs. 27–8.

result the soloist's part is greatly dependent on the orchestral part, even in matters of interpretation. Mozart clearly took steps to avoid such an unusually close relationship in the later Adagio: the orchestral introduction lays down only the soloist's first four bars, after which he is left to his own devices. If, then, K. 261 is the Adagio written for Brunetti, his objection to the original slow movement of the A major Concerto must therefore have concerned its structural and formal complexity. Yet the same spirit governed Mozart in both; the concerto was finished on 20 December 1775, so the date of '1776' that Leopold Mozart gave the later piece could mean that it was composed very soon afterwards.

Mention of Brunetti raises the question of whom Mozart wrote his violin concertos for. 'For himself' is one answer, another is for Brunetti and other virtuoso violinists in Salzburg. Certainly Brunetti and Mozart both had the same works by Mozart in their repertories and also had their own sets of the parts for use in performance. The evidence is in letters that passed between Mozart and his father in autumn 1777, when Mozart was on his way to Paris for the second time. From Augsburg he wrote: 'In the evening during supper I played the Strasbourg concerto. It went a treat. Everyone praised my beautiful, pure tone' (24 October 1777). Only eighteen days earlier, however, when Mozart was in Munich, his father wrote from Salzburg that Brunetti had to play a concerto during an interval in the theatre, 'and it was yours with the Strasbourg tune'.

There is no reason to doubt that by 'your concerto with the Strasbourg tune' and 'the Strasbourg concerto' father and son meant the same work, but identifying it has caused some head-scratching. At one stage the answer was thought to have been found when the finale of the D major Concerto, K. 218, was discovered to contain reminiscences of a 'Ballo Strasburghese' in a symphony by Dittersdorf. There is a much more plausible connection, however, with a melody entitled 'An incomprehensible song "ad notam Strassburger"', which was found in a collection of Hungarian songs and is identical in every respect with the lively folktune Mozart uses in the Rondo of the G major Concerto.[7] This must be 'the Strasbourg concerto'—and its performance in Augsburg in October 1777 could well explain not only why the processes of the Violin Concerto in G major plainly influenced the concertante works for flute composed during the journey of 1777–8,[8] but also the similarities that have already been men-

[7] D. Bartha, 'Zur Identifikation des "Straßburger Konzerts" bei Mozart', in A. A. Abert and W. Pfannkuch (eds.), *Festschrift Friedrich Blume zum 70. Geburtstag* (Kassel, 1963), 30–3.

[8] See Abert, *Mozart*, i. 513.

tioned between this concerto and the Sinfonia Concertante for violin and viola, composed shortly after the return to Salzburg: it is likely that in the latter Mozart developed structural ideas that he had been thinking about during the journey.

Shortly before setting off on that journey, Mozart may have composed a sixth violin concerto (in D major, K⁶ 271*i*) for himself to play. It has survived only in a curious version from early nineteenth-century Paris, but that may possibly go back to a torso of Mozart's original.[9] It fits very comfortably into the biographical data: the lost autograph is said to have been dated 16 July 1777; the Salzburg Court Councillor Joachim Ferdinand von Schiedenhofen mentions in his diary for 25 July the rehearsal for a concert that Mozart was arranging that same evening in honour of his sister, with a violin concerto on the programme. If the concerto's authenticity could be established, we would thus have an eyewitness for the date of its first performance.

The significance of this is that several of Leopold Mozart's letters refer to Mozart's having once composed a violin concerto for a player called Kolb (opinions are divided about his first name and hence about his exact identity). Some commentators have identified that putative sixth concerto as the work in question,[10] but what is known about its composition does not support the hypothesis. The B flat major Concerto, K. 207, has also been mentioned as a candidate, but since it became clear that that was Mozart's very first concerto it has looked most improbable that he would have written one for another person to play before having composed any others. Furthermore the B flat major Concerto could have been referred to more plainly, from a rondo which was composed for it—apparently another example of Mozart's bowing to Brunetti's wishes (that, at least, is a possible reading of the mention of a rondo in Leopold Mozart's letter of 25 September 1777). There remain the two concertos in D major, K. 211 and 218; K. 218 is the most likely candidate of all, because the authentication of its autograph differs from that of the other concertos: all the others are signed and dated in full by Mozart himself, but the inscription on K. 218 was unmistakably written by Leopold Mozart;[11] moreover, he gave only 'October 1775' as the date, without being precise as to the day on which it was finished.

It is thus conceivable that Mozart wrote his violin concertos in the first place for himself, or perhaps for Brunetti as a leading member of the court

[9] See Küster, *Formale Aspekte*, 203–8.   [10] C. H. Mahling in NMA V/14, vol. i, p. ix.
[11] Plath, 'Beiträge 1', 84–5. I am indebted to Wolfgang Plath for additional information.

orchestra, and that he wrote a new E major Adagio for the A major Concerto at Brunetti's wish, perhaps soon after finishing the work itself. The only one that might have been written for a third person is the one in D major that he did not sign and date himself (as he did all his other Salzburg manuscripts).

There is one distinct obstacle in seeking the answers to these questions. These concertos differ from many of Mozart's works, from various periods of his life, in that references to them in letters or other documents are found only at some distance from the date of their composition (apart from such rare and lucky coincidences as the entry in Schiedenhofen's diary). That is because they were composed during the longest continuous period that Mozart spent in Salzburg after 1762, from 7 March 1775 (return to Salzburg from Munich after the completion of *La finta giardiniera*) to 23 September 1777 (departure for Paris). The importance for biographers of the letters written during the composer's absences from home could hardly be more awesomely demonstrated.

6

The Salzburg Symphonies: Especially K. 183 in G minor and K. 201 in A major

When Mozart wrote his first symphony in 1764, the genre was not as well defined as it is today, when our conception of it is strongly coloured by what it became in the nineteenth century. In the mid-eighteenth century the word 'symphony' was still also used of the instrumental movements encountered in the course of a large-scale vocal work, especially at the beginning of an opera or cantata. One well-known example is the Pastoral Symphony with which the second cantata in J. S. Bach's *Christmas Oratorio* opens: a single-movement instrumental piece with features that are better described as concertante than symphonic in any standard classical–romantic sense. Yet this is the tradition on which Mozart's symphonic style builds, and the foundations are even clearer in another of Bach's choral works: the *Easter Oratorio*. This begins with a concertante 'sinfonia' in not one but two movements; the first is fast and major-mode, the second slow and minor, which arouses expectations of a third, and final, movement (fast and major again), but the oratorio's first vocal movement ensues instead.

It is not we alone but also listeners of Bach's own time who might have expected a third orchestral movement at that point. Three movements are the rule in Neapolitan operatic overtures, and concertante elements (even whole movements) are by no means rare in them. There is a purpose, too, in the 'incompleteness' of Bach's two-movement overture: instead of the 'sinfonia' being something complete in itself, its introductory function is underlined, when what might yet seem at first to be a third movement suddenly unmasks itself as the opening movement of the vocal work proper. Mozart must have been alive to all these considerations.

He composed his first symphony in London, not long after Johann Christian Bach had settled there. Bach had made his name above all with three operas that had first seen the light in Turin and Naples. His six symphonies, Op. III, each in three movements, were first published in 1765 and reprinted several times, with title-pages that sometimes called them symphonies ('simphonies' in the first edition) and sometimes overtures. Works that J. C. Bach originally composed as operatic overtures were also later published as independent instrumental pieces. The Neapolitan opera composer Niccolò Jommelli was also greatly admired as a symphonist on the strength of his three-movement overtures, and it was clearly Jommelli who broke the ground for the pioneering symphonic style of the Mannheim School; indeed, he outshone the Mannheimers in the opinion of some contemporaries. Jommelli spent many years in Stuttgart, and an inventory of music there, compiled in 1808, lists nine symphonies by Joseph Haydn, seven by Karl Ditters von Dittersdorf—and six by Jommelli, who thus takes third position even in that company, and exclusively on the strength of operatic overtures.[1] This shows that at the very time when Beethoven was working on his Fifth and Sixth Symphonies (both were performed for the first time in 1808) there were places where the old traditional connection between symphony and operatic overture was still upheld.

Mozart was aware of the tradition; when he writes from Italy that he has 'composed four Italian symphonies' (4 August 1770) he clearly means works distinguished by characteristics of Italian style, the most obvious of which is being in three movements. But his symphonic writing had other origins as well, and some instances show him taking different, more independent paths even then. He had another example in the symphonies of his own father (which are variously in three, four, or more movements, but follow the Viennese fashion in a fondness for including a minuet), and he also knew works of the Mannheim School, which was pre-eminent in this field. Mannheim symphonies already had four movements, from the inclusion of a minuet before the finale (there was a single, early precedent for this in a work by the Viennese composer Mathias Georg Monn, dating from 1740[2]). Mozart continued to honour both forms throughout his life: the number of 'Neapolitan' three-movement symphonies is not significantly less than that of four-movement 'Mannheim' or 'Viennese' works, and even the 'Prague' (K. 504, 1786) 'lacks' a minuet. Even so, it is not surprising to note that he composed his first four-movement symphonies in Vienna (1767–8: K⁶ 42*a* and 45*b*, K. 43, 45, 48).

---

[1] On Jommelli as a symphonist, see H. Hell, *Die italienische Opernsinfonie in der ersten Hälfte des 18. Jahrhunderts* (Tutzing, 1971), 359–60; 487–501. On Stuttgart at that period, see K. Küster in *Baden und Württemberg im Zeitalter Napoleons* (exhibition catalogue; Stuttgart, 1987), i/2, 878 (item 1454); 919 (item 1501).

[2] J. LaRue, 'Symphonie', *Die Musik in Geschichte und Gegenwart*, xii (Kassel, 1965), col. 1811; see also LaRue's contribution to 'Symphony', *The New Grove Dictionary of Music and Musicians* (London, 1980), xviii, 438–53, esp. 443.

Mozart was a more productive symphonist in Salzburg than later in Vienna. It is true that between the 'Haffner' Symphony (K. 385, 1782) and the 'Jupiter' (K. 551, 1788) he wrote the classics of his later symphonic output, but the six Viennese symphonies (among which the 'Haffner' is a special case) represent only a small proportion numerically out of the fifty-odd that survive altogether. The 'symphonic period' in his career can be defined even more narrowly: the great majority of the symphonies were composed between the start of his second journey to Vienna (1767) and the end of 1774: nearly forty in seven years (these numbers have to be given as approximates because there is no means of confirming the authenticity of works of which only the opening bars have survived, with an attribution to Mozart). This illustrates incidentally that not only in Vienna but in Salzburg too the musical life of the city set its own individual imprint on the symphonies.

Some among Mozart's early three-movement symphonies belong intrinsically to the operatic tradition of the symphony, rather than merely in the general, music-historical sense. Each of Mozart's early operas was consistently followed by the composition of separate symphonic movements, with which he seems to have 'completed' the overtures to make symphonies of them. Some of the overtures were in more than one movement to begin with; in *Ascanio in Alba* (K. 111, 1771) and *La finta giardiniera* (K. 196, 1775), Mozart did exactly the same as J. S. Bach did in the *Easter Oratorio* (in *Ascanio* the opera even begins during the slow movement, with a ballet). The process was actually reversed in the case of *La finta semplice* (1768), Mozart's first Italian opera, the overture of which was adapted from the four-movement symphony K. 45, written half a year earlier (the minuet was omitted). And because Mozart's symphonic output is distributed so unevenly through his *œuvre* as a whole, we have to confront the almost grotesque fact that even among his last twelve symphonies, two, and perhaps a third, were composed in immediate association with operas: as well as the extensions of the overtures of *La finta giardiniera* and *Il re pastore* (K. 208, 1775), there is the 'symphony' K. 318, whose three movements are played without a break and which may have been written as the overture for an opera.

Mozart's early symphonies are relatively short and formally modest. Their first movements can already be described in terms of that 'sonata form' inseparable from the classical–romantic symphony, but as yet they are innocent of the process whereby the principal theme prepares the ground for the subsidiary theme. This process requires that after the first statement of the principal theme it should be re-commenced, but this time it should not go on to its original conclusion but must be diverted and steered towards the dominant, and so to the second subject. But this is never exactly what happens in Mozart's symphonies, even in the late, Viennese ones.

To refer to the dominant as the goal, the achievement of which enables the second subject to come into existence, is ambiguous, because the dominant can be expressed in either of two ways. On the one hand it is a component of the standardized cadential sequence of tonic, subdominant, dominant, and repeated tonic, which together define a tonality; in that context the dominant has neither finality nor self-sufficiency, for it requires to be completed by the final return to the tonic. On the other hand, it can also stand in a merely 'dominant relationship' to the tonic key of an entire symphonic movement and as such, after appropriate modulation, assume the role of main key for a limited period (can serve, that is, as a new tonic for practical purposes, and a fit goal for a cadence). In Mozart's early symphonies the second subject is usually prepared in the first, more primitive of these ways: after a dominant half close it enters freely in the dominant, which is established only at this point, together with the theme itself. Things go differently in the middle and late symphonies: there, the entrance of the second subject is preceded by a section which serves solely to establish the dominant (this is without reference to how Mozart shapes the melodic means of the transition from one theme to the other).

Only two of the Salzburg symphonies qualify for the description 'famous': the G minor, K. 183, and the A major, K. 201; and they both belong in a period when Mozart's ideas of motivic and harmonic structures were in transition—and, moreover, one when the symphonic boom, for him, was long past its height (in terms of quantity, at least). In these two works, Mozart combined his extended understanding of tonality with his ideas about thematic development, and they both also draw near to the classical–romantic norm in being in four movements. He continued to think well of them after leaving Salzburg: early in 1783, in a letter to his father, he asked to have them sent to Vienna, as well as two others, because he intended to perform them.

The letter in question (4 January 1783) is rewarding reading, for it illustrates a number of aspects of Mozart's life and way of working (see Pl. 4). He identifies the four symphonies he wants by their incipits: first he writes the opening bars of the D major Serenade, K. 204 (more of this in Chapter 7); on the second stave, left, the theme of the A major Symphony,

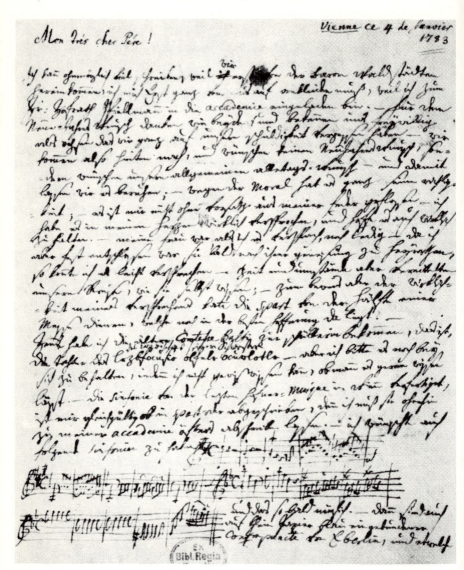

PL. 4. Letter from Mozart to his father, Vienna, 4 January 1783, with the opening phrases of the D major Serenade, K. 204, and three symphonies: A major, K. 201, B flat major, K. 182, and G minor, K. 183. A coded reference to 'the Archbishop's sister' (with Nissen's decoding above it) is five lines above the first line of music.

K. 201, with that of the G minor Symphony, K. 183, immediately below it; on the right-hand half of the middle stave, finally, he writes the opening of the B flat major Symphony, K. 182, a close sibling of K. 183 in date of composition. He wrote the themes out from memory; the last two notes in the second bar of the excerpt from the A major Symphony are G♯ instead of F♯ (this is probably only a slip of the pen), and the trills in that from the B flat major Symphony are in shorter notes than in the score, but we must bear in mind that it was ten years since he had composed them. We can see how well he remembered them, though in other circumstances it might be different, as with the 'Haffner' Symphony, which he wrote in haste and of which he was forced to confess after only six months, in another letter to his father: 'The new Haffner Symphony took me quite by surprise—I didn't recognize a note of it' (15 February 1783).

Another feature of the letter of 4 January 1783 is that it contains an example of the code the Mozart used for anything that might catch the eye of Archbishop Colloredo's censor (all letters were liable to be opened in those days). Words were made incomprehensible by replacing individual letters with 'wrong' ones. Beginning seven lines above the music staves, and ending with the first word in the fourth line above them (readers unfamiliar with eighteenth-century German script may nevertheless be able to make out the words 'Die Sinfonie' with which the next sentence begins), Mozart writes: 'I have acquired a new pupil today in the elder Countess Balfi [Pálffy], that is, the daughter of the Archbishop's sister, but I beg you to keep it to yourself, because I'm not at all sure that they [her family] want it to be known.' Written in clear, the phrase 'the Archbishop's sister'—or rather, in a now archaic idiom, 'the Archbishop his sister'—would be 'des Erzbischofs seiner Schwester'. But in the code, E is substituted for L, I for F, H for U, and S for O, and vice versa, and Mozart actually wrote '[des] lrzbfocusio olfnlr ocuwlotlr'. His biographer (and the second husband of his widow) Georg Nikolaus Nissen decoded the phrase and wrote it above the line on the manuscript.

Back to the symphonies: to what extent do they express the new aspects of Mozart's symphonic style?

In the first movement of the G minor Symphony we encounter a peculiar situation—Mozart was in the same position fifteen years later in his only other minor symphony, also in G, K. 550. In symphonies (and sonatas) in the minor, the second subject enters in the relative major key (that is, a minor third above the tonic); as a result there is not only a change of key between the first and second subjects, but also a change of mode, and hence of the entire character and colour of the sound. It is necessary, therefore, for the minor character to be asserted unmistakably at the start: if the composer abandons the minor region too soon the whole piece comes to lack the proper tonal relationships and even the underlying minor coloration. The task of the symphonic 'theme' is thus twofold: not only must it present motivic material that can be elaborated as the movement proceeds, but also, and perhaps even more important, it must establish an underlying mood through the character of the musical sound. It is therefore almost inevitable in minor-mode symphonies that the first subject will be re-commenced during the transition, but will be altered and directed towards a different ending. In K. 183 the music breaks off suddenly after twelve bars; the dominant prepared by the orchestral unison (as an imperfect cadence, not yet as a 'new tonic') demands resolution in the minor, tonic key. The demand is duly met—but by the recurrence of the theme that Mozart used to identify the symphony in the letter to his father, only the bass line is different, and horns have been added to the orchestration. Is this a new beginning or an 'answer' to the phrase broken off so abruptly? The listener probably hears the first four bars of what comes next as an answer, but then the mood changes, as the dynamic drops to **p**. Unlike its first full statement, the theme starts again—for a third appearance, that is—now played by a solo oboe. This has been playing the theme with the other instruments from the beginning, without dissolving it in syncopations; instead it has played only the essential melodic substance of the four bars in semibreves, and that is what it does now. The frenzy of the theme gives way to an almost icy stillness. The oboe continues the four bars of the theme, following the outline of the original continuation (as in the last of the bars Mozart quoted in his letter, but still in long note-values). Beginning on a low *g'*, it jumps a complete octave with the next note to *g''*, and then, as in the original theme, rises by a major third to *bb''*. By this route, the music reaches another fermata in bar 28, and once again it comes after another half close on the dominant, just as it did sixteen bars earlier. But now the situation is completely altered: no 'answer' can be expected this time; the tonic has been presented unequivocally, and the fermata itself was prepared differently (**pp**, not in a unison **f**). Now it is safe to change the mood by every means possible: from **pp** to **f**, from minor to major, from the icy motionlessness of the last few bars to an excited buzz (set off by the tremolos of the accompanying second violins and violas). It is still too early perhaps for a second subject to make its entry, for that too needs a stable foundation—or so the relatively young Mozart of 1773 has evidently decided; a surprise would cancel out the stability. Having arrived in B flat major, the music starts off again with an octave leap, as it did when the solo oboe began its continuation of the first subject. Mozart develops this into a contrapuntal section, lining up the first violins and the two oboes against the might of the B♭ horns and the low strings (in whose part the octave is reduced to a seventh, which has the effect of making the motivic material seem more tense). The transition that emerges from this is characterized by the forceful rhythms of the bass; this too is not sprung as a surprise but is associated with the octave leap each time the major section recurs—moreover the first violins suddenly reintroduce the syncopations of the first subject. After this transition the ground has been well and truly prepared for the entry of the tripping second subject, but the situation is now quite different from what it was before the startling incursion of the major mode; the B flat major of the second subject is preceded by its own dominant (F major, but in the form of an imperfect cadence), and once again there is a brief fermata.

This kind of thorough working is rare in Mozart's earlier symphonies. Either they are too short-winded to prepare the second subject over so long a span (it does not enter until bar 59 in this case), or the motivic material is not shaped coherently enough (although a unifying, underlying mood, at least, is always discernible). The same structural principle is found in the late G minor Symphony, where, too, the music first travels to a half close on the dominant, after which the first subject begins again; here, however, in the kind of evolution more typical of this transitional passage, it goes directly to the major, without pausing at another fermata. Even in this mature symphony, however, Mozart prepares the ground for the second subject more economically and reaches that goal by bar 42, significantly sooner than in the earlier work. Although K. 550 is Mozart's only other minor-key symphony, the structural principle is one he put to use in others among his 'late' symphonies: the path taken by the first few bars (leading to the dominant, whether the key signature is minor or major) is always constructed along the same lines. No more than the later work, the early G minor Symphony does not have what can really be called an opening 'theme': instead, still employing the technique he used in his first London symphony, Mozart strings together motivically discrete blocks (first unison syncopations, next the thematic ascent quoted in the 1783 letter, then the immediate preparation of the imperfect cadence). The impression is gained that in this work Mozart's symphonic forms are enriched by the acquisition of a whole new element, namely the 'evolution as transition' inserted between the 'old' half close on the dominant and the 'old' second subject ('old' meaning what is found in the expositions of the earlier symphonies). In the 'old' form the minor character at the start of the movement could not have been made distinct enough; only the 'new' form allowed Mozart to write a symphony in the minor mode at all—and hence, almost unnoticed, it opened the door to the form of his 'great' (and longer) symphonies.

The dense thematic construction is characteristic of the rest of the movement. In the development section Mozart again allows the pulse to freeze, by varying the ominous oboe version of the first subject, and in the recapitulation the double imperfect cadence (bars 128 and 144) makes it possible for the originally major transition to switch abruptly, and without any preparation, into the minor, which is as unexpected as the sudden onset of the major in the exposition, although the resulting sequence dominant–tonic is the most normal thing in the world. In the late G minor Symphony that particular step cannot be taken so directly and the original modulation must be appropriately 'manipulated'.

The second movement is in E flat major—not in B flat, which is G minor's relative major and used for the second subjects of both the first and fourth movements. Mozart had good reason to choose the submediant: the underlying mood of E flat major, the key of operatic 'ombra' (shade) scenes, is very close to that of minor modality (Mozart's first symphony, K. 16, is in E flat major overall, but its middle movement is in a minor key). The 'shadowiness' spreads to the instrumentation: the juxtaposition of muted violins and bassoon gives the music a unique tone quality.[3] After the B flat major of the first movement's second subject, the E flat major represents another of G minor's major-mode relatives; in the Trio, finally, between the two outings of the Minuet, we encounter a third: this time Mozart sticks with G, but major not minor. Thus major modality is seen in three of its aspects—and Mozart repeated the pattern in the late G minor Symphony. There is also an odd feature in the instrumentation of the Trio of K. 183 which is unusually appropriate to the movement title: almost throughout, there are obbligato parts for each of the two oboes, and one for both bassoons, while the horns play only supporting harmonies, and the strings do not play at all; but at one point Mozart briefly divides the basson part, and one of the two horns joins company with the second oboe.

---

[3] On a similar instance in *La finta giardiniera*, see Kunze, *Mozarts Opern*, 58–9.

The G minor Symphony, K. 183, shows how far Mozart's symphonic style had progressed by 1773, not only in formal respects but also in instrumentation. The latter aspect can be illustrated by reference to the A major Symphony of the following year, and in particular to the conclusions of its movements. There is least to be said about the first movement, at the end of which the first subject in its most characteristic form, as quoted by Mozart in his letter of 4 January 1783, is absorbed in a separate coda-like tutti. (It is out of this form, too, that the first subject evolves into the second, though the process is not punctuated by fermatas as in the late symphonies and the early G minor.) Things are different in the second movement, where—as in K. 183—the strings are muted. Like fitting a soft-focus lens, this has the effect of instantly disguising the fanfare quality of this movement's opening motif; it is most easily recognizable in the two violin parts, then all of a sudden it rings out in the oboe, in sharp focus and a high register. It puts an end to the contemplative mood, the violinists remove their mutes, and a few bars later the movement is over, before that astonishing effect has faded. It is a matter of opinion whether the oboe's incursion here is destructive or valedictory: at all events it unmistakably sounds a signal. The third movement plays its own game with the idea of ending: the first two sections of the Minuet end with a figure for wind (oboes and horns) which is purely rhythmic, without a trace of melodic character; the musicologist Jan LaRue once said that the 'witty last word' is left to the oboes and horns.[4] But that is not all: it also serves as a 'first word', as the strings demonstrate after the caesura in the middle of the Minuet, where Mozart starts the second part of the movement off just as wittily (if not more so) with the same purely rhythmic figure. Finally, listening to the fourth movement, we may well ask if it can ever end at all: each section ends with the violins playing a rising scale in small note-values, a figure typical of the Mannheim School, aptly named the 'rocket'. The figure seems to preclude any ending, to insist on continuation. Undeterred, when he reaches the coda, Mozart follows it with the movement's first subject, played in unison by the entire orchestra, and the listener may well imagine that the ending is not a problem after all. But suddenly the texture divides again, and the confounded rocket is fired once more (albeit a fifth lower than previously); then comes the end, two simple chords: dominant, tonic—as if Mozart wanted to say 'The simpler the better'. Indeed, and it could scarcely be wittier.

[4] LaRue, 'Symphonie', col. 1818.

7

Music for Salzburg's Patrician Families:
Serenades and Finalmusiken

One of the four 'symphonies' that Mozart (writing from Vienna on 4 January 1783) asked his father to send him was the Serenade, K. 204, or rather, a version of it reduced from seven movements to four. The second, third, and fourth movements—two concertante movements with solo violin and a minuet—had been dropped, leaving a four-movement symphony made up of the opening Allegro, an untitled slow movement, a Minuet, and an Allegro finale that begins with an Andantino grazioso. Mozart adapted other works similarly. In the case of the 'Posthorn' Serenade, K. 320, on the other hand, he extracted the concertante movements to form a small concerto. Writing again from Vienna, on 29 March 1783, he told his father that he had included 'the little concertante symphony from my last final Musique' in the programme of a concert given in the Burgtheater; the movements in question are even marked 'concertante' in Mozart's autograph.

There were other serenades which might have been quarried for the material for either a symphony or a mini-concerto, and sometimes the concertante movements amount to a completely self-sufficient unit within the work as a whole. In the two D major serenades, K. 185 and 203, these 'concertinos' are in F major and B flat major respectively—relatively remote from the home key. The sequence of the movements in K. 203, in particular, is very similar to that of K. 204, the serenade mentioned at the start of this chapter, and it too could have been turned into a symphony— but there is no sign that that ever happened.

The 'Posthorn' Serenade does not get its popular title from Mozart. He called it a 'final Musique', which raises the complex question of the nomenclature of serenades, divertimentos, cassations, 'Nachtmusiken', and 'Finalmusiken'—a question to which no one had a wholly clear-cut answer even in the eighteenth century.[1] Take Mozart's Cassation, K. 63, as an

---

[1] See G. Hausswald in NMA IV/12, vol. ii, pp. vii–ix.

example. The composer refers to it by that name in one of his letters, and it is the title on an early manuscript copy of the work from Stift Lambach; the title on Mozart's autograph, however, written in the hand of Leopold Mozart, is 'Divertimento',[2] and finally, there is a set of parts from Kremsmünster, on which the title is 'Serenata'. 'Serenada' is the title on the autograph of a work in C minor for wind (two each of oboes, clarinets, horns, and bassoons: K. 388), but in a letter Mozart calls the same work a 'Nacht Musique'. *Eine kleine Nachtmusik*, K. 525, is also a serenade, and it was first printed with that title, but the familiar name goes back to Mozart himself.

The distinctions are thus not very precise. 'Serenade' means 'evening music' (from Italian 'sera'), and similarly 'Nachtmusik' means 'night music'. A 'divertimento' is essentially something meant to entertain, or 'divert'. On the other hand, the etymology of 'cassation' is uncertain: one theory is that it derives from the big drum ('cassa') which lends its pomp to the marches with which the musicians arrive and depart—but such marches, with big drum, are also a feature of serenades and divertimentos. Other features such as the types and order of movements, or the instrumentation, are no more definitive: sometimes a divertimento is a work for full orchestra in several movements, but it is not uncommon to find the title given to works for wind ensemble alone; Mozart even used it (entirely in keeping with the tradition of the genre) as the title for a three-movement piano trio, K. 254. A 'serenata' can be a purely instrumental affair, or it can assume quite different traits: Mozart's 'opera' *Ascanio in Alba* is actually subtitled 'serenata teatrale'.

Clearly there were different terminological traditions which ran so closely alongside each other that they are hard to disentangle. From time to time, however, musicians of the era must have chosen one of the terms because they had a quite specific idea of the context in which the work would have its first performance. This is fully borne out in the correspondence of the two Mozarts, where compositions are identified briefly but unambiguously, above all in the use of the expression 'Finalmusik' not primarily to define form or instrumentation but to designate a regular event in the Salzburg calendar. Every year, at the end of the summer examinations, the students of the philosophy faculty at the university 'serenaded' the Archbishop and their professors: the 'logicians' (first-year students) on one evening, and the 'physicians' (second-year students) on another. Both

---

[2] I am indebted to Wolfgang Plath for bringing the different writers' use of these terms to my attention.

events filled an entire evening, as each work was performed twice, once outside the Archbishop's palace, Schloss Mirabell, and once outside the college, where the professors lived (if they were priests). Interested members of the public used to follow the musicians through the city to hear both performances: in 1776, when the work was not by Mozart, Joachim Ferdinand von Schiedenhofen was among them. He wrote in his diary: 'It was the logicians' Final Music tonight . . . I heard it in both places.'[3] Or, as Mozart's sister reported in August 1775, referring to K. 204: 'The rehearsal of the Final Music my brother composed for the logicians was on the 8th . . . The Final Music was on the 9th. It left us at 8.30 [p.m.] for the Mirabell, where it lasted until 9.45, and from there to the college, where it went on until after 11.' The Mozarts lived at that date on Hannibal-platz (today Makartplatz), which was on the right bank of the Salzach, like Schloss Mirabell. The college, like the castle and the cathedral, was on the other side of the river, close to Mozart's birthplace. Of course a march, or something like one, was necessary to be played before and after the serenade itself, to accompany the procession through the city. Sometimes the same piece was played twice, but on other occasions—as in the case of the 'Posthorn' Serenade—two marches were provided.

Like most works that can be grouped under the general heading of 'divertimentos', Finalmusiken were written to commission. They were nothing to do with the university officially, but were a private matter for each generation of students. In several cases it can be established who gave Mozart the commission, as for example in 1773, from a letter Leopold Mozart wrote to his wife from Vienna, where he had accompanied his son: 'I must close to give myself time to write a few lines to young Herr von Andretter and send him the opening of the Final Musik' (21 July 1773). 'Young Herr von Andretter' can only be Thaddäus, the eldest son of Johann Ernst von Antretter, who was Provincial Chancellor and a member of the War Council of the court of Salzburg. Thaddäus had left the Latin School in 1772, and presumably went straight to the university, so that in the summer of 1773, when he was 20, he would have just finished his first year. The only work by Mozart that fits the date is the D major Serenade, K. 185, framed by the March, K. 189, played both before and afterwards. They are scored for two woodwind and four brass players, plus the 'normal' string complement, and Mozart rings the changes within that ensemble very effectively: not only is there the self-contained F major

---

[3] See O. E. Deutsch, 'Aus Schiedenhofens Tagebuch', *MJb* 1957, 15–24.

'concertino' for violin mentioned above, formed by the second and third movements, but also, for example, the Trio of the first Minuet is scored for flute, two violas, and bass alone.

It looks as though another serenade by Mozart was performed in the Antretters' family circle only a few days earlier. The D major Divertimento, K. 205, is probably the work Leopold Mozart meant when he once referred to one of his son's works as 'the music for Frau Andretter': if that is so, then it would have been composed for St Anne's day (26 July), the name-day of Thaddäus's mother, Maria Anna von Antretter. It is on a smaller scale than K. 185 in every respect. It contains no independent 'concertino' and it is scored for only violin, viola, bassoon, bass, and two horns. Broadly speaking, however, both works are constructed on the same typical serenade pattern: an opening Allegro (with a slow introduction in K. 205) followed by a Minuet and Trio, a slow movement, a second Minuet and Trio, and a fast Finale (with an Adagio introduction in K. 185). The 'final music' has, additionally, the two concertante movements immediately after the first movement; in other works of the same type that slot may be occupied by another slow tutti movement, but Frau Antretter's serenade has nothing extra there.

The two serenades K. 203 (1774) and 204 (1775) were also Finalmusiken, but there is no surviving evidence to indicate who commissioned either of them. In 1769 Mozart wrote Finalmusiken for both the 'logicians' and the 'physicians', which were played only two days apart (6 and 8 August). It is usually assumed that K. 100 was one of those two pieces, but as it is in eight movements, while there are two more works of the same year which are both on the same six-movement pattern, it is quite possible that they were the two in question (K. 63 and 99). The two are also scored for the same ensemble, though admittedly they lack the trumpets required by both K. 100 and the Antretter Finalmusik. On the other hand, perhaps no typological similarity was intended and the number of instruments and movements was governed purely by what the client was prepared to pay. Any two of these three works could have been the two Finalmusiken, and it may well never be possible to say which of them was not.

Whenever Mozart calls one of his serenades a Finalmusik we can be sure that he means that it was composed for one of those unofficial end-of-term occasions. So his reference to the 'concertante symphony' from the 'Posthorn' Serenade as part of 'my last final Musique' (quoted in the first paragraph of this chapter) tells us all we need to know about the occasion of the work's composition. It is sometimes said to have been written for the Archbishop of Salzburg's name-day (30 September), but it was finished on 3 August 1779, just right for the usual time when the Finalmusiken were performed, and it was to be the last piece he wrote for students of Salzburg University. The part for posthorn in the penultimate movement (Trio II of the Minuet) may be an allusion to the students' imminent departure on vacation.[4]

Later performances of a work in a different context will scarcely have been enough reason for Mozart to change its title. It is more likely that an outsider, or even Leopold Mozart, could have erred in recalling the occasion for which one of these works was composed, but when father and son concur there should be no grounds for doubt. It follows that the D major Serenade, K. 251, was a Finalmusik from the outset, for that is what both the Mozarts call it. It is the only Finalmusik by Mozart with a 'concluding rondo' (letter of 2 October 1777), and it also has an 'Andante and Trio with oboe solo' (23 November 1778). In these circumstances it is unlikely that it was composed originally for Nannerl Mozart's name-day in 1776 and only recycled as a Finalmusik in the following year,[5] for surely Mozart would then have referred to it by something on the lines of 'my music for Nannerl which I turned into a Finalmusik'. Admittedly, the chronology is problematic: according to Leopold Mozart, who dated the autograph, it was composed in July 1776, but according to Schiedenhofen's diary neither of the Finalmusiken that year was by Mozart. On the other hand we have Schiedenhofen's testimony that Mozart wrote a second Finalmusik in 1775—and that work has not been identified.

The D major Finalmusik K. 251 is in only five movements; it differs from a four-movement Viennese symphony in having an extra minuet and trio before the slow movement. This demonstrates that there really was no hard and fast pattern of movements in a Finalmusik, and neither the presence nor absence of concertante movements is a clear indication that a particular serenade was one or not. There is a 'concertino' in the 'Haffner' Serenade, K. 250, which was undoubtedly written for a wholly non-academic occasion—for performance on 21 July 1776, the evening before the wedding of the merchant Franz Xaver Späth and Elisabeth Haffner,

---

[4] C. Bär, 'Zum Begriff des "Basso" in Mozarts Serenaden', *MJb* 1960–1, 133–55, esp. 135.
[5] C. Bär, 'Zum "Nannerl-Septett" KV 251', *Acta mozartiana*, 9 (1962), 24–30. Other clues in Mozart's correspondence to the identification of K. 251 are mentioned by A. Dunning in NMA VII/18, preface. Mozart's punctuation confirms that by 'Rondeau auf die lezt' he did not mean a work with a rondo as the final item in the concert in question.

daughter of Sigmund Haffner, merchant-factor, sometime burgomaster, philanthropist, and 'Salzburg's wealthiest citizen', who had died four years earlier. Schiedenhofen provides a concise account of the event: 'After dinner I went to the Bridal Music which young Herr Haffner had ordered for his sister Liserl. It was by Mozart and was done in the garden-house at Loreto.' The said garden-house still exists.

'Young Herr Haffner' ought to have been reasonably pleased with the abundant and inventive work the serenade turned out to be, containing not only a concertino for solo violin but also not one, not two, but three minuet-and-trio movements with varying structures such as are also found in symphonies of the Salzburg years. In the first the framing Minuet is in the minor and the inner Trio in the major; in the second the Minuet is in the major and the Trio in the minor; in the third the Minuet's two appearances are separated by two trios, and all three sections are in the major. The serenade was framed by two playings of the same march, K. 249, which is dated, in Mozart's hand, '20 Luglio 1776 prodotta 21 luglio': he did not finish it until the eve of the performance.

Mozart later wrote a second work for the younger Sigmund Haffner: the 'Haffner' Symphony, K. 385, of 1782. The occasion for it was his elevation to the nobility, yet the work may well be only a torso. It is evident that its four movements (Allegro con spirito, Andante, Minuet and Trio, Presto) are parts of a second 'Haffner Serenade', for Mozart wrote from Vienna to his father about the work: 'You will be astonished to see only the first Allegro; . . . I will send the two Minuets, the Andante, and the last movement on Wednesday the 31st—if I can—a march as well' (27 July 1782). The Andante, a Minuet, the Finale, and even the March (K. 408/2, posted to Salzburg on 7 August), have survived, and the march leaves no doubt as to the serenade character of the whole. There is, however, no second minuet (which would probably have gone between the first and second movements). It could actually have been separated from the autograph and lost: the 'other' minuet survived as an extraneous section, not physically connected to the rest of the score. Theoretically it is conceivable (as Neal Zaslaw has argued) that by 'the two Minuets' Mozart meant merely the one surviving movement, as though he thought of minuet and trio as two elements; but it had been a very long time since he had used the terminology in that way. The fact that the surviving instrumental parts include only one minuet (plus trio) also tells us nothing about Mozart's original intentions, but only about one particular perform-ance; cutting serenades to make symphonies was clearly normal practice for

Mozart (as in the case of the D major Serenade, K. 204). The question mark over the 'Haffner' Symphony remains, therefore.[6]

Further contacts between Mozart and Salzburg's patrician families are also illustrated in commissions for serenades. Mozart refers in letters of 1782 to 'the Robinig music': Georg Siegmund von Robinig belonged to a mill-owning family, with which Leopold Mozart had long been friendly. (This has traditionally been identified as K. 334, but it is by no means certain that that is correct.) Two Nachtmusiken, K. 247 and 287, were written for the name-day (18 June) of Countess Antonia Lodron in successive years, 1776 and 1777. Other works that Mozart composed for Countess Lodron include the Concerto for Three Pianos, K. 242, which is believed to take into consideration the relative abilities of the original soloists: the Countess, her daughter Aloysia, and a younger daughter, Giuseppina, who was not yet as expert as her mother and sister (the third part's importance in the ensemble as a whole can be judged by the fact that Mozart omitted it when he later adapted the work for two players).

Another keyboard concerto, that in C major, K. 246, was written for Maria Antonia Countess Lützow, niece of the reigning Prince-Archbishop and, from 1772, wife of the commandant of Salzburg Castle.[7] With the Lodrons, the Firmians, and the Kuenburgs, the Lützows belonged to the very small number of noble families in Salzburg society, and, like Countess Lodron, Countess Lützow seems to have been a proficient keyboard-player (and to have been so already when she arrived in Salzburg as a 22-year-old bride, which casts doubt on the hypothesis that she was a pupil of Leopold Mozart). The concerto Mozart wrote for her was first performed at a family gathering at Whitsun (26 May) 1776; the composer thought highly of it and kept it with him later in his career, like a number of other works, not all of them concertos, which had begun life in Salzburg as occasional commissions. In this respect the nobility and patricians of Salzburg were more than clients: the works he wrote for them helped him to cut a dash as both composer and interpreter when he went to Paris in 1777–8, and later in Vienna.

---

[6] Zaslaw, *Mozart's Symphonies*, 381.

[7] H. Schuler, 'Zur Dedikationsträgerin von Mozarts "Lützow-Konzert" KV 246', *Mitteilungen der ISM*, 33 (1985), 1–10.

8

Visiting-Cards: Who was Mozart in 1777?

In August 1777 Mozart asked the Archbishop's leave to resign from his post in Salzburg. He applied pressure: he was planning a journey and needed to start it before long, 'in order not to be exposed to bad weather in the cold months which will soon ensue'; he also reminded the Archbishop that several requests by Leopold Mozart for leave of absence for the two of them had been refused. Since his employer was a prince of the church, he saw fit to cite Scripture: all he wanted, he said, was to use the gifts which God had given him to improve his circumstances, as 'the Gospels teach us to multiply our talents'. Salzburg was not the best place for this, as the petitioner knew full well, 'because Your Highness was graciously pleased to declare three years ago, when I sought leave to travel to Vienna, that I had no hope here and would do better to seek my fortune elsewhere'. It is not clear which journey Mozart was referring to in that sentence: he had last visited Vienna between July and September 1773, that is, four years previously; nothing is known of any plan to go back in the following autumn, and it would have been unlikely, because he had to finish a commission for Munich that winter (*La finta giardiniera*). He (or perhaps his father, who drafted the letter) was thus 'honest' enough to refer to their last leave of absence but substituted a mention of the imperial court in Vienna for the electoral court in Munich, in the (no doubt correct) hope that it would have more influence on the Archbishop—all the more necessary, because the journey he now planned was again to the west.

The request elicited a positive response, although it was different in one point from what Mozart had expected. The court did indeed issue a statement that he had 'leave to seek his fortune elsewhere', and his request to be 'favourably' discharged from service was also not refused. This was essentially a purely legal statement; we would say today that his service was terminated by mutual consent. The forms of words used in documents of this kind are illustrated by the one issued to Bach in 1723, when he wanted to move to Leipzig after five and a half fruitful years at the court of Anhalt-Köthen: 'Whereas . . . the said Bach, wishing now to seek his fortune elsewhere, has accordingly most humbly petitioned Us to grant him a most gracious dismissal, now therefore We have been pleased graciously to grant him the same . . .'. Bach's career also provides an example of an unfavourable dismissal, in 1717, when, after having applied several times to the Duke of Weimar to be released from his service, he was imprisoned for four weeks until finally he was 'freed from arrest with notice of his unfavourable discharge'.[1] Employing someone dismissed in those terms was an open affront to the former employer, and Archbishop Colloredo evidently did not want to place that hurdle in Mozart's way.

But Colloredo's decree reached beyond Mozart alone, and shows a snappy reaction to the biblical allusion. Mozart's petition is annotated: 'To the exchequer, with the instruction that father and son have permission to seek their fortunes elsewhere, according to the Gospels.' In other words, not only was Mozart dismissed, at his own request, but also his father, who had not requested it. Leopold Mozart was deeply shocked, as Schiedenhofen discovered: 'In the afternoon . . . I called on the Mozarts where I found the father in worse health because he and his son have been dismissed on account of the latter's memorandum to His Highness requesting leave to travel' (diary, 6 September 1777). The Archbishop withdrew Leopold Mozart's dismissal on 26 September, that is, before the next payday, when it would have taken effect; it is quite possible that it was never intended as anything more than a warning. Mozart himself had already left Salzburg three days before that, travelling without his father for the first time in his life, but his mother was with him. No one could have foreseen then the outcome of this journey: Maria Anna Mozart never saw Salzburg again, and Mozart did not obtain a new appointment until he returned. Their goal was Paris, but *en route* they spent several weeks, or even months, in Munich, Augsburg, and Mannheim.

Naturally the 21-year-old Mozart's bags contained a substantial number of his own compositions—which these were can be deduced from the reports he sent his father about the concerts he was giving and from the latter's advice about the programmes he should play. The scores he chose to take had a particular significance now that he had been discharged from office in Salzburg: they were, in effect, his artistic visiting-cards, with which he had to make a good impression regarding his proper status as a composer, as the means to 'seeking his fortune elsewhere'. But who was he in 1777? How did he see himself, and how did he want others to see him?

---

[1] H. T. David and A. Mendel (eds.), *The Bach Reader: A Life of Johann Sebastian Bach in Letters and Documents*, 2nd edn. (London, 1966), 89 and 75.

What were the pieces of music with which he introduced himself to the audiences in the different places he visited? To answer this question, we need to form a picture of what his *œuvre* amounted to by 1777.

At that date he had written none of the 'seven great operas' (the phrase comes from the title of a book by Aloys Greither), and none of the 'ten famous string quartets' (the title of published editions and countless recordings). He had composed five (a good fifth, that is) of the twenty-three keyboard concertos, although one of them was judged by Alfred Einstein to be 'below the highest level' (K. 242 for three pianos),[2] while only with the most recent, in Charles Rosen's view, had he achieved 'his first large-scale masterpiece in any form'[3] (the E flat Major concerto, K. 271, which Mozart composed early in 1777, perhaps for the virtuoso Mlle Jeunehomme). Of the fifty-four symphonies accepted as his by the editors of the Neue Mozart-Ausgabe, forty-three already existed, but, as Eric Blom remarks in his book on the composer, following Mozart's gradual development as a symphonist through these early works is 'interesting more to the writer and his colleagues than to the general reader, perhaps', although he makes an exception for the Symphony in G minor, K. 183, and the Symphony in A major, K. 201.[4] It is difficult to assess Mozart's early keyboard sonatas, as quite a few seem to have been lost, not merely K[6] 33*d–g*, which are known only by their incipits. Of the better-known works in the genre, he had composed only six, K. 279–84, all of which probably date from 1775, while more than twice that number were yet to be written at the time under consideration. A very much larger proportion of his sacred works date from the years in Salzburg up to 1777, yet these too are not familiar pieces; not until immediately after his return from Paris did Mozart begin the series of works which are well known today, from the 'Coronation' Mass, K. 317, and the two cycles of Vesper psalms, K. 321 and 339, to the *Ave verum corpus*, K. 618, and the Requiem, K. 626. There is only one category, including some 'famous' pieces, that was entire and complete before Mozart set off for Paris in the autumn of 1777, and that is the violin concertos.

A summary like the above says nothing about the quality of the early part of Mozart's *œuvre*, but something about posterity's view of him. That, however, is precisely what we must put out of our minds if we want to understand the outcome of the Paris journey, and also the lukewarm reception Mozart got in some of the places he visited. At that time he was

---

[2] Einstein, *Mozart*, 287.   [3] Rosen, *The Classical Style*, 198.   [4] Blom, *Mozart*, 190.

no longer a child prodigy, but he was not yet the composer of the works by which posterity chiefly knows him, and the jury was still out on his early works. In Munich the Elector of Bavaria advised him to go to Italy and write operas, and Mozart's reply—that he had been to Italy three times and had composed three operas for opera houses in that country—went unheard.

The three operas he had written for Italy were *Mitridate*, the 'serenata teatrale' *Ascanio in Alba*, and *Lucio Silla*. He took only the last of these with him on this journey, and when he reached Mannheim, as well as falling in love with the 17-year-old Aloysia Weber, he coached her in arias from it (he later married her sister Constanze). But he also packed the score of *Il re pastore*, which had been performed in Salzburg in 1775, and lent it, while in Munich, to the Bohemian composer Joseph Mysliveček, whom he had first met in Italy in 1770. Mysliveček, the 'divino Boemo', was one of the most celebrated figures in Italian opera at that time. The programme of a concert Mozart gave in Mannheim included the overture of *Il re pastore* as well as arias from it, sung by Aloysia Weber. Those, therefore, were the two operas he chose to show off his abilities as a composer of opera: the last of the three he had composed for Italy, and the most recent of all. Both belonged to the category of *opera seria*; although his later fame owed much to the *opere buffe* which he composed on librettos by Lorenzo Da Ponte, on this occasion Mozart did not see fit to carry either *La finta semplice* or *La finta giardiniera*, the comedies he had written in 1768 and 1774–5.

That concert in Mannheim on 13 February 1778 represented the broadest survey of Mozart's work to date, so far as we know. Everything on the programme was his, except for the first item, a symphony by Christian Cannabich, the conductor of the Mannheim orchestra. Cannabich's daughter Rose, who took keyboard lessons from Mozart for a time, played the B flat major Concerto, K. 238; 'then Herr Ramm (to make a change) played my oboe concerto, for the fifth time'. After an aria from *Lucio Silla*, sung by Aloysia Weber, Mozart himself performed 'my old D major Concerto' (for keyboard, K. 175); it was only four years old but he evidently considered it *passé*, and played it 'because it's a favourite here'. 'Then I improvised for half an hour, and after that Mamselle Weber sang the aria "Parto, m'affretto" [from *Lucio Silla*] to great applause. We finished with my symphony from the *Re pastore*' (to Leopold Mozart, 14 February 1778).

Mozart was content to display a narrower range of his work in other concerts. Thus he wrote from Munich some four months earlier:

The day before yesterday, Saturday the 4th . . . we had a little concert here; it began at half past three and finished about eight o'clock. . . . We began with [Michael] Haydn's two quintets . . . Then I played the concertos in C, B flat, and E flat [K. 246, 238, and 271], and then my trio [the Piano Trio, K. 254] . . . Last of all I played my last cassation, in B flat [the second of the serenades composed for Countess Lodron, K. 287]. That was an eye-opener for them all! I played as if I was the greatest violinist in all Europe. (6 October 1777)

It was as a violinist that Mozart made his first appearance in Augsburg, as mentioned in Chapter 5, playing the 'Strasbourg' concerto (probably the one in G major, K. 216). He also played one of his piano concertos there, and the three-piano concerto depreciated by Alfred Einstein was heard in both Augsburg and Mannheim: in the former the soloists were Mozart himself, the cathedral organist, Johann Michael Demmler, and the piano-maker Johann Andreas Stein; in Mannheim it was played by Mozart's pupils, Rose Cannabich, Aloysia Weber, and Therese Pierron.

Mozart presented himself, therefore, first and foremost as a composer of concertos and a virtuoso on both the violin and the piano. He could also shine on the violin in serenades, in the concertante movements, and on the piano in solo music—not only in improvisations but also in his six sonatas and above all in the Minuet, K. 179 (variations on a theme by the celebrated oboe virtuoso Johann Chrisitian Fischer). From Mannheim, moreover, he wrote home for two sonatas for piano duet (probably K. 358 and 381). He does not say anything concrete about performances of any of the symphonies; possibly he laid greater emphasis on the divertimentos, for references in the letters make it clear that he took with him from Salzburg the two written for Countess Lodron and the 'Haffner' Serenade (they may not even have been the only ones, however, and Leopold Mozart later sent him not only some dances and the two single movements for solo violin and orchestra but also the Antretter Finalmusik, K. 185). Chamber music seems to have been relatively poorly represented: apart from the perform-ance of his trio in Munich, Mozart only mentions having his first String Quartet (K. 80) and his String Quintet (K. 174, the only one he had composed at the time) copied in Mannheim for the diplomat Baron von Gemmingen. He does not appear to have carried much more in the way of church music, either: the letters to Leopold Mozart mention only the

Mass in F major, K. 192, the 'Spatzenmesse', K. 220, and the offertory *Misericordias Domini*, K. 222, which Mozart lent to monks in Augsburg to copy. The overriding impression is that he wanted to make his mark above all as a composer of bravura music: operas, concertos (in the wider sense), and technically demanding solo keyboard music.

His ability to deliver in that field is confirmed by his comments on his own playing. A letter from Augsburg contains an ebullient account of his improvising, demonstrating his ability to assess instantaneously the possibilities of a composition before it even existed: to know how and when to integrate a spontaneous idea into the musical process at the very moment when he was developing it on the keys, in what was undoubtedly already a stupendous form, and to do it with the panache to sweep the audience along with him.

Then they brought in a small clavichord and I improvised, and played a sonata, and the Fischer variations. Then the others hissed in the Dean's ear that he should just hear me play in the organ style; I asked him to give me a theme, he demurred, but one of the monks gave me one. I took it out for a run, and in the middle of it (the fugue was in G minor) I began in the major, something very jolly but in the same tempo, and then at last went back to the theme, but arsy-versy. Finally I asked myself whether I couldn't also use the jolly tune as the subject [i.e. as the countersubject] of the fugue—no sooner thought than done, and it fitted as perfectly as if Daser [an Augsburg tailor] had made it to measure. The Dean was beside himself. 'It's gone, there's nothing to be done about it,' he said, 'I couldn't believe my ears, you're a very fine fellow.'   (23–5 October 1777)

'Mozart's most signal triumphs took place . . . in the dramatic forms of the opera and the concerto, which pit the individual voice against the sonority of the mass', Charles Rosen has written.[5] Mozart was already showing a strong inclination in that direction, but it is significant that at the time of his journey to Paris the works that many today probably think of first in connection with 'his most signal triumphs' had yet to be written. The keyboard, however, was already his kingdom, as it was to remain. It may have been by pure chance that the operas turned out to be so useful; at all events Leopold Mozart does not appear to have rated their importance for Paris very highly. In every other respect he agreed with his son on the most effective repertory with which to storm the French capital. At the end of February 1778 he wrote to his wife in Mannheim with instructions on the subject of luggage that are entirely in accordance with

[5] Rosen, *The Classical Style*, 185.

the musical successes of the journey so far: 'You must get another trunk, and in it you must pack only a few good winter clothes, especially for Wolfgang, all your linen—in short, the most necessary things, then his piano concertos, some of the best symphonies [including, presumably, the serenades], the concertone, etc.: in a word, the essentials.'

Mozart and his mother had spent three weeks in Munich and approximately two in Augsburg; they stayed in Mannheim for four and a half very important months. These stages in their journey call for deeper delving into the events which marked their stay in each place. We will select two aspects and look at them more closely in context: Mozart's activities as a jobbing composer and as a teacher.

9

Down to Earth with the Dilettante: The Flute Quartet, K. 285, and the Flute Concerto, K. 313

'The purpose of the journey, the sole purpose, was, is, and must be to obtain a position or earn some money.' Writing on 27 November 1777, when his son and wife had been away for two months, Leopold Mozart made no bones about the fact that he was not satisfied with the reports they had sent him of their successes and their efforts so far. His son, on the other hand, only a few hours earlier, had ended a letter to him with the words: 'Bapa cross not pe must with me, I today this like just feel, I help it can't, warefell. Night good, weep slell. Text nime, I shall sensible more writely' (26 November 1777). This will only have confirmed Leopold Mozart's impression that his son did not appreciate how serious the situation was, and after a further three months nothing had changed. In December the prospect brightened, however—for a time.

The month began badly. On 8 December Mozart was told that there was no likelihood of his finding employment in Mannheim, at the court of the Elector Palatine. 'Well, here's someone who has met the usual kindly destiny from the court' was the comment of the flautist Johann Baptist Wendling, according to Mozart (10 December 1777). He had made friends with Wendling, and only a few days previously had composed the wind parts for a flute concerto for him. It was the same story as in Munich: it was the worst possible time to be trying to find a court post in Munich or Mannheim, centres of musical life though they both were. The Elector of Bavaria, Maximilian III Joseph, died on 30 December, and was succeeded by his next of kin, Karl Theodor, who was Elector Palatine. Under him Bavaria and the Palatinate were united, and Karl Theodor moved his seat of government, and his court, to Munich. Nobody could have foreseen, even so, that the faint hopes of employment that might still linger would be destroyed by the prospect of such a comprehensive rearrangement of the situation.

But all was not gloom. In the same letter in which Mozart passed on the bad news from the court, he also reported:

Yesterday I went to dine at Wendling's as usual, and he said to me 'Our Indian' (that's a Dutchman who lives on his means, a lover of all learning, and a great friend and admirer of yours truly) 'is a rare bird, he will give you 200 florins if you will write him three little, easy, short concertos and a couple of quartets for the flute. Through Cannabich's good offices you can have at least two pupils, who will pay well; you should write some duets for piano and violin, for subscription, and have them engraved.' (10 December 1777)

Wendling had made other, similar suggestions of ways in which Mozart might make a living in Paris, which had been reported in a letter written a week earlier. The flautist was developing a concept of employment that was to have a crucial influence on Mozart—albeit only after the passage of another three and a half years, when he finally left Archbishop Colloredo's service for good and moved to Vienna. During 1781 Mozart again raised with his father the possibility of making a living from composing sonatas for subscription editions, teaching, opera commissions (something else that he hoped to attract during the journey of 1777–8), and the income from concerts. He met old friends from Mannheim when he visited Munich at the end of 1780 to prepare the première of *Idomeneo*: did that lead to a revival of the old plans?

Back to the 'Dutchman' with overseas property, whose name was first spelt 'De champs' by Mozart (27 December 1777) and later 'De jean' (from 4 February 1778). Both forms were essentially phonetic, and for that reason a certain Willem van Britten Dejong was long regarded by Mozart scholars as the likely patron (Karl Ditters von Dittersdorf had dedicated a symphony to him ten years earlier). But 'De jean' turns out to be the correct transcription: the travels of one Ferdinand Dejean had brought him to Mannheim in 1777.[1] He had been born in Bonn but lived in Leiden (which made him Dutch), was an employee of the Dutch East India Company, and had worked as a physician for many years in Eastern Asia and the South Seas (which may be why Mozart thought of him as an 'Indian'). In 1773 he had qualified as both doctor of medicine and doctor of philosophy (which made him a 'lover of all learning'). At all events, the suggested fee of 200 gulden was a powerful bait: at the time he left Salzburg, Mozart's annual income as a vice-concert-master had stood at 150 gulden (although he did not have to support a household on that, since he lived with his parents); when he was appointed court organist in Salzburg in 1779, after his return from Paris, the sum was tripled—but even

---

[1] F. Lequin, 'Mozarts "... rarer Mann"', *Mitteilungen der ISM*, 29/1–2 (1981), 3–19.

then, Dejean's 200 gulden would have represented nearly half a year's salary. It would certainly have paid for the two months to be spent in Mannheim before Wendling went to Paris (Mozart planned to travel with him) and should have provided a useful basis for launching himself in the French capital.

But Mozart's business sense in December 1777 was not up to the task of working out the mundane consequences. Dejean evidently planned to stay rather longer in Mannheim than Wendling, and Mozart clearly thought he could take his time. He appears not to have discussed the matter with Dejean in any further detail, but to have accepted the commission in the form in which Wendling conveyed it to him. That same letter of 10 December to his father ends with a résumé of his compositional plans: 'Now I must go to bed. I shall have my hands full during the two months: three concertos, two quartets, four or six keyboard duets, and then I'm also thinking of writing a new grand mass and presenting it to the Elector.' The reader of the letter is left in no doubt that Mozart had understood the comission to be for literally 'a couple' of quartets, rather than 'a few'.

Everything went well to begin with. As early as 18 December Mozart was able to write to Salzburg that 'one quartet for the Indian Dutchman, the true philanthropist, is almost finished'. This must have been the D major Quartet, K. 285, the manuscript of which is dated 25 December 1777. Two days after that Mozart again referred to the 'gallant Dutchman' and sought to allay any doubts his father might have as to Dejean's reliability. Then he did not mention the matter for five and a half weeks until he wrote: 'I'm getting on quite comfortably with finishing the music for De jean' (4 February 1778). Leopold was aghast: 'I was astonished to read that you were "quite comfortably" finishing the music for M. De Jean. Haven't you delivered it yet? And you're still intending to leave [for Paris] on 15 February?' (11–12 February 1778) In the end Mozart set off on 14 March, but Dejean left Mannheim on 15 February, when Mozart had still not completed the commission. 'Herr De jean, who is also leaving for Paris tomorrow, has given me only 96 florins (falling 4 florins short of half) because I've written no more than two concertos and three quartets for him. But he must pay me in full, because I've already arranged with Wendling to send the rest after him' (14 February 1778). Leopold Mozart wrote back irately:

Just when I think everything is on a better footing and going well, yet another foolish, half-baked notion enters your head, or it turns out that the business was different from what you first told me. Am I right again this time? You've only been paid 96 florins instead of 200? And why? Because you've written only two concertos and three quartets? How many were you supposed to write, if he's only paid you half? Why did you lie to me, writing that you were supposed to compose only three little, easy concertos and a couple of quartets? Why didn't you heed me, when I wrote expressly that you must supply this gentleman's wishes as quickly as possible? Why? So that you would be sure of getting those 200 florins, because I know mankind better than you do. (23 February 1778)

It is quite clear that Leopold Mozart, too, took the phrase 'a couple' literally—or he would not be accusing his son of having lied to him at this stage.[2] He would have expressed doubt sooner. Indeed, it is not at all clear how Dejean calculated the fee. Finally, there is the question of what Mozart meant when he wrote to his father from Nancy, on his way home from Paris, specifying 'the three quartets and the flute concerto for M. De jean' (3 October 1778)—that is, just one concerto. How many pieces did he write for Dejean, and when? Do the works themselves yield any information? Did Mozart in fact lie to his father, and from the first?[3]

Mozart wrote at least two new works for Dejean: the Flute Quartet, K. 285, and the G major Flute Concerto, K. 313. The Flute Quartet, K. 285*a*, may have been a third, although it is in only two movements, whereas K. 285 is in three. (K[6] 285*b* is altogether later.) The second concerto mentioned by Mozart in February 1778 can also be identified: he must have meant his transcription of his C major Oboe Concerto, K. 314, which he had composed the previous year and had with him on this journey. (The only question about the version for flute, in D major, is whether it, too, dates from 1777: a flute concerto by Mozart was played to celebrate his sister's name-day that summer, but nothing more whatever is known of any work in that genre composed by that date.) So if we take Dejean's commission in the form of words in which Wendling passed it on to Mozart, it appears that, while he was one concerto short, he had supplied one quartet more than had been ordered (the fact that no third quartet has survived does not in itself mean that one never existed). So did Dejean have any sound reason for paying less than half the agreed fee for what he got?

---

[2] 'A couple' does not always mean literally two. Confusion is more likely in German, because the ear does not distinguish 'ein paar' ('a few') from 'ein Paar' ('a couple'), and in the Mozarts' day the distinction was not always made consistently in writing. [Translator]

[3] W.-D. Seiffert, 'Schrieb Mozart drei Flötenquartette für Dejean?', *MJb* 1987–8, 267–75.

The reference in the letter from Nancy appears to offer one possible solution. The group of works listed there (one concerto and three quartets) enables the fee to be divided in a way that makes arithmetical sense, at least, using the promised fee and the sum actually paid as factors in a pair of simultaneous equations. The agreed fee (200 gulden) can be divided into three times 60 gulden for the concertos, and two times 10 gulden for the quartets; by that reckoning Mozart received 60 gulden for one concerto and 30 gulden for three quartets: a total of 90 gulden. He could hardly have sold Dejean the transcribed oboe concerto as a new work, for the court oboist Friedrich Ramm had already played it five times in Mannheim, where it had been received with enthusiasm: 'it is now Herr Ramm's *cheval de bataille*' (14 February 1778; see above, Chapter 8, p. 70). Dejean could scarcely have been unaware of it, and Mozart might therefore have been unable to ask more than a copying fee for a new version of this popular war-horse. As he told his father on another occasion, in Mannheim the going rate was 24 kreuzer per sheet (four sides), three times what it was in Salzburg (29 November 1777). There were 60 kreuzer to the gulden, so 6 gulden, the difference between the 90 gulden calculated above and the 96 gulden actually paid, equals 360 kreuzer, or the fee for copying 15 sheets. That is little more than the two oldest surviving manuscripts of the Flute Concerto (they date from the nineteenth century), one of which comprises ten sheets and the other eleven.

But was it justified to pay for a new quartet only one-sixth of the fee for a new concerto? It is possible that Dejean and Mozart had fundamentally misunderstood each other; it certainly looks as if Mozart knew, by the end of January 1778 at the latest, that Dejean did not want three concertos and only two quartets for his money, but expected six of the latter. Or had Wendling been unclear about the exact number of works wanted when he passed the message on to Mozart? Shortly before Mozart resolved to finish 'the music for De jean' 'quite comfortably', he left Mannheim for a short excursion, during which he wrote to his mother a rhyming letter (dated '1778th January anno 31'). In it he refers to the possibility that Wendling is cross with him for having composed nothing, but on his return:

> I'll write the four quartets so quick
> he'll have no cause to call me a prick.
> I'll leave the concerto till Paris town,
> where I'll crap it first time I sit down.

In other words, at the end of January he still had one concerto and four quartets to write for Dejean. He had finished one quartet on 25 December 1777, which means Dejean was expecting at least five quartets, but six, the usual number in such cycles, is more likely. By that reckoning a second quartet (perhaps K. 285*a*, perhaps an unknown piece) was ready by the end of January, and when Mozart told his father a few days later that he would finish the commission 'quite comfortably', he must have been in the middle of the third. The fact that, writing to his father from Paris on 20 July 1778 (after Mannheim and before Nancy), he said that he would send him two flute quartets need not be interpreted either as a contradiction of what he had already said or as having anything at all to do with the Dejean commission.[4] As Dejean had packed the works Mozart had given him in Mannheim in the wrong trunk, after all, or so Mozart wrote from Nancy, they did not reach Paris. On that occasion, therefore, Mozart can only have meant some new works, or at the very least new versions of two of the original ones, written down from memory (perhaps for the Comte de Guines,[5] who also commissioned the Concerto for Flute and Harp); it is more likely, however, that he had written two more, with the intention of completing the Dejean commission as agreed with Wendling in February.

Mozart had, at all events, supplied more than half of what Dejean had ordered: two concertos out of three (even if one was an arrangement of the oboe concerto) and three quartets out of six. Even if the D major Flute Concerto earned only a copyist's fee, it is impossible to deduce anything sensible from the named fees, paid or promised; arithmetically, it almost works out at 24 gulden per quartet and 18 gulden per concerto, but that is still nonsense, musically speaking. Obviously Dejean wanted to pay less than half the fee because the new works composed for him amounted to only half the number of quartets and one-third of the number of concertos he had expected; did Mozart argue that with the second concerto, inasmuch as it was an arrangement of an existing work, he had fulfilled exactly half the commission? The reproaches of Leopold Mozart seem justified at least to the extent that his son had undertaken the commission in too guileless and imprecise a spirit; there can be no doubt, however, that both Mozarts originally understood that only two quartets were wanted.

[4] Ibid. Seiffert's hypothesis is that by the end of January the outstanding commission was only for four quartets, none of which had been written, but that overlooks K. 285, which had been composed by then. Thereafter Seiffert only takes account of the two concertos in his calculations.
[5] Sometimes referred to incorrectly as the Duc de Guines.

The disappointment drove Mozart to his desk, in spite of Dejean's departure, and he buckled down to write violin sonatas as Wendling had recommended. After two weeks' work he announced that four were ready (K. 301–3 were finished; the fundamental structure of K. 304, the E minor Sonata, was probably also in place), but then he came to a halt, because there was no prospect of getting them published in Mannheim. It was not until he had got to Paris that he completed the set of six (by finishing K. 304 and composing K. 305 and 306),[6] and had them engraved; finally, in late autumn 1778, he presented them to the former Electress Palatine, now Electress of Bavaria.

If we look for reasons that might have hindered Mozart from doing any work at all, we inevitably light upon the Weber family. Mozart wrote about them to his father for the first time on 17 January 1778, and Leopold soon came to suspect that the non-completion of the Dejean commission was connected with the new friendship (see his letter of 12 February 1778). But if we look at the D major Quartet and the G major Concerto more closely, other possible causes for his dilatoriness become apparent.

Mozart himself was able to name some reasons: 'Of course I could sit and scribble day in, day out; but something of this kind will reach the world at large, and I want not to need to be ashamed of it, if my name is on it. And as you know I always dry up when I'm supposed to write for an instrument I can't abide' (14 February 1778). That last remark was enough to damn his Mannheim flute works in the eyes of posterity, which took it literally and regarded them as inferior—although some biographers had to tie themselves in knots to reconcile the remark with the undoubted qualities of some of the works. Hermann Abert, for example, wrote of the two concertos: 'They yield to the violin concertos in depth and originality of ideas, but they astonish us with a whole number of highly poetic and individual characteristics.'[7] Albert Einstein wrote of the G major Concerto: 'We know that Mozart approached the task of writing it without pleasure, since he did not like the flute. But the longer one knows the work, the less trace one can find of his dislike.' Of the quartets, on the other hand, he wrote that 'Mozart wrote them . . . without feeling impelled to any high flight of the imagination'; even so, the one in D major 'gave full value'.[8]

The D major Quartet begins with an intensively worked-out Allegro: harmonic progressions and motivic material correspond perfectly. At first the movement behaves in something of the manner of a concerto exposi-

---

[6] Plath, 'Beiträge II', 170. [7] Abert, *Mozart*, i. 513.
[8] Einstein, *Mozart*, 283; 178.

tion, with two modulating groups to smooth the passage from the presentation of the first subject to the onset of the second; by this means Mozart gives the flute a soloistic function part of the time, while violin and viola are bracketed together above a simple bass, and at other times he allows one of these two to follow where the flute leads or to alternate with it as an equal partner. Towards the middle of the development section he suddenly, for no apparent reason, elaborates the theme with which the modulatory section of the exposition began; this leaves him free, however, to ignore it in the recapitulation; as this section of the movement has to stay in the tonic, unlike the exposition, it does not need the material which modulated there. Thus the first movement is as concise as it is elegant, nothing is done without reason, and the resulting musical structure is both very logical and highly attractive.

The same can be said of the minor-key middle movement, in which the flute develops its magical line in three sections, supported by the strings' pizzicato. Each of these sections starts without preamble, each steers towards a different 'close', yet never reaches a genuine close. As a result the movement as a whole has an open ending: the music pauses at a one-bar fermata, after which it launches straight into the rondo finale, where Mozart returns to the demanding instrumental variety of the first movement (such as the alternating play of flute and viola in the middle section). To echo Einstein's verdict on the G major Concerto, the longer we contemplate this work, the less trace we can find of Mozart's distaste for the task of writing it—if, indeed, he ever felt any.

Perhaps the G major Concerto itself gives even more reason to doubt the alleged distaste. There are details where Mozart produces ideas which he did not use again until composing the Vienna keyboard concertos seven years later.[9] After the soloist has made his entry with the first subject, and the orchestra has rounded off the soloist's opening passage with the usual tutti interjection, the music suddenly switches to the minor. Instead of allowing the soloist to approach the modulation from the tonic, Mozart begins the following section a third lower, in G major's relative, E minor. Then, by repeating the corresponding melody line a whole tone lower, this route brings him, after all, to his goal: the dominant (from degree I—or VIII—of the scale, he has descended via VI to V). The route is straightforward enough, and Mozart had followed it in his arias from a relatively early date, but this is the first time he took it in a concerto; in his Salzburg

---

[9] Küster, *Formale Aspekte*, esp. 95; 129–31.

concertos he normally started from the tonic, but that became a rarity in the Vienna concertos. There are other aspects in which this movement anticipates the formal complexity of the Vienna piano concertos: the start of the development, for example, which Mozart makes unusually broad and develops unexpectedly from a closing group that has seemed almost stereotypical.

If the first movement is virtuosic, the second, with its expansive arcs, presents formidable challenges to the soloist's breath control. Its formal layout is no less significant than that of the first movement, for, instead of repeating the progression of the first solo section in accordance with the tradition of the genre, the recapitulation draws on the harmonic potential of the opening tutti—which also follows tradition in not abandoning the tonic, and that is usual for a recapitulation too. There are good practical reasons for the innovation here—and Mozart did not go back to the traditional way until he was writing the first movement of the E flat major Piano Concerto, K. 482. The rondo finale of the Flute Concerto is perhaps the most inclined, of the three movements, to remain within the framework of formal conventions, but that scarcely diminishes its enchantment for players and listeners.

The D major Quartet was finished on Christmas Day 1777. If, in the course of the following six weeks, a shadow fell over the zest with which Mozart had gone to work on the Dejean commission—allegations to the contrary notwithstanding—then the G major Concerto must also have been composed at a comparably early stage, perhaps also by Christmas. At the same time, however, the fate that appears to have befallen the work may provide a clue as to when Mozart 'dried up' and had nothing more in view than 'quite comfortably' finishing the music for Dejean, who abruptly ceased to be a 'true philanthropist'. Obviously Dejean was not satisfied with Mozart's work, because the composer had not observed the small print. As quoted by Wendling, Dejean wanted 'little, easy, short concertos', and none of those adjectives fit the G major Concerto. Possibly Mozart sought to make it easier by modifying the tempo markings. The word 'maestoso' puts a brake on the 'Allegro' of the first movement, but is 'majestic' really the right word for this vivacious and elegant movement? The second movement's 'Adagio' is made a little faster, on the other hand, by the addition of 'ma non troppo'. But the problems this movement presents could not be solved by such means, it seems, for (as in the case of the A major Violin Concerto, K. 219) Mozart composed a new middle movement, the C major Andante, K. 315. The tempo is significantly faster than the Adagio ma non troppo of the original slow movement, and the formal structure is also much simpler.

There is no escaping the impression, therefore, that Mozart was hauled down to earth from the high flights of his imagination with a bump and forced to wear the fetters of the amateur player's technical limitations. This would have made him 'dry up', especially when writing for an instrument for which he may indeed have had no great affection. We can probably assume that he would have carried out Dejean's commission within the appropriate technical limits if Leopold Mozart had been in Mannheim with him. His father was every inch a teacher, and he would have been readier than his son proved to be in this particular case to adapt his style, even in so exposed a field as the solo concerto, to the abilities of a patron who was evidently deficient across the board. Mozart himself was prepared to 'rescue' his concerto with a simpler second movement, but then his enthusiasm wilted: he managed to compose two more quartets (probably short ones, with dimensions comparable to those of K. 285a) and then he may well have just had someone else copy the flute version of his Oboe Concerto. It looks as if Mozart did not write the Italian arias that survive from this stay in Mannheim until after Dejean had left the city and he felt free of the commission which he had hailed with such initial delight but came to find a burden.

10

The 'Little Cousin' and the Weber Girl: The 'Cannabich' Sonata, K. 309, and how Mozart became a Singing Teacher

One of the people who most impressed Mozart during his stay in Augsburg was the piano-maker Johann Andreas Stein. Born in Heidelsheim, not far from Karlsruhe, he had served an apprenticeship as an organ-builder under Johann Andreas Silbermann in Strasbourg and later worked for the piano-builder Franz Jakob Spaeth in Regensburg, before settling in Augsburg. When his daughter Nanette and her husband Johann Andreas Streicher inherited the company they moved it to Vienna, where they became close friends of Beethoven.

Nanette Stein, born in 1769, was already famous as a child prodigy at the keyboard. Mozart had this to tell his father about her:

She is 8½ years old, and still learns everything by ear. Something may come of her: she has talent. But she will never be anything if she continues as at present. She will never gain much speed, because she works hard at making her hands heavy. She will never gain the most necessary, and the hardest, and the most important thing in music, which is tempo, because from childhood she has concentrated on not playing on the beat. Herr Stein and I spent a good two hours talking about this very point, but I have more or less converted him by now. Now he asks my advice about everything. (23–5 October 1777)

Teaching students of keyboard instruments, especially young ladies (though not many were quite as young as Nanette Stein), was an important plank in the scaffolding Mozart was building as the means—especially the financial means—of clawing his way to Paris. Nanette Stein was probably not the first to benefit from his activity in this field, although he necessarily had little time in which to give lessons while he was travelling, but her case shows that he was ready to give intensive theoretical consideration to the things he thought warranted it. Nanette's father was not the only person to find himself at the receiving end of his advice.

Stein and Mozart's relationship was based on mutual respect. A week earlier Mozart had written to Salzburg:

I must begin with Stein's pianoforte. Before seeing any of Stein's work I liked Spaeth's pianos best, but now I have to award the palm to Stein's, because they damp much better than the Regensburg ones. When I strike hard, whether I leave my finger down, or lift it, the sound always stops at the instant when I produce it. I may come at the keys as I will, the tone is always the same, it doesn't clatter, it isn't sometimes stronger and sometimes weaker, it doesn't not sound at all; in a word, everything is even. It's true that he doesn't sell a pianoforte like that for less than 300 florins, but his pains and the care he takes are beyond price. (17 October 1777)

Three hundred florins: twice Mozart's annual salary in Salzburg (a florin was the same as a gulden). Other things about the instrument that he admired included the double escapement (on the earliest forms of the pianoforte the player had to release a key completely before it could be struck a second time, but Stein had invented a means of letting the hammer drop back automatically to its starting position immediately after striking) and Stein's practice of leaving the wood from which his soundboards were made out of doors in all weathers until it cracked—'then one can be sure that nothing more will happen to it', because the tensions in the wood had been allowed to relax. The damper action, operated by the right pedal on the modern piano, and by a lever below the keyboard pressed by the player's knee on many instruments of Stein's era, also earned Mozart's unstinting praise, especially when he played his 'Dürnitz' Sonata, K. 284, on it: it 'sounds incomparable on Stein's pianoforte. The mechanism you press with your knee is better made on his than on others. I scarcely need to touch and it works; and as soon as you move your knee away only a little bit you can't hear the least reverberation' (17 October 1777).

We learn that Mozart had already found some female pupils in Munich from one of the notorious letters to his 'Bäsle', his 'little cousin' in Augsburg. Maria Thekla was the then 19-year-old daughter of Leopold Mozart's brother, Franz Alois. Mozart allowed his fondness for writing nonsense in a style not uncommon at the time (one example has already been quoted, in the opening paragraph of Chapter 9) to run riot in his letters to her. The earliest to survive was written soon after he reached Mannheim: here are just two paragraphs from it.

Dearest Coz Buzz,

I have received believed your highly esteemed letter, from which I learn earn that my uncle furuncle, my aunt shan't, and you moo are very well bell; we too, God be praised and thanked, are in good health stealth. The letter fetter from my

Papa Haha has also dropped plopped into my talons this very day. I hope you have also had bad my earlier letter setter from Mannheim. All the better, better all the . . .

Now something really sensible! . . . I ask you, why not?—I ask you, dearest silly, why not?—that when you next write to Mme Tavernier in Munich you present my compliments to the two Mamselles Freysinger, why not?—Strange! Why not?—and I beg very sincerely the pardon of the younger, Fräulein Josepha, why not? Why should I not beg her pardon?—Strange! I know not why not!—I beg so very sincerely her pardon for not yet having sent the sonata I promised her, but I will dispatch it as soon as possible. Why not?—what?—why not?—Why should I not send it? Why should I not dispatch it? Why not?—Strange! . . . (5 November 1777)

The sonata he had promised was probably the one in D major, K. 311, which was composed in Mannheim, where the 13-year-old Rose Cannabich became his next pupil. Her father Christian Cannabich, as director of the orchestra, was a central figure in the second generation of the Mannheim School, and Mozart called on him on 31 October, the day after his arrival in the city.

Four days later Mozart told his father that he visited Cannabich's house every day. 'He has a daughter who plays the piano quite nicely, and to make him my good friend I'm now working on a sonata for mamselle his daughter, which is almost ready except for the Rondo. When I'd finished the first Allegro and the Andante I took them round and played them; Papa cannot imagine how much the sonata is applauded' (4 November 1777). Then: 'I was at Herr Cannabich's house this morning, where I wrote the Rondo for his daughter's sonata and after that they wouldn't let me leave' (8 November).

Leopold Mozart promptly asked his son to have the sonata copied and send it to his sister, but Mozart sent the autograph and asked his father to get it copied, as the cost of copying was exorbitant in Mannheim. The sonata pleased both Mozart and the Cannabichs immensely: for several weeks there is scarcely a letter in which it is not mentioned. Above all, Mozart wrote more about the composition of the work and about how he got on with teaching it to Rose Cannabich, which led to remarks on its interpretation.

Mozart's father and sister both noticed at once that the sonata paid homage to one particular style. Nannerl wrote: 'Anyone can see that you wrote it in Mannheim' (8 December 1777), and Leopold: 'Is the sonata a curiosity? It has something of the mannered Mannheim goût in it, but not

enough to spoil your own good style' (11 December). The two comments
show the pains Mozart took to make a 'good friend' of Cannabich,
combining the local style with his own in such a way that both were still
identifiable; the Mannheim mannerisms he adopted in this piece are not so
much the formulas for which the music written for the Mannheim orchestra was celebrated (and on which Mozart had drawn in his A major
Symphony, K. 201—the 'rocket' and the 'roller', the crescendo in thirds),
but rather the ornamentation that today might (a little superficially) be
labelled 'galant'. But Mozart went a step further in suiting the musical
language to his individual Mannheim ends, as he revealed almost incidentally when he followed a description of Cannabich's treatment of him with
a pen-portrait of Rose Cannabich, in which the sonata again makes an
appearance:

His daughter, who is 15 but the oldest child, is a very pretty, sweet girl. For her
age she has a lot of good sense and maturity; she's serious and doesn't say much,
but what she says is spoken gracefully and amiably. Yesterday she again gave me
indescribable pleasure by playing my sonata quite—excellently. She played the
Andante, which must not go fast, with all the feeling possible. Moreover she enjoys
playing it. You remember that I'd already written the first Allegro on the second
day I was here, that is, when I'd only seen Mamselle Cannabich once. Then young
Danner [Christian Franz Danner, violinist and a composition pupil of Mozart's in
Mannheim] asked me how I intended to do the Andante; 'I will do it exactly in the
character of Mamselle Rose.' When I played it it was extraordinarily well liked.
Young Danner told this story afterwards, and it's quite true, she is like the Andante.
(6 December 1777)

So Mozart was able to adapt himself to the Mannheim style in a matter
of hours (it was not altogether new to him) and it took him scarcely any
longer to assess the character of a particular player. As a whole, what he
says about the genesis of the 'Cannabich' sonata can be taken as a reliable
yardstick of the speed at which he could write music even in intensely busy
circumstances: we must remember that in those first days in Mannheim he
also had to carry out an extensive, quasi-official programme of visits, first
and foremost to other musicians and to the Intendant of the orchestra. The
Rondo seems to have been written in the course of a single morning,
according to the account quoted above.

What lies behind both the style and the content is thus on record—
and we can scarcely doubt that the sonata also reveals the influence of
the pedagogic instincts Mozart inherited from his father and had already
exercised on Johann Andreas Stein.

The Andante will give us the most trouble, for it is full of expression, and must be played accurately with taste, forte, and piano, as written. She is very adept and learns easily. The right hand is very good, but the left, alas, is completely spoilt. I often feel very sorry for her, I can tell you, when I see her often labouring so hard that she gets completely out of breath. It's not that she's clumsy but that she can do no other, because she is used to it, because no one has ever shown her how to do it differently. I've told her mother, and her too, that if I was her regular teacher, I would lock away all her music, cover the keyboard with a handkerchief, and make her practise with right and left hand separately, very slowly to start with, nothing but passages, trills, mordents, etc., until both hands were fully fit. (14 November 1777)

For all the abundance of documentation, however, there was one thing that was still a mystery after the lapse of nearly two centuries—no one knew which sonata it was: K. 309 in C major or K. 311 in D major. Only the methods and new approach of a younger generation of Mozart scholars (in the persons of Wolfgang Plath and Wolfgang Rehm) have produced a definitive solution.[1] We know that Mozart sent the autograph to Salzburg from Mannheim by post (and that it was returned to him one sheet at a time), so the manuscript must bear traces of having been folded for posting; the autograph of K. 309 has not survived, but that of K. 311 shows no such evidence.

Furthermore, a copy of the work, made in Salzburg, ought to exist—and one does in the case of K. 309. It is actually in the hand of Leopold Mozart, for whom copying it himself was a means of studying the work's construction in the closest possible detail, for he literally did not miss a note. It follows that the 'Cannabich' sonata is K. 309.

Teaching the piano remained a very important part of Mozart's activities during the whole of this journey of 1777–8 (in Paris, for example, he taught the daughter of the Comte de Guines, who also played the harp: it was for her and her flute-playing father that Mozart composed his Concerto for Flute and Harp), yet while still in Mannheim he was able to exercise his pedagogic skills in a new field, namely singing.

He did more than teach singing. He wrote arias, one for the celebrated tenor Anton Raaff (who later created the title-role in *Idomeneo*), and one for the soprano Dorothea Wendling, wife of the flautist; he also wrote two French songs for their daughter Elisabeth Augusta Wendling ('Oiseaux, si tous les ans', K. 307, and 'Dans un bois solitaire', K. 308). The aria for Dorothea Wendling ('Ah, non lasciarmi', K^6 295a, on a text from

[1] W. Plath and W. Rehm in NMA IX/25, vol. i, pp. xiii–xv.

Metastasio's *Didone abbandonata*) uses material from a setting of the same text by Baldassare Galuppi; the borrowings of melodic and textural features (at the beginning and end of the first vocal section) may have been accidental, but that is unlikely; as Wolfgang Plath has remarked, Mozart was probably using another composer's material consciously, perhaps at the prompting of Dorothea Wendling, who may have had a special fondness for it.[2]

So far as Mozart was concerned, however, the most important pupil he had during the entire journey was Aloysia Weber, who was about 17 years old when he met her. He wrote an aria for her, too:

As an exercise, I have written an aria 'Non sò d'onde viene etc.', which has been set so beautifully by [Johann Christian] Bach, for no other reason than that I know the Bach so well and like it so much that it is forever in my head. I wanted to find out whether, in spite of that, I was capable of writing an aria that was not the least like Bach's—and it isn't a bit like his, not the least bit. At first I thought of writing this aria for Raaff, but the opening struck me immediately as too high for him, and I liked it too much to want to change it. Also, in view of the instrumentation, it seemed to me that it would be better for a soprano, and in sum I decided to write it for the Weber girl.   (28 February 1778)

As with the 'Galuppi' aria, there is a possibility that Mozart was expressly asked to write 'Non sò, d'onde viene' (K. 294): Anton Raaff had sung J. C. Bach's setting in the première of Bach's opera *Alessandro nell'Indie* in 1762 in Naples. The question of 'borrowing' is different in this case, however, for Mozart, 'knowing the Bach so well', was interested in extending stylistic possibilities in a piece of vocal music in accordance with his own inclination—rather as he had done in the 'Cannabich' sonata. As a result, his setting of the words is indeed 'not the least like Bach's'.[3]

J. C. Bach was still based in London, but he had been commissioned to write two operas for the court of Mannheim during the recent past: *Temistocle* (1772) and *Lucio Silla* (1776). Mozart placed Bach's operatic music at the centre of the singing lessons he gave Aloysia Weber, not only studying with her Bach's 'Non sò, d'onde viene' but also making her work on the nineteen vocal cadenzas which he had written some time before for three arias by Bach (K. 293e); he had his father send these from Salzburg,

[2] W. Plath, 'Mozart und Galuppi: Bemerkungen zur Szene "Ah non lasciarmi, no"', in E. Egg and E. Fässler (eds.), *Festschrift Walter Senn zum 70. Geburtstag* (Munich and Salzburg, 1975), 174–8.
[3] S. Kunze, 'Die Vertonungen der Arie "Non sò d'onde viene" von J. Chr. Bach und W. A. Mozart', *Analecta musicologica*, 2 (1965), 85–111.

together with arias by Bach for which he had composed coloratura ornamentation. Clearly, the lessons were concerned above all with the notated
'raw material' of an aria and the various ways in which the singer might
transform it with improvised ornamentation, as he or she was expected to.
Not surprisingly, therefore, Mozart's 'Non sò, d'onde viene' survives in
both 'plain' and ornamented versions.

Aloysia Weber was the daughter of Fridolin Weber, a member of the
musical staff at the court of Mannheim as singer, prompter, and copyist.
(He was also an uncle of Carl Maria von Weber.) It was as a copyist that
Mozart first encountered him, when he copied four arias that Mozart
wanted to present to the Princess of Orange at Kirchheimbolanden during
the short trip he made away from Mannheim in the second half of January
1778. Fridolin and Aloysia Weber accompanied him on that excursion, and
Aloysia sang thirteen times in all. At that stage Mozart came very close to
abandoning all his travel plans and setting off in a totally different direction.

My advice is that they ought to go to Italy ... I would wager my life on her
singing ... I will gladly write an opera for Verona for 50 zecchini, just so long as
she makes her name; for if I don't I fear she will be crucified. By that time I shall
have made so much money from the other journeys we plan to make together that
I won't be the loser. I think we will go to Switzerland, and perhaps also to Holland.
Write soon and tell me what you think.   (4 February 1778)

Leopold Mozart had no difficulty responding to that request. He
despaired at his son's vacillation and lack of ambition. He pointed out how
short-lived and impractical each of the things he had taken up so far on this
journey had been, from his notion of setting up a German opera in
Munich (now only Italian opera interested him), through the merry life he
had led in Augsburg with his 'little cousin', to Rose Cannabich and his
friendships with the Wendlings and now the Webers. He appealed to his
son's reason, although he can have had little hope of making any headway
with that, in the light of what he had just outlined.

You intend to introduce her to Italy as a prima donna. Tell me if you know of one
prima donna who has made her debut in the Italian theatre as a prima donna
without first having performed frequently in Germany ... The proposal to set off
on the road with Herr Weber and NB TWO daughters made me fear for my reason.
My dearest son! You did not dream up this horrifying idea for yourself: how can
you entertain it for a single hour? Your letter reads like a romance. Could you
really resolve to travel the world with strangers? To set at naught your reputation,
your aging parents, your sister? To expose me to the mockery and laughter of our

ruler and the whole city which loves you? Yes, expose me to mockery and yourself to scorn, for I've had to say to all the people who continue to ask about you that you will be going to Paris; and now you propose after all to take off on a hare-brained adventure with strangers? No, a moment's reflection will make you come to your senses. (11–12 February 1778)

Those last few lines make it obvious that the problem was not so much Mozart's relationship with the Webers as Leopold Mozart's relationship with people in Salzburg. He had been certain that his son would reach Paris, and had taken his success, once there, for granted. His nervousness grew by the minute as the prospect loomed of that success being delayed, or prevented altogether. If that happened he would be a laughing-stock; it was Mozart's duty to save his father's face, and make good his boasts. That aspect has not been sufficiently acknowledged in other commentaries on this incident, which tend to treat it as an everyday father–son dispute.[4] What had Leopold Mozart himself said at the start of their first journey to western Europe? 'One must . . . always have a plan in view for months ahead—but a plan that one can alter at a moment's notice if circumstances change' (22 February 1764). He appears not to have reckoned with a change of circumstances during this journey undertaken by his son. That he had a practical objection to the possibility of change is found in the reproaches he makes Mozart for having not yet finished the Dejean commission.

The change of plan evaporated, but Mozart's thoughts of marriage did not. Their paths brought him and Aloysia Weber together again in Munich at the end of 1778; but before the next year was out she was engaged as a principal at the Court Opera in Vienna, where, in 1780, she married Joseph Lange, actor and part-time painter (he painted the unfinished portrait of Mozart at the keyboard). Mozart met the Langes in Vienna in 1781; later, Aloysia Lange sang the role of Konstanze in *Die Entführung aus dem Serail*, and in August 1782 Mozart married her younger sister Constance.

---

[4] It is not even explored in F. Langegger, *Mozart, Vater und Sohn: eine psychologische Untersuchung* (Zurich and Freiburg, 1978).

11

The Concert Spirituel, and a Fatal Illness: The 'Paris' Symphony, K. 297

'Off with you to Paris! And be quick about it, show yourself in the company of great men—*aut Caesar aut nihil*': thus Leopold Mozart wrote on 12 February 1778 to Mannheim, where his son, in his opinion, lingered too long. But Mozart took his time: it was not until 14 March that he and his mother got on the road again, and another nine days before they arrived in Paris, which was to be the centre of his musical activities for almost exactly six months. Even so, the tangible products of those activities are surprisingly few: apart from the continuation of works which had been started in Mannheim, those that can definitely be ascribed to the six months in Paris include the Concerto for Flute and Harp, K. 299 (commissioned by the Comte de Guines), the music for the ballet *Les petits riens*, K^6 299*b*, a few sets of variations, and some single movements for symphonic forces. His contacts with Joseph Le Gros,[1] the director of the Concert Spirituel, were the most fruitful factor, leading to the composition of movements to augment a *Miserere* by the Mannheim composer Ignaz Holzbauer, K^6 297*a*, a Sinfonia Concertante for flute, oboe, bassoon, and horn with orchestra, K^6 297*B*, and the 'Paris' Symphony, K. 297. Mozart's mention of having composed a second symphony while in Paris (lost; see the letters of 11 September and 3 October 1778) is sometimes interpreted as an attempt to hoodwink his father,[2] but the evidence put forward is not very convincing. The four piano sonatas once ascribed to the Paris period (K. 330–3) were composed later, in fact, and we shall return to them.

Neither Le Gros, De Guines, nor the ballet-master Jean Georges Noverre, for whom *Les petits riens* was written, was among the acquaintances the Mozarts made in Paris in the 1760s. Did Mozart fail to cultivate the right people in 1778, and might that be the reason why he had no

---

[1] On Le Gros's first name, see the letter by Frances Killingley, *Musical Times*, 119 (1978), 939.

[2] Tyson, *Mozart*, 113; N. Zaslaw, 'Mozart's Paris Symphonies', *Musical Times*, 119 (1978), 753–7.

success? Whatever the reason, the discrepancy between the entries in Leopold Mozart's diary of 1763–6 and the outcome of the 1778 visit is out of all due proportion, and Leopold Mozart's hopes were sorely disappointed. Yet while his son was still in Mannheim he had sent him a list of names headed 'These are our Paris acquaintances, all of whom are looking forward to seeing you' (5 February 1778).

There is a danger here of overlooking something. For all his dawdling on the way from Salzburg, once Mozart got to Paris he clearly tried to build on the successes of his earlier visits, but it was twelve years since he had last been there. On the day after his arrival in 1778 he got in touch with Baron von Grimm, as if expecting him to open all doors as he had done so effectively in November 1763. This time, too, Grimm gladly went to Mozart's aid, but had less success. The question is, who, in fact, was 'looking forward to seeing' the 22-year-old Mozart? On his first visit, the simple fact that he was only 9 years old had attracted attention that was not aroused so easily when he was just one more musician in early manhood trying to get into the swim of Paris's crowded and multifarious musical life.[3]

A second question is whether Mozart carried with him either the expectations or the music that would most have helped him to build on the successes of 1763 and 1766. Leopold Mozart had been in the best possible position to observe his son's development since then, and not only knew but also approved the scores he had packed in his bags for this journey; he should perhaps have known how far Mozart had left behind him the kind of thing that had so much pleased Paris more than a decade earlier. Leopold Mozart cannot be blamed for not having followed in detail the changes in Parisian musical fashion during those years, from distant Salzburg or from the places he had visited since 1766; but is it possible that, caught up in the daily round in Salzburg, he had lost the objectivity to recognize that his son had changed? In 1763 and 1766 Mozart had made the rounds from one salon to another, showing off his skills at the keyboard as performer and composer, but since then he had acquired formidable experience as a composer of symphonies, concertos, and operas. His old field of activity was now too narrow for him, and if he was to show himself off it must be across the entire range of his abilities, as he had been doing in the immediately preceding months in Mannheim and in recent years in Munich and Vienna. The child prodigy's success was guaranteed in the

---

[3] See R. Angermüller, *W. A. Mozarts musikalische Umwelt in Paris (1778): Eine Dokumentation* (Munich and Salzburg, 1982).

atmosphere of the salons of Paris in the later years of the *ancien régime*, but it was not the appropriate platform for the new Mozart.

Nevertheless, Mozart had not forgotten his earlier visits and did not ignore the experience gathered during them. As in the spring of 1764 he had some sonatas for keyboard and violin published, this time the set that he had started in Mannheim, dedicated to the Electress Palatine Elisabeth Auguste; like the earlier pair (K. 6 and 7) they were numbered 'Op. 1'. The dedication to a German princess, however, carried little weight in Paris. The problem was that Mozart was not in the position to capitalize on the ways in which he himself had altered in a city that had certainly altered; an ex-wunderkind, making his first tour as artist and impresario in one, he scarcely stood a chance of making a bold impression on the musical life of a vast metropolis whose variety must have been bewildering for an out-sider. The nervous strain the situation put on him is reflected in his mother's letters to her husband. Two weeks after their arrival in Paris she wrote:

Wolfgang has so much to do, he has to write a *Miserere* by Holy Week for the Concert Spirituel, which must have three choruses, and a fugue, and a duet, and all the rest, with very many instruments. It's supposed to be finished by next Wednesday [8 April] to allow for rehearsals. He's writing it at the house of M. Le Gros, the director of the Concert . . . After that he has two concertos to write for a duke, one for flute and one for harp, and then he must write an act of an opera for the French theatre.   (5 April 1778)

As Mozart explained in the note he enclosed with his mother's letter, Noverre did not want just one act but hoped to commission a whole opera. Furthermore he was adding not three but five choruses to Holzbauer's *Miserere* (one with tenor solo), not a duet but a trio, and also two recitatives (one with oboe and flute obbligatos); Maria Anna Mozart may not have been able to gauge the full extent of her son's work, since she was catching only glimpses of it. Her mention of the Concerto for Flute and Harp (which she took to be two separate works) is probably symptomatic.

Mozart was busily pursuing his contacts with Baron Grimm, Le Gros, Noverre, and the Marquise d'Épinay (another acquaintance made in the 1760s, when she had had a liaison with Grimm), and was undoubtedly concerned about getting some musical ground under his feet—but that does not mean that his mother was in a position to follow closely what he was doing. She reports of herself:

As for my own life here, it is not at all pleasant. I sit all day alone in a room, like being in prison, and besides it is so dark, looking out on a little yard where you can't see the sun all day, so that I don't even know what the weather is like. I can do a little knitting with great difficulty in what daylight reaches down to me, and we are paying 30 livres a month for this room! The entrance and the stairs are so narrow that it would be impossible to get a piano up here. That is why Wolfgang goes to M. Le Gros's house to compose, because there is a piano there. So I don't see him all day long, and I shall probably lose the use of my tongue completely. (5 April 1778)

Mozart's situation in those weeks was in fact hopeless, for all his busyness. He recognized as much, and said so succinctly in this same letter: 'If a man can't write in his own home, and is in a hurry as well, it is damnable.' It is all the worse if the hopes and the work are in vain: nothing came of the opera commission and two of the *Miserere* choruses were not performed in the end. The same fate befell the Sinfonia Concertante for wind, which Mozart also started early that April, if we can believe his letters (there is no evidence to disprove them). But he was drawing his bow at a venture and all his hard work was wasted: in a matter of weeks he wrote sadly 'I don't expect to be the toast of Paris' (1 May 1778). Once on the way home, he wrote from Nancy: 'I'm not bringing much new music with me, because I haven't written very much' (3 October 1778). It is very unlikely that the reason for that was negligence on his part: in early April, he expected a quite different outcome from his visit to Paris, but by early May he was questioning his illusions. Disappointment was not the only thing to hinder his creativity, however: another cause presented itself shortly after he had finished the 'Paris' Symphony.

The history of the symphony's composition is well documented—so well, in fact, that the quantity of material has actually caused confusion. Broadly speaking, the sources belong to one or other of two strands. The first is connected directly to Paris and came to a provisional but tangible halt in 1788 (ten years after Mozart's stay in the city) when the work appeared there in print for the first time; the other remains connected to Mozart himself. The most obvious difference between the two strands is the second movement, the Andante. In the score published in Paris it is a fifty-eight-bar movement in 3/4 time, while the manuscript that stayed in Mozart's hands has a different movement, ninety-eight bars long and in 6/8. There has never been any doubt that both Andantes are by Mozart, for in addition to the sources both are mentioned in the composer's letters to his father, where he reports Le Gros's opinion and gives his own as well:

Le Gros is so pleased with it that he says it is his best symphony. Only the Andante did not have the good fortune to satisfy him—he says it has too many modulations, and is too long. He only says that because the audience forgot to clap as loud and as long as they did after the first and last movements, for the Andante is the one that most pleases me, all connoisseurs and music-lovers, and most listeners. It is exactly the contrary of what Le Gros says, it is quite natural, and short, but in order to please him (and others, according to him) I have written another one. Each is right in its own way, for each has its own character—but I like the second one even better. (9 July 1778)

Until quite recently no one doubted that the compound-time Andante preserved in autograph was the earlier, and that the one published with the first edition was the later. It was with the supposedly later Andante too, that the symphony was published in the Neue Mozart-Ausgabe. But in 1964 a sheet of sketches was discovered, on which there was a draft of that triple-time version of the slow movement, also in Mozart's handwriting. With Alan Tyson's new evaluation of the sources (1981) it became evident that the true situation was the reverse of what had formerly been thought.[4]

The sheet of sketches also has an early version of a section of the symphony's finale; that means that the slow movement in 3/4 published in the first edition had already been conceived when Mozart first sketched the finale. Furthermore, two drafts of marches composed for *Les petits riens* are also to be found on the same sheet, which means that the sketches can all be dated earlier than 11 June 1778, when the ballet was first performed. The first performance of the 'Paris' Symphony took place a week later, on 18 June, the feast of Corpus Christi. We should also allow for a certain period of rehearsal time, and the ballet would probably have needed longer than the symphony; it all makes it even less likely that the Andante in 3/4 sketched on the same sheet is the one Mozart composed as a substitute. In any case, Mozart told his father that he had finished the symphony in a letter of 12 June; the sketch—with its early version of details of the last movement—must therefore date from before that.

There can be no doubt, however, that the first performance took place with this Andante—according to Mozart's account Le Gros's criticism of the movement, which led to the composition of the other Andante, was a reaction to the audience's reception. The parts used by the orchestra (apparently no fewer than fifty-five players[5]) must have had the three

---

[4] Tyson, *Mozart*, 106–13.

[5] R. Angermüller, 'Wer spielte die Uraufführung von Mozarts "Pariser Symphonie" KV 297?', *Mitteilungen der ISM*, 26/3–4 (1978), 12–20.

movements (including the slow movement in triple time) in consecutive order, without space to spare, and substituting the one in 6/8 must have meant inserting an extra page in each part. The date 15 August was chosen for the first performance of this new version of the symphony, as Mozart informed his father: 'The symphony will be performed for the second time, with the new Andante, on 15 August, the feast of the Assumption' (9 July 1778). Perhaps the single leaves with the new movement became separated from the rest, or perhaps it was regarded as a later addition: for one quite understandable reason or another, when the symphony was published ten years later it had the original slow movement and not the substitute. It is also understandable that the autograph which remained in Mozart's possession contained the substitute and not the original, because, as he told his father, he preferred the second one. To that extent it is even right that the symphony should be performed as it always is, with the later of the two; but we should bear in mind that that does not represent Mozart's original intentions, and we owe it only to Le Gros's intervention.

This new evaluation of the sources of the Andante of the 'Paris' Symphony serves to weaken further the speculations that Mozart may have told his father that he had composed more in Paris than he actually had. If the autograph of the score that he kept included the original slow movement, rather than the substitute, then the suggestion that the substitute was lost by accident from the sources of the first edition could apply to Mozart's score also, and the loss would be as insignificant as in the case of the Paris edition. But we know now that the version kept by Mozart included only the substitute Andante, and that gives us concrete evidence in support of the case that the autographs of works composed in Paris, for whose existence there is secondary evidence, did not survive complete. Perhaps there was a Sinfonia Concertante for wind instruments and orchestra,[6] perhaps Mozart did compose a second 'Paris' symphony—K[6] 311A.

Of course Mozart told his father about the first performance of *the* 'Paris' symphony.

The symphony began . . . and straightaway in the middle of the first Allegro, a passage that I had been sure would please, the entire audience was carried away and there was a great burst of applause. But I knew as I wrote it that it would make that kind of impression, and so I brought it back again at the end, and the applause, too, was repeated da capo. The Andante [i.e. the original one in 3/4] also pleased the

---

[6] W. Plath in NMA X/29, vol. i, p. xi; on the doubts about the existence of another symphony, see Tyson, *Mozart*, 113, and Zaslaw, 'Mozart's Paris Symphonies', 753–7.

audience, but not as much as the last Allegro. Because I had learnt that last allegros here always begin like the first, with all the instruments playing together and usually in unison, I began it with two violins alone, playing piano for eight bars, and then a sudden forte. The audience (just as I expected) went 'shh' during the piano, then came the forte—and hearing the forte, of course they clapped their hands. After the symphony I went straight to the Palais Royal to celebrate, had an excellent ice, said the rosary I had promised, and went home.   (3 July 1778)

The 'Paris' was Mozart's first symphony for three and a half years (the last had been K. 200, 12–17 November 1774). His orchestral style had developed in the interval, but in some ways he harked back to earlier stages in his development as a symphonist than the one he had reached in 1774. For one thing, the work conforms to the Italian manner rather than the Viennese in being in three movements; and for another, in the most forward-looking of the Salzburg symphonies, those in A major and G minor (K. 201 and 183), the symphonic expositions are characterized by elements of thematic development, but in the 'Paris' Mozart returned to forming the two outer movements from distinct motivic blocks, a procedure which accommodates huge melodic variety but is rather schematic, while the 'development' is all in the harmonic treatment. Yet that aspect, too, is not very adventurous: the second subject enters at, harmonically speaking, the earliest possible moment (as soon as a half close on the dominant has been reached). In these respects the symphony derives unquestionably from the earlier Salzburg symphonies. It is not even the first time he had given a finale a quiet opening, for he had done something very similar in the C major Symphony, K. 200, and the string unison in the G minor, K. 183, is also piano.

Mozart's celebration was cut abruptly short: there was not even time to answer his father's letters. The day after the première of the 'Paris' Symphony his mother was taken ill. The initial symptoms—diarrhoea, fever, and headaches—were attributed by Mozart to her having drunk polluted water. He wanted to call a doctor, but at first she refused to hear of it. When she finally agreed, it was on condition that it was a German doctor. Meanwhile a week had already gone by: the illness had entered its second stage, and she lost her hearing. A week later, during the afternoon of 3 July, she went into a coma, and died late that same evening without recovering consciousness.

Immediately after her death, Mozart wrote his father the letter in which he told him about the 'Paris' symphony's première, among other things, but he also broke to him 'the very painful and sad news' of his mother's illness. He followed it, at 2 a.m. on 4 July, with a letter to Joseph Bullinger, a former Jesuit who had been employed as a private tutor since the dissolution of his order, and a close family friend, whom Mozart now asked to tell his father the full truth.

The news had still not reached Leopold Mozart ten days later, when he started a letter to his wife and son, to wish Maria Anna well on her name-day. At 10 a.m. on 13 July he received his son's letter informing him of her illness, and gave spontaneous expression to his concern; at this point he wrote the reproaches to his son that have sometimes been interpreted as having been written after he knew of his wife's death. But it was not until 3.30 p.m. that he learnt the truth from Bullinger. The reproaches ceased at once, and Leopold Mozart ended his letter by imploring his son to let him know every detail of the illness. Mozart complied but was so anxious to spare his father that he broke off the account at the point a week before his mother died and did not continue it in his next letter (although he had promised to do so). 'I went about in a daze. I had all the time I could have wished for composing there [in their rooms], but I was not in the condition to write a single note', he wrote of his state of mind during her illness (31 July 1778). Yet he must have composed the substitute Andante of the 'Paris' Symphony then (perhaps straight after the performance on 18 June).

Mozart had no reason to stay in Paris any longer. Baron Grimm wrote to his father on 17 July, saying that he could not see any opportunity for the young man there. Leopold Mozart was stricken, for his son's return home would mean that he would be forced to admit to himself and to the population of Salzburg at large that the prestigious undertaking had failed. Earlier in the year he had reproached his son for always assuming, 'without sufficient reflection', that everything could be 'accomplished as satisfactorily and infallibly as if it must necessarily turn out well of its very nature' (12 February 1778), but he himself had something of the same propensity. He had miscalculated after all, and the journey had developed its own dynamic. He had not allowed for the intervention of personal factors—not merely the accident of meeting the Weber family in Mannheim but also his wife's death—and he could not have foreseen, in 1777 and from Salzburg, the effect of an event like the Elector Palatine's succession to the duchy of Bavaria or the state of musical affairs in Paris.

It is perhaps something of a surprise to find him writing 'You are not happy in Paris, and I have come to the conclusion that you're not altogether wrong' (31 August 1778). An opportunity had arisen which allowed Mozart to return to Salzburg. With that a weight was evidently lifted from the father's heart, but Mozart himself could see nothing good about the change of circumstances. Only a week before his arrival home, he wrote from Munich 'I swear to you on my honour that I cannot abide Salzburg or its inhabitants (I refer to the people born there); I find their speech, their whole way of life, unendurable' (8 January 1779).

The letter from his father smoothing his path back to Salzburg reached Mozart just as he had returned to Paris (he remained there for another four weeks) from Saint-Germain, where he had met Johann Christian Bach. As on his first journey to western Europe, on the leg of it that took him to London, so on the second he spoke face to face with the composer he still regarded as an unquestionable authority, even though he himself was now, on the whole, a successful composer. He does not reveal what they talked about, but their conversation appears to have centred on quite specialized musical questions: among others, perhaps, techniques of motivic construction. In one minuet (which Einstein wrongly assigns to the Eight Minuets with Trio, K^6 315g) Mozart elaborates a theme which he had 'learnt from Bach', as he wrote later. Bach had travelled to Saint-Germain in the company of his friend the castrato Ferdinando Tenducci, for whom Mozart composed a 'scena' (recitative and aria) for soprano and twelve instruments. This was yet another of the works written in Paris that failed to survive. It is possible, as with the scena 'Non sò, d'onde viene', that Mozart modelled the piece on a work by the older composer, and that they collaborated closely, rather as master and pupil might. Bach clearly gave Mozart some new ideas about concerto techniques, which he tried out at once in the first concerto he composed after returning to Salzburg, the one for two pianos K. 365.[7] In the first movement, for the first time in any concerto, Mozart did not bring back the second subject from the opening tutti in the solo exposition but used a new one in its place; the theme from the opening tutti appears at the end of the development instead. Trivial as this may appear at first glance, it had long-term (and mixed) consequences for his later concertos: the first innovation opened his eyes to new possibilities in concerto form, which he did not work out fully until the middle part of his time in Vienna; the second, on the other hand, remains the unique instance in all his concertos. Both are something exceptional when set against the concertos he had composed up until then, but both are found in J. C. Bach's Keyboard Concerto in B flat major, Op. 13 No. 4, first published in 1777.

---

[7] Küster, *Formale Aspekte*, 111–13, 146, 233–5.

12

Easter Masses and Coronation Masses: 'Coronation' Mass, K. 317, and Missa Solemnis, K. 337

What must have seemed inconceivable in autumn 1777 came to pass in the middle of January 1779: Mozart re-entered the service of the Archbishop of Salzburg—and, truth to tell, in doing so fell on his feet. Colloredo evidently exacted no conditions in offering him the post of cathedral organist, which had become vacant on the death of Anton Cajetan Adlgasser on 21 December 1777 (he suffered a stroke in the organ loft while playing for a service, an event described in graphic detail by Leopold Mozart). The new appointment brought three times the salary Mozart had given up when he resigned in September 1777, but he felt humiliated, nevertheless, by being obliged to accept the position. For Leopold Mozart it was the best of the currently available options, and the Archbishop had the satisfaction of seeing that one of his subjects, of whose qualities he may well have been convinced, had learnt a lesson.

In fact, Colloredo appears to have agreed to conditions made by Mozart. On first hearing of the offer the latter wrote:

If the Archbishop does not allow me to travel every two years I cannot possibly accept the engagement; a mediocrity remains mediocre whether he travels or not—but a man of superior talent (which it would be impious of me to deny that I am) goes to seed if he always stays in the same place . . . There is only one thing I want in Salzburg, and that is that I should not play the violin as I used to—I no longer claim to be a violinist; I want to conduct, and accompany arias, from the keyboard . . . (11 September 1778)

He was given leave of absence before the first two years were up (he went to Munich for *Idomeneo* in November 1780), and his engagement was as a keyboard-player: not the piano alone but also—in the nature of the post—the organ. It all happened quickly. Having left Munich (his last staging-post on the journey from Paris) on 13 January 1779, Mozart must have reached Salzburg on the 15th, and his application was processed on the 17th. He was charged to carry out his duties in the cathedral, at court, and in the chapel in return for the same salary as his predecessor; further, he was expected to supply 'the court and the church as and when possible with new compositions by himself'. Let us take a look at how well he acquiesced in his new lot.

One yardstick of how assiduously he tried to satisfy expectations is provided by the number and nature of the compositions he wrote in his official capacity. The court does not appear to have provided an opportunity to compose an opera (not, at all events, in the twenty months or more during which Mozart actually did the work associated with the post). There is no sign in the two symphonies, K. 319 and 338, that he wanted, or was able, to initiate another phase comparable, perhaps, to the flowering observed in the symphonies of 1773–4. A work like the 'Posthorn' Serenade was, presumably, a Finalmusik and hence a private commission from students at the university, nothing to do with his archiepiscopal appointment. A better indicator is found among his sacred compositions, the two masses in C major, K. 317 and 337 (the 'Coronation' Mass and the Missa Solemnis), and the two cycles of vesper psalms, K. 321 and 339 (*Vesperae de dominica* and *Vesperae solennes de confessore*).

The 'Coronation' Mass, K. 317, was finished on 23 March 1779, a matter of weeks after Mozart took up his new appointment. For a long time it was uncertain what occasion it was composed for: probably the most romantic hypothesis was that it was written for the pilgrimage church of Maria Plain which overlooks Salzburg to the north, and where, since 1751, the image of the Virgin had been crowned in an annual ceremony on the fifth Sunday after Whitsun. The available evidence speaks against that idea, however; in 1779 that Sunday fell on 27 June, more than three months after the mass was completed, making a quite exceptionally long interval for a work of this size. But these very dimensions are an indication that the work, like the Missa Solemnis, K. 337, was composed for Salzburg Cathedral. Both works are scored for a full wind ensemble in addition to the usual 'church trio' of strings (in K. 337 there are obbligato passages for the cello); the text is not reduced to the scale of a missa brevis, but neither is it treated as expansively as in a true missa solemnis; the Gloria and the Credo do not start at 'Et in terra pax' and 'Patrem omnipotentem' respectively (after the intoning of the opening words by the celebrant), but set the text in full and even include some purely orchestral bars of introduction—although the fixed time limit is not exceeded. If Mozart had the duty to compose music for masses celebrated in Salzburg Cathedral within the permitted limits, it is understandable that he would do so in a form that would attract the Archbishop's notice. This means that his interest would focus on masses for feast-days when the Archbishop himself was the celebrant, rather than on ordinary Sundays with their more austere musical regulations. A feast when the archbishop was due to celebrate came shortly after Mozart finished the 'Coronation' Mass on 23 March 1779: Easter Sunday fell on 4 April.[1]

This hypothesis is borne out by analogy: it was a year later, in March 1780 (unfortunately the exact date is not recorded), that Mozart finished his other mass in C major, K. 337, usually called his Missa Solemnis. Easter was relatively early in 1780, on 26 March, but there is nothing in the approximate date to argue against the likelihood that the mass was, once again, composed for Easter Day. Mozart did not compose an Easter mass for Salzburg in the following year, 1781; he had spent the winter in Munich, where he had seen *Idomeneo* into the world for the carnival, and he had been summoned straight from there to Vienna, where Colloredo was staying; by Easter (15 April) his relations with his employer were fast approaching their catastrophic end, and he finally wrote his letter of resignation on 10 May.

Thus the two masses composed by Mozart during his time as court organist in Salzburg can be linked to the same liturgical situation, but they are not the only sacred works of that period. There are church sonatas which can be dated in the immediate proximity of each mass. The autograph of K. 328, also in C major, is on a type of paper that Mozart did not use after about the time of the composition of the 'Coronation' Mass;[2] admittedly it is not dated, but the possibility exists that it too was composed for Easter 1779. There is an even closer connection between the Church Sonata, K. 336, and the Missa Solemnis, K. 337. Again, the two works are in the same key, but in addition Mozart used the same form of words to date them, 'nel Marzo 1780', and they have an instrumental feature in common: unusually, the organ is assigned a concertante role in the church sonata, and similarly it has an obbligato to play in the Agnus Dei of the mass.

There is yet more: both in 1779 and in 1780 Mozart composed a cycle of Vesper psalms, the *Vesperae de dominica*, K. 321, and the *Vesperae solennes de confessore*, K. 339. The dates on the autographs consist only of the year

---

[1] K. Pfannhauser, 'Mozarts "Krönungsmesse"', *Mitteilungen der ISM*, 11/3–4 (1963), 3–11; E. Hintermaier, 'Die Familie Mozart und Maria Plain', *Österreichische Musikzeitschrift*, 29 (1974), 350–6.

[2] Tyson, *Mozart*, 172.

and the titles are neither authentic nor, in the case of the *Vesperae de dominica*, liturgically correct.[3] The titles by which the two cycles are known are more properly used to distinguish cycles with different sequences of texts, yet these two cycles are constructed from the same texts in the same order, as set out here (psalms numbered according to the Vulgate):

1. Dixit Dominus Domino meo: Psalm 109
   'The Lord said unto my Lord'
2. Confitebor tibi Domine: Psalm 110
   'I will give thanks unto the Lord'
3. Beatus vir qui timet Dominum: Psalm 111
   'Blessed is the man that feareth the Lord'
4. Laudate pueri Dominum: Psalm 112
   'Praise the Lord, ye servants'
5. Laudate Dominum omnes gentes: Psalm 116
   'O praise the Lord, all ye heathen'
6. Magnificat anima mea Dominum: Luke 1: 46–55
   'My soul doth magnify the Lord'

In a true 'Vesperae de dominica' Psalm 113 ('In exitu Israel') should come fifth, instead of Psalm 116; the substitution follows the pattern of a 'Vesperae solennes de confessore'. The cycle shows something else: it is only in the Roman breviary that Vespers has five psalms, which means that a Benedictine foundation, such as St Peter's in Salzburg, can be ruled out as the institution for which Mozart composed his two cycles, because there are only four psalms in the order for Vespers in the Benedictine breviary.

A sung Vespers with this text can, in addition, only be performed on the appropriate feast-day itself, not on the eve; as the liturgy further distinguishes between the feast of a 'bishop and martyr' (confessor pontifex) and that of a plain martyr (confessor non pontifex), and the psalm cycle listed above is that for Vespers on the feast of a 'confessor non pontifex', it becomes clear that both works conform to the same type of liturgy.

Other works that Mozart may have composed for Salzburg Cathedral in 1779–80, such as the *Regina coeli*, K. 276, cannot be pinned down to that period with complete certainty. The most that we can be sure of in each of the two years is thus a mass for Easter Day, a church sonata, and a cycle of Vesper psalms for the feast of a martyr not of episcopal rank. The decree appointing Mozart to his post had required him to carry out his duties

---

[3] All terminological discussion of the Vespers is based on: K. G. Fellerer and F. Schroeder in NMA I/2, vol. ii, pp. vii–viii.

'irreproachably, with assiduity and diligence'. He probably took it up on 1 February 1779, for it was only at the end of February that the order authorizing payment of his monthly salary as court organist was sent to the Court Pay Office. Not just over Easter in the first year but for the best part of two years, he carried out his duties 'irreproachably' but doggedly; the works he wrote 'as and when possible' conform to a pattern that meets the requirement of irreproachability, not fewer than were expected, but not a note more. Can he be said to have fulfilled his duties only to the letter?

Even if he did, the musical quality of the works in question did not suffer: all are outstanding examples of their respective genres. The composer himself thought very highly of the masses, in particular, and for posterity, too, they proved to be pioneering works.

On 13 November 1780, Mozart wrote to his father from Munich, where he had gone to prepare *Idomeneo*:

Please be good enough to send me the full scores of the two masses I've brought with me, and also the Mass in B flat, because Count Seeau [Intendant of music at the court of Munich] is going to mention them to the Elector. I would like people to find out what I can do in that style as well. I've heard only one mass by Grua— the sort of thing that anyone could turn out by the half-dozen every day.

It is likely enough that the two masses of which he had, evidently, brought away only the parts were the two most recent, namely those composed for Easter in 1779 and 1780; by the 'Mass in B flat' he probably meant the one composed most recently before them, the Missa Brevis (et Solemnis), K. 275. We can be sure that he was only interested in showing off the current state of his development as a composer, rather than anything earlier. His dismissal of the efforts of Franz Paul Grua, composer and later Kapellmeister at the Munich court, demonstrates his confidence that the music he was now writing, as represented by his two most recent masses, was well above the average.

After his move to Vienna, Mozart again asked his father (several times) to send him the scores of his masses. An unusual relationship is manifested between the two in C major of 1779–80 and some of the Viennese works, specifically in the way the two Agnus Dei in the masses, both of them soprano solos, throw musical bridges across to soprano solos in the operas composed in Vienna. The start of the Agnus Dei of the Missa Solemnis is melodically identical with the start of the aria the Countess sings at the beginning of Act II of *Le nozze di Figaro* ('Porgi amor qualche ristoro'), while her aria in the middle of Act III ('Dove sono i bei momenti'.

No. 19) 'adopts' the opening phrase of the Agnus Dei of the 'Coronation' Mass, but it is transposed up a fifth and converted from triple to duple time; at the same time elements of the accompaniment are also adopted, inasmuch as rests in the vocal line are bridged by the oboe (by strings, initially, in the 'Coronation' Mass). As the last section of the mass, the Agnus Dei ends with the words 'Dona nobis pacem'; in the 'Coronation' Mass Mozart brings back motivic material from the Kyrie at this point. He starts the Kyrie off with an Andante maestoso, quickening it to 'più andante' in the seventh bar. It is the motivic material of the 'più andante' that he uses for the 'Dona nobis pacem' (Andante con moto) and raises to an Allegro con spirito when the chorus enters. That same material turns up again in *Così fan tutte*, in Fiordiligi's great aria 'Come scoglio immoto resta' (No. 14, after the Act I sextet). As in the Kyrie of the 'Coronation' Mass, there is an Andante maestoso before this material (given to the soprano and the clarinets) is brought in to launch an Allegro ('Così ognor quest'alma è forte').

Accident or intention? It would be hardest to prove intention in the case of the link between the 'Coronation' Mass Agnus Dei and 'Dove sono': it is a matter only of a two-bar fragment which could indeed have found its way from the mass to the opera by accident, for it completely lacks the individuality that might bear out the idea that it was done deliberately. The differences in the accompaniment in the two pieces do not even allow it to be said that Mozart's spirit of invention trod the same path twice. The common ground from which the openings of the two arias spring is too common for the similarity to have a particular significance. It is different with the correspondence between the 'Dona nobis pacem' of the 'Coronation' Mass and *Così fan tutte*: here it actually is a matter of treading the same path twice, although Mozart arrives at a different place in each case. The same applies to the third connection, that between the Missa Solemnis and 'Porgi amor', and it is even more difficult to doubt that the link was intended. There is a early draft for 'Porgi amor' in which it is quite different, so Mozart appears to have decided to make the aria in the opera similar to the one in the mass only after exploring other possibilities. All three instances, however, demonstrate that the thematic structures which Mozart created in his masses of 1779–80 remained very much alive for him for the rest of his life. There is extramusical evidence that the two works continued to occupy his mind throughout all his years in Vienna.

Both masses possess an extraordinary musical variety. Both give the orchestra unusual prominence—as much as could be permitted within the framework of a missa brevis et solemnis. The short text of the Agnus Dei—expansively delivered, however, by the soloist—allows the composer the luxury of an orchestral introduction (as does the Benedictus of the 'Coronation' Mass, which is similarly constructed), but Mozart also wrote orchestral introductions for the Kyrie and the 'Dona nobis pacem' (which is not even a complete section) in the Missa Solemnis, and the Credo, long though the text is, in the 'Coronation' Mass. Mozart emphasized the cyclic form of the mass in bringing back the melody of the Kyrie for the 'Dona nobis pacem' in the 'Coronation' Mass; in the Missa Solemnis he broke with the convention of setting the Benedictus as a solo and wrote an elaborate choral fugue, which is rather unusual in a missa brevis et solemnis. The two masses do not offend against the papal requirement for greater liturgical brevity, but nevertheless they give the music greater prominence than it usually has in the circumstances. It becomes more than the vehicle for the text, and develops its own, independent structures, yet remains concise. This must be one of the reasons why both works continued (and have done so to this day) to be sung in churches on feast-days—sometimes on very great occasions indeed.[4]

It is highly probable that the two C major masses of 1779–80 were among the works performed for the coronation of Franz II in 1792. The ceremonies were threefold: homage of the Austrian nobility in St Stephen's Cathedral in Vienna on 25 April, coronation as King of Hungary in Budapest on 6 June, and coronation as Holy Roman Emperor (he was to be the last) in Frankfurt am Main on 14 July. Copies of the scores of the three masses, K. 258, 317, and 337, were put on sale in Vienna close to all three dates. But Franz II came to the throne only two years after the succession of Leopold II, and as a result 'almost the same compositions were performed as at the ceremonies in 1790, since this event, occurring so unexpectedly and so soon, did not allow the time for new music to be written', according to Ignaz Franz von Mosel in his biography of Salieri (1827). That means, however, that Mozart's masses were promoted to 'coronation masses' in 1790 rather than 1792—or, at the latest, in September 1791, when Leopold II was crowned King of Bohemia in Prague. In addition, we know (from a note on the title-page of a manuscript copy) that Mozart's offertory *Misericordias Domini*, K. 222, the work he once sent to Bologna, was performed in 1792.

---

[4] Pfannhauser, 'Mozarts "Krönungsmesse"', 3–5.

It is thus possible that the 'Coronation' Mass, K. 317, earned its nick-name from an event that took place in the last months of the composer's life; he himself never called it by that name, and the first recorded instance of anyone doing so is as late as 1873. Surprisingly, the first time one of his masses was referred to as a 'coronation mass' was half a century earlier than that, in 1823, and the work in question was the Missa Solemnis, K. 337. As the activities of Vienna's music-dealers in 1792 suggest, however, both masses were probably equally entitled to the name. Just as the two piano concertos K. 459 and 537, composed in 1784 and 1788 respectively, were posthumously published as 'coronation concertos', because Mozart was supposed to have performed them in Frankfurt in 1790 on the occasion of Leopold II's coronation, so, too, the (unauthentic) nickname attached itself to the two masses on account of particularly prestigious performances, even if only one of them kept it.

Evidently Mozart planned to perform his 'Coronation' Mass in St Stephen's in Vienna early in June 1791. He had been appointed adjunct Kapellmeister of the cathedral on 9 May, and he was due to conduct a mass there on the Sunday after Whitsun; Anton Stoll, choirmaster in Baden near Vienna, had the parts, and Mozart wrote to ask for them, but in the end the performance did not take place. So even before the ceremonies in Prague later that year, and a full twelve years after its composition, there is evidence that this one, at least, of the two masses continued to hold a central position in Mozart's own estimation of his work.

13

'A symphonie concertante': The Sinfonia Concertante, K. 364, and its Context

Mozart composed his Flute Concerto in G major for Ferdinand Dejean in Mannheim around the turn of the year 1777–8; it was almost five years later, probably in the autumn of 1782, that he finished another concerto for one soloist, the Piano Concerto in A major, K. 414, the first of the series of keyboard concertos which he composed in Vienna. He had started two solo concertos in the mean time but failed to finish either of them: in Mannheim in November 1778 on his journey home from Paris (perhaps with Friedrich Ramm in mind again), he began one for oboe (K. 293), but got little further than the first tutti interjection during the solo exposition; and he did no more than sketch the first movement of a horn concerto (K. 370*b*), in Vienna in 1781. (In 1856 his son Carl Thomas Mozart broke up this sketch into separate sheets and leaves—even halves of leaves—which he distributed as rewards for notable contributions to the celebration of the composer's centenary; some of these fragments have been lost and the rest are scattered far and wide.) Otherwise, he had composed three concertos for more than one soloist: the Concerto for Flute and Harp, K. 299 (1778), the Concerto for Two Pianos, K. 365 (early 1779), and the Sinfonia Concertante for violin and viola, K. 364 (a little later in 1779). In this category, too, there were unfinished works: a concerto for violin, piano, and orchestra (K⁶ 315*f*, begun at much the same date as the unfinished oboe concerto), and a sinfonia concertante for violin, viola, and cello (K⁶ 320*e*, begun around the same time as K. 364). There is also every indication that Mozart composed another sinfonia concertante—for flute, oboe, horn, bassoon, and orchestra—in Paris in 1778, shortly after the Flute and Harp Concerto. Thus, apart from the early Salzburg Concertone for two Violins, K. 190, and the Triple Piano Concerto, K. 242, all Mozart's concertos for more than one solo instrument came into being within a very short period of time, from April 1778 to the summer of 1779, and amount to four finished works and two unfinished.

This was not a matter of chance. At most, the word 'chance' could be used of the Concerto for Flute and Harp, which Mozart composed immediately after his arrival in Paris for Adrien-Louis Bonnières de Souastre Comte de Guines and his daughter; the former, according to Mozart, played the flute 'incomparably' and the latter played the harp 'magnificently' (14 May 1778)—so he was probably aiming at the same level of proficiency as in the case of the triple concerto he wrote for the Lodron family. On the other hand he entered new stylistic terrain when he responded to a commission from Joseph Le Gros for the Concert Spirituel, as he wrote to his father: 'Now I'm going to write a symphonie concertante for flute wendling, oboe Ramm, Punto horn, and Ritter Bassoon' (5 April 1778). (It is altogether unlikely that either the gradual rise from lower-case initials to capitals, or the abrupt switch in the order of players' and instruments' names, is unintentional.) The 'symphonie concertante' was a popular form, cultivated especially by Le Gros and the Concert Spirituel, and it developed according to its own laws: among other things the motivic material of the solo instruments is always largely independent of that presented by the orchestra in the opening tutti.[1]

The work whose progress was plotted by Mozart in his letters has fuelled the fires of research for generations. The discussion over whether or not it could be identified with a surviving but anonymous sinfonia concertante for oboe, clarinet, horn, and bassoon went on for decades. However, the differences between the work described by Mozart and the anonymous work, and, in particular, the striking divergences between the formal characteristics of the latter and those typical of Mozart's concerto style[2] rule out attribution of the anonymous work to Mozart. He had to leave his score with Le Gros, who, however, did not perform the work. Mozart told his father that he would rewrite it from memory (3 October 1778) but evidently nothing came of this.

Mozart used the term 'symphonie concertante' or 'sinfonia concertante' of three works: the lost one he composed for Le Gros, the unfinished one for violin, viola, and cello, and—the only one that was both finished and not lost—the one for violin and viola, K. 364. Even in those days he used the word concerto for works with keyboard soloists, like the Concerto for Two Pianos, K. 365, and the unfinished concerto for violin, piano, and

---

[1] B. S. Brook, 'Symphonie concertante', *Die Musik in Geschichte und Gegenwart*, xii (Kassel, 1965), cols. 1899–1906, esp. 1901; see also B. S. Brook, 'Symphonie concertante', *The New Grove Dictionary of Music and Musicians* (London, 1980), xviii. 433–8.

[2] Küster, *Formale Aspekte*, 208–14.

orchestra, K⁶ 315f, just as he had a few years earlier for the Triple Concerto, K. 242. Similarly he called the work for flute and harp a 'concerto', but he called the early work for two violins with supporting oboe and cello, and orchestra, a 'concertone' (large concerto) on account of the multiple soloists. Clearly, for Mozart the 'sinfonia concertante' genre specifically excluded any work involving an instrument, like the harp or the piano, that can play melody and harmony simultaneously. The distinction seems to have held good for him further afield, for example, when he referred to the 'little concertante symphony' from the 'Posthorn' Serenade, K. 320, meaning those movements which have 'concertante' parts for various wind instruments (29 March 1783; see above, p. 60).

We must assume that when he set about composing the first of his works in the sinfonia concertante genre, for Le Gros, Mozart observed the rules that were to govern his concerto style for several years to come. It was not until around the middle of his Viennese period that, for example, he again wrote concertos in which all the motivic elements of the opening tutti reappear during the course of the opening movement. He might have had difficulty combining this stylistic trait of the sinfonia concertante with his own personal concerto form, which reckoned with two themes remaining 'constant' throughout the movement (in addition to the ideas in this particular area which he may have absorbed from J. C. Bach). The Sinfonia Concertante for violin and viola, K. 364, which will be discussed below as his only surviving work in the genre, observes the rule of tutti–solo motivic contrast to a very marked degree.

This contrast may be a survivor from an old tradition. The Italian 'ritornello' ('little return', that is, a short passage that returns several times without alteration) and the Greek 'epeisodion' (in a tragedy, a segment of the action between two choruses) already indicate the nature of the differences (including motivic ones) between ritornello and episode in the concerto. But the distinction had become less sharp by Mozart's day: it had long been possible for an episode to refer back (as recapitulation, for example) to material from an earlier episode, and for ritornello and episode to be linked motivically (for example, by a similar opening).

The motivic separation of solo and tutti, however, allowed Mozart to take a fresh look at the construction of solo sections. The fact that there is always more than one soloist in a sinfonia concertante makes it possible to give less prominence to the soloist–orchestra relationship and more to the relationship of the soloists to each other. In the Concertone Mozart clipped the wings of his two solo violins by giving solo status to instruments from the orchestra as well; in the Triple Concerto the orchestra stands well back, but the three soloists make no bones about developing their own part out of motivic material presented to them in the orchestral introduction. In the Sinfonia Concertante, on the other hand, not a single phrase from the opening tutti returns in the solo exposition: even its principal theme is brushed only fleetingly. At the same time Mozart sticks to the system of punctuation he had derived from aria form. The fact that he does not use material from the opening tutti even for the tuttis that separate the solo passages is not exceptional in itself (concertos where it is not done are, nevertheless, in a minority), but the technique gains a special meaning here because, as in the G major Violin Concerto of four years earlier, Mozart denies the listener a loud conclusion to the opening tutti and allows it to ebb away quietly.

The finale of the Sinfonia Concertante also represents a modification of a common form. It is essentially a rondo but without the usual alternation between episodes using new material and a refrain which is always the same (and differs from the ritornello of a first movement by remaining in the tonic). The refrain behaves as usual in a rondo, and the varying of its last occurrence with snatches of 'alien' material is typical of Mozart, but constructing both episodes from the same material is against all rules. (In textbook terms, the form is not the conventional ABACA but ABAB^{1}A^1.) As in the first movement, here too the reciprocal play between the two soloists is placed in the foreground. Numerous elements of the music make their first appearance in one of the two solo parts and are then repeated in the other, sometimes with slight variations. This process of repetition needs a lot of space to unfold properly, and Mozart duly allows his five-section rondo to expand to a grand total of 490 bars. The repetition is also responsible for one structural detail in the final refrain: in the last 'snatch' of new material which appears in this section, Mozart gives each soloist in turn a cadenza which is like a caricature of a cadenza in an aria. A vocal cadenza might be sung within the range of a fifth. In the middle of the first movement of *Exsultate, jubilate*, the vocal range is increased by putting the A into a higher octave. But here the range between the highest and the lowest notes is increased to two and a half octaves in the viola part and to three and a half octaves in the violin (Ex. 13.1). This presented a test of technical agility to players at the time of the work's composition, when there were no chin-rests to keep instruments in place during changes of position: as the hand moved towards the body and then rapidly away again there was a real danger of dropping the instrument (see Pl. 5).

Ex. 13.1
(a) *Exsultate, jubilate*, K. 165, 1st aria, bars 60–5.
(b) Sinfonia Concertante, K. 364, 3rd movement, bars 448–56 (solo violin).

The aria and operatic style also have a special influence on the slow middle movement, which falls into two sections of approximately the same length (sixty-two and sixty-eight bars). It follows the pattern of many binary arias, in the second half of which the text of the first is repeated while the harmonic arc which drew away from the tonic during the first half is led back to it; during this process the thematic material and the musical structure remain essentially the same (elaboration may extend the second half). This two-part structure was very common in arias and had a long tradition behind it: even in the da capo aria the main section is frequently binary.

As in the two outer movements, the two soloists again engage in dialogue with one another, but in the aria-like structure of this movement the dialogue takes much the form of a duet. Operatic duets can be stationary, illustrating merely that two characters have something in common, or they can promote the action and bring the two characters closer together by stages. The premiss is that the two are still relatively far apart to begin with and present their own musical and verbal statements in fairly substantial solos; at a second stage these alternating solos come closer together in dialogue until the third stage is reached, at which they sing together in harmony. This duet schema, relying on the synthesis of the thesis and antithesis presented initially, can shape an entire movement, or it can equally well be employed in each of a movement's two parts, but

PL. 5. Portrait of Leopold Mozart, on the title-page of his book *Versuch einer gründlichen Violinschule* (1756). It shows the playing position and the absence of a chin-rest.

then the opposition of the thesis and the antithesis will not be so marked in the second part. It is this second form (the vocal equivalent of which will be examined in a later chapter with reference to *Don Giovanni*) which is encountered in the middle movement of Mozart's Sinfonia Concertante.

This is one of the very rare instances in Mozart's concertos of a middle movement in the minor. After the early Piano Concerto in G major, K. 41, which Mozart put together from movements from separate sonatas, the three outstanding examples are all in E flat major: the Sinfonia Concertante, and two of the piano concertos, K. 271 and 482. On the other hand there are two other keyboard concertos in E flat major which have middle movements in the major (the Double Concerto, K. 365, and K. 449), and these are balanced, as it were, by two in other keys which have middle movements in the minor (K. 456 in B flat major and K. 488 in A major). These slow movements in the minor give off an air of sadness which is in the greatest possible contrast to the vivacity characteristic of most of the outer movements in these concertos. If that sadness is a reflection of Mozart's overall mood at the time of composition in each case, does it mean that those were especially oppressive moments in his life? How much sadness can go into a composition, framed between two movements which appear to be full of the joy of life, if the whole is to be regarded as artistically integrated?

As a matter of sober fact, at times of especially deep sorrow Mozart composed nothing. What he wrote to his father from Paris, describing his mother's last illness, has already been quoted: 'I went about in a daze. I had all the time I could have wished for composing . . . but I was not in the condition to write a single note' (31 July 1778). And eleven years later, almost to the day, at a time when serious financial problems were made worse by his wife's illness, he wrote to his friend Michael Puchberg, 'I'm sure I don't need to tell you again that this unhappy illness prevents me from doing any kind of remunerative work . . . But as it now appears that my dear . . . wife is getting a little better day by day, I should soon be able to work again' (12 July 1789). Yes: we can assume that the sadness in the Sinfonia Concertante is sincere, and, probably, that its expressiveness is deepened by personal experience; but then personal experience must be given some credit in the cheerful outer movements as well. We should accept, as a fundamental principle, that Mozart was more intent on giving an adequate form to musical situations than on using them for the expression of his personal emotions, without exercising any artistic control. The propensity of E flat major to fall into a melancholy, 'minor' mood has already been mentioned (p. 58); that would in itself be a musical explanation for the C minor of the middle movement here. Furthermore, it may be a greater artistic experience for us to allow an unsurpassable dramatist like Mozart to plunge us into a particular mood than to imagine that he would allow himself to be influenced so directly by a personal emotion while composing any one movement. The composer who moves almost imperceptibly from the C minor of the middle movement of this work to build up the 'redeeming' E flat major of the finale proves, at all events, his sovereign command of moods—not his own mood alone, which he must restrain, but primarily that of the listener, whom he wants to reach.

14

Heroic Isolation and Divine Directives:
Idomeneo, re di Creta, K. 366

The first performance of *Il re pastore* was given in Salzburg on 23 April 1775; the interval between then and 29 January 1781, the date of the next première of a full-length opera by Mozart, *Idomeneo*, is the longest between any two of his operas (his only work for the theatre in the mean time was the incidental music for *Thamos, König in Ägypten*). But unlike *Il re pastore*, *Idomeneo* is reckoned among Mozart's great operas, so there is every reason to look at what had changed during that gap of nearly six years. Had Mozart's conception of musical drama developed only in terms of his personal style, or was something more fundamental involved?

In 1777, in Mannheim, he had petitioned Elector Karl Theodor for a commission to write an opera. 'I said, "I commend myself to Your Serene Highness's grace, my dearest wish would be to write an opera here; I beseech Your Highness not to forget me entirely. I know German too, God be praised and thanked", and I smiled. The Elector answered, "It may easily be possible"' (to Leopold Mozart, 8 November 1777). But destiny carried Karl Theodor off to Munich, and any artistic plans for Mannheim were swamped in the political upheaval.

Mozart had discussed the idea of setting texts in the German language earlier on this journey, in Munich, where, as in Mannheim, he tried to obtain an appointment or commissions to write operas before moving on. He thought it would be feasible to write 'four German operas a year, some *buffe*, some *serie*, and I should have one *sera* [a benefit evening] from each, or a share of the proceeds; that's the custom, and that alone would bring in at least 500 gulden, and with my salary that would already be 800 gulden, but I'm sure it could be more' (to Leopold Mozart, 2 October 1777).

His Munich proposal, in particular, gives the impression that he was thinking of combining elements of typically Italian styles (*opera buffa* and *opera seria*) with German texts. This had already been attempted by other composers with some success. One example was the opera *Günther von*

Schwarzburg by Ignaz Holzbauer, Kapellmeister at the court of Mannheim, where Mozart attended a performance, of which he reported back to his father with enthusiasm (14 November 1777). *Günther von Schwarzburg* even has recitatives; Mozart's remarks do not reveal whether he would have taken a work like Holzbauer's as his model if he had been given the commission he wanted in 1777, whether in Munich or Mannheim. However, his ideas seem to have undergone a fundamental change during the following three months. Perhaps it was becoming acquainted with the Weber family that made him suddenly start to prefer Italian opera to German, and perhaps the three Italian arias he composed at the end of February 1778 before leaving Mannheim reflect the change of mind. A German opera by Mozart in the style of *Günther von Schwarzburg* seems to be out of the question from that date forward; he found the very idea of recitatives in German problematic, given the close connection of the musical form with the Romance languages. A solution presented itself during his return journey from Paris, when he was again in Mannheim, and heard the melodramas of Georg Anton Benda. They caught his imagination as a model for a German equivalent to recitative, in which most of the text would be spoken to an orchestral accompaniment, while recitatives should be sung 'only occasionally, when the words lend themselves to being expressed in the music' (12 November 1778). When he came to write his two German operas, however, he fell into line with the practice of the German Singspiel, very occasionally linking accompanied recitatives to arias and choruses but otherwise leaving the dialogue to be spoken without orchestral participation.

Mozart returned to Salzburg in January 1779 without a single opera commission. One arrived from Munich, however, during the summer of 1780—really quite soon, considering the political and organizational problems that had attended the union of the Palatinate and Bavaria. The result was *Idomeneo*, composed for the Munich carnival in 1781. The commission was a 'scrittura' (as it probably would have been if it had come from Mannheim), meaning that the composer was contracted in connection with the one work for the length of time it would take to be written and staged; it was not an engagement so much as a hiring, for the composer would remain in the service of his current employer. Mozart's earlier opera for Munich, *La finta giardiniera*, had been commissioned on similar terms, and so had the two works for Milan, *Mitridate* and *Lucio Silla*. The document offering the new commission has not survived, so we do not know the exact terms and conditions attached, but they obviously included a number of official stipulations. One concerned the choice of subject, for which Munich wanted to turn to a French source (as in the case of the carnival opera of 1780, Franz Paul Grua's *Telemaco*).[1] It was normal practice at that date for the commissioner of an opera to choose the subject. The librettist was Giambattista Varesco, chaplain at the court of Salzburg, who had a bad press for a long time; it is now recognized that he carried our his task of translating and adapting the French original (written for an opera produced in Paris in 1712) scrupulously, and enriched it with material from other classical and biblical sources.[2] Nevertheless, there are undeniable weaknesses in Varesco's text, for example, the fact that all the characters suffer their fates in total isolation: they react to divine directives but rarely come together in relationships that move the action on. Even when they do, possibilities that would have been developed by the librettist of a typical *opera seria* are neglected. We look in vain for the intrigues characteristic of this kind of drama or for any exploitation of the dramatic potential of a love-duet. Varesco wrote the libretto in Salzburg, so that Mozart was able to start the composition before he left for Munich on 5 November 1780.

It looks at first sight, therefore, as though *Idomeneo* picks up the thread of Mozart's operatic career at the precise point where he had left it with *Il re pastore* and his reflections durng the winter of 1777–8.[3] The new opera seems to belong in the world of *opera seria*, borne out by the description of it in the announcements of its first performance as a *dramma per musica*, which is a synonym for *opera seria*, just as *dramma giocoso* is for *opera buffa*. The very title is typical of the world of *opera seria*, in using the name of a single, sublime ruler from the pages of history, Idomeneus, King of Crete at the time of the Trojan Wars: the fact that the classical versions of the tale contain a strong element of legend does not undermine the 'historical' aspect. An *opera buffa*, on the other hand, is more likely to be designated by a type of human being (as with *La finta giardiniera*—The Pretended Garden-Girl), or by some form of reference to typical human behaviour or traits (both in *Così fan tutte*—All women do the same). A personal name is found in the title of an *opera buffa* only when it is part of the description

---

[1] On Munich carnival operas, see D. Heartz in NMA II/5, xi/1, p. vii.

[2] K. Kramer, 'Das Libretto zu Mozarts *Idomeneo*', in R. Münster (ed.), *Wolfgang Amadeus Mozart, Idomeneo, 1781–1981* (Munich, 1981), 7–43, esp. 22.

[3] On *Idomeneo* in general, see Kunze, *Mozarts Opern*, 112–74.

of the content (as with *Le nozze di Figaro*—Figaro's Wedding). *Idomeneo, re di Creta* is, in this respect, analogous to *Lucio Silla* or, especially, *Mitridate, re di Ponto*, Mozart's two earlier *opere serie*.[4]

Other typical *opera seria* elements are the number of acts (three: two is the norm for an *opera buffa*) and, up to a point, the composition of the cast. The cast of an *opera seria* is usually headed by two couples (primo uomo and prima donna, and secondo uomo and seconda donna), customarily forming two pairs of lovers. The primo uomo (first man) is always a castrato (sometimes the secondo uomo is, too). These four characters confront a tenor who plays a king; in spite of his rank he is not the principal dramatic character in the work to which he gives his name but yields, in particular, to the primo uomo (as in *Lucio Silla*, see above, p. 27). A sixth character, the ultima parte (last [musical] part), is often a bass playing a member of the royal household.[5] There are seven characters in *Idomeneo*, in addition to the chorus and its soloists, but that is not a significant departure from the norm. Idomeneus (the king) is a tenor, and his son Idamantes (primo uomo) was originally sung by a castrato (mezzo-soprano). The question of who is the prima donna is more problematic, however. Is it Ilia, the daughter of King Priam of Troy, or Electra? The latter is a more central character in the myth of Troy as the daughter of Agamemnon, who urges her brother Orestes to avenge their father's murder (committed by their mother Clytemnestra and her lover Aegisthus). This background is set out by Ilia in her first recitative and explains Electra's presence on Crete, for which there is no classical authority. The mythological unauthenticity might be regarded as evidence in itself that Electra cannot develop into the prima donna but is doomed to be no more than Ilia's rival for Idamantes' love. On the other hand her position gives Electra a certain advantage over Ilia in Act II, so that the uncertainty over the prima donna question is almost a driving force of the action as a whole. The third male character, Arbaces, is described in the cast-list as 'the king's confidant'—a typical ultima parte, were it not that the part was originally written for a castrato. The bass role is that of the Voice of the Oracle, a minimal part in the drama as a whole, and there is finally the even smaller part of the Priest of Neptune, another tenor, but certainly not a secondo uomo. The cast as a whole is, therefore, already

---

[4] On these categories, see Kunze, ibid. 41–2, 113; on the typology of titles, see Osthoff, 'Opera buffa', 682–3.

[5] Ibid. 705, after Saverio Mattei, 1781. On other specifics, see also Lühning, *Titus-Vertonungen*, 38–40, after Giovanni Baretti, 1763.

somewhat atypical in construction, indicating a more pragmatic than schematic approach to the *seria* subject, and the further we go into the dramatic structure of *Idomeneo* the more deviations from the norms appear.

The opera is set in Crete and begins immediately before the return home of Idomeneus from the siege of Troy. He has sent Ilia, a Trojan princess and now a captive, to Crete ahead of him. She laments her fate, especially her fear that the Greek Idamantes, whom she loves, will naturally prefer the Greek Electra to herself. Idamantes fails to set her mind at rest, even though he makes an important gesture of friendship towards the Trojans: having grown gradually into royal responsibility during his father's absence, he takes it on himself to order the prisoners of war to be released from their chains, to celebrate Idomeneus' return. Electra opposes this: she hopes that by taking a strong pro-Greek line—against Ilia—she will win the approval of Idomeneus, so that he will make her his son's wife. Word comes that Idomeneus has been shipwrecked in a storm off the coast of Crete, and Electra expresses her despair in an aria.

The scene moves to the coast, where the storm rages, but suddenly Idomeneus reaches the shore. We soon learn that he saved himself by vowing to Neptune, the god of the sea, that he will sacrifice the first person he meets when he sets foot on land, a necessity that he understandably deplores. In their wisdom, the gods decree that that person is Idamantes. When Idomeneus recognizes him, he abruptly recoils from him, leaving Idamantes perplexed. The first act ends with an intermezzo (March and Chorus) depicting the landing of the Cretan troops who sailed with Idomeneus.

The central concern of the two remaining acts is Idomeneus' attempt to come to terms with his vow. At first he tries to evade it by sending Idamantes far away across the sea to ascend the throne of Argos, with Electra as his queen. But Neptune intervenes: a sudden storm prevents them from taking ship. The people witnessing it are horrified, especially when Idomeneus reveals at the height of the storm that it is all his fault; he prays to implacable Neptune to spare his son and accept the sacrifice of his own life instead. The third act opens with Idamantes alone: he believes that Ilia spurns him as resolutely as his father avoids him. Neptune, we learn from his soliloquy, has sent a monster to ravage Crete; Idamantes has resolved to fight the beast, even if it means his own death. But he wins, and it looks as if Idomeneus has no choice but to fulfil his vow and kill his son. At the moment when he raises the knife Ilia throws herself between them and begs to die in Idamantes' place: surely heaven cannot desire the death of the sons of Greece, but only that of the (former) enemies of Greece. At that the Voice of the Oracle is heard, giving the resolution to the action. Idomeneus must abdicate in favour of Idamantes, who must marry Ilia. All that is left is for very nearly everyone on stage to rejoice. Only Electra departs in anger. She has lost the contest for the role of prima donna; the dramatic standing given to her final outburst (originally an aria, but Mozart turned it into recitative before the first performance) puts her in the same position as the Queen of the Night and her followers at the end of *Die Zauberflöte*.

The conventional structure of an *opera seria* separates the dramatic progress from the musical splendours. The action moves forwards in the recitatives, creating the opportunity at the end of a scene for a big aria in which a singer demonstrates his or her vocal prowess and earns a round of applause at the end of it. In a normal *opera seria* this applause does not disturb the flow of the action because the end of the scene brings a break in any case; furthermore, such arias are frequently in da capo form, in which the action hangs fire for musical reasons, so that the applause does not increase the interruption, even when it is so tempestuous that the singer is obliged to repeat the aria. On top of that, the singer usually leaves the stage after the aria, for which reason this type of aria is often called an 'exit' aria. The splendour of such an aria is spread out, it can be said, alongside the unrolling of the dramatic course of events; the fact that a singer sometimes launches into an extensive exit aria even when he is supposed to be fleeing for his life may be contrary to dramatic sense but conforms wholly to the musical structure of an *opera seria*. Finally, an exit aria can be dramatically satisfying: no one will take exception to Leporello's 'catalogue' aria in *Don Giovanni* on the grounds that it is an exit aria. Those who regularly attended *drammi per musica* in Mozart's day expected exit arias as the showpieces of vocal art.

In the case of *Idomeneo* that expectation was largely disappointed. Most of the arias provided by Varesco and Mozart serve a completely different kind of dramatic concept—so much so that some are not even musically independent, closed numbers. Almost every aria in Mozart's later operas can be taken from its context and performed unaltered as a self-sufficient item, but several of those in *Idomeneo* would need to have at least the closing bars rewritten, for in their original position they run on into the next section of the music—usually, that is, into recitative. As a result the music moves on inexorably, and its progress would be disrupted by applause at the end of a scene. In 'normal' *seria* opera the aria is an action-free zone, which the singer can dominate, rather like a concertante instrument, but in *Idomeneo* the action continues during the arias, and the arias make individual contributions to the action; even the postlude of an aria is the accompaniment to the next phase in the action.

This tension between traditional *opera seria* and the new ideas in *Idomeneo* is illustrated by Idomeneus' great aria in Act II, 'Fuor del mar ho un mar in seno' ('Escaped from the sea, I find a sea in my breast'). Mozart composed it for Anton Raaff, then 66 and the star tenor of old-style *opera seria*, whom he had got to know during his 1777–8 visit to Mannheim, and at first he wrote an aria of such length and such extreme virtuosity that it was more than the poor man could cope with, so it had to be shortened. The first version ends with a perfect cadence: its singer (it is supposed) will deserve applause. The removal of the virtuoso figuration that would justify the applause, however, places the aria on the same footing as those sung by other characters, and of course it receives the same dramatic treatment as they do. It too, now, does not come to a full close: at the point where there might have been one a new character has already entered, the situation has taken a dramatic new turn, and interruption of the action for a round of applause is out of the question.

Mozart makes his intentions quite clear with the very first aria in the work, which is sung by Ilia. It has no precise start but grows directly out of the accompanied recitative that went before it. Such a start is not uncommon, but Mozart also denies the piece a precise ending and that is unusual. At the point where the aria might come to a full close, Ilia, torn between sorrow for her dead father and brothers and her love for Idamantes, is interrupted by Idamantes himself, and her shock at suddenly seeing him causes the aria to turn into secco recitative with equal suddenness. But even the recitative that has preceded this aria is unusual: almost the entire action before the aria begins has been conducted in recitativo accompagnato—accompanied, that is, by the strings, in the style usually employed to raise the emotional temperature from that of the normal, harpsichord-accompanied secco recitative. Secco recitative is what one expects at the beginning of an *opera seria*, and it is only towards the end of the work (or an act) that excitement rises sufficiently to justify the introduction of accompagnato. But Mozart abandons secco in the third bar, giving a clear indication of the manner in which he is going to stretch the *seria* norms. He starts with excitement already running high, and even later Ilia drops back into secco only for brief intervals at a time, for example, at the point where she tells herself that Idamantes does not love her: this disenchanted observation calls for a corresponding sobriety in the musical expression. By these means Varesco and Mozart portray Ilia reacting to her fate but thrown helplessly to and fro by it, and in doing so they reject the *seria* convention of establishing one emotion as fundamental to a recitative, even if it is then allowed to vary. Librettist and composer obviously recognized that the situation would not tolerate that kind of emotional uniformity and based their dramatic treatment on a foundation hitherto unusual for *opera seria*—although it did not necessarily lead to more finely delineated characterization.[6] In other respects the conventional expressive resources of recitative are utilized from traditional—if notably intelligent—standpoints. When it seems desirable, Mozart selectively heightens the accompagnato to arioso, and this allows the aria itself to take off fairly unexpectedly from one of these ariosos (the fact that the bassoons suddenly join in with the strings gives the game away). By this means 'aria', as a musical form, becomes merely a manifestation of the possible ways forward open to recitative; on the one hand it sees a certain repose enter the oscillations of Ilia's emotions, on the other hand it serves to spotlight the climax in the course of their development. Nowhere else in Mozart's operas can this stringent intensification of recitative to aria be observed, except perhaps in Don Alfonso's short arias in *Così fan tutte*, but even those have regular beginnings and endings.

Mozart also played with the ranking of the different forms of recitative in the reverse direction; falling back from accompagnato to secco is always dramatically very strongly legitimized, as in the instance in Ilia's aria described above. There is a particularly convincing example towards the end of *Idomeneo*. Long stretches of the third act are dominated by accompagnato, because the scenes leading up to the sacrifice of Idamantes are, in the nature of things, intensely exciting. Mozart wrote to his father about it: 'My head and my hands are so full of the third act that I shouldn't wonder if I turned into a third act myself. This act on its own takes more effort than an entire opera, for there is scarcely a scene in it that is not extremely interesting' (3 January 1781). Ilia's intervention prevents the sacrifice: at the moment when the accompagnato tension has risen to its height, she enters with down-to-earth secco. Idomeneus, Idamantes, and the High Priest want to see the king's vow fulfilled, and as they react to the interruption the music naturally returns to accompaniment by the strings. Once more Ilia speaks up, again in sober, secco tones; then she explains the

[6] See Kunze, *Mozarts Opern*, 127, 132.

reasoning behind her offering of her own life, and now the strings enter to give her words a more 'solemn' accompaniment. She kneels at the altar to receive the fatal blow, and here the accompagnato is as appropriate as it was when Idamantes was the sacrificial victim. But now the voice of Neptune's oracle is heard, and they are all released from their ordeal.

Arguably Mozart spoilt the oracle's intervention. The first version he composed was seventy bars long; the autograph shows that the cuts which he several times asked his father to ask Varesco to make led next to a thirty-one-bar version, and finally to one only nine bars long.[7] But, as the Munich sources show, including the final, printed version of the libretto, by the time of the performance it had grown back to forty-four bars (and had lost the trombones which feature in all the earlier versions). This eliminated a weakness in the nine-bar version, in which the Voice of the Oracle functions only as a *deus ex machina*. But even the final Munich version dropped Varesco's original idea: the words with which the passage opens in the first and second versions in the autograph are 'Ha vinto Amore' ('Love has conquered'). According to Varesco, that is, the hopeless position that the action has reached is resolved not by the words of the oracle but by Ilia with her (secco) intervention. Neptune himself, in this version, would have become nothing more than a reactive element in the drama, a force for opposition overcome by Ilia (with Amor's aid). Varesco's opera would suddenly have transported itself from the world of *seria* to a new one for which the French Revolution has usually been held responsible: the world of the 'rescue opera', of which Beethoven's *Fidelio* is the best-known inhabitant.[8] In that opera Florestan, the political prisoner, is saved from the pistol of Pizarro only by the physical intervention of Leonore, not by the approach of the minister, who brings about the general relaxation of tension like a *deus ex machina* (similar to the case of Ilia, Idamantes, and the oracle in *Idomeneo*).

Mozart thought the text of the third act was too long 'and therefore the music is too' (18 January 1781), and for that reason he made cuts in the material preceding the sacrifice scene, including, among other things, Idamantes' aria of farewell (yet another number without a regular beginning or ending). There remained seventy-seven bars of rising accompagnato tension before Ilia's startling secco intervention, and this overload of tension increases the surprise of the secco. The very fact that

---

[7] See Heartz in NMA II/5, xi/1, pp. xiv–xv.

[8] See also D. Charlton, 'On Redefinitions of "Rescue Opera"', in M. Boyd (ed.), *Music and the French Revolution* (Cambridge, 1992), 169–88.

secco, the common musical currency of a *seria* action (almost a temporal more than a musical component), becomes a theatrical event, a dramatic rhetorical figure, demonstrates the originality of Mozart's music for *Idomeneo*. But it was the much derided Varesco who created the premisses for it. The man of whom it has been said that 'unfortunately, [he] had no sense whatever of the stage'[9] nevertheless laid the foundations for Mozart's integration of the arias into the course of the events; it is he who (so far as we know) deserves credit for the idea of introducing action on the stage which snatches exit arias from the jaws of their predictable final cadences at the last minute. It was Mozart who refined the technique which pushed *opera seria*, an unmitigated type of number opera, to its very limits (without, of course, going so far as the through-composed technique of Wagnerian opera), but he did so by seizing the formal opportunities Varesco had created for him and bringing the situations—more than the characters, perhaps—to musical life.

Mozart and Varesco seem to have been positively fixated on the musical forms whereby these goals were to be reached. That is made especially clear by the consequences of the decision to reduce the virtuosity of 'Fuor del mar'. But it is equally obvious that their ideas were allied to developments which were special to the Wittelsbach courts in Mannheim and Munich. Some of the elements found in *Idomeneo* are also present in *Günther von Schwarzburg*, that *seria* opera with a German text. It too begins with a scene in which a female character (the Countess Palatine) is alone on the stage and starts to sing a recitative which is accompanied—from bar I—by strings. It too has exit arias, the postludes of which are swept up in the advancing action, and which fall back into accompanied recitative without coming to a full close (I.iii, Rudolf's aria; II.vi, Asberta's aria). That is not to say that a stylistic phenomenon of this kind is likely to have been specified in the 'scrittura'. The Munich carnival opera of the year before *Idomeneo*, Franz Paul Grua's *Telemaco*, is a dyed-in-the-wool *opera seria* so far as its musical forms are concerned (despite the French influence on its libretto) and betrays no ambition to follow the example of *Günther von Schwarzburg*, that of the following year, Antonio Salieri's *Semiramide*, stays wholly within the limits of *seria* convention in respect of differentiation of tempo and the dramatic functions of secco, accompagnato, and arioso.[10]

---

[9] Dent, *Mozart's Operas*, 34.

[10] The MSS of the Munich versions of the Grua and Salieri operas are in the Bayerische Staatsbibliothek, Munich.

Archbishop Colloredo went to Vienna early in 1781 to be with his father, Imperial Vice-Chancellor Rudolf Joseph Prince Colloredo, who was ill. The recent death of Empress Maria Theresia was another reason why it was opportune for the Archbishop of Salzburg to be in the capital. Mozart, on the other hand, remained in Munich until March, but he was clearly already by mid-December trying to provoke the Archbishop by prolonging his stay deliberately: the 'scrittura' may even have been limited to six weeks.

By God, if it was left to me, before leaving home I should have wiped my behind with the last decree. On my honour, it's not Salzburg, it's His Highness—the haughty nobility—that becomes more intolerable by the day. I would be only too pleased if he would have somebody write and tell me that he no longer requires my services. (To Leopold Mozart, 16 December 1780; not surprisingly, parts of this letter are in the usual code.)

But instead the Archbishop sent word that he required his services urgently and ordered him to leave Munich and come straight to Vienna. As a result Mozart had the score of *Idomeneo* with him and lost no time in circulating it in Vienna, but he was doomed to disappointment. He quickly found out that the subject was unacceptable in the imperial capital, where, as he told his father within a month of his arrival, 'people prefer comic pieces' (18 April 1781). He raised the question of language again; after another five months he wrote that he wished *Idomeneo* could have been translated into German as Gluck's *Iphigénie* had been: 'I would have completely changed the role of Idomeneus, and rewritten it for Fischer in the bass, and made quite a lot of other changes, and brought it more into line with French style' (12 September 1781). Johann Ignaz Ludwig Fischer was the bass who later created the part of Osmin in *Die Entführung*; it would certainly have been a very different Idomeneus from the one heard in Munich. It was not until 13 March 1786, five weeks after the first performance of *Der Schauspieldirektor* and seven weeks before that of *Figaro*, that *Idomeneo* was performed in Vienna, for the only time in the composer's lifetime; it was given before a private audience in Prince Auersperg's palace.

It may appear, with the wisdom of hindsight, that *Idomeneo* only approaches the threshold of the style of the great operas Mozart composed in Vienna. On the other hand his own comments testify that the climate in Vienna at that date was unsuitable for that particular sapling to thrive. *Idomeneo* is therefore truly unique among Mozart's works; its style was developed for it alone, and the immense changes in the conditions in which Mozart began working shortly after its première forced him to make equally fundamental changes of course in a number of areas. Writing from Munich about his wish that the Archbishop would dismiss him, he had continued: 'With the great protection I have here now, I should be sufficiently assured for my present and future circumstances' (16 December 1780). But Mozart in Munich would presumably have been, for a while at least, Mozart without the style of the Da Ponte operas, and would perhaps have done more and gone further in the style of *Idomeneo*. Manfred Hermann Schmid, in his study of Mozart's work in Salzburg, writes that the *Vesperae solennes de confessore* belong, with *Idomeneo* and the Sinfonia Concertante, K. 364, to the works which complete a first major section in Mozart's *œuvre*; the Vespers, he declares, are completely isolated when they are compared with works by Eberlin, Adlgasser, and Michael Haydn, which represent the Salzburg tradition.[11] Mozart gave the appearance of settling back into the Salzburg scene in 1779 but did not really surrender his intention of leaving it again. The circumstances he found in Vienna two years later, however, were new to him and he had to accommodate himself to a different set of local traditions. Against this background, it is too soon to look for signs of the Vienna *œuvre* in Mozart's works of 1779–80, but the Salzburg style is already *passé*. The result is a tension which affects not only the Vespers and the Sinfonia Concertante, as already shown, but also *Idomeneo*. The period between Mozart's return from Paris and his finding his feet in Vienna is thus a completely separate stage in his artistic development.

---

[11] Schmid, *Mozart und die Salzburger Tradition*, 247, 229.

15

Pupils and Fugues: Paths to the C minor Fugue for Two Pianos, K. 426

The Archbishop of Salzburg's court organist arrived in Vienna from Munich on 16 March 1781. Although from that moment onwards he was no longer an independent traveller but had to comport himself as a dutiful member of the Archbishop's household, Mozart did everything in his power to hold on to his former liberty. He made new contacts and, especially, looked up old acquaintances like the Weber family and the schoolmaster Joseph Mesmer (a cousin of Franz Anton Mesmer who gave his name to mesmerism). Eventually Mozart succeeded in arranging an appearance at a concert of the Society of Musicians on 3 April, but the Archbishop stopped him from going ahead with a concert he had wanted to promote on his own account, from which he had expected to make 100 ducats (= 450 gulden, that is, 50 gulden more than the annual salary he received from the Archbishop). The 'second Salzburg period', which had started when Mozart returned there in January 1779, seemed to be over as far as he was concerned; in a postscript to a letter to his father he wrote: 'Believe me, this is a splendid place—and for my profession the best place in the world' (4 April 1781).

Mozart poured it all out in one letter: what Vienna was like, his anger at the loss of earnings from the abandoned concert, and an account of the concert he did give. The recognition that the life he had once dreamt of making for himself in Mannheim could become a reality in Vienna must already have struck him in those first two weeks. But he did not want to be the one to take the first step in breaking with Colloredo, perhaps out of concern for his father, who would have to stay on in Salzburg (as in autumn 1777), perhaps because he did not want to quarrel with his father. It is even conceivable that he attached some importance to a favourable dismissal this time. 'I do not know as yet that I am supposed to leave—for until Count Arco tells me himself I shall not believe it' (4 April 1781). But Count Arco, the Archbishop's chief steward, kept Mozart waiting.

Mozart was longing for one final feather to drop and tilt the balance, and while he waited his conviction about 'the best place in the world' grew. He wrote again to his father:

The subscription for the six sonatas has now opened and that will bring me in some money. All is going well with the opera too [*Zaide*, K. 344]. Come advent, I shall give a concert, and then it will go on like that, getting better and better, for there is always good money to be earned here during the winter. (19 May 1781)

And a week later: 'About pupils: I can have as many as I want; but I don't want that many. I want to be better paid than others are, and preferably have fewer' (26 May 1781).

Works for publication and sale, concerts, operatic projects, and teaching: Mozart spent the first weeks in Vienna sniffing out the prospects of putting the ideas he had formed in Mannheim into practice. By 6 May it was probably too late for him to retreat in his disagreement with the Archbishop, but Count Arco had refused to accept his petition for dismissal. 'He told me that I could not resign without your permission, father' (12 May 1781). By 9 June that hurdle had been cleared. Taking leave from Count Arco may have surpassed his expectation.

What's it to him if I want my dismissal? If he really has such a good opinion of me he should persuade Somebody of the reasons for it—or just allow the matter to take its course, but not call me names, and hustle a fellow out of the door with a kick in the backside. But I'm forgetting that maybe it was on His Highness's orders. (9 June 1781)

That sealed Arco's reputation in the eyes of posterity, once and for all. 'I shall always be there beside Mozart's radiant figure like a threatening shadow, hatred in my eyes, envy in my heart . . . As long as Mozart's name is spoken, I too shall be remembered.' Franz Farga placed these words in the mouth of Salieri at the end of his romantic novel *Salieri und Mozart* (1937), but the kick set Arco up there with the other traditional villains of Mozartian biography.

One of Mozart's first pupils was Josepha Barbara Auernhammer, daughter of Johann Michael Auernhammer, an official in the service of the imperial government. She was the dedicatee of the six violin sonatas that were published by subscription in autumn 1781. Mozart was not very complimentary about her on the whole, for example: 'The young lady is a fright! But she plays enchantingly; the one thing she lacks is the true, fine, singing touch in cantabile—she snatches at everything.' At the end of this letter he asks: 'Please have the B flat sonata for four hands and the two two-piano concertos copied for me and send them to me as soon as possible' (27 June 1781).

These works—the Sonata, K. 358, the Double Concerto, K. 365, and the two-piano version of the Triple Concerto, K. 242—were needed for both tuition and performance. For instance, Mozart and Josepha Auernhammer played K. 365 at a private concert in her parents' house at the end of November, together with the D major Sonata, K. 448, also for two pianos, the middle movement of which would have ideally served Mozart's purpose of helping his pupil to acquire 'the true, fine, singing touch in cantabile'.

During this first period in Vienna Mozart was not only a teacher, however, he was also finding an enormous amount to learn—in spite of the fact that at the age of 25 he had already acquired experience of the whole musical world. Three years before moving to Vienna, he had written to his father from Mannheim: 'I am, as you know, pretty well able to assimilate and imitate every manner and style of composition' (7 February 1778). That may sound like bragging, but even if his twenty-second birthday was barely a week behind him, he was already entitled to make the claim. He had been brought up in the traditions of Salzburg, which, as both an archiepiscopal seat and a university town, occupied a leading position in the Catholic, southern part of the German-speaking world; he knew his way about in the two cities, Vienna and Mannheim, that were currently the most important centres of musical life in central Europe, melting-pots where he had moreover been given a taste of more exotic influences—that of Bohemia in Mannheim, and of the further regions of south-eastern Europe in Vienna; he had travelled the length and breadth of Italy from Milan to Naples in quest of modern Italian style and had seen for himself how that went down in England; and at the time of writing he was on the point of returning to Paris to find out what French musical life had to offer him. He could rightfully claim to possess both a theoretical and a practical overview of the musical situation in Europe. He had not merely surveyed the scene, he had composed everywhere he went, and thus tested his own affinity to musical life in each place in turn. What had he missed in the central European scene of the 1770s and 1780s? Dresden perhaps, but former glories were fading there as the great age of Johann Adolf Hasse, the chief proponent of Neapolitan style, drew to its close—and Mozart had met Hasse. He had a nodding acquaintance, at least, with the music of other northern German composers, too, such as Carl Philipp Emanuel

Bach, as we know from his reworking of a sonata movement by the Hamburg composer in the finale of the Piano Concerto, K. 40. And his encounters with the conservative, contrapuntal 'church style' of the music still performed in the papal chapel in Rome, and championed by Padre Martini in Bologna, had put him in touch with musical history—although it is not certain that that is how he saw it himself: he heard Gregorio Allegri's *Miserere* in Rome as an antiquity (it was composed in the middle of the seventeenth century) and simultaneously as part of a living repertory. His experience in Bologna was similar: Martini was working on a history of music (which was never finished: only the section on classical antiquity ever appeared in print), but when Mozart was obliged to pass a test in Renaissance polyphony in order to obtain admission to the Accademia Filarmonica it must have seemed to him an exercise in a musical style which was still cultivated, élitist though it might also be. (He failed to master it well: the Accademia made allowances for his youth and admitted him none the less.) So, at 22, Mozart knew something of this aspect, too, of the musical life of his time: the survival of a historical style in daily use, long before the idea of 'early music' existed as a separate concept.

Yet there were still new lands for Mozart to discover in Vienna. He came across the music of J. S. Bach, apparently for the first time, and he now began a more intensive study of Handel, although he had encountered and played his music as early as 1764, when he was in London. In 1781 there were parts of Europe where Bach's fugues and Handel's oratorios were still 'contemporary' music. The English enthusiasm for Handel was undiminished, and would give rise before long to the great centenary celebration of 1784 (when he would have been 99). Bach's compositional techniques had continued to be developed along an undeviating straight line by pupils such as Johann Ludwig Krebs (1713–80) and some of his sons: the fugues of Wilhelm Friedemann Bach (1710–84) came to Mozart's attention for the first time now, in Vienna. *The Well-Tempered Clavier* was put in front of the young Beethoven in Bonn, in this same year of 1781, and parts of the cantatas were performed in Hamburg by Bach's second son, Carl Philipp Emanuel Bach (1714–88), throughout his years as director of music in the city. Emanuel and his brother Wilhelm Friedemann supplied much of the information which Johann Nikolaus Forkel, director of music at the University of Göttingen, included in his biography of their father. All this was happening at the very time that Mozart was in the process of leaving Salzburg and settling in Vienna; the interest in the music of Bach and Handel was thus not necessarily in any sense 'historical' but a reflection of facets of everyday, contemporary musical practice. Mozart's reaction to it is typical: as so often before, the new interest stirred him to compose. This time, however, the stimulus seems to have been far more fruitful than his earlier encounters with Bolognese or Roman church style.

The key figure in this new encounter was Gottfried van Swieten (1733–1803), the son of Maria Theresia's personal physician, who had been Austrian ambassador to the court of Prussia from 1770 to 1777. He subsequently became prefect of the court library in Vienna and, from 1781, chairman of the commission on education and censorship. In connection with an organ recital given by Wilhelm Friedemann Bach in 1774, the Bach family had come up in conversation between Swieten and Frederick the Great, as Swieten had later reported to the Austrian Chancellor, Prince Wenzel Anton von Kaunitz. (Kaunitz was another music-lover, but it was probably part of Swieten's ambassadorial duties to report all his conversations with the King of Prussia.) It is not certain from the report that this was actually the first time that Swieten had ever heard of J. S. Bach, as is sometimes claimed, and he had certainly had contacts with pupils of Bach before then: C. P. E. Bach's six string symphonies of 1773 were commissioned by Swieten, and he may have had music lessons during his years in Berlin from Friedrich Wilhelm Marpurg and Johann Philipp Kirnberger, two music theorists whose writings would be scarcely conceivable without the examples from the works of J. S. Bach. All that the report demonstrates is that Swieten could not take it for granted that the name of Bach would be known in Vienna, and that it was Kaunitz, if anyone, to whom it might have been new.

Among other matters, [the King] spoke to me about music and about a great organist called Bach, who was visiting Berlin at the time [i.e. Wilhelm Friedemann]. This artist possesses a significant talent in respect of everything that I have heard or can imagine in profundity of harmonic knowledge and power of execution. Those who knew his father, however, consider that he is not his equal. The King shares this view, and in support of it sang to me lustily the theme of a chromatic fugue which he had given the older Bach, who had at once composed a fugue on it with four, then five, and finally eight [actually, six] obbligato parts.[1]

The King was of course referring to Bach's visit to Potsdam in 1747 and the propitious incident which gave birth to the *Musical Offering*.

---

[1] The original report was in French. The excerpt here is translated from the German version in P. Nettl, *Mozart, 1756–1956* (Frankfurt am Main, 1955), 139.

Mozart had met Swieten before, in 1768; they met again now in Vienna on an occasion when the composer, at the keyboard, introduced his new opera, *Idomeneo*, to a private audience. Their association grew closer in the early months of 1782. Mozart wrote to his father:

Apropos: I meant to ask you, when you return the Rondeau [K. 382, the new finale for the first Piano Concerto, K. 175], please send me also the six fugues by Handel, and the toccatas and fugues by Eberlin. I go to Baron van Swieten's every Sunday at noon, and nothing but Handel and Bach is played there. I'm building a collection of Bach fugues just now—not only Sebastian's but also Emanuel's and Friedemann's. Also of Handel's . . . And I would like to have the Baron hear Eberlin's as well. I expect you've already heard that the English Bach has died? Sad news for the musical world!   (10 April 1782)

We learn three things from this passage. First, that Handel was known to both the Mozarts as a great composer (that Mozart was only now beginning to study Handel's fugues does not affect that assumption). Second, both of them associated the name of 'Bach' first and foremost with the 'English' Bach, Johann Christian; it is therefore not surprising that it occurs to Mozart, when he is writing about the Bach family in general, to mention that news has reached him of the death of Johann Christian (on the New Year's Day just past). Third, the thought of fugue reminded Mozart of the music he had been brought up with in Salzburg, especially (he was, after all, studying 'historical' music!) the works of Johann Ernst Eberlin, who had become court and cathedral organist in 1729 at the age of 27, been promoted to the office of court Kapellmeister in 1749, and died in 1762. It is likely, however, that when Mozart wrote he had not had an opportunity to look closely at the fugues performed 'every Sunday' at Swieten's house; possibly there had not yet been very many such Sundays, and the 'collection' of which he boasted may have existed in intention rather than reality. His active engagement with the fugues of Handel and the Bachs may thus as yet not have got beyond an early stage; he was eventually to arrange five fugues by J. S. Bach for string trio and six more for string quartet, and also write a string trio version of one by W. F. Bach (K. 404*a*, 405), but that was probably some time later.

At all events Mozart soon changed his mind about Eberlin's fugues. Only ten days later he wrote to his sister: 'If Papa has not had the works by Eberlin copied yet, so much the better. I've been working on them and—I had forgotten—I saw, alas, that they're much too puny and really don't deserve to be set beside Bach and Handel' (20 April 1782). He enclosed with that letter his recently composed Fugue in C major, K. 394 (and a prelude to go with it), which shows just how thoroughly he had been studying *The Well-Tempered Clavier* in the mean time. The new technical aspects which he encountered in Bach's work did not cause him to write off the traditions of Salzburg composers completely, however. There is every reason to concur with Manfred Hermann Schmid when he writes of the Salzburg influence on Mozart's fugal technique: 'Modest pedal-points and chaste strettos are the fugue's only ornaments. Mozart knows nothing of northern German theory's demand for every sort of artifice.'[2] In spite of the experience of April 1782, nine months later Mozart wrote to his father once again:

There are also some contrapuntal pieces by Eberlin on small paper, bound in blue, and a number of . . . things by [Michael] Haydn, which I should like to have for Baron van Swieten, whom I visit every Sunday from 12 till 2. Can you tell me if there are fugues of any consequence in Haydn's last mass, or vespers, or both? If there are, you would oblige me greatly if you would get them both copied for me, by degrees.   (4 January 1783)

Mozart's interest in fugue seems to have lasted just as long as the new year of 1783 itself. The Fugue in C minor for two pianos, K. 426, which he finished on 29 December, marks the conclusion of an intensive, specialized preoccupation with fugal techniques; later, with a new introduction and re-scored for strings, the piece became part of his Adagio and Fugue in C minor, K. 546. Exactly six weeks after the two-piano version of the fugue, however, the first of the Viennese series of great piano concertos was completed: that in E flat major, K. 449. It was followed, during Lent, by the most productive period of concerto composition in Mozart's career to that date. The surge of interest in fugue in 1782–3 did not necessarily amount to 'a crisis in his creative activity',[3] therefore, but may equally well have been a special enrichment of his art, one facet of the process of exploring the opportunities open to him in Vienna; in the nature of things, it was going to take him a little time to find his niche there in order to work as a free-lance musician. Thus, Mozart's 'fugal period' runs from the composition of the Fugue in C major for solo keyboard, finished ten days after his first mentioning J. S. Bach, to that of the Fugue in C minor for two pianos at the very end of 1783.

The C major Fugue illustrates the speed with which Mozart could, as he had said, 'assimilate and imitate every manner and style of composition'. It

---

[2] Schmid, *Mozart und die Salzburger Tradition*, 53.   [3] Einstein, *Mozart*, 151.

comes remarkably close in some rather isolated details to fugues in *The Well-Tempered Clavier*, actually going beyond 'northern German theory's demand for every sort of artifice'. One instance is the appearance, shortly before the end, of a pedal-point—a bass note sustained throughout several changes of harmony; another is Mozart's use of stretto, introducing a subject in a second part before its statement in a first has been completed, sometimes with only a very small measure of time between the two entries. The piece offers only one other of the 'artifices' of fugal technique, but it is an uncommonly telling one, and illustrates how profoundly Mozart must have penetrated to the essence of Bachian fugue. Shortly before the middle he has the subject enter in augmentation (lengthening all the notes to double the value they have in the subject's original form); augmentation—like a pedal-point—is a means to intensification at the end of a piece: augmentation leads the subject towards a certain apotheosis, a pedal-point (usually on the dominant) demands resolution on the tonic, creating the opportunity for conclusion. But the augmentation here does not lead to the conclusion; instead, following it, Mozart reduces the number of the parts to the two top ones, while the bass rests, and then he has the subject enter yet again in the top part. A look at the piece as a whole shows the significance of that, for it is sixty-seven bars long, and that renewed entry of the subject in the top part occurs in the middle of bar 34, marking exactly the start of the second half of the piece, and thus the augmentation marks the conclusion of the first half.

But that is not the only form of articulation which is characteristic of Bach. The fugal 'subject' does not normally reign alone; its entries are interspersed with episodes, the motivic material of which may well resemble that of the subject but does not actually cite it. In order to differentiate the 'genuine' thematic expositions from the free episodes, it is necessary to determine where the subject is stated in its entirety, from which may be deduced the relationship between thematic sections and episodes in the work's structure. Mozart's fugue is sixty-seven bars long; exactly half of it (thirty-three and a half bars—or, better, sixty-seven half-bars) is taken up with statements of the subject, but it does not appear in the other sixty-seven half-bars. Thus the piece is divided exactly in half on a second plane: not only midway through its duration but also in the distribution of the musical material. Mozart's subject is in fact two bars long, which makes sixty-seven half-bars appear to be a very odd total, but there is a simple explanation for it, in that each half contains one passage of stretto and one of augmentation. Mozart might have discovered this double division-by-two, of both duration and material, in numerous places in Bach's fugues.[4]

He did not follow the Bachian model in every respect. He ignored the element of goal-directedness, with its signalling of the approaching end by regaining the tonic (with an entry of the fugal subject, like ritornello form in a concerto): the passage of augmentation immediately before the midpoint of the work is already back in the tonic, which must therefore be abandoned again soon afterwards. Furthermore, Bach usually treats the parts equally but Mozart does not: of the sixteen entries of the subject, he gives only two to the middle part, while the outer parts have seven each. And he pursues other goals than Bach in the details of the tonal progression: in the first half of the piece alone, he has the subject appear on every degree of the scale except one (the seventh) and thus touches a majority of tonal regions: nothing so comprehensively picturesque is to be found in any fugue by Bach.

The fugues show yet again how Mozart reacts to the encounter with the music of the past as a practical musician: he writes a piece of music in order to get a better grasp of the structures of what he has learnt by making his own version of it. If the three-part C major Fugue, K. 394, sounds like imitation Bach in places, in the C minor Fugue for two pianos Mozart cuts himself free from his model. The repertoire of 'artifices' has grown. Mozart has a shot at writing the subject in inversion, that is, inverting the intervals between the notes, so that the downward leap by a fifth with which the subject begins in its original form becomes a rising fifth, and so on. That is not all: he has the inversion enter in stretto, and then both the original version and the inversion in stretto; once with both parts played on one instrument, and a second time with one part played on each. Finally the original form and the inversion enter simultaneously, without any lapse of time at all. Mozart's delight in experimentation has obviously reached independence by this stage: it is no longer a question of following a model but simply of having once encountered one; Mozart has absorbed the impressions he received from Bach, and recast them.

Yet Mozart rests this example of pure fugal art on a stereotyped foundation.[5] Once again, in the C minor Fugue he uses a two-bar subject; the first part of it establishes clearly and unmistakably the minor character of the key (in the fifth at the start of the phrase and the diminished seventh

---

[4] See U. Siegele, 'The Four Conceptual Stages of the Fugue in C minor, WTC I', in D. O. Franklin (ed.), *Bach Studies* (Cambridge, 1989), 197–224.

[5] See K. H. Wörner, 'Über einige Fugenthemen Mozarts', *MJb* 1954, 33–53.

at the end), the second derives from a descending sequence of semitone steps (reordered to some extent, and lacking an E♮ between A♭ and B♮). The acquaintance with Bach was not crucial to either part: a subject resembling the first part dominates the 'Laudate pueri dominum' of Mozart's *Vesperae solennes de confessore* (1780), and a subject resembling the second opens the last movement of his String Quartet, K. 173 (1773). He could have found a model for the combination of the two (including the semitone scale in the original form) in Bach, however, namely the subject of the *Musical Offering* (which was not unknown to Swieten, at least). Frederick the Great, of the same generation as Bach's sons, and probably lacking much practical experience in fugal composition, was capable of writing a subject consisting of the kind of classical fugal elements fit to be put before an acknowledged master of the art of fugue. Mozart's choice of subject should be judged in that light. (See Ex. 15.1.)

Whereas the three-part C major Fugue was written for one instrument, Mozart wrote his C minor Fugue in four parts and for two keyboards. He

Ex. 15.1. Fugue subjects.

(a) C minor Fugue for two pianos, K. 426.

(b) *Vesperae solennes de confessore*, K. 339, 'Laudate pueri'.

(c) String Quartet in D minor, K. 173, 4th movement.

(d) J. S. Bach, *Musical Offering*, 'Thema regium'.

may have had two reasons for this: firstly, the 'art' of the strict fugue is easier to follow with just one part notated in each of the four systems (Bach himself may have been influenced by a similar concern for clarity when he published *The Art of Fugue* in score). For another thing, Mozart could again have had his work as a teacher in mind: the travels of the fugal subject not merely about the two systems of one keyboard part but also from one instrument (the pupil's) to another (the teacher's) may have struck him as a more diverting means of instruction. Or perhaps he played it with Constanze Weber, whom he had married on 4 August 1782. At the beginning of the 'fugal period', in April 1782, he wrote in one letter: 'When Constanze heard the fugues she fell in love with them. Now she will hear nothing but fugues, but above all in this field, nothing but Handel and Bach' (to his sister, 20 April 1782). That Mozart did play duets, on two instruments, with Constanze is proved by the sketch of a sonata-movement, which has the heading 'Sonata à 2 cembali par la Sig:ra Costanza Weber—ah—'. This must date from before their marriage, but that does not rule out the possibility that they later played the C minor Fugue together on two pianos.

Mozart maintained the association with Swieten, even when the latter found new interests to pursue. An important phase in their relationship was reached several years later, between 1788 and 1790, when Mozart occupied himself with Handel's oratorios. Swieten had encountered these in England not long before he was posted to Prussia, and he must have brought them to Mozart's attention at a relatively early date; his outstanding contribution to keeping oratorio in the style of Handel alive came after Mozart's death, however, for it was he who provided the texts for Haydn's oratorios *The Creation* and *The Seasons*. In his biography of Mozart, published in 1828, Georg Nikolaus Nissen writes of Mozart's role in the performances of Handel's oratorios which Swieten organized in the 1780s, employing 'the talents of our Mozart, who knew how to bring Handel's great ideas to life with the warmth of his own feeling, and to render them enjoyable for our own age by the enchantment of his instrumentation'.[6] Nissen's viewpoint was very likely Mozart's own, in his approach to the music of Bach and Handel: his study of counterpoint added a new facet to Mozart's style, and he gained new stimuli from what he found in the work of earlier masters. The C minor Fugue for two pianos, at the latest, is therefore a Mozartian composition through and through. This is confirmed by the estimation

[6] Nissen, *Biographie*, 540.

Mozart himself expressed of it when he transcribed it for strings and wrote the following entry in the catalogue of his works in 1788: 'A short Adagio à 2 violini, viola, e basso, added to a fugue which I wrote a long time ago for 2 claviers'. The fugue was therefore not merely a study but had become a fully fledged work, which Mozart was ready to acknowledge as such even after another four and a half eventful years.

16

'What our German poets are thinking of...': *Die Entführung aus dem Serail* as Singspiel and Mozart Opera

Idomeneo won Mozart an ally in the director of the Vienna Court Theatre, Franz Xaver Wolf Count Orsini-Rosenberg, whom he had first met in Florence in 1770, and it also earned him the attention of Gottlieb Stephanie, actor and stage-manager of the Court Theatre (often referred to as 'Stephanie the younger' to distinguish him from an older brother). The first tangible outcome of this was already taking shape by the end of Mozart's first month in Vienna, when he wrote to his father: 'The younger Stephanie is going to write me a new libretto, and a good one, or so he says' (18 April 1781). These negotiations were already in train, therefore, while Mozart was still in Archbishop Colloredo's service: he was not literally kicked out until 8 June. Once again, it looks as if he made sure of his prospects before taking a step which would lead to the termination of his employment. The new opera for Stephanie had no bearing on any such step, however: the libretto could have been sent to be composed in Salzburg, and the circumstances of a production in Vienna need not have been any different, essentially, from those of the production of *Idomeneo* in Munich. (Mozart believed that the subject-matter of *Die Entführung* made it unsuitable for any city other than Vienna, but the productions elsewhere in his own lifetime proved him wrong.)

Stephanie's 'new libretto' was in fact an adaptation of a text by Christoph Friedrich Bretzner and appears to have kept quite close to the original to begin with. Even after the changes asked for by Mozart, it retained the essential features of a Singspiel: the German language and the mixture of spoken dialogue with inserted musical numbers primarily in song forms. Stephanie delivered the libretto to Mozart just over three months after promising to write it. As the composer told his father: 'The subject is Turkish, and it is called "Belmont and Konstanze, or The Seduction[1] from the Seraglio"' (1 August 1781). On the first day alone,

---

[1] *Sic:* 'Verführung', not 'Entführung' ('Abduction').

he wrote two arias (Belmonte's 'O wie ängstlich, o wie feurig' and Konstanze's 'Ach, ich liebte, war so glücklich') and the trio with which Act I ends (Belmonte, Pedrillo, Osmin: 'Marsch, trollt euch fort'). The work's first performance took place in Vienna on 16 July 1782; it had been planned for mid-September 1781, but at that point Mozart had composed little more than the first act—it must have become clear not long after he had received the text that operas by other composers were going to be given priority.

Mozart sent his father some music in September—'I wanted to give you at least an idea of the first act, so that you can form an impression of the whole'—and followed the package with a letter (26 September 1781) in which he wrote about the material in more detail, and explained how he had influenced the text and overall dramatic structure, which was comparable to what he had done nine months earlier in the case of *Idomeneo*.

He had sent only fourteen bars of the Overture—presumably the first fourteen, consisting of the opening piano phrase and its forte continuation. To help his father 'form an impression of the whole', he now wrote: 'Of the Overture you have only fourteen bars. It's quite short, and alternates forte and piano throughout, with the Turkish music entering on every forte. It modulates through the keys—and I don't believe anyone will sleep through it, even if they've missed an entire night's sleep.'

In Bretzner's original text, the Overture is followed by a monologue spoken by Belmonte who, in the search for his beloved Konstanze, finds himself before the walls of Selim Pasha's palace. There he runs across Osmin, whose song 'Wer ein Liebchen hat gefunden' ('When a man has found a sweetheart') is the first vocal number. Stephanie had followed Bretzner's lead and introduced Belmonte by words spoken, not sung, and the Turkish element stole the limelight of the first musical number. Mozart thought otherwise, and wanted Belmonte, too, to have an entrance aria: 'The opera had begun with a monologue, and so I asked Herr Stephanie to make a little arietta out of it.' Nor did it suit him that the first exchanges between Belmonte and Osmin were also spoken: early in the work as it was, he wanted to heighten the drama of the encounter by setting it to music, following directly after the solos with which first Belmonte and then Osmin had introduced himself. Once again, Stephanie had been asked to turn the original prose dialogue into verse.

Thus from the very start Stephanie's Singspiel text had taken a different path from the one Mozart wished his opera to follow. The composer

PL. 6. Belmonte interrupts Osmin at his fig-picking. Vignette on the title-page of a vocal score of *Die Entführung aus dem Serail* (1828).

closed the gap between them in accordance with the principle he expounded to his father in another letter: 'In an opera the poetry simply must be the music's obedient daughter' (13 October 1781). The means he employed give us some exemplary insights into his fundamental ideas about music-theatre. How does Mozart translate the growth of hostility between Belmonte and Osmin into music? What was the concrete musical goal that he was able to reach by way of the text he asked Stephanie to rewrite as arias?

Belmonte tries to stop Osmin singing his song and make him talk to him instead. He speaks his question, 'Is this the palace of Selim Pasha?', but, being a polite and musical young man, he waits until Osmin has completed each stanza of his song before speaking again. (He never interrupts before

Osmin's 'Trallalera' refrain: some modern directors fail to observe this.) But Osmin refuses to let himself be interrupted, and Belmonte loses patience and his temper. For Mozart this is the moment to have Belmonte enter the musical action, abandoning speech because it has reached its dramatic threshold; it is the moment at which, if he had been writing recitatives as in *Idomeneo*, Belmonte would abandon secco recitative. Mozart makes sure the point is understood: Belmonte destroys Osmin's song by the way he tears into it and literally throws the singer off the beat. He appropriates the 'Trallalera' melody but, not content with accelerating Osmin's 'andante' to an 'allegro', he also replaces the 6/8 metre with 4/4 (see Ex. 16.1). Osmin will never be able to recover his song, for Belmonte's musical assault is psychologically invincible, so adroitly is it carried out; not even the change of tempo, which Mozart was obliged to notate at a precise spot in the score, is fully detectable—as late as the word 'Liede', Belmonte's music is still in the triple metre, and common time is established only in the following bar. After this devastating rudeness on Belmonte's part, it is almost a miracle that Osmin gives any answers at all—brief though they

Ex. 16.1. *Die Entführung aus dem Serail*, No. 2, bars 49–57. Transition from Osmin's song to his duet with Belmonte.

are—to the questions which follow more calmly. The calm is doomed to be short-lived, for as soon as Belmonte mentions the name Pedrillo Osmin stiffens. Belmonte has lost the advantage he had, while Osmin is not so easily discountenanced by another as Belmonte was by him. But the revelation that Belmonte has lost this round is conceivable only in Mozart's musical version, in which Osmin's song turns without a break into the duet (not into spoken dialogue). It is only in the musical form that Belmonte exposes his weak side to Osmin, while in the original version the impression is given that Belmonte acquiesces in his fate and waits patiently until the librettist gives him the chance to speak.

Osmin does not boil over until much later, when Pedrillo arrives to add to his annoyance. Still sustained by consciousness of his position in Selim's household, he starts his aria 'Solche hergelaufne Laffen' ('Fops and nobodies like these'), which reaches a highpoint in the coda 'Ich hab auch Verstand' ('I too have brains'). Normally a coda comes at the end of a movement, but in this case it is not the end, for Osmin becomes heated—at his own words, be it said. The adulation of Osmin's 'brains' is followed, therefore, by an extension of the aria, which eventually reaches a new coda ('Drum beim Barte des Propheten . . . nimm dich wie du willst in acht'; 'So, by the Beard of the Prophet . . . watch out for yourself'). The warning is musically unmistakable, but Pedrillo is oblivious to his danger and dares to open his mouth; only then does Osmin's patience snap ('Erst geköpft, dann gehangen'; 'Beheaded first, then hanged').

Mozart sketched this scene too to his father, and outlined the reasons for the compositional decisions he had taken. '"Drum beim Barte des Propheten" is in the same tempo but with quick notes'—in the first coda the notes are crotchets, minims, and semibreves, in the second they are semiquavers, quavers, and crotchets, so it is four times as quick. That is not all:

Since his anger continues to wax—just as you think the aria is already over—the Allegro assai ['Erst geköpft, dann gehangen'], in a completely different metre, and in a different key, cannot fail to make the best possible effect; for a man in such a violent rage goes beyond all order, proportion and purpose, he is beside himself—and the music too must be beside itself. But the expression of passions, violent or not, must never go so far as to cause disgust, and music, however horrifying the situation, must never offend the ear but continue to please, consequently it must always remain music. For that reason I did not choose a key alien to F (the aria's tonic) but one of its friends—not the nearest, D minor, but the next nearest, A minor.

That is, not the minor but the major third (mediant).

The Belmonte–Osmin duet which Mozart systematically develops instead of the original spoken dialogue is musically quite tame compared to what happens in the course of this first great aria of Osmin's. Again there is nothing comparable in Bretzner's original text. Mozart told his father: 'In the original libretto Osmin has only the one little song ["Wer ein Liebchen hat gefunden"] to sing, and nothing else apart from the trio and finale'. (In fact it also included the Pedrillo–Osmin duet, 'Vivat Bacchus'.) In Mozart's opera, on the other hand, Osmin is a central character, and the initiative for making him one was entirely Mozart's. The composer presented his librettist with a *fait accompli*: 'I told Herr Stephanie exactly what I wanted for the aria: most of the music had already been composed before he knew anything about it.'

There were other places in the first act where Mozart found it necessary to change the text, as emerges from the long letter to his father. He preceded Belmonte's aria 'O wie ängstlich, o wie feurig' with a short accompanied recitative ('Konstanze, dich wiederzusehen'), in place of the spoken words provided. The text of the aria itself fascinated him because of the opportunities it gave for musical depiction (the throbbing of the lover's heart, the trembling, the faltering, the heaving of the swelling breast, the whispering, the sighing). He was less well pleased with parts of Konstanze's first great aria, of which the last four lines were originally:

> Doch im hui schwand meine Freude,
> Trennung war mein banges Los,
> und nun schwimmt mein Aug in Tränen,
> Kummer ruht in meinem Schoß.

('But my joy vanished in a jiffy, my sad fate was separation, and now my eyes are bathed in tears, sorrow reposes in my bosom.')

Mozart commented:

I changed the 'hui' to 'schnell' as follows: 'Doch wie schnell schwand meine Freude' ['But how swiftly my joy vanished'] etc. I don't know what our German poets are thinking of. Even if they don't understand the theatrical side of opera, at the very least they shouldn't make the characters speak as if they were addressing swine. 'Hui'—what a sow!

In a later letter he found fault with the last line: 'Sorrow can't "repose"' (13 October 1781). But here Stephanie appears to have stood his ground.

Mozart said he had 'sacrificed Konstanze's aria a little to Mamselle Cavalieri's agile throat'. The sacrifice seems to have consisted in finally bursting the bounds of Singspiel-like simplicity which he had already stretched somewhat in the early scenes with Osmin. 'I have tried to express "Trennung war mein banges Los, und nun schwimmt mein Aug in Tränen" as well as an Italian bravura aria allows.' Despite appearances, Catarina Cavalieri was no Italian but a born Viennese, whose real name was Cavalier. For her, Mozart put an Italian aria into his German Singspiel, and subordinated the stylistic principles of Singspiel to those of the Italian aria. It was a pragmatic thing to do: Konstanze has lived for some time in extreme isolation in Selim's palace, and as a European she is a complete stranger in the Singspiel world of the seraglio, so it is right that she should express herself musically in a style radically different from that of her environment.[2]

Now the trio, i.e. the finale of the first act. Pedrillo has passed his master off as an architect, to give him the opportunity to meet his Konstanze in the garden, and the Pasha has taken him into his service. Osmin, the overseer, doesn't know about it, and being a rude lout and arch-enemy of all foreigners he is impertinent and won't let them into the garden. The opening where this is shown is very abrupt, and because the text lent itself to it I've written it in three parts rather well ['Marsch, trollt euch fort']. But then the major pianissimo passage [the C major insert in the C minor ensemble, setting the same text] begins immediately and that must go very fast—and the conclusion will be very noisy indeed. (26 September 1781)

That was all that Mozart had done at that stage, for he had given the second act back to Stephanie for rewriting. All he told his father was that he was not satisfied with the way the numbers were placed at the end of the second and beginning of the third acts. 'At the beginning of the third act there is a charming quintet—or rather, finale, and I would prefer to have it at the end of the second act.' In other words, he wanted an ensemble that would make a good finale in the proper place for it. But 'in order to bring that about a big alteration is needed, in fact a whole new intrigue'.

Leopold Mozart's response to all of this has not survived, but Mozart's reply to it has. It looks as if the father tried to dampen the son's euphoria over several points, for Mozart wrote that although his father's comments

---

[2] Kunze, *Mozarts Opern*, 210.

were correct in general, they did not really affect the special case of *Die Entführung*. It is perhaps no accident therefore that as Mozart went on with the composition he did not manifest again the urge to communicate which he had felt in September 1781.

All the evidence indicates that Mozart continued to play the major part in shaping the action and the text. The 'big alteration' he had mentioned led to a completely different outcome, and it starts to take effect well before the finale, at a relatively early stage in the second act, during which Blonde, Pedrillo's beloved, has to fend off Osmin's lecherous advances, Pedrillo makes Osmin drunk with Cypriot wine, and Belmonte and Konstanze are reunited. Mozart extended the first scene by following Blonde's aria 'Durch Zärtlichkeit und Schmeicheln' ('By tenderness and compliments') with a duet for her and Osmin ('Ich gehe, doch sage ich dir . . .'; 'I'm going, but let me tell you . . .'). Much of the drinking scene was left unchanged, but the meeting of Belmonte and Konstanze became the starting-point of a new act-finale, containing much more than the expressions of hope that made up the scene in the original version. (The hopes are largely moved on to the opening of Act III, to Belmonte's aria 'Ich baue ganz auf deine Stärke'—'I trust entirely in your strength'.) The finale of Act II, which according to Mozart's original idea should have fed on the dramatic potential of Act III, by including the escape scene, did acquire something of a 'new intrigue', or at least a new twist: the (unfounded) suspicions of Belmonte and Pedrillo as to their lady-loves' fidelity. If Mozart's wish had been fulfilled, the third act would indeed have needed a 'new intrigue'—but what new action could it have contained?

Even as it stands, the changes made to the second act go deeper into the heart of the work. Blonde's duet with Osmin is an addition to Bretzner's original text, but in Act II of that she had a duet with Konstanze (an invocation of the consoling power of hope, placed near the middle of the act). However, forcing Konstanze's Italian style to combine with the Singspiel nature of Blonde in a duet would probably have taken something away from essential elements of Konstanze's character, so Mozart gave Blonde a duet with Osmin in compensation, while seizing the opportunity to 'sacrifice' another aria to 'Mamselle Cavalieri's agile throat'. The first of Konstanze's second-act arias, 'Traurigkeit ward mir zum Lose' ('Sadness has become my lot'), originated with Bretzner (though he did not provide it with a recitative introduction), but Mozart broke all operatic rules by following it almost immediately with another, 'Martern aller Arten mögen meiner warten' ('All kinds of tortures may await me'). Neither is any less Italianate than her first-act aria, and Belmonte's arias, too, are increasingly infected with the Italian style (at first in 'Wenn der Freude Tränen fließen'—'When tears of joy flow'—and even more markedly in 'Ich baue ganz auf deine Stärke'), as if Konstanze's isolation is dissipating as the opera advances, bringing Belmonte closer to her.

As Gerhard Croll has shown,[3] Mozart did seriously entertain the idea of moving the elopement scene forward from the third act to the finale of the second, for a sketch survives in which the scene is set to music in the style of a finale. Once again, however, Stephanie must have prevailed, but the upshot is almost as far from Bretzner's original conception as it would have been if the alterations wished for by Mozart had been carried out. Mozart evidently insisted on moving the 'charming quintet' which he thought more appropriate to a finale from the start of Act III to the end of Act II. The quintet should have contained the attempted abduction, but in the compromise reached by librettist and composer that scene takes the form of spoken dialogue, without any music. In other words, the event promised by the work's title is not realized in music at all, only the preparations for it at the end of Act II. The only musical number whose text and function are taken entire from Bretzner's original is Pedrillo's romance. 'In Mohrenland gefangen war ein Mädchen' ('A maiden was held captive in Moorish lands'), which is the agreed signal for the escape from Selim Pasha's palace. Even when Osmin wakes up (in spite of his earlier potations) the scene continues to be spoken, although in some places the revised text borrows material from the original which was meant to be sung, for example Osmin's repeated exclamation 'Gift und Dolch!' ('Poison and poignards'). Mozart turned his musical attention instead to writing another aria for Osmin ('O wie will ich triumphieren'; 'Oh how I will celebrate'). Only the opening line was penned by Bretzner, in whose text the rhyme was given to Pedrillo ('Ich will gern kapitulieren'—'Gladly I capitulate'), and followed by two more lines ending in '. . . ieren'. Bretzner had a duet in which Belmonte and Konstanze vow fidelity in spite of the hopelessness of their situation, but the text was different from Stephanie's and Mozart's 'Meinetwegen sollst du sterben' ('You must die because of me'), and it was followed by another aria for Konstanze. In Mozart the finale immediately follows the duet and again differs from Bretzner's original, which found no room for the reprise of Osmin's enraged 'Erst

---

[3] In NMA II/5, vol. xii, pp. xviii, xxxi.

geköpft, dann gehangen'. Finally Mozart (and Stephanie?) rejected Bretzner's idea of having Belmonte turn out to be the son of Selim; making him the son of the Pasha's arch-enemy is just one more piece in the great mosaic of alterations to the overall dramatic disposition.

Mozart started to compose *Die Entführung* in summer 1781, scarcely half a year after finishing *Idomeneo*. That he began by setting three isolated numbers from Act I appears an unsystematic way of going about it, but they took him straight to the heart of the differences between his conception of Singspiel and that of Stephanie and Bretzner. Belmonte's aria raised the question of recitative in the German language, and Konstanze's aria that of the virtuosic Italian style, while Osmin's position in the drama is carved out in the Belmonte–Pedrillo–Osmin trio. The work's strengths emerged almost incidentally. The aria 'Ach, ich liebte' gives musical reality to Konstanze's isolation, which thus becomes more than an abstract dramatic idea; no other character's music could manifest the same traits. Belmonte comes nearest to her in his music, but his aria establishes him as a primo uomo within the Singspiel, and the other stock *seria* characters are also to be found here: Pedrillo and Blonde form the second couple, and Osmin is the typical 'member of the royal household'. The Singspiel genre differs from *opera seria*, however, in allowing Mozart to give each of the types of character his or her individual musical form to sing in. Only Konstanze consistently sings with 'Italian bravura', only Pedrillo and Osmin sing songs in the usual style of Singspiel—not, however, as musical numbers inserted in the action but only when the action truly requires a song (from Osmin while he picks figs, and from Pedrillo as the signal for the escape). Like secco recitative in *Idomeneo*, material which is specific to the Singspiel genre (that is, the song) is examined for its dramatic uses, and used only where it passes the test. To that extent, so far as musical dramatic construction is concerned, *Idomeneo* with its apparent paucity of plot and *Die Entführung* with its abundance take off from the same considerations.

This extends also to the details with which Mozart fleshes out his schematic cast, applying not only to the musical forms but also to the musical language in which each character develops his or her wholly personal means of expression. Even the speaking role of Selim Pasha is affected. Potentially the tenor 'king' who might have given his name to the work in a *seria* treatment, the only apparent reason why he does not sing in Mozart is that his wisdom, the world his thoughts occupy, make him as isolated a figure in the musical-comedy setting of the seraglio as the musical forms of *opera seria* make Konstanze; it would be quite easy to forget that speech is one of the standard components of Singspiel. This brings us, in fact, to the crucial 'advance' that *Die Entführung* makes over *Idomeneo*. A month after his arrival in their city Mozart had made up his mind that the Viennese preferred comic operas, and that notion made him turn from *seria* to Singspiel, the less rigid conventions of which enabled him to give musical individuality to each member of the cast. Almost without medi-ation, therefore, Mozart was catapulted beyond the position that he had reached in Munich the previous winter, to what proved to be the basis of a great deal of the popularity of the three Da Ponte operas: the delineation of character.

The crucial step was the upgrading of Osmin from a standard buffo figure, the comic servant, to a major character.[4] Osmin sings three arias, as many as Konstanze and only one less than Belmonte, and he is involved in five ensembles, the same number as Belmonte (Pedrillo comes next with four, the two women trail with three each). Stephanie might share responsibility for this at the superficial level, but the richness with which Osmin is characterized in musical terms comes wholly from Mozart: the ominous exoticism of his minor-key entrance song, the increasing loss of restraint in the melodic shaping of his first great outburst of wrath, the 'Turkish' music that accompanies it. Osmin assumes a human face. True, he is depicted as a person wholly alien to the citizens of Vienna but he is a realistic and recognizable human being, even if the fact emerges primarily in his knee-jerk responses to the events that enrage him. There is some-thing subtler behind them, however, rendered in the details: Osmin is not primarily evil or violent, merely easily provoked. He cannot hear Blonde get away unscathed with calling him an unbearable animal ('ein unerträgliches Tier', in a phrase from the original text of the vaudeville that ends the opera, which tends to be changed nowadays) without falling into his 'Erst geköpft, dann gehangen'—which owes its existence to Mozart's intervention in the first act. For all that, Osmin is a 'rude lout' as Mozart said, but it is Mozart's characterization that makes him one, not beginning as late as the composition of the first notes but from the conception of his role in the drama: it is dramatically necessary for Osmin to be someone who behaves without decorum and cannot control his emotions. It is the

---

[4] See C.-H. Mahling, 'Die Gestalt des Osmin in Mozarts "Entführung": Vom Typus zur Individualität', *Archiv für Musikwissenschaft*, 30 (1973), 96–108.

means Mozart uses to express this characterization that blow sky-high the neat little songs and ariettas of Singspiel style. Then, from the composer's point of view, it followed as day follows night that the same also applied to the other roles, such as Konstanze's with her Italian bravura arias.

17

A Promise Kept? The C minor Mass, K. 427

Unfinished works are unpopular on the whole: they are thought of as sketches, false starts, dry runs. A few, admittedly—especially ones that were cut short by their composer's deaths, like Bach's *Art of Fugue* and Mozart's Requiem—exercise an uncommon attraction on posterity and tend to generate anecdotes. Then there are works which were literally set aside while the composer turned to other projects and were never picked up again. One such is Schubert's 'Unfinished' Symphony, begun six years before his death, of which he wrote only two movements and a fragment of a third; another is Mozart's Mass in C minor, which he set aside eight years before his death and did not return to even in the last months of his life, when sacred music once more became a central preoccupation.[1] Schubert's symphony and Mozart's mass also have in common the fact that their composers regarded them as performable in their unfinished state: Mozart had sections of his mass performed while he was visiting Salzburg in the summer and autumn of 1783, and in giving away the two completed movements in 1823 Schubert must have been aware that they might be performed when they were no longer in his own keeping. The title 'The Unfinished' suggests, indeed, something similar to what lies in the unfinishedness of, say, *The Art of Fugue*. Posterity's attitude to Mozart's mass is remarkably sober, by contrast; it has collected few anecdotes, and is even referred to as if it was complete (although it was not finished by another hand, as the Requiem was): it is simply 'the' C minor Mass.

It is not only the mass's fragmentary status that raises questions; even its genesis is obscure. The first we hear of the work from Mozart is in a letter to his father, where he is plainly confirming and commenting on something they both already know about and have discussed before. The relevant passage is as follows:

I meant what I said about morality—it was not without intention that it flowed from my pen. I really promised in my heart, and really hope to keep my promise.

[1] See Tyson, *Mozart*, 26–7.

My wife was still single when I made it, but as I was firmly resolved to marry her soon after her recovery it was easy for me. Time and circumstances frustrated our journey, however, as you yourself know. Let the score of half a mass, which lies there hopeful of conclusion, serve as proof that my promise was real.   (Lines 8–16 of the letter reproduced as Pl. 4, p. 54; 4 January 1783)

What did he mean by 'morality' (or a 'moral obligation': 'die Moral')? Leopold Mozart must have raised an objection to some remark, which he must now confirm was written 'not without intention'. What had he 'really promised'? He goes on to mention marriage, a journey, and a mass. The promise preceded the marriage, a journey (to Salzburg) was delayed, and a mass he has started to compose proves that the promise was genuine. There was a connection, therefore, between the journey and the mass. Mozart must have vowed to travel to Salzburg after his marriage and there perform a mass that would be composed for the occasion. The matter of 'her recovery' is briefly drawn into the equation, too, implying that his fiancée's life was threatened by illness, and that that was the immediate reason for making the vow.

Mozart had been married on 4 August 1782, in St Stephen's Cathedral in Vienna, to Constanze Weber, born in 1762, the younger sister of Aloysia Weber (who had married the actor Joseph Lange in 1780). When they met in Mannheim in the winter of 1777–8, Mozart and Aloysia Weber had dreamt of a future together, but Leopold Mozart had expressed strong disapproval of their plans. He had also opposed his son's intention to marry Constanze Weber when it was revealed to him in December 1781. Mozart seems to have been trying to allay some of his father's misgivings when he assured him parenthetically 'I must also tell you that when I resigned [from the Archbishop of Salzburg's service] our love did not yet exist' (15 December 1781). The marriage took place before Mozart had received his father's blessing: the letter giving it did not reach him until the day after the ceremony. Baroness Martha Elisabeth Waldstätten, Mozart's adviser from the first months of his taking up residence in Vienna, saw to the wedding breakfast, and had also helped him with other preparations. Leopold Mozart wrote to her over the following weeks, confiding his worries about his son's life-style and future. It is plain that he had not found it easy to give the match his blessing. Mozart, on the other hand, ended his account of the wedding with the assurance that 'now my dear Constanze is looking forward to visiting Salzburg a hundred times more even than before! And I wager—I wager—you will rejoice in my good fortune when once you have got to know her!' (7 August 1782)

The journey to Salzburg was delayed further, and the young couple did not set off until late July 1783, a year after their wedding and six months after the letter which for us today represents the earliest mention of Mozart's vow to write a mass. The connection between the journey and the performance of a mass is confirmed. Mozart's sister noted in her diary on 23 October: 'In the Kapellhaus, for the rehearsal of my brother's mass, in which my sister-in-law is singing the solo', and three days later: 'To St Peter's for the office, my brother's office was done. All the court musicians took part.' There is little doubt that the 'office' in question was the C minor Mass, and it is interesting to note that the court musicians performed in it, although it was given in the church of St Peter's Abbey, which lay outside the Archbishop's jurisdiction.

In the circumstances, keeping the promise which linked a journey to Salzburg with the mass has the appearance of an act designed to conciliate Leopold Mozart, who was undoubtedly worried and at times displeased. It is likely, too, that the mass was influenced by emotions Mozart described not long after his wedding, in another letter to Salzburg: 'I have found that I have never prayed so fervently, or made my confession and taken communion so devoutly, as at her [Constanze's] side' (17 August 1782). Of course this remark, too, may have been made 'not without intention', this time of making a good impression on his father—but there were other things which he may have hoped to impress upon his father by the mass. In composing it, Mozart must have felt obliged not only to express piety in general but also to demonstrate the blameless conduct of his life, including the practice of his art, and to do that he needed to exhibit the musical skills he commanded now that he was freed from extramusical restraints. All Leopold Mozart's worries about his son, concerning both his marriage and also his artistic development now that he was no longer subject to his father's scrutiny, were to be set at rest at once. Leopold Mozart had expressed his fears to Baroness Waldstätten:

I would be completely reassured if only I did not find a major failing in my son, and that is that he is far too patient or somnolent, too complacent, perhaps sometimes too proud, or whatever name you care to give to the combination of all these things which makes a person idle—or else he is too impatient, too hotheaded, and will brook no delay at all. There are two opposing principles which have the upper hand in him—too much or too little, and no middle way. When he has all he wants, at once he is content and becomes complacent and idle. If he is forced into activity, then he thinks a lot of himself, and wants to make his fortune at once. Nothing must stand in his path—and, alas, it is precisely the most gifted people, the extraordinary geniuses, whose paths are strewn with the most hindrances. (23 August 1782)

Whatever else the C minor Mass is, it is not a product of idleness. In early January 1783, when Mozart wrote the letter in which it is mentioned, he was busy completing three keyboard concertos (K. 413–15), preparing for the Lenten season of concerts (he had less to do in 1783 than in the two following years), and also working on the vocal score of *Die Entführung*. Yet according to him he had also written half the mass—a statement that can be checked against the surviving autograph. This consists of the finished Kyrie and Gloria, half the Credo (that half is scored, whereas not even the words are set from 'Crucifixus' onwards), and the finished Sanctus and Benedictus; there is no Agnus Dei.

The Sanctus and Benedictus appear not to have been composed in Vienna, for they are written on Salzburg music paper, identifiable by its having ten staves on a side, whereas the paper Mozart bought in Vienna has twelve. Probably, therefore, he wrote this section after travelling to Salzburg in July 1783, so that his claim that the mass was half written (and scored) was arithmetically correct. Two of the six sections of the mass were finished (including the Gloria, with its long text) and half of the Credo (which also has a long text); but he had not yet set the Sanctus, Benedictus, and Agnus Dei (which all have relatively short texts). The work did not get any further between January and July 1783, admittedly, apart from some elaboration or revision of the Gloria's opening chorus and the end of the Kyrie, indicated by an anomaly in the order of the pages.[2]

Mozart undoubtedly intended the C minor Mass to be performed in the framework of a church service, had he but finished it, but the movements he completed are already of a length that goes against the Enlightenment wish for some control over baroque proliferation in liturgical music. Mozart must have felt that this expansiveness was necessary to allow him to show off the musical skills that he now commanded on the scale and in the abundance that only refusal to be restrained made possible. In order to achieve this, he needed to have recourse to a genre which was extreme even within the framework of a missa solemnis: the 'cantata mass', in which the six sections are further subdivided into separate musical movements.

[2] For more detailed discussion, see M. Holl and K.-H. Köhler in NMA I/1/1, vol. v, p. xiv, and Tyson, *Mozart*, 84, 96.

An important element in the composition of the mass seems to have been Mozart's assimilation of what he had learnt during those Sunday afternoons at Baron van Swieten's. It can be seen in the development of fugal techniques on the northern German model, although showing the same personal modifications as are found in the C minor Fugue for two pianos (here, in the 'Cum Sancto Spiritu' of the Gloria). Another instance is the homophonic cries of 'in excelsis' in the Gloria's opening movement, which are reminiscent of the 'Hallelujah' chorus in Handel's *Messiah*. The pregnant, constant rhythmic patterns of the 'Gratias agimus' and the 'Qui tollis' may also testify to an acquaintance with Handel's oratorios. However, the 'Qui tollis' has other baroque ancestors as well, which left it with something very like a 'basso quasi ostinato'. The texture of the piece rests on a distinctive bass ground only a few bars in length; this does not remain constant, it is not repeated unvaryingly beneath changing upper parts (that would be 'basso ostinato'), but its persistent presence is felt, largely in its rhythmic shape, while its melodic content changes—although there are regular recurrences of the original theme, the old-fashioned figure of a chromatic descent through a fourth. Somewhere in the ancestry of this combination of a 'basso quasi ostinato', a constant accompanimental rhythmic pattern, and a text from the mass, stands the 'Crucifixus' from Bach's Mass in B minor: did Mozart know it?[3] Unlike his baroque predecessors, however, Mozart does not employ this bass merely to support his structure; instead he illustrates one of the changes that took place in conceptions of compositional technique under Viennese Classicism, by treating the melody as genuinely thematic material and using it to launch each of the movement's four forte choral segments (on the words 'Qui tollis' or 'Qui sedes').

This disposition of the 'Qui tollis' refers back to yet another baroque practice: the bass theme expounded in the orchestral introduction recurs later as a component of greater importance than the thematic material of the choral writing—it is as if the choral parts were inserted into pre-existing, purely instrumental structures. (When this characteristic was identified in Bach's cantatas in modern times it was christened 'Choreinbau' or 'Vokaleinbau'—there is an analogy with 'built-in' or fitted cupboards.[4]) It

---

[3] The idea is suggested by W. Plath, 'Zwischen Bach und Händel: Bemerkungen zum "Qui tollis" aus Mozarts c-Moll-Messe' (unpublished paper read at the conference 'Alte Musik als ästhetische Gegenwart', Stuttgart, 1985).

[4] W. Neumann, *J. S. Bachs Chorfuge* (Leipzig, 1938), 2nd edn. (1950), 53–75; A. Dürr, *Die*

is even more in evidence in later movements of Mozart's C minor Mass, especially in the duet 'Domine Deus' sung by the two soprano soloists, which positively begs to be considered as an exercise in the technique. The first soprano enters to the 'accompaniment' of the first violins playing the melodic material with which the orchestral introduction opened (at first the violas and low strings provide the other parts), later the other melodic elements enter; the vocal material runs in the contrary direction to the instrumental material (see Ex. 17.1*a*). Normally such a difference is deemed necessary only when the instrumental material is unsingable, but that is precisely not the case here: a little later the second soprano enters with the first-violin melody ('Domine fili unigenite'). Thus Mozart did what he did here not because he had no choice but after mature consideration of what he wanted to do.

That he was writing as he wanted to is illustrated perhaps even more convincingly by another aspect of the 'Domine Deus'. In each of the individual vocal segments the start (whether the first-violin melody or the contrary material) is followed by a passage in which the voice moves in large note-values only (the first instance is soprano 1, 'Deus Pater'). The orchestra appears to have all the musical relevance here, while the singer has only one note to deliver in each bar, a high one and a low one alternately. The appearance is deceptive, however, and gradually, during the course of the movement, the sense of thematic material flowing in the contrary direction takes on a deeper significance. By the middle of the movement, Mozart has both singers conjoin in one of these long-note passages, the first starting with a high note, the second with a low—the parts are thus designed to cross, advancing contrariwise, like the two alternative main themes of the whole movement (Ex. 17.1*b*). The climax is reached shortly before the end, when the second soprano takes the place of the first on each high note in turn (Ex. 17.1*c*): hence the two parts are melodically complementary in this respect, and the impression is created (in the ideal performance) that the high note is being held for two bars instead of only one as heretofore.

Yet Mozart appears not to have gone for the 'ideal performance'. His sister's note that her sister-in-law sang 'the solo' must mean that Constanze Mozart sang one of the soprano parts in the 'Domine Deus', but Mozart probably did not envisage another woman taking the other part but a man,

Kantaten von Johann Sebastian Bach (Munich and Kassel, 1971), i. 33. For an 18th-century view, see J. J. Quantz, *Versuch einer Anweisung die Flöte traversiere zu spielen* (Berlin, 1752; repr. Leipzig, 1983), 296.

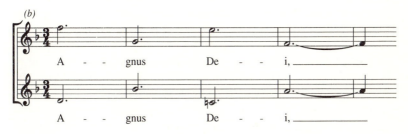

Ex. 17.1. C minor Mass, 'Domine Deus'.

(*a*) Soprano 1 entry in the contrary direction to the orchestral material of the introduction (bars 14–15).

(*b*) The two soprano parts crossing for the first time (bars 60–4).

(*c*) Soprano 2 replacing soprano 1 on the high notes (bars 82–6).

that is, a castrato. He could have had in mind either Francesco Ceccarelli or Michelangelo Bologna, both of whom were friends of the Mozarts.[5] The combination of female and castrato sopranos was not a completely new phenomenon in Salzburg. According to Nannerl Mozart's diary again, Ceccarelli 'sang a duet with the English Miss' on 3 April 1783 (the 'English Miss' is not identified), and eight days later 'Jommelli's *Miserere* was done at court on the 11th, Haydn and Bologna sang it'. 'Haydn' refers to Maria Magdalena Haydn, a singer in the Archbishop's employment and wife of Michael Haydn. If Mozart had already made up his mind while still in Vienna to write one of the soprano parts to suit a particular singer, then it must have been Ceccarelli, whom he could have heard in Salzburg in 1777, whereas Bologna had only been there since the summer of 1782 and Mozart would therefore not yet have made his acquaintance.

In composing the mass, then, Mozart may have thought from the first of the shimmering juxtaposition of the two fundamentally differently constituted vocal timbres: the castrato and the female soprano. Soprano castratos were famous for their range, lightness, and virtuosity, and that finally allowed the play of the range of vocal colours to extend even further: a tenor voice is added to the two types of soprano in the 'Quoniam tu solus sanctus'. At the same time, these three voices represent the principal vocal timbres in *opera seria*: primo uomo and prima donna in the two sopranos, and the 'king' in the tenor (but without the associated hierarchy), and so the operatic connection is not denied. Thanks to his wide compass, the soprano castrato can take part in the extended interplay with the female soprano in 'Domine Deus' and also be ranged with the tenor; the tenor part also crosses one of the sopranos at one point (bars 93–4). All three voices eventually come together in unison for 'Quoniam tu solus' (bars 107–9).

Against this background, much of the Benedictus, composed for four solo singers only after Mozart had reached Salzburg, gives the impression of being a 'normal' quartet, with the castrato, presumably, taking the second part in the place of an alto, as in the ensembles in the Gloria. It is hard to tell which of the sopranos sang the 'Laudamus te' in the Gloria. We have Nannerl Mozart's word for it that her sister-in-law sang 'the solo', but an aria in the style of Neapolitan opera would also have been eminently well suited to a castrato.

Only the Kyrie, Gloria, and Sanctus with Benedictus were sung in St

---

[5] Holl and Köhler in NMA I/1/1, vol. v, p. xi.

Peter's in Salzburg on 26 October 1783. We have no idea what music was performed for the Credo and Agnus Dei—perhaps these movements were taken from one or more of Mozart's earlier Salzburg masses. The young couple left the city early the very next day: Mozart's vow must have been presumed honoured in full. But the music of the new mass went into cold storage and made no contribution towards Mozart's career: he had no use for it in Vienna, either as a mass in itself or as a fragment. He thought of it again at a time when he was evidently snowed under with work, the spring of 1785, when the Vienna Society of Musicians gave him a commission for a psalm-setting to be performed at their concerts on 13 and 15 March. The contact which led to the commission had already been set up the previous summer, when he wrote to ask his sister to have his old oratorio *Betulia liberata* sent to him: 'I have this oratorio to write for the Society here—I might be able to use bits of it in places' (21 July 1784). It would certainly be interesting to see what the mature Mozart would have done with the work of his teens. What he composed for the Society of Musicians in the end was not a psalm but, in the words of the publicity for the concert', 'a wholly new cantata, suited to the present time', *Davide penitente*. The text of this cantata includes material from the penitential psalms, but freely rewritten: this was necessary because the librettist (already possibly Lorenzo Da Ponte) had to make the words fit music from the Kyrie and Gloria of the C minor Mass, in a way that served both the sense of the text and the lie of music originally composed for a different use. This was nothing new: most of the arias and choruses in J. S. Bach's *Christmas Oratorio*, for example, originated in cantatas composed in honour of the Elector of Saxony and members of his family; one difference in the case of *Davide penitente* is that the movements were kept in their original order, with new arias inserted before and after the original 'Qui tollis', one for tenor and one for soprano, so that the three soloists had an aria each. In this work both soprano parts were intended for women.

Mozart did not make an autograph score of *Davide penitente*; all that survives is a copyist's version, made on the basis of raw material provided by the composer. He may later have considered revising the work and producing a fresh score, for among sketches that are thought to be for the A major Piano Concerto, K. 488, there is one on a page headed 'Davide penitente' which was written at least nine months after the work itself (see below, Chapter 24). But with concerto deadlines to be met in the spring of 1786 and the première of *Figaro* fast approaching, Mozart was at least as much pressed for time then as he was in the previous spring.

18

A Letter: The 'Linz' Symphony, K. 425

On Monday 27 October 1783, the day following that on which it is generally accepted that the unfinished Mass in C minor had its first performance, Nannerl Mozart wrote in her diary: '9.30, my brother and sister-in-law left'. She also noted: 'A beautiful day', so his birthplace must have looked its best as Mozart took his leave of it, so far as we know, for the last time. On the only journey later in his life that took him west from Vienna, to Frankfurt for the coronation of Leopold II, he travelled along the Danube on the outward leg, via Linz and Regensburg, and returned via Munich and the Inn valley, leaving Salzburg to the south (as in 1781, after the Munich première of *Idomeneo*).

Even for someone who was in no great hurry, and wanted to rest along the way, the journey from Salzburg to Vienna in those days took no more than five days. In 1767, when the Mozarts went to Vienna for the second time, they made only four overnight stops, in Vöcklabruck, in Linz, in Strengberg, and in St Pölten. This time the young couple took the same route but they made a halt on the second day, and by the fourth they had got no further than Linz. Mozart wrote to his father:[1]

> Linz, 31 October 1783
> We arrived here safely at nine o'clock yesterday morning. The first day, we spent the night at Vöcklabruck. We got as far as Lambach the next morning, and I was just in time to accompany the Agnus Dei on the organ during mass. The abbot was overjoyed to see me again. He told me the anecdote about him and you in Salzburg.

Lambach is one-third of the distance from Vöcklabruck to Linz. The friendship between the Mozarts and the Benedictine abbey there probably went back earlier than the family's visit in the autumn of 1767; the abbot, Amandus Schickmayr (1716–94), had studied at Salzburg University and may have known Leopold Mozart as a fellow-student. The manuscript of one of Mozart's early symphonies (K⁶ 45*a*, composed in The Hague in

---

[1] The letter is quoted in its entirety in the course of this chapter.

1766[2]), was given to Lambach in 1769. No doubt Mozart and Schickmayr had much to talk about: for one thing, the composer would surely have congratulated the abbot retrospectively on his name-day. St Amandus was the second patronal saint of St Peter's in Salzburg, where his feast had been celebrated two days earlier by the performance of Mozart's C minor Mass. Then there was that 'anecdote', which remains a mystery to this day and presumably concerned some incident during the thirty years before the younger Mozart's first visit to Lambach on 12 September 1767.

Posterity has good reason to be glad that the traveller was in less of a hurry this time: if he had gone on his way as he did in 1767, we might have been the poorer by a great symphony. That a symphony would be the journey's outcome was not foreseen, however, and for the moment Mozart had more to report about his visit to Lambach:

> We stayed there all day, and I played the organ and a clavichord. I heard that an opera was being performed the next day in Ebelsberg, at the house of Prefect Steurer (whose wife is Frau von Barisani's sister), and that almost all Linz would be there.

Ebelsberg, to the south-east of Linz, and now a suburb of the city, was a scant day's journey from Lambach along the Traun valley, and, as acquaintances of the Salzburg physician Silvester Barisani and his family, the Mozarts will have had no difficulty in obtaining an invitation to attend this private performance. The letter continues:

> I made up my mind to see it too, and off we went. No sooner had we arrived than the young Count Thun (brother of the Vienna Thun) came to see me, saying that his father had been expecting me for the past fortnight, and would I drive straight on to his house, for I must stay with him. I said I would be quite happy to put up at an inn. But the next day, when we reached the gates of Linz, there was a servant waiting to drive us to old Count Thun's, and that is where we are now lodged.

We do not know the first name of 'the young Count Thun' but we know quite a lot about his family, the counts of Thun-Hohenstein. They had close connections with Salzburg: one member of the family had been Archbishop of Salzburg at the turn of the seventeenth to the eighteenth century, and a Dean of Salzburg of the same name was made Bishop of Trento in 1776. Another member of the family was the Prince-Bishop of Passau, with whom the Mozart family stayed during their first journey to Vienna. Thus Mozart's association with the Counts Thun went back to

---

[2] Allroggen, 'Mozarts erste Sinfonien', 392–4.

1762, and it endured for the rest of his life. Four weeks after that stay in Passau, he paid a call on Count von Ulfeld in Vienna (no doubt he went through his musical paces); this was the father of Maria Wilhelmine Countess Thun, whom Mozart may very well have met then, therefore, during his first childhood visit to Vienna. In 1781 she took him under her wing and showed a lively interest in the composition of *Die Entführung*.[3] In 1762 she had just married Franz Joseph Count Thun, 'the Vienna Thun' of Mozart's letter from Linz, who—like 'the young count' of the letter—was a son of 'old Count Thun': Johann Joseph Anton Count Thun (1711–88) had married a Princess von Hohenzollern-Hechingen, but had been widowed at the age of 34. He divided his time between Linz and Prague— where he played a not insignificant part in assisting Mozart's later career.

Mozart was not the only person to benefit from the family's love of music, of which the most prominent manifestation was Countess Maria Wilhelmine's salon in Vienna, where Haydn and Gluck were frequent guests. Her sister was a pupil of Muzio Clementi for a time, and her daughters in due course acquired names that are well known from the life of Beethoven: one married Andrey Kyrillovich Razumovsky, the other Karl Count Lichnowsky (the last-named was also Mozart's pupil and accompanied him on his journey to Berlin in 1789).

Why 'old Count Thun' had been waiting a fortnight for Mozart to reach Linz is unknown. Perhaps he had an informant in Salzburg who had told him that the composer was there, but it would be odd if the informant knew nothing about the performance of the C minor Mass in St Peter's. Was the decision to perform the mass taken at short notice? Was the opportunity to combine it with celebration of the feast of St Amandus seized as a happy chance? Had that 'chance' caused the Mozarts' return journey to be delayed?

At all events, the overnight stop at Ebelsberg (we do not know what opera they saw) was the reason why the Mozarts reached Linz at the odd hour of nine o'clock in the morning (as Mozart noted in the opening sentence of his letter). From the moment of his warm reception at the Count's house he had been busy.

I cannot say enough about the courtesy which has been heaped upon us in this house. On Tuesday—that's 4 November—I am to give a concert in the theatre here, and because I haven't got a single symphony with me, I'm writing a new one

---

[3] See A. Orel, 'Gräfin Wilhelmine Thun (Mäzenatentum in Wiens klassischer Zeit)', *MJb* 1954, 89–101.

neck and crop, which must be ready by then. I must close now, because I must work. My wife and I kiss your hands, beg your forgiveness for causing you inconvenience for such a long time, and thank you once again for all your kindness. Farewell now.

The Mozarts had reached 'old' Count Thun's house on the morning of Thursday 30 October, and the new symphony (the one now known as the 'Linz') had to be ready by the evening of the following Tuesday. All the arrangements for the concert must have been agreed on the Thursday, in order that the preparations could be completed within the six-day period—not just the composition alone but also the copying of orchestral parts, which would have required at least the same amount of time, and then rehearsals—if there were any. As if that was not enough to be getting on with, Mozart appears to have been fired to make the formal experiment of giving the first movement of his symphony a slow introduction. He had had them in serenades in the past, but now he not only composed a symphony with one for the first time, but also wrote one for a symphony by Michael Haydn, which was evidently played at the same concert (unless it was done at a concert in Vienna not long afterwards). Was the idea a reaction to a stimulus received in Linz at Count Thun's house? A little over three years later, after meeting the Count once again in Prague, Mozart wrote to his friend Gottfried von Jacquin: 'After dinner old Count Thun regaled us with a serenade played by his own people, lasting nearly one and a half hours' (15 January 1787). Was there a serenade after dinner in Linz on that day in October 1783? Did something else (perhaps music in the Count's library) trigger a reaction in Mozart? Or was it the case that the Count provided the opportunity for him to do something he had been contemplating for some time? Not many symphonies with slow introductions had been composed at that date: even in Joseph Haydn's symphonies of the period they are the exception, not the rule.[4]

Mozart almost certainly began the composition of the 'Linz' Symphony by writing the introduction, so he had perhaps already made up his mind about it when he started the letter to his father on 31 October; it is almost beyond belief, at all events, that it did not already exist when he started to compose the Allegro spiritoso that follows it. Writing the first movement must have given Mozart especial pleasure, for it contains a number of other things he had not tried before: presenting the second subject, for example, not as a lightly scored, lyrical element in the dominant (major) key but as

---

[4] Sadie, *Mozart Symphonies*, 70.

a hefty forte element in the dominant's relative minor, is absolutely out of the ordinary symphonic run of things. The 6/8 slow movement, beginning with such song-like lightness but reaching out into such mature, expressive depths, shows that same innovatory tendency. Mozart also found the time to cater to Viennese taste by adding a minuet to the other three movements, while the last is one of those Mozart finales above which he might well have written 'as fast as possible' (as he described, in a letter, the last movement of the 'Haffner' Symphony).

There is no evidence that the symphony was anything but a success. Leopold Mozart, having had the score sent to him for copying, wrote to his daughter: 'We had a big concert at Barisani's, at which I presented your brother's new, excellent symphony' (17 September 1784). (In the intervening months Nannerl Mozart had married Johann Baptist von Berchtold zu Sonnenberg, Prefect of St Gilgen. Her grandfather had held the same office, so she was now living in the house where her mother had grown up.)

The orchestral parts copied for the Salzburg performance have survived, unlike Mozart's autograph or the parts used in the first, Linz performance. The Salzburg parts appear to be as close as we can get to the work in its original form—and they reveal that Mozart revised the symphony at some later stage, fine-tuning details of dynamics and phrasing. The occasion for this was probably a performance during Lent 1785, which in turn was probably the reason why the Vienna music-dealer Johann Traeg was offering the parts of the symphony for sale, in manuscript copies, in April 1785. Thus this revised version of the work circulated in Mozart's lifetime. It was probably one of Traeg's copies that the composer sent to the court of Prince von Fürstenberg at Donaueschingen in summer 1786, along with several other works which he described as his 'latest offspring'. (The 'Linz' Symphony was nearly three years old by then, but Mozart had compiled a list of works to offer to Prince von Fürstenberg, which were the most recent in their respective genres—it was another six months before the 'Prague' saw the light of day.) The 'Vienna' version of the 'Linz' survived in the Donaueschingen copy, which, during the twentieth century, came to be regarded as 'the only demonstrably authentic source for the work'.[5] On the other hand, it is now recognized that the Salzburg parts represent

[5] On the different versions, see C. Eisen, 'New Light on Mozart's "Linz" Symphony', *Journal of the Royal Musical Association*, 113 (1988), 81–96. On Mozart's offer to Donaueschingen, see K. Küster in *Baden und Württemberg im Zeitalter Napoleons* (exhibition catalogue; Stuttgart, 1987), i/2, 893–4 (item 1471).

the 'Linz' version. Without the letter Mozart wrote to his father on the last day of October 1783 we would not know as much as we do about how the different versions came into existence, and the symphony would surely not be known as the 'Linz'. It is yet another instance of the crucial part Mozart's correspondence plays in our understanding of his music.

Mozart stayed in Linz until late November. It appears that neither the composition itself nor his surroundings induced any 'creative torment' in him. Pressed for time as he must have felt, he nevertheless did not end the letter without a flurry of messages for three youngsters from Munich who were living in Leopold Mozart's house as boarders and pupils, Margarethe Marchand, her brother Heinrich, and Maria Johanna Brochard. (Margarethe Marchand was studying singing: it is not certain whether or not Mozart heard her in her subsequent successful career.) So, after having written 'Farewell now', he went on:

Our warmest regards to Gretl, Heinrich (about whom I've already said a great deal here), and Hanni. Tell Gretl from me especially that she shouldn't be coquettish when she sings, for incessant simpering and pouting is not agreeable. Only silly asses will be taken in by that sort of thing. I at least will sooner put up with a farm-boy who is not embarrassed to shit and fart in front of me, than let my head be turned by such artifices when they're so exaggerated that they're transparent. And so adieu. We both kiss our dear sister with all our hearts. I am always your most grateful son,

W. A. Mozart

19

Theme and Variations, Minuet, and Alla turca: The Piano Sonata in A major, K. 331

In the summer of 1881 Johannes Brahms mentioned a new composition in a letter to his friend Theodor Billroth: 'I'm enclosing a few little piano pieces'.[1] What he meant by that was the four movements of his Second Piano Concerto, which is undoubtedly a single work rather than the sum of four 'little pieces'. We also think of Mozart's A major Piano Sonata as a single work, but in this case it is perhaps harder to explain why we should.

A Mozart keyboard sonata usually has three movements: a fast opener, a slower middle one, and a fast finale. Those individual types can vary considerably, and the rule formulated by nineteenth-century music theorists, to the effect that a first movement is always in 'sonata form' and followed by a cantabile middle movement and a rondo finale, is by no means always observed. The most egregious offenders are: the E flat major Sonata, K. 282, which has an Adagio first movement and two minuets before the final Allegro; the D major 'Dürnitz' Sonata, K. 284, composed probably early in 1775 for a Bavarian nobleman, Thaddäus von Dürnitz, in which the opening Allegro is followed by a 'Rondeau en polonaise' and a theme and variations; and the A major Sonata with the Turkish March, K. 331. In this last, a theme and variations form the first movement, which is an Andante, moreover, and the work continues with a minuet and the famous 'Turkish' rondo. The conclusion to be drawn from this—as in the case of Brahms's Second Piano Concerto—is not that, strictly speaking, the A major Sonata is not a true sonata at all, and not an integrated single work either, but rather that our ideas about the form of piano sonatas may be too restricted when we come to consider Mozart's.

In fact the word 'sonata' was used, and even defined, in Mozart's day without the question of form necessarily arising. The most notable instance is the entry under that heading in one of the most important early musical

---

[1] *Billroth und Brahms im Briefwechsel* (Berlin and Vienna, 1935), No. 136, p. 311.

reference books, the *Musikalisches Lexikon* (1802) by Heinrich Christoph Koch (1749–1816):

Sonata. The general designation of instrumental pieces for two, three or more parts, consisting of a number of sections of different characters, in which are expressed the sentiments of a single person, or of several separate persons [corresponding to the number of parts], wherefore in performance each part is customarily played by only one instrument.

If each movement of a sonata is to possess a distinctive character, or express a specific sentiment, it cannot consist of the kind of loosely linked separate melodic sections which together—as is usually the case with the so-called divertimento, for example—amount to the kind of whole which contains merely an agreeable mixture of sounds to please the ear, or an unspecific tone-painting from which our imaginations can create whatever they please according to local circumstances. On the contrary, if a sonata movement is to assert a specific and sustained character, it must consist of fully interlocking and cohering melodic sections which develop one out of the other in the clearest palpable way, so that unity and the character of a whole are achieved, and the imagination, or rather the sentiment, is not diverted along byways.

A piece of music of a specific character, that is, a piece of music intended to express a specific sentiment, is meant to do more than merely, so to speak, brush the nerves of that sentiment. Rather, its purpose is to represent the intended sentiment to a certain degree of satiation, or to a certain degree of effusion from the heart. If this is to occur, and if the listener's heart is simultaneously to feel sympathy with the expression of that sentiment and its modifications, then the substance and the form in which it is clothed must be sufficiently attractive to ensure that interest grows steadily. It is therefore not enough for the principal subject or theme of each section of a sonata to contain the expression of a specific sentiment; in order to have the substance to sustain and prolong that sentiment, it must also present itself, together with the secondary ideas associated with it, in ever new and interesting variations and combinations, so that the succession of the whole captures the attention, and the expression of the sentiment in all its modifications gains in interest for our hearts.

The claim that a sonata, though it is merely an instrumental piece, can be invested with this interest and a specific character has long been advanced by the sonatas of C. P. E. Bach, and the works of Haydn and Mozart provide more recent evidence to strengthen it.[2]

It would, of course, be overstating the case to present Mozart's A major Sonata as Exhibit A in Koch's reflections on the sonata, and Mozart's

---

[2] H. C. Koch, *Musikalisches Lexikon* (Frankfurt-am-Main, 1802; fac. repr. Hildesheim, 1985), cols. 1415–17.

conception of the divertimento was obviously also too much inclined towards the symphonic to be described in terms of 'unspecific tone-painting'. In Koch's day writing about musical theory and aesthetics, even when it took lexicographic form, usually started from a subjective, rather than a scientific, standpoint and the desire to put the writer's own view and experience of particular topics into words. Koch, a musician at the little court of Rudolstadt in Thuringia, was not describing 'the sonata' of C. P. E. Bach, Haydn, or Mozart (let alone Beethoven); rather, like the music composed with that title, his definition was an expression of what was possible at the time—and we should remember that an enormous amount of it was in circulation, thanks to the triumphal progress the evolving pianoforte was making through the rapidly developing institution of the middle-class salon. Back to Mozart's A major Sonata: in the particular respects of expressing a 'sentiment to a certain degree of satiation' and making the 'substance and form' of the expression 'sufficiently attractive to ensure that interest grows steadily' Mozart takes an unusual path in this work, as closer study reveals.

The subject of the variations in the first movement is not exactly what is normally meant by an 'original' theme. It bears some resemblance to the theme of a keyboard sonata by Domenico Scarlatti, although that is more generously proportioned and its separate elements occur in a different order from that of Mozart's theme. (If the motivic material of the opening bars in Scarlatti's piece can be labelled ABAB . . . , then in Mozart's it is AABC–AAB¹C¹.) Nevertheless, the points of similarity are clear enough. Scarlatti's sonata has the heading 'Pastorale'. and the Scarlatti scholar Alessandro Longo discovered that its theme draws on a Neapolitan Christmas carol. The same must be true of Mozart's theme, but then the question arises as to whether a connection exists between Mozart's theme and Scarlatti's, or whether Mozart got his directly from the carol and then elaborated it, much as Scarlatti had. For the time being, that question goes unanswered.[3]

The material of the variations does not consist of the carol melody alone but includes the bass line also, a procedure that has been called 'Doppelgerüst' (dual framework) technique.[4] There are six variations in all.

[3] T. van Huijstee, 'Naar aanleiding van Mozarts KV 331: Scarlatti's K 513', *Mens en melodie*, 33 (1978), 148–56; M. Boyd, *Domenico Scarlatti, Master of Music* (London, 1986), 172–3.

[4] R. Flotzinger, 'Die Klaviervariationen W. A. Mozarts in der Tradition des 18. Jh.s', *Mitteilungen der ISM*, 23/3–4 (1975), 13–27.

They employ the obvious techniques of varying the mode (No. 3 is in the minor) and tempo (No. 5 is an Adagio, and No. 6 an Allegro, subjecting the basic Andante to a kind of stretto process), but the player's virtuosity is also enlisted: the second variation, for example, has a triplet accompaniment which is passed to and fro between the hands, while in the fourth the hands cross, as the left-hand part lies alternately below and above that of the right hand. The first variation sees the theme dissolve into the kind of 'sighing' motif so characteristic of music of mid-eighteenth-century 'Empfindsamkeit', but that is not all: it also sets out the dynamic framework for the remaining variations. The theme itself is presented *p* apart from a few *sf*s, changing to *f* only in the last two of its eighteen bars. In the variations, however, a *f* is reached in the fifth bar, and that is also associated with changes in harmony and sonority in all but the fourth variation. For all that, the dual framework of melody and bass is not called into question anywhere in the variation process.

With six variations, the movement has fewer than are often found in Mozart's self-contained sets of variations. The two based on themes of Antonio Salieri (K. 180) and Giovanni Paisiello (K. 398) also contain six only, but others are much more capacious, above all the ones he composed in Paris in 1778: the cycles on 'Ah vous dirai-je, maman' and 'La belle Françoise' both number twelve.

Thus a Neapolitan influence seems to be at work in the first movement, irrespective of whether the theme came from the anonymous carol or from the sonata by the Neapolitan Domenico Scarlatti. The variations themselves are not 'Neapolitan': that much is immediately made clear in the first with its 'empfindsam' coloration. The second movement (most unusually, also in the home key) can be regarded as owing something to French style, typologically, only once again Mozart refuses to be tied down to any particular stylistic 'model'. The Minuet is very generously proportioned, contains a large number of musical phrases, and might more accurately be headed merely 'Tempo di menuetto', for it stands at some remove from the dance character of a true minuet. The D major Trio which provides the inner section of the 'minuet-and-trio' complex repeats the hand-crossing technique from the fourth variation.

The third movement, finally, is a rondo built from 'Turkish' elements, presented in a particularly pure state. Mozart alternates pure major and pure minor phrases and sticks quite closely to a basic rhythmic formula made up of two minims, two crotchets, and a third minim, which is characteristic of a Turkish cavalry march and which he had already used before, as part of the 'Turkish' colouring of the finale of the A major Violin Concerto, K. 219 (1775).[5] In the Turkish music from which this figure derives, the rhythm is built up from the interplay of several different percussion instruments, each playing its own rhythmic pattern, and it is the total of these which produces the pattern used by Mozart—who puts it all in the left hand. The rhythm in the major-mode sections could be even more sharply accented on some instruments of Mozart's day, which had a special pedal to operate a cluster of percussion instruments fixed to the frame. This *'alla turca* register' added to the exotic coloration.

With these three movements Mozart achieved what Heinrich Christoph Koch defined twenty years later as the essential character of the sonata, for the processes of variation and rondo form, with their reliance on the recurrence of musical elements, undoubtedly succeed in expressing a 'sentiment to a certain degree of satiation'. The same thing can be achieved in other musical forms, of course, such as the 'sonata form' typically associated with first movements, to which dialectical qualities are attributed (the first and second subjects, as 'thesis' and 'antithesis', are brought together to achieve 'synthesis')—and sonata form is the very thing that Mozart draws close to in his expansive minuet. Thus the three movements of this sonata are particularly telling in their illustration of the manifold possibilities 'the sonata' could explore in the eighteenth century, without the sacrifice, by any one individual work, of its inner integrity.

With the exception of works from the first decade of his life, it is clear that Mozart wrote his early keyboard sonatas in groups. The composition and publication of such groups (threes, half-dozens, full dozens) were common throughout the eighteenth century and beyond, from Corelli's twelve *Sonate da camera* to Schubert's three sets of twelve German dances (D. 128, 420, and 790). Mozart wrote a first set of six sonatas in Salzburg and Munich in 1774–5 (K. 279–84). During his travels in 1777–8 he wrote two in Mannheim (K. 309 and 311) and one in Paris (the A minor, K. 310), to make a set of three. For many years the A major Sonata, K. 331, together with the C major, K. 330, and the F major, K. 332, was also ascribed to the Paris period, but Mozart's handwriting and the type of paper he used indicate that it was composed several years later, around the time of the visit to Salzburg in late summer 1783.[6] The three works were

---

[5] K. Reinhard, 'Mozarts Rezeption türkischer Musik', in H. Kühn and P. Nitsche (eds.), *Bericht über den Internationalen Musikwissenschaftlichen Kongreß Berlin 1974* (Kassel, 1980), 518–23, esp. 519–20.

[6] Tyson, *Mozart*, 30; Plath, 'Beiträge II', 171.

printed by the Viennese firm Artaria only a short time later. From then onwards Mozart's keyboard sonatas became, so to speak, more individual: the B flat major Sonata, K. 333, probably written only a little later than the group K. 330–2, was not printed with them; later sonatas are entered in Mozart's catalogue of his works as separate compositions. This 'individualization' is not confined to the keyboard works but is an important aspect of what has been called 'the mature Mozart'—the character which stamps the music of the last years in Vienna, above all, but is already manifest in his assimilation of fugal techniques or his tackling of dramatic construction in *Idomeneo* and *Die Entführung*.

20

New Paths for the Concerto: Twelve Keyboard Concertos, from K. 449 to K. 503

The musical life of Vienna in the 1780s befitted the standing of one of the world's great cities, and it operated by its own laws. With all his experience of the world, Mozart was reasonably confident that he would be able to make his mark on it, when he settled there at the age of 25, but it took him an astonishingly long time before he had learnt how to exploit all the possible ways of doing so. He encountered problems in the field of opera to begin with, for in spite of the success of *Die Entführung*, no comparable new commissions followed in its wake. Concerts were another important area of musical life where he had to establish his footing. The major season for concerts was in the winter months, divided between Advent and Lent. Concerts (or 'academies') took place in the private houses of the rich and well-born, but they were also arranged on a private basis in public venues by individual artists (with the co-operation of others). Such ventures could yield considerable sums; that was one of the reasons why Mozart was drawn to Vienna, as his anger at being prevented from earning that kind of money during his first few weeks in the city shows. By arranging the events on a subscription basis the artist could have a certain idea of the proceeds in advance.

When Mozart arrived in Vienna from Munich in 1781, the Lent concert season was already well under way. He is known to have performed works of his own at concerts put on by himself in the following two years, but it is also known that they were not new works, for the most part. It was 1784 before he seized the opportunity to shine as both performer and composer, by writing new concertos especially for his own academies. The fact that he finally recognized the benefits of combining both aspects of his gifts must be connected with the appearances he made at other people's academies, but perhaps what he learnt from the composition of three keyboard concertos for publication (K. 413–15; 1782–3) was an even more important factor. He appears to have started a fourth concerto around the same time—the E flat major, K. 449[1]—and may have intended to get it printed with the other three, for he added a postscript to a letter to his father to say that 'only three concertos' were being published (4 January 1783); unfortunately the letters that might explain that 'only' have not survived.

It was another two years before the E flat major Concerto was ready: Mozart finished it (on 9 February 1784) for his 18-year-old pupil Barbara (Babette) Ployer, who gave the first performance shortly afterwards. There must have been some connection between finishing it and Mozart's decision to seize his chance as both performer and composer, because in March he himself was the soloist in the premières of two further concertos, the B flat major, K. 450, and the D major, K. 451, finished a week apart on 15 and 22 March. He finished yet another, the G major Concerto, K. 453, on 12 April—it was Easter Monday, and Lent was over. It too was composed for Barbara Ployer, who learnt it in two months. Her circumstances were such that she was able to give the first performance during the summer, when Vienna normally eschewed concert-going.

Barbara Ployer came from Upper Austria, from a family whose eldest sons held important posts in the customs service at the Danube port of Sarmingstein. This was where goods that had made the dangerous passage past the Danube whirlpools at Grein on small boats were transferred back on to barges, as well as being cleared for transit from Upper to Lower Austria. The younger sons mostly left home for careers in government service, like Barbara's great-uncle; it was with his son, Gottfried Ignaz Ployer, agent in Vienna for the court of Salzburg, that she went to live in 1779, and his house in the country, at the village of Döbling, was the scene of the first performance of the G major Concerto, on 13 June 1784.[2] Today Döbling gives its name to the XIXth district of Vienna, which also includes the popular 'Weinort' of Grinzing as well as Beethoven's Heiligenstadt. The 'Pastoral' Symphony was composed in Döbling, and Gustav Mahler died there.

In 1784, then, Mozart embarked on a self-appointed task which dominated his production for the next two years. Between the first weeks of 1784 and Easter 1786 he composed no fewer than eleven keyboard concertos, and he completed the round dozen in style during Advent 1786 with the C major Concerto, K. 503. At the turn of the year 1785–6 he was

---

[1] Tyson, *Mozart*, 153–5.

[2] See W. Senn, 'Barbara Ployer, Mozarts Klavierschülerin', *Österreichische Musikzeitschrift*, 33 (1978), 18–28.

doubly burdened, still composing new concertos and now also preparing for the performance of two operas, *Der Schauspieldirektor* and *Figaro*. The end of the period in which he wrote the great concertos coincided with the end of the years when there were no operas, and when the opera-composer came back to life the concerto-composer retreated to the background. Let us set aside, for the time being, the question of whether these two facts were interdependent; there could have been a number of reasons why the run of great concertos came to an end, and the link with the beginning of the period of the great operas could be of secondary import-ance, or even purely coincidental. We should remember that only a few years later, in the last year of his life, Mozart worked practically simul-taneously on at least two concertos and two operas, apparently without any sense of conflict.

Let us look more closely at Mozart's intensive concentration on the concerto. As we have already seen with the violin concertos, the preoccu-pation led to rapid advances in compositional technique. But it is also important to note that in the midst of stylistic innovation Mozart did not fundamentally renounce what he had written previously; the new works took up a prominent position in his concert-giving but earlier ones did not disappear altogether. So how did his concerto style change?

Mozart described the concertos he had written over the previous three months in a letter to his father on 15 May 1784. He was afraid that 'they will be of little use to you: except for the concerto in E flat [K. 449] (which can be done *a quattro* without wind instruments), the other three [K. 450, 451, and 453] are all scored with obbligato wind, and you seldom have such forces at your disposal'. The E flat major was not the only concerto that could be played *a quattro* (with just a string quartet ac-companying the soloist);[3] there would have been little profit in publishing K. 413–15 if the same had not been the case with them. Leopold Mozart was not the only musician who did not have a larger ensemble at his com-mand: rather, it was the rule, and Mozart had composed all his earlier keyboard concertos under similar restraints. It was different in the case of his concertos with violin and wind soloists; they had generally been scored with obbligato wind parts, the omission of which would have a deleterious effect on a performance. The G major Violin Concerto, for example, could not be played without oboes, because they play the second subject in the solo sections of the first movement, and without them there

---

[3] See C. Wolff, 'Mozart 1784: biographische und stilgeschichtliche Überlegungen', *MJb* 1986, 1–10, esp. 6.

would be nothing but 'accompaniment'. There is nothing similar to that in Mozart's keyboard concertos before 1784. The advancement of individual instruments out of the orchestra gives a wind or string concerto a textural richness and variety which, in a keyboard concerto, can be provided by the solo instrument playing—as it always does—polyphonically.

The E flat major Concerto, begun around the time of the composition of K. 413–15, was a late example of that earlier practice. Mozart did not finish it then, perhaps because it grew too big for what he wanted—the opening tutti alone, with its eighty-eight bars, implies criteria other than those which apply in the other three, which are between fifty-six and sixty-three bars long. It was a year before he took it up again and finished it for a pupil, but he first experimented with the orchestral accompaniment in a work for himself, the B flat major Concerto, K. 450. His idea seems to have led to a build-up of pressure in him, and he could not wait, apparently, to expound his new technique at full stretch: even as early as in the first two bars, an ensemble reduced to *a quattro* forces would produce nothing but the tonic, B flat, repeatedly, for everything else is given to the oboes and bassoons. Perhaps Mozart does not quite keep the promise he makes there, for long stretches of the solo sections—as in later concertos—could conceivably be accompanied *a quattro*, without wind. The presence of a keyboard soloist sets other criteria but the new conception of the orchestra keeps on flaring up.

Scarcely had Mozart got thus far when he took a further step forward, and enlarged the wind contingent as such. The B flat Major Concerto, K. 450, calls for two oboes, two bassoons, and two horns, but in the D major Concerto, K. 451, these are joined by a flute, two trumpets, and timpani, apparently without any particular reason. All of those instruments, except the flute, had already been included in the C major Concerto, K. 415 (although there, as Mozart said, the wind is optional), but the presence of the flute was the most significant innovation here: never before had Mozart included a flute in the accompanying orchestra in a concerto, but from now on he always had one, and so the flute became part of the standard wind complement in all the later concertos, alongside two each of oboes, bassoons, and horns. Once again, however, this provision was not final: all the concertos Mozart finished in the following fifteen months (with the exception of the A major Concerto, K. 488, of which more below, in Chapter 24) were in keys that allowed the inclusion of trumpets and hence timpani—but there are some special cases among them. It is not wholly clear whether or not Mozart composed trumpet and timpani parts for the F major Concerto, K. 459 (finished on 11 December 1784); in the thematic catalogue of his works that he was keeping by then he mentions them in the instrumentation, but the autograph score, which survives, does not include them. That is not necessarily significant, for, as in the case of the D minor Concerto, K. 466, lack of space could have led to their being notated on a separate sheet, which has been lost. In the case of the E flat major Concerto, K. 482, again, those particular parts may have been written later, but in that work the orchestra differs in another respect: finished on 11 December 1785, it is the first concerto to have clarinets, which replace oboes. Only in the C minor Concerto, finished a few months later, is the wind palette used in its entirety: one flute, and two each of oboes, clarinets, bassoons, horns, and trumpets.

The enlargement of the sound world which was the direct consequence of the enlargement of the orchestra brought its own limitations with it, however. Trumpets and clarinets could only be used in certain keys: the former in B flat, C, D, E flat, and F, the latter in A, B flat, and related keys. The two areas overlap only in the E flat major and C minor concertos (K. 482 and 491), and the A major Concerto, K. 488, is the only one to stand apart from the series of works in keys accessible to the trumpet, But Mozart's conception of instrumentation had evolved since 1782–3; not only were his scores longer and his orchestras larger but the textures also take account of the consequences. The increasing tendency to 'think big' was not confined to the orchestration, either, but affected the musical structures too.

Even the opening themes of the concertos were now sometimes proportionately large in scale.[4] Formerly Mozart often began concertos with concise, fanfare-like material (as now still in the D major Concerto, K. 451), or with a brief unison forte (as still in the E flat major Concerto, K. 449), which then at once gave way to material of a completely different character, in accordance with the usual motivic processes. Now he subjected these thematic forms to unprecedented demands. For example, when he conceived the C major Concerto, K. 467, around the turn of the year 1784–5, he had two ideas for concerto opening themes in C major, both of which were representative of his new thinking, and he developed complete opening tuttis from both of them. One of these he used at once to launch the concerto under his hand, the other he set aside for two years,

---

[4] See Küster, *Formale Aspekte*, 236–9.

and only then put it to work in K. 503. In K. 467 he was content with a relatively short first subject, a unison, as in earlier concertos; the only odd thing about it is that it is marked *p*. For the time being, evidently, he did not want anything as potentially expansive as the other theme, the one kept in reserve until he wrote K. 503: this was fanfare-like in character, yet it was already eighteen bars long, by contrast to, say, the two-bar fanfare of K. 451. Eighteen bars for a first-subject statement: again, the criteria are new. In the 'concerto' Allegro of the Serenade, K. 203, of 1774 the entire opening tutti was only twenty-two bars long, the entire movement only 156; in the C major Concerto, K. 503, the opening tutti is ninety bars long, the movement 432.

In the continuation of these first movements, Mozart gets as far away as possible from the tradition of alternating blocks of tuttis and solos. Now he sometimes has symphonic development in mind as he constructs the opening tutti, so that new musical situations do not develop by perceptible stages but each proceeds smoothly out of the one before (this is especially evident in the two concertos in minor keys, K. 466 and 491, and in the C major, K. 467); and in addition he gets to work on the 'punctuation' of the solo exposition. By having the modulating sections start in relatively remote keys he lends them much more weight than they had in earlier concertos, in which their logical function completely dominated the musical course of events. In the Mannheim Flute Concerto, K. 313, of 1777–8 Mozart went, for the first time, straight into a minor key (from tonic to relative minor) to begin the modulation; in the C major Concerto, K. 503, in a similar situation, he selects the even more remote E flat major as the starting-point for the modulation and thus gives the process as a whole an unexpected coloration.

The blurring of the frontier between the end of the exposition and the start of the development is another innovation (K. 503 actually boasts a 'thematic' development section): either Mozart carries over the thematic material of the tutti with which the exposition ends into the solo with which the development begins (as is particularly evident in the A major Concerto, K. 488, in which he writes an orchestral episode specially for the purpose), or the tutti is not allowed to finish properly but is swamped by the soloist's entry, as in the D major Concerto, K. 451. The natural consequence of this is the tendency to step outside the tonal norms (more extensively than in the solo exposition), but we have to wait for the most extreme example of that until the B flat major Concerto, K. 595, in which, without having come to a formal full cadence, Mozart plunges suddenly, by way of two steps, each the interval of a third, from the F major of the tutti into a diametrically contrary B minor.

Mozart did not bring this large-scale restructuring to a halt when he reached the recapitulation. It is a solo section, and, in accordance with the traditional alternation of tuttis and solos in concerto-form movements, it must relate to another solo section, namely the solo exposition. A recapitulation is tonally stable: it begins and ends in the home key. The solo exposition, on the other hand, moves away from the tonic (to the dominant, when in the major). The usual procedure is to make appropriate adjustments in the recapitulation, but Mozart recognized that there was another section—albeit a tutti—which stays within the same harmonic bounds as the recapitulation: the opening tutti begins, naturally, in the tonic and also ends in it, leaving the business of harmonic elaboration to the soloist. One step at a time, from the D major Concerto, K. 451, onwards, Mozart worked out a technique whereby the first half of a concerto-form recapitulation follows the same course as the opening tutti. The process ended with a phenomenon that could hardly be more characteristic of Mozart in his middle and late years in Vienna: instead of making his solution to the 'problem' a new foundation-stone of his formal technique in orchestral works, he used it in just one, the E flat major Concerto, K. 482. Then, it seems, he looked round for new challenges, rather than resting on the achievements of old ones.

The wind of experimentation which blew through the first movements is just as much in evidence in the middle movements, and from the first bars. Up to and including the concertos of 1784, the usual thing in Mozart is for the orchestra to start a middle movement on its own. That changes in 1785. In the two great concertos in C major, K. 467 and 503, and in the E flat major, K. 482, the middle movements begin in the traditional way, but in all the other keyboard concertos they begin with the soloist in solitary state (in the concertos for horn and clarinet the orchestra is playing, but not on its own). In these works—for example, in the A major Concerto, K. 488, or the two in minor keys—Mozart prepared a deliberate surprise for his contemporaries.

Concertos in minor keys: one of the far-reaching consequences of Mozart's rethinking of the concerto was the ability to compose one in a minor key at all. He wrote two: the D minor, K. 466, and the C minor, K. 491. The obstacle that had to be overcome was the problem of the sequence of tonalities, not only in the first movement but also in the last. In a first movement the problem is most acute in the tonal relationship of the first and second subjects: in the opening tutti they are both in the tonic; in the solo exposition of a concerto in a major key, the first is in the tonic and the second in the dominant, and both retain their major character. In a concerto in a minor key, however, the second subject would have to be able to change its modality, in order to be minor in the opening tutti but major in the solo exposition.[5] But not every subject lends itself to transformation from minor to major, and there is also the question of the conditions on which such transformation is desirable at all. Mozart brought the prime ingredient of the solution with him from Paris in 1778 and used it for the first time in his Sinfonia Concertante, K. 364: the second subject of the opening tutti can be replaced by a new theme in the solo exposition. Nevertheless, he tried two alternative solutions in the two minor-key concertos. In the D minor he breaks the rules by having the second subject in the opening tutti enter in the major mode, though it lacks the power to determine tonality that would normally be expected in a second subject playing its usual role at the end of a solo exposition; for that reason he still has to introduce a 'second' second subject at that point. In the C minor Concerto, the second subject is in the minor in the opening tutti, and that meant that Mozart had to write a new theme to fill the major-mode spot in the solo exposition—and then transpose it into the minor in the recapitulation!

Choice of a minor key presents a completely different set of problems in finales. Can a virtuoso soloist be asked to sign off a concerto in the minor mode? Mozart's answer in the D minor Concerto is 'No', and he switches the music into the major just before the end. The same thing happens in Beethoven's Third Piano Concerto and in Chopin's F minor Concerto. The finale of the C minor Concerto, on the other hand, is in the minor, but it differs from Mozart's other concerto finales in another respect, for instead of being the usual (since 1774) rondo it is a variation movement (its only forerunner is the G major Concerto, K. 453). Even so, the major mode is not banished altogether, and provides the destination for two of the variations. In a minor-key concerto, this was obviously the only alternative for Mozart to the rondo in which the transition to the major was avoided until the coda.

A look outside the concerto genre, finally, suggests a third option. The G minor Piano Quartet, K. 478, was composed between the D minor and C minor concertos. It begins with an Allegro in G minor, which is in

---

[5] For a discussion of this topic in K. 491 as a whole, see E. Badura-Skoda, *Wolfgang Amadeus Mozart, Klavierkonzert c-moll KV 491* (Munich, 1972), 24–5.

typical sonata form in all details. The middle movement, an Andante in B flat major, is similarly conventional. Unlike the string quartets of the same period the work is in three, not four, movements, and that gives it something in common with the violin sonata—and the concerto. The juxtaposition of a keyboard instrument and a group of strings encourages a certain affinity to the concerto, and the rondo-finale does in fact express itself in forms that could go into a concerto with hardly any alterations. The movement is in G major throughout. The switching of an entire concerto finale into the major is, again, known in the music of Chopin—his E minor Concerto, for example. There are times in this quartet, therefore, where it comes on like a concerto, and thus adds an important and forward-looking extra facet to the concertante style appropriate to works in minor keys.

21

Leaving the Beaten Track: The Violin Sonata for Regina Strinasacchi, K. 454

In the early part of his time in Vienna Mozart composed very few new works for other musicians to perform, although he had contact with them: witness the fact that he played in their concerts. Evidently he had not yet fully discovered the possibilities of concerts as a showcase for new compositions. Teaching Barbara Ployer seems to have been what set him on that road; his earlier experience with Josepha Auernhammer had not had the same effect. The number of works he composed for virtuosi during this period is very small indeed: a horn concerto for Joseph Leutgeb, who was a friend from Salzburg, and individual arias for the singers who took part in the first performances of *Die Entführung*. Then, in 1784, he produced a concerto for the blind pianist Maria Theresia von Paradis (1759–1824), in all probability the B flat major Concerto, K. 456, completed on 30 September. Before that, however, he had written a sonata for the Italian violinist Regina Strinasacchi (1764–1839); this was the B flat major Violin Sonata, K. 454, which Mozart himself dated 21 April 1784 in the thematic catalogue of his works. Three days later, however, he wrote to his father: 'We have the famous Strinasacchi from Mantua here at present, a very good violinist; her playing shows a great deal of taste and feeling. I am at this moment writing a sonata, which we will perform together in the theatre on Thursday at her academy' (24 April 1784). That was a Saturday, but even five days later, at the concert itself, it still seems that the work was not as ready as the date in the catalogue—that is, the Wednesday eight days earlier—asserts. According to a later account by Constanze Mozart, which is not contradicted by the evidence of the autograph, Mozart played most of the keyboard part straight out of his head; from this it would appear that he did not actually complete it until later, probably expressly for its publication, which was announced very soon afterwards, on 7 July 1784.

This kind of pressure of time was nothing new to Mozart and probably did not worry him. Even in the case of one of his earliest concerts in

Vienna, when he was still in Archbishop Colloredo's employment, he could send his father this kind of report:

Today—for I'm writing this at eleven o'clock at night—we had an academy. Three pieces by me were done. New ones, of course—a rondo for a concerto for Brunetti, a sonata with violin accompaniment for myself—which I composed last night between eleven and twelve, but wrote down only the accompaniment for Brunetti, so as to have it done in time, but kept my own part in my head—and then a rondo for Ceccarelli.   (8 April 1781)

In the case of the 'Coronation' Concerto, K. 537, composed some years later, there are long stretches where Mozart never got round to writing down more than the part for the right hand, in spite of the fact that he gave several performances of it. Unlike that, he did later complete the violin sonata he wrote for the concert on 8 April 1781, the one in G major, K. 379, so that it could be published—like the B flat major sonata of 1784, although in very different circumstances. Violin sonatas are a constantly recurring factor in Mozart's biography, and one stamped more than most by commercial considerations. It was something Mozart had learnt in early childhood, when the first of his compositions to appear in print, in Paris in 1764, were the four sonatas, K. 6–9, issued in pairs as Opp. 1 and 2; Opp. 3 and 4, which followed shortly afterwards, also consisted of sets of violin sonatas, six each this time: K. 10–15 (London, 1765) and K. 26–31 (The Hague, 1766). The first ten of these sixteen works were all described on the title-page as 'Sonates pour le clavecin qui peuvent se jouer avec l'accompagnement de violon': keyboard pieces, that is, with an optional violin accompaniment. This applies in particular in the case of the London set, in which the violin part can equally well be played on a flute, and a cello can also be added to the ensemble, while the four published in Paris were originally composed for keyboard alone, and the violin parts were added later.

Mozart took the lesson—that violin sonatas were publishable—to heart. It was when he was spending the winter of 1777–8 in Mannheim, looking for some means of earning a living, that he composed the six Violin Sonatas, K. 301–6, which he had engraved in Paris in summer 1778 (as a second Op. 1) and presented to the former Electress Palatine (now Electress of Bavaria) in the following winter, on his return journey. When he moved to Vienna, he again resorted to publishing violin sonatas, and another six (another Op. 2) duly appeared in November 1781. These were, moreover, relatively old works: the G major Sonata which he had conjured out of the air seven months earlier was the newest of them, while the C major, K. 296, went back to March 1778 (it was composed in Mannheim on the outward journey); the other four were K. 376–8 and 380.

Violin sonatas were the kind of works that could be dedicated to people from whom Mozart hoped to obtain some help or advancement in the place where he happened to be. On a wider front, they attracted public interest, especially when they could truthfully be described as 'keyboard sonatas with violin accompaniment', in that they did not present an overwhelming degree of technical difficulty. In fact, Mozart never lost sight of the idea of adding a violin part later to something he had already written for keyboard: as late as 1788, the F major Sonata, K. 547, followed the same path as that which led from keyboard pieces to the very first Paris sonatas of 1764.

The history of the sonata for Regina Strinasacchi bears a superficial resemblance to that of the earlier sonatas, to the extent that it was printed together with two 'genuine' keyboard sonatas (K. 284 and 333), but Mozart struck out on a new path with this work, in two respects. Firstly, it can be assumed that it was printed in order to capitalize on a successful first performance, which was almost certainly not the case with the earlier violin sonatas. Secondly, Mozart composed this sonata for himself and a virtuoso violinist, and not primarily for amateurs in the general public who might buy a printed edition to play for their own pleasure. Consequently he was able to take account of other musical considerations than those which prevailed when the violinist could not be expected to do more than 'accompany' the keyboard player. Leopold Mozart called the B flat major Sonata a 'duetto' for that reason. The G major Sonata of 1781 was composed on broadly similar terms, but it is much less ambitious in several respects than the 'Strinasacchi' Sonata.

Ten of the twenty-two violin sonatas which had appeared in print by the end of 1778 comprised only two movemetns, including five of those in the set of six published that year as Mozart's second 'Op. 1'. One of those, the C major Sonata, K. 303, anticipates the layout of the G major Sonata, K. 378, in that, while both works are essentially in two movements, a slow introduction precedes the Allegro 'first' movement. The third sonata that Mozart composed with a slow introduction was the 'Strinasacchi' Sonata, but here the Allegro is followed by two more movements, not one. A sonata which was just one of three new works to be performed in the residence of old Count Colloredo (but probably massaging the Archbishop's self-esteem at the same time) was all very well in its way, but three years later Mozart must have taken a different view of a work (obviously the only one) which he composed especially to perform with a visiting celebrity. There is another factor to consider, too: Leopold Mozart wrote to his daughter some time later, after he had heard Strinasacchi play in Salzburg,

She does not play a single note without feeling, even in the symphony [the opening movement of a concerto] she plays with expression, and nobody could play adagio with more feeling and more movingly than she does. Her whole heart and soul is in the melody she plays; and her tone is just as beautiful, and strong too. (7 December 1785)

Is it likely that those qualities had no effect on the composition? And is it possible to discover what the reasons for that beauty of tone may have been?

The words about Strinasacchi's 'feeling' echo what Mozart himself had said in April 1784. He could well have been as impressed as his father was by her adagio playing, in which case both the Largo introduction and also the slow middle movement with its wide melodic arcs (Andante, but originally an Adagio) may have formed part of his conception of the work from the first. Above all, the middle movement is harmonically very elaborate; the 'development' in a middle movement is often little more than the transition from the dominant back to the tonic, but here it provides an especially clear illustration of Mozart's aims. He chose a complex but highly effective course, which exploits, even extends, the harmonic possibilities of developmental working in a special way. One of the common developmental techniques is sequence, that is, a theme is 'shunted' up or down by fifths, by thirds, or by chromatic steps. Here, at about the movement's midpoint, Mozart moves from the dominant, B flat major, into B flat minor for a brief period before having the theme that is to be treated sequentially enter for the first time. He then uses an extended cadential formula to screw it higher—a semitone at a time, following the chromatic scale, contrary to the 'normal' musical construction methods of the age. By this means he reaches first B minor (melody in the violin), then C minor (melody in the keyboard). C minor is the relative of the tonic, E flat major, to which it is thus possible to return painlessly. This employment of chromatic progression, the conscious crossing of what other musicians of the time would have regarded as a closed frontier, and which they would in any case probably not have chosen in preference to some simpler construction, is characteristic of Mozart's later Viennese style: at a technically not very significant spot he leaps off the beaten track and leads performers and listeners alike straight up a beetling cliff-face. As later in the B flat major Piano Concerto, K. 595, at the transition from the exposition to the development, here too he disrupts the muscial flow, so that for a while the goal is almost lost from sight, and carries the problem of his own making towards its solution in such a manner that we finally reach it in a state of far greater alertness than a stereotyped, 'classical' construction could induce.

It was perhaps no accident that the young player's tone made such a special impression on Leopold Mozart. There is every indication that Regina Strinasacchi played a Stradivari (which is thought to have belonged at a later date to Louis Spohr), but it is not certain whether she already had it in 1784.[1] At that time Stradivari violins were not yet regarded as beyond question the best. Only ten years earlier, in his manual of violin-playing, Georg Simon Löhlein had remarked on their 'firm, penetrating, oboe-like, but withal thin tone' and ranked them below the instruments made by the Tyrolean Jakob Stainer and by the Amati dynasty. In Paris the sound of a Stradivari was perhaps first hailed as a sensation in 1782, in the hands of Giovanni Battista Viotti (1755–1824), but Viotti had earlier made his début in Berlin, where Mozart was to have a further fruitful encounter with instruments by Stradivari: it was there, in 1789, that he received the stimulus which led to the composition of the 'Prussian' Quartets. It is not inconceivable, therefore, that in the B flat major Sonata Mozart was reacting for the first time to the sound of a Stradivari, especially as hearing one in Berlin later had a comparable effect on him. There is also the fact that Leopold Mozart, himself the author of a violin manual, praised Strinasacchi's tone, which was obviously quite new to him. It is consistent with the triumphal progress throughout the world on which Stradivari's instruments were even then embarking.

---

[1] S. Stookes, 'Some Eighteenth-Century Women Violinists', *Monthly Musical Record* (Jan. 1954), 14–17, esp. 17. Liner notes with the recording of K. 379, 350, and 454, made by Eduard Melkus and Paul Badura-Skoda in 1962, Harmonia Mundi HM30630. W. H. Hill, A. F. Hill, and A. E. Hill, *Antonio Stradivari* (London, 1902; repr. Great Missenden, 1980), 256–7. G. S. Löhlein, *Anweisung zum Violinspielen* (Leipzig, 1774), 2nd edn. (1781), 132.

22

Equal but Different: The Six 'Haydn' Quartets

Early in 1785 Mozart finished the last in a series of six quartets which he dedicated to Joseph Haydn. The dedication creates a highly unusual association between two of the three great composers at the heart of 'Viennese Classicism'. What was their relationship like in its earlier stages? What contacts did either of them have with Beethoven? Are there any traces of the association between Haydn and Mozart in the actual musical substance of those six quartets?

'Haydn, Mozart, and Beethoven have evolved a new art', proclaimed the poet, composer, and writer on music E. T. A. Hoffmann as early as 1814.[1] Only six years younger than Beethoven, and twenty years younger than Mozart (whom he admired so greatly that he changed his own third name, originally Wilhelm, to Amadeus), Hoffmann belonged to the next artistic generation. All the romantics revered the 'big three', but as a musician Hoffmann also felt the pressure their existence exerted on lesser composers. Only a few months earlier, in a piece about a piano sonata by Johann Friedrich Reichardt (1752–1814), he had written:

The composition of instrumental music having been raised to such heights by the genius of great masters like Haydn, Mozart, and Beethoven, the condition each and every piece must now fulfil is that, as well as the more—nay, most—ingenious harmonic textures which are possible only in pure instrumental music, where the restraints natural to vocal music are unknown, the instruments should also exhibit themselves in their most individual individuality, in the fullest splendour of their inward wealth, in the highest power they can command.[2]

In 1814 Mozart had been dead for more than twenty years, Haydn for five; Hoffmann joins Beethoven's name to theirs, although the works that we think of as his 'late' ones, in which the instruments certainly display 'their most individual individuality', had yet to be written. Mozart's 'Haydn' Quartets undoubtedly played their part in setting these high standards.

[1] E. T. A. Hoffmann, 'Alte und neue Kirchenmusik', in *Schriften zur Musik* , ed. F. Schnapp (Munich, 1977), 230.
[2] E. T. A. Hoffmann, 'Johann Friedrich Reichardt, Klaviersonate f moll', ibid. 204.

The three co-stars heading the bill of Viennese Classicism were unalike. Haydn came from Rohrau in Burgenland, the rural area south-east of Vienna, Mozart and Beethoven from cities ruled by prince-archbishops (Bonn was the capital of the electorate of Cologne). Unlike the great baroque pair Bach and Handel, the three knew each other personally. When Beethoven set off for Vienna in 1792, his patron Ferdinand Count von Waldstein wrote in his album the assurance that if he worked hard he would 'receive Mozart's guardian spirit from Haydn's hands', but he had made an earlier journey to Vienna, in 1787, and according to the testimony of several of his friends he did meet Mozart himself. He is supposed to have gone to Vienna in order to study with Mozart, but it is not altogether certain whether he did or not.

Mozart will have heard about Haydn on his earliest visits to Vienna, and have heard his music in Salzburg, where Michael Haydn, Joseph's younger brother, worked. When their first meeting took place is unknown, but it must have been well before the occasion on 15 January 1785 when Haydn was a guest in Mozart's house, of which we know only at second hand, from Leopold Mozart's passing on the news to his daughter in St Gilgen: 'This very moment have received ten lines from your brother, in which he writes . . . that last Saturday he let his dear friend Haydn and other good friends hear his six quartets, which he has sold to Artaria for 100 ducats' (22 January 1785). The last of the six, the 'Dissonance' Quartet, K. 465, had been finished only the day before, 14 January. When Artaria brought them out in the following September, the composer dedicated them 'Al mio caro Amico Haydn', echoing the words used by Leopold Mozart, who perhaps picked them up from his son's (lost) letter of the previous January. It is safe to conclude that the acquaintance was already of quite long standing by then.

Mozart and Haydn sincerely admired each other, but there was a curious lack of sympathy in the way they regarded each other's chosen course in life. Mozart addressed Haydn, his senior by twenty-four years, respectfully enough as 'Papa', but, as the more experienced traveller, advised against his first journey to London. According to Haydn's early biographer Albert Christoph Dies, he told him that 'you have not been educated in the ways of the great world, and you don't speak enough languages'.[3] Purely in terms of music history, during Mozart's lifetime Haydn's relationship to him was such as to justify the 'Papa'. The works that set him at Mozart's

---

[3] A. C. Dies, *Biographische Nachrichten von Joseph Haydn* (Vienna, 1810), 78.

side in the pantheon of Viennese Classicism—the Op. 76 String Quartets (which include the 'Emperor'), the twelve 'London' symphonies, Nos. 93–104, the oratorios *The Creation* and *The Seasons*, the great masses—were not written until after the younger man's death, at a time when Haydn was able to reap the harvest of his travels. It is true that Haydn took some decisive steps in the direction of his late *œuvre* during the 1780s, with the 'Russian' Quartets published in 1781, for example, or the six 'Paris' symphonies, Nos. 82–7, but viewed purely in the light of what was yet to come—and this is crucial for determining Haydn's place in history—such works are sometimes regarded as transitional. Haydn was actually three years older than Johann Christian Bach, Mozart's early mentor, who died in 1782. If Haydn too had died at the age of 46, posterity would probably label him, as it does Bach, 'pre-classical'. Haydn seems to have been fully aware, however, of the particular generation gap between him and Mozart. Shortly after the première of Mozart's *Don Giovanni* in Prague, in 1787, when Haydn was 55, he too was approached with an offer to stage one of his operas in the Bohemian capital. He refused because his earlier operas had been tailored too closely to the forces at Prince Esterházy's court for which they had been written, and added: 'It would be quite a different matter to have the invaluable opportunity of composing an entirely new work for your Theatre. Even then it would need courage to run the great risk of putting myself in competition with such a man as Mozart.'[4]

But even Haydn could not think himself into Mozart's way of life. He did not understand the significance that his existence as a freelance composer in the Austrian capital had in periods of success like January 1785 and autumn 1787, and he did not foresee its effects for later generations. 'I am simply furious', he wrote in the same letter, 'that this unique Mozart has not yet been engaged by an Imperial or Royal Court. Pardon my speaking out of turn—Mozart is a man very dear to me.' Twenty-one years later, when Beethoven was offered the post of Kapellmeister at the court of Jerome Bonaparte, King of Westphalia, he turned it down, preferring to remain a freelance in Vienna, with the support of three patrons; in 1787, at the age of 16, Beethoven probably had the opportunity to observe Mozart's life-style for himself. He took lessons from Haydn during the latter's last years of greatness in Vienna, and perhaps he fulfilled Count Waldstein's wish more fully than it was intended: 'Mozart's guardian spirit

---

[4] The letter is given in full in Niemetschek, *Life of Mozart*, 60–1.

still mourns and weeps for the death of its nursling. It took refuge with the indefatigable Haydn, but found no occupation there; it seeks, through him, to be united with someone once more. Through incessant industry may you receive Mozart's guardian spirit from Haydn's hands.'

Musically, the dependence between Mozart and Haydn, from the middle of the 1780s onwards, was a matter of complementaries. Each had something to say to the other, but they had different problems to overcome. Mozart may have been inspired in the composition of his 'Haydn' Quartets by Haydn's 'Russian' Quartets, Op. 33; there are notable similarities in the area of melody and motif. But in these quartets Haydn worked out the solution to a problem that was personal to him, and evidently irksome. He appears to have had difficulty in finding inventive constructions with which to conclude the short periods of a minuet; the increasing frequency with which he resorted to the 'emergency brake' in the shape of stereotyped concluding formulas became an embarrassment for him.[5] He solved his problem by calling into question the periodic structure which was a fundamental element of minuet form, and composing scherzos instead (changing the title as well as the form). Mozart was completely unaware of this as a problem: his earliest music lessons had played their part in ensuring that he never had any difficulties with minuets. But Haydn's severance of a personal Gordian knot had consequences for Mozart too: the distortion of the dance character of the minuet challenged him, but on a quite different plane. Anyone who wanted to dance a minuet to the music of the 'minuet' in even the first of the 'Haydn' Quartets (K. 387, finished on New Year's Eve 1782) would have to do it in spite of the music. From the third to the eighth bar Mozart sees to it that the 3/4 beat jumps the rails: every second crotchet of the melodic line (first violin alone to begin with, then cello as the bottom line) is marked *f*, which alternates with a *p* in accordance with 2/4 structure—and thus contradicts the minuet tempo. At this stage it is only a matter of weakening the tempo, but in bars 13–14 it develops into the real joke (see Ex. 22.1). The second violin enters with the theme in bar 13, and the viola follows in bar 14: for both the first note is marked *p*, as in bar 3. But from the viola entry onwards the pattern of alternating emphases slips from our grasp, for its first note coincides with the violin's fourth note, marked *f*. For a bar, therefore, the two instruments not only alternate the stresses from one note to the next within each of their melodic lines according to a pattern which is 'wrong'

---

[5] On this and other matters relating to the minuet, see W. Steinbeck, 'Mozarts "Scherzi"', *Archiv für Musikwissenschaft*, 41 (1984), 208–31, esp. 212 and 214.

Ex. 22.1. String Quartet in G major, K. 387, Minuet.
(*a*) Violin 1, bars 1–4.
(*b*) Contrary emphasis in violin 2 and viola, bars 11–15.

for a minuet, but they also arrive at mutually contradictory solutions to the problem.

The dance movements of the other quartets demonstrate the same quirkiness. In the second of the six (K. 421, in D minor), Mozart suspends regular periodic structure,[6] and in the fifth (K. 464, in A major), after the four-bar period with which the second part opens, there is a fermata lasting a whole bar before Mozart continues, and as a result the next four-bar period occupies bars 6–9 rather than bars 5–8. Nevertheless, the movement as a whole adds up to an apparently regular structure made up from four-bar periods (72 bars = 18 × 4).

Mozart also picked up the thread of one of Haydn's earlier experiments with minuet form—the inclusion of elements of sonata form—at a point where the older man had dropped it. It is not a feature of his 'Russian' Quartets, but in the earlier Opp. 17 and 20 sets Haydn introduced new 'themes' to draw attention to the fact that new keys had been reached.[7]

[6] S. Leopold, 'Mozart, KV 421: Ein Menuett über das Menuett', *Musica*, 43 (1989), 42–3.
[7] Steinbeck, 'Mozarts "Scherzi"', 221 ff.

Mozart—or so it appears—continued along the path that Haydn had abandoned, but he adopted the innovations at which Haydn arrived only after his change of course. Perhaps this was one of the things that made Haydn burst out with the earliest recorded of his enthusiastic comments about Mozart, as repeated by Leopold Mozart in a letter to his daughter. While he was visiting Vienna early in 1785, Haydn said to him after a private performance of three of Mozart's quartets: 'I tell you before God, as I am an honest man, your son is the greatest composer I know either in person or by repute; he has good taste, and more than that, he has the greatest knowledge of composition' (16 February 1785). That knowledge, as represented in the 'Haydn' Quartets, would be scarcely conceivable without Haydn; while Mozart's music may well have been a spur to Haydn himself.

Setting aside the ways in which Mozart orientated himself by the light of ideas already considered by Haydn, let us turn to the question of when he decided to dedicate six quartets to Haydn. He was the second composer to do so, in a line that eventually numbered sixteen.[8] The first was Ignaz Pleyel, who dedicated his Op. 2 to Haydn (it was advertised in the *Wiener Zeitung* on 15 December 1784). That Mozart was already acquainted with Pleyel's first set of quartets, his Op. 1, published in 1783, and with his career (which will have illustrated the usefulness of Haydn's quartets as a model for a composer), is revealed in a letter to his father:

Some quartets have come out by a certain Pleyel, who is a pupil of Joseph Haydn. If you don't yet know them, try to get hold of them: it's worth the trouble. They're very well written and very pleasing: you will also recognize his master in them. Good—and lucky for music, if Pleyel is able to replace Haydn for us in the fullness of time! (24 April 1784)

It is likely, therefore, that Mozart immediately registered the appearance of Pleyel's Op. 2 quartets when they were published eight months later. Pleyel went about the business of dedicating his works in a systematic way. Op. 1 was inscribed to the patron who had paid for his tuition from Haydn, Count Ladislaus Erdödy (to whom Haydn dedicated his Op. 76 quartets); dedicating Op. 2 to his teacher was an obvious next step. Mozart's dedication of his quartets to his 'caro amico' was of a different order, yet it is possible that it was only Pleyel's example that put the idea into his head. In the dedicatory preface Mozart wrote (in Italian): 'You

[8] H. Walter, 'Haydn gewidmete Streichquartette', in G. Feder and others (eds.), *Joseph Haydn: Tradition und Rezeption (Kongreß Köln 1982)* (Regensburg, 1985), 17–53.

yourself, my dear friend, expressed your satisfaction [with the quartets] during your last visit to the capital. Your praise gave me the courage to present them to you now.' That 'last visit' must have been in January 1785, a few weeks after the publication of Pleyel's Op. 2. The suspicion that Mozart was swept up in the wake of that earlier dedication is thus not particularly far-fetched.

If we assume that Mozart first thought of dedicating a set of quartets to Haydn in December 1784, we must take account of the fact that the first of the set was already two years old (the G major Quarter, K. 387, of 31 December 1782). It is true that he was planning to compose a series of six, but at that date he had not settled on getting it printed in Vienna by Artaria, or on dedicating it to Haydn. It was to the Parisian publisher Jean-Georges Sieber that he first mentioned that he was working on string quartets, not least because he was 'not altogether satisfied with the standard of engraving here' (26 April 1783). A dedication to Haydn, however, would not have done anything to promote sales of the quartets in Paris until after the immense success of the 'Paris' symphonies, which were not commissioned until early in 1784; in 1782–3 a dedication to Haydn would have made better sense in Austria—more exclusively so than in 1785. It seems clear, therefore, that Mozart's decision about the dedication was taken at least later than the composition of the first of the six quartets.

Moving on from the dedication and the influences emanating from Haydn's own quartets, the 'Haydn' Quartets represent stations in a continuous evolutionary process. The technical and musical premisses altered for each of the quartets during the course of the two years and more that passed between the composition of the first and the last, so that in the end the set is more striking for the diversity of the six works than for representing variants of a uniform musical type. The question of sonata-form typology in the minuet arises, for example, only in respect of the first, the G major Quartet, K. 387, where it does so, moreover, in the context of more general experimentation with sonata form. This is most apparent in the fourth movement, where Mozart writes two fugal expositions in place of first and second subjects, enabling the questioning usual in a sonata-form final movement to be combined with the experiences of contrapuntal working. The fact that, come the recapitulation, the two thematic groups do not enter singly again but are joined in the manner of a double fugue, and in place of 'the second subject', and only the episode and the closing group from the exposition return in their original forms, shows how important that combination was for Mozart: yet he did nothing similar in any of the other five quartets.

One constant in all six is the play with the phrase-structures in the minuet, in the manner of a Haydn scherzo. Another thread running through them all is the deployment of unexpected suspensions, mutually contradictory elements of passagework, and other examples of harmonic audacity in the four-part writing, which actually stirred up doubts about the works' quality. The 'offending' passages are most frequent in the slow movements,[9] and they are at their height in the slow introduction of the sixth quartet—whence its nickname, 'Dissonance'. Nissen relates some of the choicest of the criticisms:

These quartets suffered a curious fate in some places. When Artaria sent them to Italy, they were returned to him, on the grounds that the engraving was riddled with mistakes: the people there actually thought that the many unfamiliar chords and dissonances were printing errors. When Prince Grassalkovich in Hungary had these same quartets played by members of his orchestra, he cried out again and again: 'You're playing it wrong!' And when they had persuaded him of the contrary, he tore the music up, there and then.[10]

But Mozart's harmonic writing is innovatory in other ways in these works. At the start of the A major Quartet, K. 464, for example, he avoids the obvious modulating construction as a matter of principle. The normal, direct path from the first subject in the tonic to the second subject in the dominant (E major) would be, first, to skirt E major, and then to elaborate it in such a way that the process culminates in a cadence on to E major. This is not for Mozart, or not here. After stating the theme for the first time, he repeats it, but contrary to expectation it is now in A minor; an intermediate theme is then presented in C major (bars 25 ff.), which is more readily explained in terms of the A minor than in the overall A major ambience. But Mozart has his eye fixed firmly on his target: he interprets the C as an upper leading-note—and with one more semitone step he reaches B major; in conjunction with that C the continuation still has a minor tinge to it, but B major, as the dominant of the E major which is his goal, provides exactly the foundation Mozart wants for the entry of the second subject. Yet again one thing is quite clear, as it is in the keyboard concertos or in the sonata composed for Regina Strinasacchi: the film of

---

[9] For example, K. 387/3, bs. 8–9; K. 428/2, bs. 15 ff.; K. 458/3, bs. 14 ff. For a survey of some detailed discussions see J. A. Vertrees, 'Mozart's String Quartet K 465: The History of a Controversy', *Current Musicology*, 17 (1974), 96–114.

[10] Nissen, *Biographie*, 490.

minor colouring which Mozart casts over the radiant A major of the work at this one point has nothing to do with any subjective sadness, and everything to do with Mozart's wish to explore musical possibilities that would lie beyond reach in 'normal' circumstances.

The A major Quartet was finished on 10 January 1785, four days before the 'Dissonance'. The 'Hunt' Quartet, K. 458, was completed two months earlier, on 9 November 1784, but had been lying unfinished for about eighteen months. There are places in all three of these works where we can witness another aspect of the composer's exploration of unfamiliar musical possibilities, as well as one in which the earlier and later works in the group differ: textures and part-writing.

First, though, what is a string quartet? Johann Friedrich Reichardt gave an answer in the preface to his *Vermischte Musikalien* (1773): 'I had the idea of a conversation between four people'. The principle rests on the assumption that each of the four people contributes something to the conversation. The simile falls down in so far as Reichardt did not conceive of the speakers in an actual conversation all vociferating simultaneously throughout; rather, he 'composed out' the thoughts of the silent partners as the running accompaniment to each speaker holding the floor in turn. To understand the history of the string quartet at this stage we need to recall its origins in the baroque trio sonata, for two violins and accompanying continuo, and the quartet sonata, where a fourth part is given either to a keyboard instrument in an additional accompanying role or to a third melody instrument. In these the musical interest lies primarily among the melody instruments, and rarely extends to the continuo.

Obviously, it is extremely hard to reconcile the equality which is the ideal, at least, in a conversation with the hierarchical premises of a trio sonata, and the differences in relationships affect the cello most; its role in continuo is purely accompanimental, and it scarcely ever has the chance to contribute anything to the conversation. In that respect, the tradition of the trio sonata still makes its presence felt in the three earliest of Mozart's 'Haydn' Quartets (in G major, K. 387, D minor, K. 421, and E flat major, K. 428) and in the early stages of the fourth (in B flat major, K. 458, the 'Hunt'), which can probably be dated in the summer of 1783, at much the same time as the second and third of the set.[11] In these instances the cello comes to the fore only in motoric passages, where it generates emphatic rhythmic impulses; motivic fragments from themes, or comparable melodic

---

[11] Tyson, *Mozart*, 94–105.

shapes, fall to its lot only in the context of thematic working or in fugatos, that is, when the four-part texture is subject to the laws of 'strict composition'. In no other way does the cello get to take a leading melodic role in the first three quartets. What happens in the finale of the D minor Quartet—a variation movement—is typical: the principal voice lies in the first violin in the theme and the first variation, in the interplay of the two violins in the second variation, and in the viola in the third; although the texture tends more strongly towards equality for all four parts in the last two sections (Maggiore and Coda), the melodic lead is again taken principally by the two violins—the cello does not get a turn. The ending of the A major Quartet, on the other hand, is in the style of the later works: here, in the last movement (bars 257–62), a short, stereotyped, coda-figure in quavers is heard first in the viola, then in the cello, finally in the first violin. It is the second violin which loses out this time, and it looks as if Mozart was more interested in the colours of the three instruments than in the fact that he had four of them to write for: if the second violin took its turn it could only be pleonastic. The emancipation of genuine quartet composition, achieved by promoting the cello, is now complete. It happened, we might say, in the middle of the 'Hunt' Quartet: in the summer of 1783, when Mozart wrote the beginning of the first movement and the minuet, the new way of treating the cello had not yet revealed itself, and when he finished the first movement, late in 1784, he stayed within the bounds of what he had written earlier. But he was free to change his methods in the remaining movements, and it could be said that listeners actually hear the start of a new stage in Mozart's creative chronology when the cello suddenly assumes an entirely new role in the slow movement and plays as the equal and complement of the first violin (as the other outer part). The first violin speaks out at the beginning of the movement, but the cello takes over in bar 18, while the three upper parts play an accompaniment of repeated semiquavers. There is an advance on that in the slow movement of the A major Quartet: the melody of the low pair, viola and cello, takes them so high that in the end they outtop the second violin (bar 153). From this exploration of the possibilities open in composing quartets it was only a short step to the notoriously 'cello-heavy' texture of the 'Prussian' Quartets, and Mozart had also prepared the ground for the multitudinous variety of relationships between the voices in his string quintets: the pairing of upper and lower parts, the relations of outer and inner parts, and even the crosswise coupling of first violin and viola, or of second violin and cello.

So it was only with the movements of the 'Hunt' Quartet composed in 1784 and the two quartets that followed it that Mozart reached the 'heights' which to E. T. A. Hoffmann constituted the immense challenge that Haydn, Mozart, and Beethoven issued to their successors, the requirement that 'the instruments should also exhibit themselves in their most individual individuality, in the fullest splendour of their inward wealth, in the highest power they can command'. That is the difference between the first three and the last three quartets of the set. The six works are also distinguished by individual traits: not only the slow introduction which is unique to the 'Dissonance', nor the exotic modulations of the A major Quartet, but also the early experimentation with sonata form in the G major of 1782, and everything about the D minor—of which Mozart's wife later declared that it had been composed during the birth of their first child (Raimund Leopold, 17 June–19 August 1783).

Or is the D minor simply the minor-mode component 'normal' in a published set of six works, like the E minor Violin Sonata, K. 304, in the Op. 1 sonatas of 1778, or later works that Mozart may or may not have envisaged being published in sets (the G minor String Quintet, K. 516; the draft of a quartet movement in E minor, K^6 417d, perhaps intended for the 'Prussian' Quartets;[12] or even the late G minor Symphony, K. 550)? This ties in with conventions of eighteenth-century music-publishing, when discrete works by one composer in the same or compatible genres were issued together. The usual practice is well illustrated by a famous published collection from the early years of the century, Vivaldi's twelve concertos, Op. 3, published as *L'estro armonico* in 1711. The edition divides into four groups of three concertos each, and within each group the first is written for four solo violins, the second for two solo violins, and the third for one solo violin (sometimes with an optional solo cello as well). Similar 'external' considerations even influenced J. S. Bach within a single work, the 'Goldberg' Variations: of the thirty variations, every third is a canon (except the last, which is a quodlibet), and the sixteenth variation is laid out like a 'French overture'—aptly, given its role as the start of the second half of the whole work.

Mozart, too, was not immune to the force of convention, and that probably explains why the six 'Haydn' Quartets were not printed in chronological order in the first edition (K. 428 was printed as No. 4, and K. 458 as No. 3) and why the slow movement comes second and the

---

[12] Tyson, *Mozart*, 93; Wolff, 'Creative Exuberance', 195.

minuet third in some, and vice versa in others. The overriding principle is one of simple variety: the inversion of chronology in the printed order of the third and fourth quartets (redressed by the Köchel numbers) resulted in the situation that the minuet is the second movement in the odd-numbered works and the third in the even-numbered ones. This method of constructing sets of works was not new to Mozart: the six quartets he composed in Vienna in 1773, K. 168–73, also relate to each other in similar fashion. There, the work in a minor key comes last and the two works in which a minuet is the second movement are in the middle (as Nos. 3 and 4); the minuet is the third movement in the rest.

In the 'Haydn' Quartets, therefore, we can see not only Mozart's assimilation of Haydn's influence, but also the stages of his individual development of techniques of composing for four-part string textures, documented in each work in turn. In spite of the shifting configuration of the questions he set himself to answer over the extended period of their composition, there are constants among the details, yet only to an extent that is consistent with the six components of the group maintaining the character of wholly individual, separate works at the level of musical technique. Their variety is strong enough to survive being gathered into a 'set', even though that grouping imposes additional rules of its own upon them. These stratifications, in addition to those in string-quartet textures which became more and more acute for Mozart as he worked at them, must have been the reason why the six quartets were not finished in the first few months of 1783 (as the composer had originally intended, to judge by his letter to the publisher Sieber) but took a good two years. Writing the quartets became a 'lunga, e laboriosa fatica', as he confessed in the dedication to Haydn: a long and tedious labour.

23

Lamentations and Mourning: *Maurerische Trauermusik,* K. 447

It is not certain when Mozart first encountered the ideas behind Freemasonry: it may have been while he was still in Salzburg, where he is known to have been in contact with Freemasons. What is certain about his relations with the order is that he was admitted into the Viennese 'Beneficence' lodge on 14 December 1784. Three and a half weeks later, on 7 January 1785, at the request of 'Beneficence', he was promoted from apprentice to journeyman in the 'True Concord' lodge. Five weeks after that, Joseph Haydn was admitted into 'True Concord' as an apprentice. Leopold Mozart was admitted into 'Beneficence' at the beginning of April (and reached the grade of master before the month was out). On 11 December 1784, Emperor Joseph II decreed that the number of lodges in Vienna must be reduced, which meant, in effect, that they had to amalgamate. Mozart's lodge, 'Beneficence', joined with the 'Crowned Hope' and 'Three Fires' lodges to form a new lodge called 'New-Crowned Hope', which met for the first time on 14 January 1786. Mozart is referred to as a master in the new lodge's records, but it is not known when he reached that grade.

The first and last of the dates mentioned in the above paragraph mark Mozart's first thirteen months as a Freemason, and also the period in which the great majority of his music for the Viennese lodges was composed, for the only work still to come was the 'Little' Masonic Cantata *Laut verkünde unsre Freude,* K. 623, of autumn 1791—if, that is, works which were concerned with Masonic themes but not composed directly for the lodges (like, notably, *Die Zauberflöte*) are left out of the reckoning. In the first thirteen months, on the other hand, Mozart wrote the song 'Die Gesellenreise', K. 468 (probably for the occasion of his father's promotion to the grade of 'Geselle' or journeyman), two songs (K. 483 and 484) for the first meeting of 'New-Crowned Hope', and furthermore the cantata *Die Maurerfreude* ('Masons' Joy'), K. 471, which was performed on 24 April

1785 at a ceremony of the 'Crowned Hope' lodge in honour of Court Councillor Ignaz von Born. (Born, the Master of the 'True Concord' lodge, had been made a Knight of the Realm for his invention of a new, more economical method of smelting.[1]) The outstanding work of this period, however, is the Masonic Funeral Music, K. 477, the definitive verison of which was performed on 7 December 1785, but it seems to have occupied Mozart for several months before that.

Mozart's entry for the Masonic Funeral Music in his catalogue of his works reads (under 1785): 'In the month of July. Masonic Funeral Music, on the deaths of Brothers Mecklenburg and Esterházy; 2 violini, 2 viole, 1 Clarinett, 1 Bassethorn, 2 oboe, 2 Corni e Basso.' The final version of the work has two additional basset horns and a double basson—but more about that below. The first thing to note is that brothers Mecklenburg and Esterházy did not die until November 1785, so that the work cannot have been thought of as 'funeral music' until four months later than the date in Mozart's catalogue.[2] Duke Georg August zu Mecklenburg-Strelitz, a major-general in the Austrian army, was a member of the 'Three Eagles' lodge: he died on 6 November 1785. Franz, Count Esterházy von Galantha, Court Councillor at the Hungarian-Transylvanian Chancery, died on the following day; he was a member of the 'Crowned Hope' lodge, one of the three which had been amalgamated to form the 'New-Crowned Hope' lodge; Hugo von Hofmannsthal borrowed his nickname, 'Quinquin', for Oktavian in *Der Rosenkavalier*. A first ceremony to commemorate both men was held on 17 November, and a second in honour of the duke took place on 7 December.

The discrepancy between 'July' and November is puzzling. If Mozart wrote the work in July 1785, then he did not write it as 'Funeral Music, on the deaths of Brothers Mecklenburg and Esterházy'. On the other hand, it is more than probable that it was performed at the first of the two commemorative ceremonies, with exactly the forces listed in the catalogue, and therefore it came into existence in that form shortly after 7 November, with an eye to performance on 17 November. The parts for the three additional instruments were presumably composed in late November or early December, in connection with the preparations for the second ceremony. That at least explains the difference between the list of instruments in Mozart's catalogue and the eventual scoring.

[1] See Deutsch, *MDB*, under 24 Apr. 1785 and 17 Aug. 1785.
[2] P. A. Autexier, 'Wann wurde die Maurerische Trauermusik uraufgeführt?', *MJb* 1984–5, 6–8.

The Masonic Funeral Music is regarded as the greatest achievement among Mozart's Masonic works.[3] Cast in a single movement, sixty-nine bars long, it is also the shortest of those which involve an orchestra, and only the addition of the extra instruments makes its orchestra significantly larger than that required for the two Masonic cantatas. Different aspects work together on purely musical planes: Mozart begins the work with a passage for the wind alone, in which suspensions play a central structural part, as held notes swell and ebb away through the length of a bar, and then resolve in a single crotchet. Strings enter (headed by the first violins, with the bass following later) until suddenly the oboes and the clarinet detach themselves from the ensemble for the middle section of the work. They intone a Gregorian chant associated with the Lamentations of Jeremiah, with a tradition going back to ancient Jewish sacred music. Mozart had encountered this melody at least once in a different context: Michael Haydn had set the 'Te decet hymnus Deus in Sion' to it in his requiem mass for Archbishop Schrattenbach in Salzburg in 1771 (in his own Requiem, in 1791, Mozart also set that text to a borrowed tune, a Magnificat in his case). Mozart may also have known the melody in the non-ecclesiastical context of Joseph Haydn's Symphony No. 26 (subtitled 'lamentatione'). At all events, he appears to have gone back to its roots, for he wrote it out on a sketch-sheet in its basic liturgical form, without the repetition of notes that was necessary if a different text was to be fitted to it, as in the case of Michael Haydn's requiem. Yet notes of the melody are repeated, as if it needed to fit a text, in the form Mozart gives it in the wordless Masonic Funeral Music; it is hardly likely that the repetitions are the fruit of purely aesthetic considerations, and even less likely that they are there by accident.

Why did Mozart refer to Lamentations? Does the knowledge of Michael Haydn's requiem prevent us from seeing a particular symbolic significance in the background to Mozart's choice of the melody? Philippe A. Autexier has pointed out that the subject of Lamentations is the destruction of the Temple of Solomon. Reference to this in a rite in a Masonic lodge, he writes, is 'indicative, incidentally, of Mozart's syncretism [and] can occur only at the elevation of a brother whose temple has been destroyed'.[4] Was the Masonic Funeral Music perhaps, therefore, originally intended for some other, non-funerary occasion?

[3] Landon, *Golden Years*, 118.   [4] Autexier, 'Wann wurde . . . uraufgeführt?'

On 12 August 1785 Mozart attended a meeting of the 'True Concord' lodge at which the Venetian lodge-secretary Carl von König was received into the lodge. König's lodge in Venice had been suppressed by the Inquisition in May and he had been expelled from the city. It is possible that a commission to compose a work to be performed at König's admission to a Viennese lodge was given to Mozart soon after König's arrival in Vienna, and that he had a relatively long time in which to write it, as the ceremony had to be delayed until Ignaz von Born returned from a stay at a spa.

Autexier reasons that the work was performed on that occasion with a vocal contribution: it is the only plausible practical reason for the rhythm of the woodwind theme and the note repetitions. He conjectures that two verses from Chapter 3 of Lamentations fit the melody in the form Mozart gave it:

Verse 15: Replevit me amaratudinibus inebriavit me absinthio (He hath filled me with bitterness, he hath made me drunken with wormwood)

Verse 54: Inundaverunt aquae super caput meum dixi perii (Waters flowed over my head; then I said, I am cut off)

These verses certainly give a concrete sense to the details of the woodwind melody, and yet the symbolism in Mozart's setting was not so specific as to prevent the piece from being put to use again as funeral music.[5] Mozart saw no need to fit a new text, more appropriate to the second occasion, to the woodwind melody (and presumably none of his Masonic brothers asked for it), and the associations of the melody (and the rhythm derived from the original text) were not found to be inappropriate in the new context. For Mozart and his brother Masons, therefore, even if they had the destruction of the 'temple' in Venice in mind at the first performance, the *Maurerische Trauermusik* was a fitting piece to be played on any solemn, mournful occasion. ('Trauermusik' is conventionally 'music for a funeral' but 'Trauer' means 'mourning'; in the nature of things, both words are customarily linked with funerals, but the association is not exclusive.)

Autexier's hypotheses close the circle described by the work's early history. Mozart could have composed it in July, but for one reason or another he did not enter it in his catalogue until some time later. There

---

[5] P. A. Autexier, *Mozart & Liszt sub rosa* (Poitiers, 1984), 23–6 (on the musical symbolism), 29 (on the numero-symbolic significance of the work's 69 bars as the sum of the verse-numbers 15 and 54).

were other works that year that he did not enter at the time of their writing: the G minor Piano Quartet, K. 478, composed in October, and an aria he wrote for insertion in Francesco Bianchi's opera *La villanella rapita*. When he sat down to bring his catalogue up to date, perhaps in mid-November, he remembered that he had composed the aria on 5 November, and also that he had written the piece of Masonic music in July, perhaps because the occasion for which it was composed had great importance for him, both as composer and as Mason. By the time he wrote the entry in the catalogue, however, events had overtaken the work's origins and he thought of it as the commemorative piece for brothers Mecklenburg and Esterházy. Mozart may have worked on the Piano Quartet over quite a long period of time (more of that below, in Chapter 29). According to the autograph it was finished on 16 October. Its entry in the catalogue comes between those for the Masonic Music (dated 'July') and the aria (dated 5 November), and it is dated 'ditto'—implying 'July', but perhaps meaning no more than 'around the same time'.

24

The Composer's Workshop: The Genesis of the A major Piano Concerto, K. 488

Opening the door of an artist's workshop and peering inside can smack of sacrilege; the observer is embarrassed to do anything so crass as watch the stirrings of genius with an assumption of cool objectivity, perhaps taking notes, as if creation were something that could be reduced to a mathematical formula. Yet certain works seem to challenge us to delve into the processes which brought them into existence, and not be satisfied with studying them only as a finished whole.

The composition scores of larger works often reveal composers changing their minds about matters of detail before arriving at the final version, but in the case of Mozart's A major Concerto, K. 488, the things that were changed were fundamentals, affecting substantial sections of the work. It is a classic example of how far Mozart's creative processes were concerned with conceptional questions before he settled on the final realization of a piece. Like every other concerto by Mozart, K. 488 begins with a first movement in typical concerto form; the middle movement is one of the few that he composed in a minor key (F sharp minor) and only the second that he started with an unaccompanied solo passage; the finale, as in so many other Mozart concertos, is a rondo. The very key is striking: A major meant that trumpets could not be used—but clarinets could; on the other hand, there are no oboes, although they are included far more often than not in Mozart's concertos and symphonies. Admittedly, there is nothing about the make-up of the ensemble, the tonality (including the mode of the middle movement), or the fact that the Adagio begins with a solo, to arouse special attention, but they turn out to repay closer investigation.

The first thing we should look at in the composer's workshop are his tools: paper, pen, and ink. Paper (not only music paper) is usually bought in fairly substantial quantities, and as soon as one lot is exhausted the user buys more. Paper of the eighteenth century often carries a watermark which identifies its maker. Different papermills had different marks, and they could not go on using exactly the same ones forever: when a mould had to be replaced it invariably meant a slight change in the appearance of the mark. It can happen that the score of a single work on a large scale (such as a keyboard concerto) will turn out to have been written down on sheets of paper bearing different marks. If sheets of paper having the same provenance are found in the context of more than one work, and if the writer has conscientiously dated the separate pieces of work—as Mozart frequently did—then the paper-types alone already provide enough evidence for us to reconstruct, with almost forensic certainty, a reliable historical framework of the chronology not only of the writer's use of paper but also of the progress of his work, for this historical framework is capable of showing when an individual piece of work was interrupted and resumed only months later—when the old stock of paper was exhausted and a new one in use.

Composers need music paper, and in some cases further information about the history of a work's composition can be gleaned from the number of staves on a paper-type, and from whether the staves were drawn by hand or by machine. The manuscript of the A major Concerto is uninformative in that particular respect. Finally, however, the appearance of the actual writing on the page can highlight the stages in which a score was written down:[1] it will vary according to the sharpness or bluntness of a quill pen at different times; the shade or density of the colour of the ink is another factor contributing to the impression of variability, depending on the exact mixture of the ingredients each time the ink-well was refilled. The autograph of the A major Concerto reveals beyond reasonable doubt that it is indeed a composition score: we can see that Mozart first wrote down the melody parts (principally, that is, the music for the soloist and the first violins), together with the bass and essential structural elements of the accompaniment, which could be filled in in detail later, and brief, important outlines of subordinate parts in the course of the complex of melody parts.

The first important question to be raised in reconstructing the genesis of the A major Concerto, K. 488, concerns the paper. Mozart wrote the date 2 March 1786 on the first page, but the paper he used for the first half of the first movement (including the dated side, that is) is one that he had stopped using months earlier than that. Alan Tyson, whose study of Mozart's manuscripts includes this concerto, sees no alternative to assigning

---

[1] H. Beck in NMA V/15, vii, g/6–8.

the first stage of the first movement to 1784, or early 1785 at the latest;[2] from that it would follow that in spring 1786 Mozart only finished a draft that had been started at least a year earlier. The completion was executed on paper that he had had to hand since approximately December 1785— that is, over the three-month period preceding the completion of the whole work.

But the rest of the work was not polished off in a single burst of creative energy. The first clue to that is the fact that the numbering of the sheets starts again at '1' at the beginning of the third movement. Did Mozart compose the Rondo before he had finished the Adagio (so that he did not know exactly what number to use)? Or did he perhaps sketch the Rondo quite independently of the rest of the concerto? That is not all: there are four sketches from the same period, for slow and fast movements, all of which could have gone into this concerto. Scarcely one is longer than twenty bars, and they are all of the first sections of movements, albeit in a variety of forms; three of them (K^6 488b–d) could be the openings of a rondo-finale, the fourth (K^6 488a) that of a slow movement. These are the most external of all the types of evidence about the detailed progress of the concerto; if we look deeper into the source material, some of the confusion that follows the first look begins to clear.

There is inner stylistic evidence to support Tyson's view that Mozart began the concerto in 1784. The solo sections of the first movement (up to the characteristic first tutti interjection) are laid out in a manner comparable to those of the G major and B flat major concertos, K. 453 and 456, which Mozart finished between April and September 1784, that is, between eighteen months and two years before he finished the A major Concerto. In all three works the solo exposition remains remarkably close to the thematic material which has already been introduced in the opening tutti; virtually no new material is introduced by the soloist unless we count ornamentation.[3]

The first creative phase finished in the middle of the tutti which closes the exposition, about 145 bars into the movement's total of 313. At that stage Mozart had written down only the parts carrying the substance of the music—which made it much easier for him to get back into the work later. As first conceived, the movement was to be for the same orchestra as the earlier concertos of 1784, and among the wind he had allowed for flute, two oboes, two bassoons, and two horns. But his ideas about how a

---

[2] Tyson, *Mozart*, 152.   [3] Küster, *Formale Aspekte*, 156.

keyboard concerto might sound continued to develop, and when he went back to K. 488 that orchestration no longer corresponded to what his inspiration currently prompted. He used a knife to scrape away the ink where he had reserved a stave for two oboes and substituted the direction '2 clarinetti'. Only the mark of the scraping and the new direction are now to be seen, of course, and writing the clarinet parts on the stave reserved for the oboes presented few difficulties. There were two places where Mozart had already written phrases which he had originally intended to be played by the oboes; having the clarinets play them instead was no problem, except with regard to the actual notation. Oboes are in C; when they are required to play in A major their part has to have three sharps (as does a keyboard part). Clarinets of the kind needed for this concerto are in A: the scale of their basic fingering is A major (where the oboe's is C major), so that giving their part three sharps, which would be tonally correct, will confuse the player more than it helps him. The part of an A clarinet is therefore written as fingered (both in Mozart's day and ever since): every player knows that it is notated a third higher than it is meant to sound, but regards that as fair exchange for clear notation. When the work is in A major, there are no sharps or flats in the key signature of the part given to an A clarinet: the player fingers a part that looks like C major while the instrument's construction takes care of the production of sounds in A major. The consequences of this for Mozart, going back to work on his A major Concerto, were that he had to alter what he had written earlier for oboes; he therefore put brackets round the original notation and wrote the 'correct' version, transposed for the clarinets, on a blank page further on in the score. This discrepancy in the notation contributes to the proof that the direction scratched out at the beginning of the score was for oboes.

This change of plan obviously occurred at a relatively late stage of the concerto's genesis. Indications to support this are supplied by other comparable compositions of the 1780s: the only other keyboard concertos in which Mozart uses clarinets are those in E flat major (K. 482, composed in December 1785) and C minor (K. 491, March 1786), and the only other concerto of any kind to have them is the one for horn, K. 447, which was probably written in 1787.[4] Could it have been the composition of the E flat major Concerto that gave Mozart the idea of going back to his earlier draft, which had been gathering dust for eighteen months, and remodelling it in a similar style?

---

[4] Tyson, *Mozart*, 247.

It cannot be ruled out altogether that for a time he continued to think of going ahead with oboes in the ensemble. One of the four sketches associated with this concerto, as mentioned above, comprises eleven bars of a keyboard part (K⁶ 488*d*). As with the first stage of work on the concerto, he laid out the page so that all the orchestral parts could be filled in in their proper places above and below the solo part, and the number of staves reserved for that purpose is that which would be needed if the sketch was indeed conceived in connection with K. 488. Mozart did not actually specify the individual instruments alongside the staves, but what indicates that he still had oboes in mind is the very carefreeness with which he wrote the sketch down. In all the other unfinished sketches associated with the A major Concerto he routinely wrote the appropriate clef, key signature, and time signature for each part. Once he had decided to use clarinets he always included a key signature appropriate to a part for the A clarinet (as described above)—even when he did not write a single note for the instrument in that particular sketch; perhaps it served as a general reminder. In this one particular sketch, however, he did not do so, and the obvious conclusion is that it dates from a time when he still intended to have oboes and not clarinets.

The other three sketches all, on this evidence, date from the later stage, after Mozart had decided to use clarinets. Including the versions of the Adagio and finale which he eventually wrote, he considered at least five possibilities for this concerto around the end of 1785 or the start of 1786: there was one alternative for the slow movement, and at least two (three, if we count the 'pre-clarinet' sketch) for the finale (see Ex. 24.1).

The slow movement may in fact be one of the last parts of the concerto to have been written. As stated earlier, it is in F sharp minor (A major's relative minor), and begins with a passage for the soloist alone. The alternative version in the sketch (K⁶ 488*a*) is in the subdominant, D major, and opens with the orchestra playing, apparently without the soloist. The use of the subdominant (more often than the dominant) and an orchestral opening are standard features of the middle movements of Mozart's concertos—see, for example, the one in C major, K. 467, the last-but-one concerto he composed before the A major. Its immediate predecessor, the E flat major Concerto, K. 482, has a minor-key middle movement, as does the earlier B flat major work, K. 456. On the other hand, Mozart had only once before composed a middle movement that began with the soloist playing without any accompaniment, in the D minor Concerto, K. 466— not, that is, either of the A major Concerto's two immediate predecessors.

Ex. 24.1. Piano Concerto in A major, K. 488. Openings of movements in the final version, and sketches possibly representing alternative openings.

(*a*) 1st movement: Allegro, A major.

(*b*) 2nd movement: Adagio, F sharp minor.

(*c*) 3rd movement: Allegro assai, A major.

(*d*) Alternative for the 2nd movement, D major, K⁶ 488*a* (violin 1).

(*e*) Alternative I for the 3rd movement, K⁶ 488*d*.

(*f*) Alternative II for the 3rd movement, K⁶ 488*c*.

(*g*) Alternative III for the 3rd movement, K⁶ 488*b*.

Thus the combination of a minor key and an opening by the soloist alone is completely new. Of the two features, the latter is especially significant here, because Mozart wrote only one more concerto (in C major K. 503) in which the middle movement was *not* begun by the soloist playing alone. Had Mozart already finished the E flat major Concerto (on 16 December 1785) and gone back to the A major work before he had the idea of combining the minor key (as in the E flat major) with the solo opening (as in the earlier D minor Concerto), and was it then that he cast aside the version he had already sketched (with the major key and the orchestral opening)?

Ex. 24.1. *Continued*

The D major sketch for a slow movement is in 3/4 time, while the finished Adagio in F sharp minor is in 6/8; 6/8, however, is also the time signature in one of the sketches (K⁶ 488c) that appear to have been drafted for the last movement. This gives the opportunity to establish another stage in Mozart's compositional process. Having two consecutive movements in the same tempo would have lacked the desirable contrast, especially as there are also motivic similarities between this sketch and the F sharp minor version of the slow movement. This sketch would have followed well enough after the 3/4 of the D major sketch, however—was it the dawning of the F sharp minor idea which led to its abandonment?

One sketch remains for us to consider: again, it appears to have been for the Rondo. Its tempo is 4/4, alla breve, like the final version of the movement. It is likely, therefore, that it represents a stage when Mozart was close to deciding exactly what he wanted but still capable of hesitation. Something similar happened in the case of the D minor Concerto, K. 466, where there is a sketch on the autograph itself of an alternative idea for the last movement; that too is in the same metre. The sketch K^6 488*b* was probably, therefore, drafted not long before the final version of the A major Conerto's finale—but it appears that that may have been before Mozart had finished the middle movement, because he numbered the finale's pages from '1', as mentioned earlier.

The above represents one reconstruction of the way Mozart could have arrived at his eventual—and undoubtedly satisfactory—choice of the last two movements in the concerto, but it is immediately obvious that there are other possibilities which posterity would probably have found equally satisfactory: a D major middle movement followed by the 6/8 Rondo, or the F sharp minor Adagio which Mozart realized, followed by the alla breve finale which he only sketched—either of these would have been acceptable after the first movement which he had started so much earlier. But even the first movement acquired traits in its final form which it probably would not have had if it had been finished in 1784. For a few months in 1784–5 Mozart experimented with linking the recapitulation more closely to the opening tutti rather than to the solo exposition (which was still the usual practice in concerto form). This may have been because he saw possibilities in the fact that the opening tutti and the recapitulation operate under the same harmonic terms—both are firmly in the home key.[5] The solo exposition is laid out in the A major Concerto (as in K. 453 and 456) in a way that indicates that he would have repeated the experiment there if he had finished the movement before setting it aside. The procedure reached its most extreme manifestation in the E flat major Concerto, K. 482, and after that it obviously lost all interest for Mozart. Perhaps he believed that he had exhausted its potential, and therefore never wanted to use that particular technique again. At all events, when he came to write the recapitulation in the first movement of the A major Concerto he completely ignored the idea that had preoccupied him at the time when he started the movement. Thus, even within the opening movement, the concerto took a fundamentally different course from the one that could

---

[5] Küster, *Formale Aspekte*, 154–5.

have been expected if its writing had been continuous, and the development and maturing of Mozart's ideas on concerto form are highlighted in the realization of its three individual movements.

The Mozart scholar Alfred Einstein once speculated that Mozart sometimes had to take several trial runs at blocking the movements of a work before arriving at a version that he was content to carry out and complete.[6] As Christoph Wolff has shown more recently, with reference to the string quartets, it was a little more reflective than that.[7] For Mozart, the individual movements of a work had to stand in a meaningful relationship to each other, and therefore if a fundamentally new aspect came to alter one movement it had consequences for the others as well. It looks as if Mozart's decision in favour of a slow movement in 6/8 ruled out a finale in the same metre. This demonstrates that, although he numbered its pages from '1', he did not compose the definitive finale in a vacuum but wrote it with the character and specifications of the preceding parts of the work in mind, even if he had not yet finished them. Einstein's theory of a 'trial run' does perhaps, however, hold good at least in respect of the step to that definitive version of the finale from the sketch, K^6 488b, in which the crucial choice of tempo had already been made.

It is clear that the decisions were all made within a very short space of time. All the abandoned sketches were written on paper of the same type as the last stages of the concerto autograph.[8] Mozart began to use this paper-type at a point in or around December 1785, and his stock of it lasted him about a year. He did not merely finish the concerto in the first three months of that period, therefore; he also took the final decision to have clarinets instead of oboes and conceived the idea of writing the slow movement in a minor key, for the sketch for one in D major is already written on the same paper-type.

Mozart had other work in hand during the same period, not least the preparations for the first performances of *Der Schauspieldirektor* and *Figaro*. Two things about these other activities were learnt from the manuscripts associated with the A major Concerto: one is that Mozart thought of revising *Davide penitente*, for the oratorio's title appears at the top of the sketch for a D major middle movement. (The oratorio was first performed in the spring of 1785, but Mozart was not using this paper as far back as

[6] In the preface to the *Köchel-Verzeichnis*, 3rd edn. (Leipzig, 1937), pp. xxxix–xl.

[7] Wolff, 'Creative Exuberance', esp. 197–8.

[8] Tyson, *Mozart*, 140–1, 150–2; I am indebted to Alan Tyson for information about K^6 488d, conveyed in a letter.

that.) Secondly, he also returned at this time to his earlier Piano Concerto in A major, K. 414, because he wrote down some cadenzas for it on the same sheet as the transcription for clarinets of the fragments of music for oboes which had survived from his first phase of work on the later concerto. He obviously jotted the clarinet parts down to serve as an *aide-mémoire* while continuing with other work, because, as mentioned above, he later inserted them in the score, on an empty side at the end of the second movement. It must have been his last act in composing the concerto. To that extent the manuscripts of the A major Concerto, K. 488, open the door not only to the history of the work itself but also to the daily routine on Mozart's desk.

25

Satisfaction Deferred: *Le nozze di Figaro*, K. 492

Mozart's creative circumstances can be seen to change fundamentally during the course of 1786. On 7 February a new opera by him reached the stage for the first time in four years, when the one-acter *Der Schauspieldirektor* (completed on 3 February) was partnered with Salieri's *Prima la musica, poi le parole* (First the Music, Then the Words) to make a full evening's entertainment. At about the same time the torrent of great keyboard concertos that he had been pouring out since 1784 slowed to a trickle: after the C minor Concerto, K. 491, finished on 24 March, the next was the C major, K. 503, which he completed in December on the basis of an earlier draft. He wrote only two more keyboard concertos in the remaining five years of his life: the D major, K. 537, and the B flat major, K. 595. The symphony that he composed towards the end of 1786—the 'Prague', K. 504—was the first for three years (since the 'Linz', K. 425). From that time onwards opera and the symphony came to dominate his productivity. The 'Prague' was followed by the three late symphonies (K. 543, 550, and 551), and *Der Schauspieldirektor* by five more works for the stage, beginning with the three to librettos by Lorenzo Da Ponte: *Figaro* (1786), *Don Giovanni* (1787), and *Così fan tutte* (1790). Let us not forget that during the same period Mozart also tried his hand at genres in which he had not composed before, above all the string quintet—but we will have to follow that thread separately.

The source of the opera *Le nozze di Figaro* (Figaro's Wedding, a more precise translation than the familiar 'Marriage') was the play *La Folle Journée, ou Le Mariage de Figaro* by Pierre Auguste Caron de Beaumarchais.[1] Mozart composed it without a commission for it: a rather pointless enterprise, because in those days operas had fundamentally very little prospect indeed of being staged without one. It is clear, however, that Mozart could

---

[1] On *Figaro* in general, see Kunze, *Mozarts Opern*, 222–318, and Carter, *Le nozze*. On the work's genesis, see Kunze, 230, and Tyson, *Mozart*, 114–24 and 290–327. Da Ponte published his memoirs in Italian in New York in the 1820s (Eng. tr., London and Philadelphia, 1929).

count on some support from the Emperor, Joseph II, which gave him an incentive. The libretto was the first product of Lorenzo Da Ponte's amazingly fruitful collaboration with Mozart (unless he was also the author of the text of *Davide penitente*). Da Ponte, seven years older than Mozart, was the son of a Venetian Jewish family which converted to Christianity in 1763. Ten years after that he took holy orders, but loose living led to his being banished from Venice for twelve years in 1779. He moved to Dresden, where the court was Catholic and cultivated Italian art and music, and there he met the poet to the court theatre, Caterino Mazzolà. This seems to be the only reason Joseph II could have had for appointing him to the corresponding post in Vienna in 1783, for he clearly had not written a single dramatic work at that date. His first opera libretto was for Salieri (*Il ricco d'un giorno*, 1784). His second, *Il burbero di buon cuore* (1786), for Vicente Martín y Soler, scored an immediate and huge success, and he must have produced his next two very soon afterwards. They were *Il finto cieco* for Giuseppe Gazzaniga, who shortly afterwards beat Mozart to the post with a *Don Giovanni*, and *Le nozze di Figaro*—only the fourth libretto he had written.

The idea of basing the opera on Beaumarchais's play appears to have been Mozart's. That, at least, is what Da Ponte says in his memoirs, and there is no reason to suppose that, had it been the other way round, he would have concealed it. It was a bold, even risky choice: only a short time earlier a performance of the play itself had been banned. The censors' objections were avoided in the case of the opera by Da Ponte's omitting the most obviously subversive parts of the text from his own version. It is also conceivable that in this milder form the libretto fitted in with the reforming ideas that the Emperor was working to impose on the Austrian state: given that the nobility was the only section of the population able, in any large numbers, to afford the high admission prices for opera, Mozart and Da Ponte's work held up to them the evil of the 'privilege of the first night', the custom which gave a nobleman the right to enjoy a newly married female servant on her wedding night. (The Emperor believed—probably correctly—that he himself was reasonably blameless in that particular area.) The spoken theatre was more easily affordable by a wider public, so that there *Figaro* might perhaps indeed have fomented revolutionary unrest.[2] But the significance of this one particular socio-historical aspect of the work should not be overestimated, or else it is hard to explain

[2] Braunbehrens, *Mozart in Vienna*, 209–15.

the work's popularity at court theatres throughout the remainder of the eighteenth century.

It is not very clear why the court theatre suddenly turned to Mozart at this particular time, especially as the move resulted not only in the contracts for *Der Schauspieldirektor* and *Figaro* but also in more mundane tasks such as the two numbers for insertion in the Viennese production of Francesco Bianchi's opera *La villanella rapita* that Mozart wrote in November 1785. An odd feature is that the approach was made at a time when the court theatre's schedules were full to bursting. Salieri's position was particularly strong, after the success of his opera *Les Danaïdes* in Paris in 1784; then there was Martín y Soler, who had arrived in Vienna in the early part of 1785, and whose patroness, the wife of the Spanish ambassador, was too influential for him to be overlooked when it came to commissioning new operas. To argue that Mozart had no chance of getting an opera put on would perhaps have been more plausible just then than at any other time in his life. And yet his chance came. Was it because the Emperor wanted to prevent Martín (and Salieri) being too dominant? If so, was His Majesty opposed by his own Chief Director of Theatres, Count Rosenberg, on the twofold grounds that his programmes were already full for the season and he was furthermore a member of that same aristocracy which the Emperor was trying to reform? The count could not express his opposition openly, for obvious reasons, but it would be equally understandable if he tried to keep *Figaro* off the stage of the court opera. At all events, Mozart and Da Ponte had to stand firm against the count's resistance up to the première itself; but the Emperor's support would have stiffened their resolve.

The play by Beaumarchais to which 'Figaro's Wedding' forms the sequel was already well known in Vienna, and especially to opera audiences, in the form of Giovanni Paisiello's *Il barbiere di Siviglia* (1782). Initially composed for St Petersburg, this swept Europe and entered the repertoire in Vienna in 1783 (it was still so popular in 1816 that Paisiello's adherents disrupted the first night of Rossini's opera—which was originally called *Almaviva* in the hope of mollifying them). It is conceivable, therefore, that the public—especially the opera-goers—would not have stood for a ban on an operatic version of the sequel; Beaumarchais's play had already been published in Vienna, in 1785, in a German translation which had a motto from the text on the title-page: 'Follies which appear in print only gain esteem in places where they are prevented from circulating freely. Act Five, Scene Three.' (See Pl. 7.)

Der
närrische Tag,
oder die
Hochzeit des Figaro;
ein
Lustspiel in fünf Aufzügen, aus
dem Französischen des
Herrn
Caron von Beaumarchais.

Gedruckte Dummheiten haben nur da einen Werth,
wo man ihren freyen Umlauf hindert. Fünfter Aufzug,
dritter Auftritt.

Wien, 1785.

PL. 7. Cherubino in the garden, on the title-page of Beaumarchais's *La Folle Journée, ou Le Mariage de Figaro*, in the German translation by Johann Rautenstrauch (Vienna, 1785). The motto from Act V is below the vignette.

218

The play attracted other objections, however, which had nothing to do with politics. For example, Leopold Mozart wrote to his daughter:

I have at last had a letter from your brother, dated 2 November, and all of twelve lines long. He begs my pardon, because he has to finish his opera, *Le nozze di Figaro*, post-haste . . . I know the play, it's a very laboured piece, and the translation from the French will certainly have to be liberally altered to make an opera from it, if it is to be effective. God grant that the action will fall out well: I have no doubt that the music will. (11 November 1785)

The 'action' did fall out well, and its construction gave Mozart the chance to develop a thoroughly effective concept for the opera, integrating the drama and the music. Yet the action is based on a very simple premiss: in the duet with which the work opens, Figaro and Susanna are preparing to move into a room conveniently situated between the rooms of their respective employers, Count and Countess Almaviva, so that they can both respond quickly when they are called. The only drawback is that it is equally conveniently situated for the Count to get his hands on Susanna as soon as he has sent Figaro out on some errand. Figaro and Susanna are on the point of marrying, but they still await the permission of the Count, who is doing his best to postpone giving it. The entire action of the opera stems from this situation: Figaro and Susanna use every stratagem they can think of to make the Count give his permission for them to marry as soon as possible, only to be foiled repeatedly by problems of co-ordination: each time Figaro bounds in with an idea he has hatched on his own, he misreads the scene he has interrupted; each time Almaviva has been forced into a corner and is on the point of yielding, a third party hands him yet another excuse for delay.

Mozart contributes a decisive, purely musical element to the exposition of this recurrent situation, in the form of the sequence of tonalities of individual numbers in the work. He starts the Overture in an effervescent D major, and his operas of the Vienna period encourage the assumption that the key of the opening will prove to be the tonal goal to which the work will return at the end (there is a minor exception in *Don Giovanni*, which starts in D minor and ends in D major). Even if the music moves quickly away from the overture's D major in the opening scenes of Act I, the way back to it will clearly have to be found sooner or later; the goal of the action—namely, the wedding of the title—is equally clear, but as it is continually deferred, it is understandable that there must be a link between the parallel dramatic and musical endeavours to find the way, even though both keep encountering failure, until eventually they can be allowed to succeed. There are essentially two choices for each tonal step forward along the way: either arias and ensembles can succeed each other in keys which are very closely related (at the fifth), or the composer can emphasize an unexpected twist in the action by suddenly vaulting into a remote key; the individual numbers can either still follow immediately one after the other, or be linked by recitatives.

In the first act, Mozart is at the furthest possible remove from the goal of reaching D major by fifth-steps in the scene where the page Cherubino confides in Susanna. Cherubino, whom Figaro will a little later precisely characterize as an 'amorous butterfly' ('farfallone amoroso'), presents Susanna with the text of a canzonetta he has written himself and pours out his emotions ('Non so più cosa son, cosa faccio'—'I no longer know what I am or what I'm doing'): in E flat major. After that, the B flat major of the next number, the Trio, is a step in the direction of D major: Almaviva also comes into Susanna's room (while Cherubino quickly hides) but he is surprised there by Basilio, and is forced to hide in his turn; Basilio's innuendos bring him out of his hiding-place, however, but as he fulminates at the music-master he discovers Cherubino. This heaps fuel on his rage, and he has still not recovered when Figaro bursts into the room, accompanied by a chorus of peasant boys and girls whom he has recruited to strew hymeneal flowers about the place, singing in G major. He could not have chosen a worst moment, as the audience can see for itself. G major is the subdominant of D major, the ultimate tonal goal, and it might seem that the end of the opera is in Figaro's grasp. But the G major is premature: in its relationship to the B flat major that went before it it expresses the unexpected; to reach it from B flat major by natural, organic steps, the music should have gone by way of F and C major. The marriage plans are thwarted for the time being, and the act closes in C major with Figaro's great aria 'Non più andrai'—'No longer you'll go' (chasing after the ladies), for the Count has ordered Cherubino into the army.

The main business of the second act, set in the Countess's bedroom, is Figaro and Susanna's second attempt to make the Count give his permission for their wedding. This time they gain an ally in the Countess, who feels neglected by her husband. After her sorrowful entrance aria, Cherubino 'sings' his canzonetta to her (which elicits comments from the Countess and Susanna on its performance—'Che bella voce', 'What a lovely voice'—rather than its content). The arrival of the Count sends Cherubino scurrying into the dressing-room, where he knocks a stool over with a crash that makes the Count demand to know who's in there; having locked the outer door to the Countess's room the Count takes her with him while he goes in search of an implement with which to break open the dressing-room door, and Cherubino seizes his chance to jump out of the window: throughout this scene the music remains in the C major / G major region.

The Count and Countess return and now the Countess admits that it is not Susanna (as she said earlier) but Cherubino who is hiding in the dressing-room. A characteristic situation ensues: the key changes to E flat major, as in the first act. With this, at the furthest possible harmonic remove from D major, the act-finale begins. We can assume that a Mozartian act-finale of that period will end in its tonic, so that D major is not going to be reached this time, either—and yet: a step in the right direction is taken when B flat major is heard as the dressing-room door opens to allow, not Cherubino, but Susanna to emerge (unseen by either of the Almavivas, she had returned to the bedroom before the Count locked the door, saw Cherubino jump out of the window, and took his place in the dressing-room). Once again the path is clear for the action to move by fifths—F major, C major, G major—to the goal of D major, especially as the Count is forced to apologize to his wife for his brusque and boorish behaviour. But the situation remains very delicate and once again it is ruined by Figaro, entering the B flat major environment with his ill-starred G major, to announce the arrival outside of a band of musicians ('Signori, di fuori son già i suonatori'). There is still one outstanding detail, moreover, so far as the Count is concerned: thanks to an anonymous letter he has caught wind of something which he interprets as an intrigue against himself. This was the reason why he came to the Countess's room in the first place: now the letter gives him the chance to seize the advantage again. Instead of Figaro's G major being followed by a D major resolution, Almaviva goes right about and starts interrogating his valet about the document—in C major. By this means he also bridges the gap until an ally comes to his aid in the shape of Antonio the gardener, complaining about damage to his carnations done by some fellow jumping out of the Countess's bedroom window. The key to which Antonio enters is F major—yet another fifth-step backwards away from D major. Mozart constructs Antonio's complaint in two parts, but he loads this conventional aria-form with dramatic potential. Binary arias of this type always move up by a fifth from the tonic to the dominant and then back to the tonic: in the context in which Antonio makes his intervention in *Figaro*, that means initially a step towards the ultimate goal of D major; Mozart uses this to let Figaro score a point by jeering at the gardener's fuddled condition while the music is in C major—but his triumph is short-lived. Again Almaviva turns the tables: 'Or ripetimi' ('Tell me again') he commands Antonio, and the scene continues in accordance with the musical rules, and moves back in the direction that favours the Count, unaffected even by Figaro's claim that it was he who jumped out of the window. Almaviva gains a further advantage when Antonio, in B flat major, hands him the officer's commission which must have fallen out of Cherubino's pocket as he jumped. Once again Figaro's quick wits come to his aid, as Susanna whispers to him that it is the commission, and that the seal is missing, from which Figaro is able to concoct a tale that explains how he happened to have the document on him. Once again the music has reached the midpoint of a binary structure, so that it is once again in the dominant (F major) of the current tonic, and Figaro is striving once again to win his cause—musically, at least, a vain endeavour. Almaviva has no difficulty in finding the way back to B flat major, and the return to E flat major cannot be far off: it arrives with the entrance of Marcellina, Don Basilio, and Dr Bartolo, bearing a promissory note signed by Figaro, in which he undertook either to repay a large sum of money lent him by Marcellina, or to marry her. If he marries Marcellina, he cannot marry Susanna—and with that the second act ends. So far, then, Figaro has had two practically identical shots at outwitting his master, but both, being premature, have failed in practically identical ways, although the first failure was spread over a string of separate numbers, and the second developed through the course of an elaborate act-finale—the opening key of which gave notice that the attempt was doomed from the start. It is time for a fundamental change of plan.

The new plan is inaugurated by the Countess and Susanna: the former will put on her maid's clothes and take her place in a meeting with the Count later that evening. They do not have an opportunity to explain the plan to Figaro, and the Count's suspicions are aroused when Susanna does what she can by telling Figaro only that he has already 'won the case without a lawyer'. The first case to come up, however, is the legal hearing concerning Figaro's debt to Marcellina, which is decided in his favour when it is discovered that he is the illegitimate son of Marcellina and Bartolo. On the spot the older couple decide to get married, change sides, and join the camp opposed to Almaviva.

The finale of Act III underlines the change of plan musically: the ill-omened sequence E flat–B flat–G– . . . which has led to the lovers' defeats in the earlier acts does not even get under way this time, and formally, too, fully developed vocal numbers are avoided. On the surface, the scene is permeated with the festive atmosphere of the ceremony in which the Count gives his consent to the marriages of Marcellina and Bartolo, and of Susanna and Figaro (while Susanna slips into his hand the note inviting him to the tryst in the garden). The events cannot all unfold according to their own lights, for they are penned in by the background music: the procession of the wedding parties, the chorus of peasants and huntsmen singing their congratulations, and the Fandango (for which Mozart had recourse to an original Spanish air). The situation is essentially the one which Figaro attempted to set up in the course of Act II: 'Publicity compels everyone to behave ceremonially'.[3] The circumstances are different now, however, and there are no surprises, no tables are turned. Quite the contrary: all the leading actors have something to hide, and what they say does not go beyond snatches of recitative in the overall progress of the ceremony. The music generated by the 'publicity' provides a screen behind which the secrets can remain hidden.

Secrecy is swept away at last in Act IV. Figaro, it is true, remains in a state of uncertainty for a time, because even now he is not informed of the plan which is to lead to the Count's rendezvous with his own wife. But under the surface Mozart makes it clear that Susanna really has 'won the case without a lawyer'. Her aria 'Deh vieni' ('Come, my beloved') immediately before the finale begins is in the F major that has previously been disastrously side-stepped by Figaro's entrances—although it was only on second thoughts that Mozart put it in that key. Formally, the situation at the start of the finale is similar to that at the start of the Act II finale, but it is in D major, an unmistakable sign that this time things will reach their desired resolution. Mozart makes it doubly certain as the evening wears on. Figaro witnesses the Count's success in wooing 'Susanna' (the disguised Countess) to music in E flat major, the key furthest from the realization of his hopes. E flat major is followed, as usual, by B flat major when Figaro recognizes his Susanna disguised as the Countess, and is then caught making passionate advances to her by the Count—who thinks it is his wife. On previous occasions it was Figaro's role to disrupt B flat major with an overhasty step into G major, but this time it falls to the Count to do so, as he shouts for help. Things have turned out even worse than he had foreseen in his great aria in Act III ('Vedrò, mentr'io sospiro . . .' 'While I

---

[3] Kunze, *Mozarts Opern*, 263.

sigh, shall I see my servant happy?'—in an apparently lordly D major): Figaro has not only won Susanna from him, but has seduced the Countess too! Mozart allows him to remember and revive a phrase from the aria as he denounces 'the faithless woman' (see Ex. 25.1). Figaro, it seems, has gone too far and will never be able to marry Susanna now. But then the real Countess reveals herself, the Count is forced to beg her pardon in front of the entire household (Pl. 8), and thanks to his precipitateness in choosing G major the last step to D major can be taken.

Leopold Mozart was perhaps justified in his misgivings about the 'action'. The exposition in the first act is crystal-clear, but it offers no prospect of an eventual resolution; the second act is no different. The entire third act and most of the fourth have to pass before Figaro grasps that there has been a change in his fortunes. Mozart transcends these problems by exploiting their musical potential to the full: not only in a point like abandoning verbal expression in the finale of Act III, but repeatedly in the use of the sequence E flat–B flat–G–... to convey the role of the unexpected in the drama as a whole. At the end of Act I, which does not have a through-composed finale but takes the form of a series of separate numbers, interspersed with recitative, this sequence is unfurled casually,

Ex. 25.1. *Le nozze di Figaro.*
(a) Act III, No. 17, the Count's aria, bars 70–5.
(b) Act IV, finale, the Count, bars 375–81.

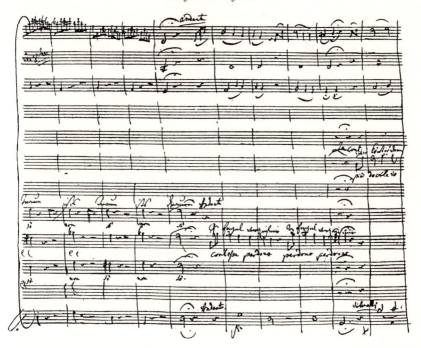

PL. 8. *Le nozze di Figaro*, Act IV, finale, bars 416–25, in Mozart's autograph. (The Count asks the Countess's pardon; German text added in another hand.)

almost as if by accident. But from there it is a clear, dramatic, evolutionary step to the finale of Act II, where the same construction is placed according to standard musical rules, in the tonal integration of a regular operatic act-finale. It is known from the outset that it will return to the E flat major which will not bring about the desired dramatic resolution, and that the path must be retraced from the over-hasty G major to E flat major, step by relentless step. The third act, like the first, has no formal finale, but this time round Mozart uses every means to show that 'Figaro's wedding' is in the balance. The end of the fourth act is once again constructed according to the rules, within the strict framework of a true finale: but this time it starts in D major, and the E flat–B flat–G sequence, though a standard feature, is integrated into the framework and directed towards a different goal from the one it had in Act II. These constructions take on, therefore, something of the character of a game with the compositional rules as they affect finales: Mozart obeys them, of course, but interprets them in a way which shows that they can serve a dramatic purpose; the musical rules, enhanced by a sequence of tonalities which can express the unexpected, become an operatic stage-property. Such developments could already be discerned in *Idomeneo* and *Die Entführung*, and after a gap of several years Mozart picked them up where he had set them down.

26

Records of a Friendship: The Horn Concerto, K. 495, and Other Works

'I can't resist making fools of people', Mozart confessed to his wife in a letter he sent her from Vienna while she was taking the waters at Baden. He had just told her of a trick he had played on a friend of his, by having himself announced as 'an old and good friend from Rome'; the victim had sent word 'that he would not keep me long, and meanwhile the poor fool dressed himself up in his Sunday best, his finest coat and his hair magnificently dressed—you can imagine how we all laughed at him' (25 June 1791).

The butt of this practical joke was Joseph Leutgeb (1732–1811), and it was not the only one Mozart played on him; but the two knew each other too well for any risk of hurt feelings. The acquaintance went back to Mozart's childhood: the family had been on their way to Paris for ten weeks when Leopold Mozart included in a letter to their friends in Salzburg a list of the people his son had said he was missing, and the name of Leutgeb is among them (20 August 1763). At that time Leutgeb was a horn-player in the Salzburg court orchestra. Later, in the early part of 1773, he met the Mozarts in Milan, when they were extending their stay for the première of *Lucio Silla* as long as they could, while he had been given leave to visit Rome (in Milan, Leutgeb stayed with the German painter Martin Knoller, who spent several summers in the 1770s painting the frescoes in Balthasar Neumann's last work, the abbey church at Neresheim, near Ulm). It appears that Leutgeb shared the Mozarts' dislike of Archbishop Colloredo: at all events, writing to his son in Mannheim nearly five years later, Leopold Mozart reported that 'Herr Leutgeb, who has now bought a little snail's house on credit, with a cheesemonger's licence, in a suburb of Vienna, wrote to you, and me, shortly after you left . . . he wants a concerto from you. But he will know by now that you're no longer in Salzburg' (1 December 1777). The 'cheesemonger's licence' seems to have been acquired primarily as a hedge against old age, when infirmity might put a stop to horn-playing.[1]

Mozart obviously remembered the request three years later. Within the first few days of his arrival in Vienna from Munich, in 1781, he sketched the first movement and the rondo of a horn concerto (K. 370*b* and 371), but did not work up either of them. The fact that later, after Mozart's death, Leutgeb knew nothing of the sketches' existence does not mean that Mozart did not have him in mind when he started them; as interpreter, he would not have needed to know of the work until it was finished. Mozart may have composed the Horn Quintet, K. 407, in place of the abandoned concerto. He finished his first concerto for the horn (K. 417) in May 1783; this was followed by a second (K. 495) in June 1786, and a third (K. 447) in 1787, although until fairly recently that was thought to date from four years earlier. The discrepancy in dating is even greater in the case of K. 412, which was long believed to have been composed in 1782, but it is now accepted that Mozart started it in the last months of his life, and left it unfinished; it was then completed (like his Requiem) by his pupil Franz Xaver Süssmayr.[2] The date on the autograph had been read as '1797' and regarded as a joke on Mozart's part, but close examination led to the discovery that it was actually '792', scribbled in haste and lacking the '1' that denotes the millennium (normal practice at the time), and furthermore that the handwriting was that of Süssmayr—and the 'joke' lost its sparkle.

Some of the jokes Mozart really made at Leutgeb's expense were more durable, for example the inscription at the top of the first Horn Concerto, K. 417: 'Wolfgang Amadé Mozart finally took pity on Leutgeb, Ass, Ox, and Fool, Vienna, 27 May 1783' (an allusion to the length of time Leutgeb's wish had remained unfulfilled). Others among the 'jokes' and 'tricks' had much more serious foundations than appear at first glance.

Leutgeb was undoubtedly a master of his instrument. The horn of his day was the so-called natural horn, which consists of a mouthpiece and a metal tube with a conical bore which gradually widens, and is coiled a few times to make it easier to hold; at the end the tube flares out to form the 'bell'. As with every other wind instrument, a note is produced by making the column of air inside the tube vibrate; a note of a higher or a lower pitch can be produced by overblowing—but the technique is subject to strict natural limitations. Any note that sounds is accompanied by the vibration of a specific range of 'overtones': the complete spectrum of

---

[1] Landon, *Golden Years*, 149.

[2] On the revision of the dating, see Tyson, *Mozart*, 246–61, esp. 246–7.

overtones (of which only a certain selection vibrate with each individual note) is ordered at fixed intervals, the 'natural harmonic series'. A brass-player of Leutgeb's time could play only the pitches in that series: he could pick them out singly as the overtones of his instrument's fundamental note by overblowing, but he could play no others (in principle, but see below). The second harmonic (first overtone) is the octave above the fundamental, then the fifth above that; harmonic no. 4 is two octaves above the fundamental and nos. 5 and 6 are the notes forming the ascending triad on no. 4; only in the fourth octave above the fundamental does the series form a half-way normal diatonic scale. There are further problems of detail: individual notes in the natural harmonic series (nos. 7, 11, 13, and 14) cannot be used as they are because they have no place in the well-tempered scale, and action must be taken to modify their pitches.

The modern horn is equipped with valves, introduced in the first half of the nineteenth century, which allow the player to alter the length of the tube and thus of the column of air that is to be made to vibrate. Pressing a key opens or closes the valve and, by extending or shortening the tube, also alters the fundamental tone. The structure of the harmonic series remains the same, whatever the fundamental is, so if the fundamental changes by, say, a semitone, all the harmonics will also change by a semitone. Thus the modern horn-player has instantaneous access to a range of notes that his predecessor could not reach. Thanks to the valves, all the notes of the chromatic scale were made available to the horn (and the trumpet).

Joseph Leutgeb could probably also change the fundamental pitch of his instrument for a movement at a time, even if it was not possible while actually playing. In order to do so he had to change the length of the tube by inserting crooks of various lengths (either between tube and mouthpiece or in a gap left in the inner coil for that purpose, as in the German-made 'Inventionshorn'). But Leutgeb—as became normal in his day—also commanded the technique of 'stopping': by varying the position of his right hand inside the bell while playing, he could modify the pitch by up to as much as a minor third. The movement of the fingers modified the quality of the tone momentarily, but it also altered the pitch of the stopped note: hitting exactly the right pitch was purely a matter of experience.

The solo part in Mozart's Horn Concerto, K. 495, lies between nos. 3 and 16 in the harmonic series (two octaves), and thus uses almost the entire range of the instrument; from no. 6 onwards, moreover, every semitone of the scale is found (Mozart dispenses only with the 'impure' harmonic

Ex. 26.1. Horn Concerto in E flat major, K. 495, 1st movement, bars 97–104. The 'impure' pitches are marked ×, the stopped ones ↑.

no. 14). The consequences of this for Leutgeb's playing can be seen from a short example taken from the start of the development section of the first movement, where it is clear that Mozart was able to take it for granted that Leutgeb would 'stop' certain notes. (See Ex. 26.1.)[3]

Presumably Mozart also took Leutgeb's breath-control into account, but expected the most from it. Horn concertos need not differ in form from concertos for, say, keyboard, but individual phrases must be shorter, and so must the overall length of a work. A comparison of the first movements of various concertos illustrates the difference these considerations can make: that of the Horn Concerto, K. 495, with an opening tutti of forty-two bars and an overall length of 218 bars, has approximately the same dimensions as that of the Violin Concerto, K. 218, composed in autumn 1775, in which the corresponding figures are forty-one and 220 bars. At probably much the same time as K. 495, however, Mozart started another concerto for horn which he did not finish, perhaps because its opening tutti of sixty-five bars would have made it impossible to continue in suitable proportions without overtaxing the soloist. By the mid-1780s he was capable of writing much more substantial concerto movements when not restricted by that consideration. For example, in the case of the first movement of the Piano Concerto, K. 503, completed late in 1786, the opening tutti alone is already half as long as the entire first movement of K. 495, and its overall length, at 423 bars, is wellnigh double.

In another respect—the notation—Mozart presented his 'fool' with a considerable challenge in K. 495. The 1964 edition of the Köchel catalogue notes that 'the autograph was written in a colourful mixture of blue, red, green, and black inks, as a joke'. Unfortunately, only six leaves of the

---

[3] For more detail, see H. Pizka, *Das Horn bei Mozart (Mozart and the Horn)* (Kirchheim bei München, 1980), esp. 44, and Landon, *Golden Years*, 149–50.

manuscript have survived (performing editions rely on an early printing), but they gave enough information to modify the hilarity, when Franz Giegling, in preparing the concerto for the Neue Mozart-Ausgabe, worked out that the 'colourful mixture of ... inks' represents a code whereby Mozart gave the player tips for performance, probably concerning dynamic nuances for which standard notation was inadequate (see the last two sides of the second movement, reproduced on the endpapers of this book).[4]

No autograph material survives of the first movement, but we have fragments of the second and third. They show that Mozart used all four colours in the second movement, but contented himself with red and black in the third. Giegling came to the conclusion that he used the red ink to make individual parts stand out in the ensemble (regardless of whether the music was loud or soft), the green to indicate a 'sotto voce'—a p that should still 'sing', and the blue (the passage of time has turned it grey) to emphasize an echo effect; the black (nearer brown in places) denotes the basis from which the others take off.

An alternative interpretation is possible, however. There is no dispute about the use of black as the colour for the 'normal' state of affairs for the accompaniment (for the soloist, too, especially when the part stays close to the tutti); additionally Mozart used red ink for passages when the orchestra was prominent and the soloist silent. This leads to the following result in the very last bars of the second movement. Four bars from the end the solo horn plays in 'red', then falls back via blue and black to green. The same sequence of colours, suggesting a diminuendo, has already been seen over several bars in the parts of the orchestral horns and basses (finishing three bars before the end); on the other hand, at the start of the two pages reproduced, the soloist is meant to hold back a little (in a green phase), compared to the preceding bars, after which the two bars of rest for the soloist (simultaneous with the start of the big diminuendo for the orchestral horns and basses) should stand out very clearly. Thus there is a gradation, in the order red, blue, black, green, which may represent the fall from f to p, or from full to fine tone. If that is so, then it appears that in the last movement Mozart dispensed with the greater refinement of the second and fourth degrees, the blue between the red and the black, and the green, the most reticent of the four.

One thing is clear, at least, and that is that Mozart did not skip about between inkpots just for fun, but in order to make some musical sugges-

---

[4] Giegling in NMA V/14, vol. v, pp. xiii–xiv, and facsimiles, pp. xxii–xxiii.

tions to the interpreters. What about the verbal 'jokes' written in Italian above the solo part in the last piece Mozart composed for Leutgeb, the Rondo of the Concerto, K. 412, which was completed by Süssmayr? Was it really as a joke that Mozart wrote 'Adagio' in the score above the horn part but 'Allegro' above all the orchestral parts, or had he originally planned to write a slow middle movement (as it is, the concerto consists of just the two fast movements), and then forgotten to cross the word out? The other remarks Mozart wrote above the horn part are undoubtedly intended to be read by someone who was a good friend of his, but they are more than pure nonsense—well, maybe the 'à lei, Signor Asino' ('Over to you, Sir Donkey') before the first solo entry is nonsense, but the rest?

First and foremost among the features that Mozart thought deserved comment are the recurrences of the rondo theme. Giving it to the soloist for the third time, he wrote 'Questo poi và al meglio' ('That's better, this time'). He broke off the theme in the fourth bar, and left a comment to serve as a warning against mechanical continuation: 'E non finisci nemeno?—Ah Porco infame!' ('And don't you ever finish? O you infamous swine!') The words might be more polite, but Mozart means nothing more by them than an analysis of his own work.

Rests are also annotated ('respira!'—'take a breather!'). Once the comment is in German: '15 Jausen'; 'Jause' is an Austrian and south German expression meaning a coffee-break—this time Mozart is just joking. Passages of idiosyncratic rhythm are marked 'ah che mi fa ridere' ('how you make me laugh') or simply 'ha ha ha'. Against this background of comments that were certainly not meaningless, it is not surprising to see that Mozart remembered the stopped notes. The first four times the soloist has to play G♯, which is not part of the natural harmonic series on D, occur over a passage of six bars. Here Mozart singles out just those four stopped notes, and no others, for the following series of comments: 'Bestia—oh che stonatura—Ahi!—ohimè!' ('You beast—oh, what an awful noise—Oh dear!—Woe is me!')

Undoubtedly Mozart's annotations of the solo horn part are amusing and written in jest, but they also make good musical sense: they highlight compositional details, draw attention to the unexpected, and show that Mozart was well informed about the instrument's limitations (the range of notes it could play, the restrictions imposed by the player's need to breathe). Leutgeb was a friend of Mozart's, and the range of colour in K. 495 and the comments on the autograph of K. 412 amount to very unusual, musical records of the friendship. In both cases the serious purpose behind what was for so long understood to be merely frivolous illustrates the musical heights of which Mozart and the fellow Salzburger who preceded him to Vienna were capable.

27

On Doctor's Orders: The 'Kegelstatt' Trio, K. 498

On 5 August 1786 Mozart finished a trio in E flat major for piano, clarinet, and viola. The oddity of the instrumentation immediately attracts attention: whatever made him think of writing a piece for those three particular instruments?

For a start, the combination has less to do with a classical–romantic piano trio (for piano, violin, and cello) than with an 'enriched' baroque trio sonata, in that it involves two melody instruments, one inclining to the soprano register, the other to the alto—descending, indeed, to the bass register in some places (e.g. bar 18 of the Minuet), and a keyboard instrument, with an obbligato part for the right hand. Mozart's ensemble in this work is comparable to that of the middle movement of the fifth 'Brandenburg' Concerto, where the three soloists—flute, violin, and harpsichord—play unaccompanied. In choosing the three instruments he did for the 'Kegelstatt' Trio, however, Mozart went about as far as he could have done from the norm of even the 'enriched' trio sonata, for they were not chosen at random, not even at random within the conventions of that norm, or as a response to a situation in which Mozart found himself composing for a given ensemble of somewhat idiosyncratic constitution. The two melody instruments share the characteristic of being able to play in two distinct registers: the clarinet in the low 'chalumeau' register (not overblown) and the high register (overblown), and the viola over a range which embraces the tenor and a very high alto (here, as high as f''), overlapping the cello in one direction and the violin in the other. The piano, of course, commands several registers. The combination of the three gave the composer the run of an uncommonly wide range of both pitches and timbres, using as few instruments as can be imagined. In that respect, the 'Kegelstatt' Trio looks like a direct continuation of his work on the later 'Haydn' Quartets; there Mozart had already experimented with registral variety, and here he went further by leaving all-string combinations behind and approaching registral variety as a musical element in itself: one that presented a challenge to which he felt entitled to respond with a hand-picked group of instruments.

This is an aspect of the work that was set aside slightly more than two years later when the Viennese music publisher Artaria announced its publication as a 'Trio per il Clavicembalo o Forte Piano con l'accompagnamento d'un Violin e Viola', adding 'or clarinet' only as an alternative to the violin; presumably this was done with Mozart's permission, even if only commercial considerations drove him to give it. Transposing the clarinet part for violin destroys all registral variety, for in this context the violin cannot be heard as anything but a soprano instrument.

The order of movements is another sonata-like feature of the work. Unlike Mozart's trios for keyboard and two string instruments, which all follow the fast–slow–fast pattern, the three movements of this trio—an Andante, a Minuet and Trio, and an 'allegretto' Rondo-Finale—make it more readily comparable to works like the early E flat major Piano Sonata, K. 282, in which an Adagio is followed by a Minuet and Trio, and an Allegro finale. But even that comparison shows how much more individual Mozart's ideas had become in every respect. The Minuet in the E flat major Sonata is perfectly 'normal' in its minuet–trio–minuet construction. Things are rather different in the 'Kegelstatt' Trio: the viola develops an idiosyncratic triplet motion in the course of the Trio section, and this persists when the Minuet is 'repeated', although there was no trace of it first time round. This is another example of Mozart assessing compositional traditions and questioning them when he thinks it is musically justified.

The Viennese writer Caroline Pichler states in her memoirs that Mozart wrote the 'Kegelstatt' Trio for performance in the house of friends of his, the family of Professor Nikolaus von Jacquin.[1] Jacquin (1727–1817) had been professor of botany and chemistry at the University of Vienna since 1786 and was also responsible for the parks and gardens of Schönbrunn Palace, and for the Botanic Gardens lying to the east of the gardens of the Belvedere Palace. His academic reputation was founded on his work in the Central American field, authorship of a chemistry textbook and a *Flora austriaca*, and his application of the Linnaean system of plant classification. Mozart's acquaintance with the family probably dated from 1783, and he became especially friendly with one of the sons, Gottfried (1767–92), and

---

[1] C. Pichler, *Denkwürdigkeiten aus meinem Leben 1769–1843* (Munich, 1914), i. 158. On Nikolaus von Jacquin, see the article by H. Dolezal in *Neue deutsche Biographie*, x (1974), 257–9.

the daughter, Franziska (1769–1850). Franziska von Jacquin was Mozart's piano pupil, and he once wrote to her brother: 'I must confess that I've never had a pupil as hard-working or as keen as she is' (15 January 1787). According to Caroline Pichler the keyboard part in the 'Kegelstatt' Trio was written for Franziska von Jacquin, and Mozart wrote other works for her and her brother. The viola part in the trio may have been intended for himself to play, and the clarinet part for the virtuoso Anton Stadler, who is mentioned in that same letter of 15 January 1787 as another friend of the Jacquins. Caroline Pichler also tells us that the Jacquins usually held their musical evenings on Wednesdays, and as the 'Kegelstatt' Trio was finished on a Saturday it can be surmised that its first performance was given on the following Wednesday, 9 August 1786. What is not clear is when this 'Jacquin Trio' became known as the 'Kegelstatt' (or 'Skittle-Alley'). The nickname suggests that Mozart wrote it while playing skittles, but that raises two questions: did Mozart compose while playing skittles (or pursuing other, similar activities)? And what consequences might it have had for the music if he did?

Mozart is supposed to have taken up physical exercise in the form of skittles, billiards, and riding, on the urging of his doctor in Vienna, Sigmund Barisani (1758–87), another friend, and son of the Salzburg Barisanis. We do not know exactly when the advice was given, but in view of Barisani's early death it is very likely that it was before that summer of 1786, when the 'Kegelstatt' Trio was composed. At all events, he treated Mozart in 1784 for renal colic, and possibly also in summer 1783 for the grippe. Shortly after that, just before Mozart took his wife to Salzburg, he wrote to his father: 'Have the skittle-alley in the garden ready for use, because my wife is very fond of it' (12 July 1783). This proves that there was a skittle-alley in the garden of Leopold Mozart's house (the 'Dancing-Master's House' on what was then Hannibal-Platz), and is a strong indication that Mozart had played the game when he still lived in Salzburg. In general, the inhabitants of Salzburg preferred 'Bölzlschiessen', in which darts were fired at a target, using a kind of airgun.[2]

Mozart himself provided evidence that he did indeed compose music at the skittle-alley, when he dated the manuscript of the horn duos, K. 487, '27 July 1786 while playing skittles'. That was just nine days before he finished the 'Kegelstatt' Trio; it is possible, of course, that the two works

---

[2] R. Angermüller, 'Bölzlschießen', *Mitteilungen der ISM*, 30/3–4 (1982), 73–8.

were later confused and that the circumstances in which one was written became associated with the other, but it is equally possible that Mozart happened to be particularly keen on skittles that summer, and wrote rather a lot of music at the same time.

Hans Redlich wrote: 'According to a quite untrustworthy legend . . . Mozart is credited with the composition of this Trio while playing a game of skittles. Hence the surviving nickname "Kegelstatt-Trio". This is all the more unlikely as the "Kegelstatt-Trio" is a serious and, indeed, a most carefully composed work in Mozart's most individual vein.'[3] While that comment is perfectly true, it is not a sufficient reason for dismissing the 'legend'. As Mozart wrote to his father years earlier from Paris: 'You know that music is—so to speak—my element, that I think about it all day long, that I like to speculate, study, cogitate' (31 July 1778). What is open to discussion is not so much whether Mozart played skittles while he composed (implying that his attention to the music would have been only superficial), but the complementary question: could he have stopped composing while he played skittles?—and that seems likely to deserve the answer 'No'.

There are two further instances of Mozart working at the same time as he engaged in a sporting activity, both connected with his journeys to Prague. In Nissen's biography we read:

In 1787 Mozart composed several numbers for his opera *Don Giovanni* while playing skittles in the garden of his friend Duschek, which lay just outside the city [Prague]. When it was his turn to play he stood up; but no sooner was it over with than he returned to his work, without being distracted by the talk and laughter of those about him.[4]

Although the horn duos, K. 487, at least, were probably composed in full at the skittle-alley, it is conceivable that Mozart was merely engaged in orchestration in Duschek's garden. However, another resident of Prague, Friedrich Dionys Weber (1766–1842), an early conductor of Mozart's music, also averred that Mozart composed parts of *Don Giovanni* 'even while playing skittles with his best friends, sketching first one thing and then another on separate sheets of paper, and only later completing what remained to be done on another sheet' (1/4 June 1829). Unfortunately, like Nissen, Weber himself did not actually witness what he described.

---

[3] From the preface to the Eulenburg edition (No. 376) of the Trio, pp. iii–v.
[4] *Biographie*, 561.

Mozart returned to Prague four years later, for the première of *La clemenza di Tito*. On this visit it was billiards that is alleged not to have interrupted his work. Nissen again:

While Mozart was writing the coronation opera *La clemenza di Tito* in 1791, he visited a coffee-house near his lodgings almost every day with his friends, to divert himself with a game of billiards. They noticed on several days in succession that while playing he hummed a motif to himself very softly, 'hm hm hm', and a number of times, while others were playing, pulled a book from his pocket, cast fleeting glances inside it, and then went on playing. How astonished his friends were when Mozart sat down in Duschek's house one day, and played to them on the piano that beautiful quintet from *Die Zauberflöte*, for Tamino, Papageno, and the Three Ladies, which begins with the very motif that had so preoccupied him while playing billiards. It was proof, not only of the incessant activity of his creative intelligence, which was not interrupted even in the midst of pleasures and diversions, but also of the immense power of his genius, which was capable of applying itself to such different subjects at one and the same time. As is known, Mozart was already at work on *Die Zauberflöte* before he set off for Prague, there to compose and perform *La clemenza di Tito*.[5]

Here, doubt stirs. The quintet in Act I of *Die Zauberflöte* (it begins with Papageno muffled by a padlock on his mouth, as punishment for lying, and ends with him forgiven and setting off with Tamino to rescue Pamina), like all the other vocal numbers of that opera, had already been composed by the time Mozart arrived in Prague. If Mozart 'cast fleeting glances inside' a book, it is rather more likely that it was a copy of a libretto than a sketchbook (in which he would presumably have written), and if Mozart was carrying a libretto about with him in Prague, even during a game of billiards, it is more likely to have been the text of *Tito*, which he had yet to finish composing. Nissen's account may well have relied on the memory of Constanze Mozart, and it is quite possible that after more than thirty years two separate strands—the composition of *Tito* and the humming of Papageno's theme, both while playing billiards—became entangled.

Strictly speaking, the Prague anecdotes describe something different from what is conveyed by Mozart's note about the horn duos, which therefore stand apart among the works considered in this chapter. There are twelve duos but only three are known for certain to be by Mozart (Nos. 1, 3, and 6); at least two other hands can be distinguished in the other nine in the manuscript. The pieces are so difficult that it was thought for a long time that they were intended not for natural horns but for basset

[5] *Biographie*, 559–60.

horns, a woodwind instrument on which, like the clarinet, for example, intonation is governed by the simpler means of stopping finger-holes. But perhaps that is precisely where we should look for the key to understanding the circumstances of their composition (as Dietrich Berke has argued in the Neue Mozart-Ausgabe[6]): there could have been an occasion when Mozart was playing skittles with at least two adept horn-players, and the conversation turned to exceptionally difficult horn parts; the matter could have been put to the test there and then, 'while playing skittles'.

But while such an occasion would have been something out of the ordinary, billiards and skittles keep on recurring in Mozart's creative life, even though there is no reason to see any kind of inner connection between playing games and composing. Billiards and skittles fulfilled the same purpose as the doctor's recommendation to work standing rather than sitting. So what does the case against a 'Skittle-Alley' trio amount to, after all? There are works whose much more innocent-seeming nicknames are much more questionable—such as the 'Prague' Symphony, which we shall look at in the next chapter.

[6] NMA, VIII/21, p. xii.

28

The Feast of St Nicholas: The 'Prague' Symphony, K. 504

'In the fall of the year 1787 Mozart set out on a journey to Prague in company with his wife, there to produce *Don Giovanni*.' So begins Eduard Mörike's novella *Mozart auf der Reise nach Prag*, first published just before the Mozart centenary in 1856. Mozart had made one earlier journey to Prague in 1787, in January, but Mörike's tale concerns the second. In keeping with his romantic (and Romantic) portrait of an artist (which gains a special orientation from the fact that the artist is a historical person), Mörike represents the reason for the second journey as follows:

It is true that, while it was being performed, the inhabitants of Vienna could hardly have enough of *Belmonte und Konstanze* [*Die Entführung*], owing to the popular elements in that piece; yet it was certainly not due solely to the intrigues of the manager that a few years later *Figaro* unexpectedly proved a sorry fiasco in rivalry with the charming, but greatly inferior *Cosa rara* [by Martín y Soler]— that same *Figaro* which the more cultivated, or less prejudiced inhabitants of Prague received immediately afterwards with such enthusiasm that, touched and gratified, the Master determined to write his next grand opera specially for them.[1]

Indeed, Mozart probably was thrilled by Prague's reception of *Figaro*. On the other hand, we cannot expect that a great work of imaginative literature will necessarily be anchored to historical fact, and it is not hard to see that gratitude alone would probably not have been sufficient to persuade him to compose *Don Giovanni*, had it not been reinforced by a firm commercial contract from the same impresario who had produced *Figaro* in Prague. The National Theatre in Prague was under the management of Pasquale Bondini in the 1786–7 season, and the success of *Figaro* made him a lot of money. Offering *Figaro*'s composer a contract for a new opera was therefore a sound investment from his point of view, while Mozart for his part obtained not only encouragement as music-dramatist but also the prospect of handsome financial gain, since in addition to the fee for the

---

[1] Tr. W. and C. A. Phillips (London, 1946), 15, 23–4.

composition (probably 450 gulden) he could look forward to an even larger sum from a benefit performance.

The exact date of the Prague première of *Figaro*, which set this chain of events in motion, is unknown, but it must have taken place early in December 1786, that is, seven months after the world première in Vienna on 1 May 1786. The magnitude of its success in Prague can be gauged from the fact that at the time people elsewhere formed the impression that the Prague première had been the world première. When it was produced in Donaueschingen in 1787 the playbills advised the public that 'the music is by the celebrated Herr Mozart'—exactly the form of words that was used in the Prague publicity of December 1786. Moreover the Donaueschingen theatre gave the work in the version first seen in Prague (who altered it is unknown), and when the score was catalogued for the Donaueschingen Court Library the opera was described as having been performed first in Prague in 1786. A copyist's score which made its way to Berlin reproduces the musical text as it was first given in Vienna, but gives 'Prague 1787' as the performance date.[2] The Vienna production passed almost unnoticed and was put completely in the shade by the one in Prague.

Mozart's invitation to Prague was probably issued when it was clear that the enthusiasm would last till he got there (indeed, it was thought that his arrival would fan the flames). He left Vienna on 7 January 1787; since the rumour that he would be coming to see his opera began to circulate in the Bohemian capital in mid-December, the invitation must have been in his hands by Christmas at the latest. He was given convincing proof of the huge scale of Prague's enthusiasm for *Figaro* on the evening after his arrival, when he attended a carnival ball. As he wrote to his friend Gottfried von Jacquin, he was too tired to dance himself,

but it was an unmixed pleasure for me to watch all these people tripping up and down in sincere enjoyment to the music of my *Figaro*, transformed into country dances and allemandes. They talk of nothing else here but—*Figaro*; they play, blow, sing, and whistle nothing but—*Figaro*; they go to no opera but—*Figaro* and evermore *Figaro*. It's certainly a great honour for me. (15 January 1787)

The enthusiasm was endorsed by officialdom. The Prague *Oberpostamts-zeitung* reported on 12 January 1787:

[2] A. Tyson, 'The 1786 Prague Version of Mozart's *Le nozze di Figaro*', *Music and Letters*, 69 (1988), 321–3. On the Donaueschingen Court Library, see K. Küster in *Baden und Württemberg im Zeitalter Napoleons* (exhibition catalogue; Stuttgart, 1987), i/2, 895 (item 1472).

Our great and beloved composer Herr Mozart arrived here yesterday evening from Vienna. We are confident that Herr Bondini will do him the honour of putting on a performance of *The Marriage of Figaro*, the popular creation of his musical genius, on which occasion our celebrated orchestra will not fail to furnish new proof of its ability, and the discerning inhabitants of Prague—notwithstanding that they have heard the opera often already—will, we are sure, attend in great numbers. We should also welcome an opportunity to admire Herr Mozart's playing.

The paper's wish was granted a week later. Franz Xaver Niemetschek was present and wrote about the event in his biography of Mozart (the first ever published):

The theatre had never been so full as on this occasion; never had there been such unanimous enthusiasm as that awakened by his heavenly playing. We did not, in fact, know what to admire most, whether the extraordinary compositions or his extraordinary playing; together they made such an overwhelming impression on us that we felt we had been bewitched. When Mozart had finished the concert he continued improvising alone on the piano for half an hour. We were beside ourselves with joy and gave vent to our overwrought feelings in enthusiastic applause. In reality his improvisations exceeded anything that can be imagined in the way of piano-playing, as the highest degree of the composer's art was combined with perfection of playing.[3]

According to Johann Nepomuk Stiepanek, later director of the Prague National Theatre, Mozart played no fewer than three improvisations on this occasion, the last of them—by popular demand—based on 'Non più andrai' from *Figaro*. Consequently the variations on the same aria which the on-stage band plays to accompany the hero's supper in the last scene of *Don Giovanni* had a special significance for the Prague audience for which that opera was written.

The details of the rest of the programme can only be pieced together and remain incomplete. In addition to Mozart's solos on the piano, there appear to have been two symphonies. Niemetschek identifies only one in the 1798 edition of his book, calling it 'the great symphony in D major', in other words the one known to posterity as the 'Prague'; then in the revised second edition of 1808 he says that one in E flat major was also played. The 'great' E flat major Symphony, K. 543, was not finished until eighteen months later however, on 26 June 1788, and the last symphony Mozart had written in that key was the early one of 1773, K. 184. It has not been possible to ascertain whether Niemetschek meant that early

---

[3] Niemetschek, *Life of Mozart*, 36.

symphony or if his reference to a work in E flat major represents only a later gloss. Another possibility is that the 'Paris' Symphony was performed that evening. There exists a first trumpet part in Mozart's hand, evidently made because the original part had been lost, which may date from in or around December 1786.[4] This can only have been needed because a performance was due to be given, but whether in Prague or elsewhere is an open question.

It is unfortunate that that trumpet part cannot be dated with any greater accuracy, for otherwise it might tell us more about Mozart's preparations for his journey, and hence also about his circumstances in December 1786. All we know about these is gleaned from a passing remark in a note Leopold Mozart sent to his daughter in St Gilgen, enclosing a 'very illegible letter from your brother' and mentioning that 'he is giving four Advent concerts' (8 December 1786). The letter by Mozart has not survived, like the great majority of those he wrote to his father in the last years of his life (the last of a relatively complete sequence is dated 9 June 1784, after which there is only one, dated 4 April 1787). Nannerl Mozart married on 23 August 1784, and all we know of the many letters Mozart sent his father after that comes from the comments on them in Leopold's letters to her in St Gilgen. Once in a while he sent them on to her, and we can be sure that she preserved them as carefully as she did her father's, but only the latter have survived. The loss of the letters by Mozart himself is a sad accident (there is no reason to suspect any sinister cause for it), but it is all the worse because it leaves us with a period in Mozart's life over which speculation about his problems and tribulations has proliferated, without sources remotely comparable to the personal letters of earlier years to control it.

Some commentators have questioned whether the 'four Advent concerts' Mozart told his father about actually took place, but the doubt seems ill-founded. True, Leopold Mozart mentions them as being yet to come, using the present tense to imply the future, but there are occasions in Mozart's concert-giving career for which the evidence is far less solid. For example, Mozart's letter to his father of 3 March 1784 lists his concert dates over the period from 26 February to 3 April: these amount to a total of twenty-two in thirty-eight days, but only in the case of one of them is there any corroborative evidence of its having taken place, while another is reported to have been cancelled. The Mozart family correspondence tells

---

[4] Tyson, *Mozart*, 140.

us about many more things than are confirmed by other evidence; if that letter of 3 March 1784 had been lost we would know virtually nothing of what Mozart did in those five and a half weeks. Why anyone should fail to seize on the evidence that does exist concerning a period in his life which is more sparsely documented than earlier periods is baffling.

In fact, in the case of the four concerts planned for Advent 1786, there is a relative abundance of indirect evidence that Mozart's intention to give them, at least, was quite serious. On 4 December he at last finished the C major Piano Concerto, K. 503, eighteen months after composing the opening of the first movement. Two days later he completed work on the 'Prague' Symphony, and from all that we know about Prague's reception of *Figaro* we have to conclude that the news of the opera's success had not yet reached him on that 6 December—the feast of St Nicholas.[5] The 'Prague', too, was not entirely new: he had composed the finale some months earlier, in the spring of 1786, that is, at much the same time as the last acts of *Figaro* and the C minor Piano Concerto, K. 491.[6] It appears, therefore, that around 3 December 1786 (the first Sunday in Advent) Mozart not only 'worked up' a substantial sketch for a concerto that had been lying fallow for a year and a half, but also extended a lone symphonic finale into a three-movement work. Was he in a hurry?

According to tradition Mozart wrote the overture to *Don Giovanni* in the course of a single night. That piece is somewhere near the same length as the first movement of the 'Prague' Symphony; a slow movement also had to be written. How long would Mozart have needed to finish the symphony? He already had some raw material for both movements, which he perhaps noted down while working on the C major Concerto. Sketches survive of the middle part of the exposition and much of the rest of the first movement, and can be seen to have made an important contribution to it in its eventual form. The second movement, on the other hand, had to be started again from scratch, as Mozart decided not to use the ten bars he had sketched earlier. If Mozart was working under pressure, could not two days have been enough to complete the symphony—especially as the third movement had already been written? Evidence that he was sometimes careless enough to allow such pressure to generate exists in the shape of a comment Leopold Mozart made a year earlier, in a letter to his daughter, about the straits the composer was in over *Figaro*. 'He will have pushed it aside continually, taken his time, as is his wont, and now all at once he's

[5] L. Somfai in NMA IV/11, vol. viii, p. ix.   [6] Tyson, *Mozart*, 22.

got to buckle down to it in earnest, because Count Rosenberg is cracking the whip' (11 November 1785). The aesthetic quality is not impaired, but the impression remains that the symphony was composed in haste. The only reason for that would have been a concert coming up in the immediate future—which cannot be connected with the journey to Prague in the following month, or with any more general future prospects (he was thinking of a visit to England). Against the background of the primary sources, the question of whether or not Mozart had already heard of *Figaro*'s conquest of Prague by that 6 December becomes secondary. The work he had to get through in connection with the Advent concert season in Vienna was far more pressing, and he may well have broken the back of it by the end of St Nicholas's Day. The visit to Prague was some weeks away, and it comes as no surprise if Mozart profited during it from work he had already done for Vienna. At all events, he clearly did not write any new music, datable to the first weeks of 1787, specifically for his first journey to the Bohemian capital.

But what made him write an isolated symphonic finale in the spring of 1786, when he was busy with *Figaro*? We might think that he conceived it as a replacement for the finale of another symphony in D major, rather than as the start of a completely new work, but then we would have to identify the symphony that did not satisfy him. It would presumably have to be one by another composer, for no other symphony in D major by Mozart is scored for the same orchestra as the 'Prague' (with double flutes, oboes, and bassoons). The 'Paris' (K. 297, 1778) and the 'Haffner' (K. 385, 1782) both require two clarinets in addition to the other wind, while none of the earlier ones need more than two pairs of wind instruments, and most of them only one. The dating of this symphonic finale to the same weeks as the composition of *Figaro* explains one of its details: its main theme begins with the same rapid triadic motif as one of the numbers in the opera, namely the duet for Susanna and Cherubino, after the page has had to hide in the dressing-room to prevent the Count from finding him in the Countess's bedroom (at the end of the duet, having literally no other way out, he jumps out of the window).

Whatever purpose the movement was originally intended to serve, it ended up in the 'Prague' Symphony, as its oldest component. The other two movements are equally theatrical, with Mozart making the most of the dramatic potential of the alternation of major and minor. This is seen not only in the slow introduction (the slowest in any of his symphonies), where the element of searching for the 'eventual' key is in the tradition of the genre, but also elsewhere, for example in the G major Andante, in which the modulation is linked to a particularly tight-packed series of independent themes: after the cadence with which the G major introduction ends, and a sudden loud wind unison, the first violins strike up a 'subject' in E minor (bar 19) and another in D minor two bars later; it is only with the B flat major motif of the next bar that the way leading to the A pedalpoint begins (and the short step from there to D major, the dominant of the movement's home key, is postponed as long as it can be).

In the main part of the first movement, having set up this theatrical framework, Mozart develops a new and particularly effective form of symphonic exposition—so effective in his own view that he returned to it for the two outer movements of the 'Jupiter' Symphony. As already described in earlier chapters, there is very little evidence in Mozart's symphonic expositions—that is, within the context of modulation from the tonic to the dominant—of the process of a 'principal theme' preparing the ground for a 'secondary' one, in accordance with the textbook principle that there must be a 'first-subject group' and a 'second-subject group', with an 'intermediate group' between them. Rather, what might be termed the 'first-subject group' in one of Mozart's symphonies is the accumulation of a number of different motivic elements; sometimes a comparable 'development' takes off from a motivic element that patently makes an appearance only after the statement of the 'first subject' (in the 'Linz', for example, where the development is not of the first subject—*p*—that introduces the Allegro spiritoso after the slow introduction, but of a later motif—*f*—in march tempo). As once before, in his early G minor Symphony, K. 183, here Mozart combines the 'development principle' with his usual technique of setting off several contrasting blocks against each other—but in an unusual manner.

At the beginning of his 'allegro' section, Mozart develops an initial idea into, not a 'subject', but five distinct motivic blocks, by way of which he arrives at a half close on the dominant.[7] He is now, in some sense, at a crossroads. In his earlier symphonies he regarded this situation, giving off no more than a hint of the dominant, as sufficient foundation for the immediate launch of the second subject (in the dominant); we find it in 1774, in the fourth movement of the D major Symphony, K. 202, and four years later, in somewhat similar, albeit more expanded form, in the 'Paris'. The consequence is that the exposition is over not much later, and that

[7] Block A, b. 37; block B, b. 51; block C, b. 55; block D, b. 63; block E, b. 69. For a fuller discussion see Küster, *Formale Aspekte*, 35–49, 79–81.

means that the movement as a whole cannot be very long. There is another way of doing it. The second subject, when it comes, is still in the tonic because the dominant was not established firmly enough to become its key, and the whole exposition thus remains in the tonic. In that case, the modulation has to come later, in another section of the movement. This is the way Mozart constructs the opening sections of his concertos and some of his arias. The third way—the one he uses in the 'Prague' Symphony and in the outer movements of the 'Jupiter'—is also based on the idea that the dominant is not yet strong enough to sustain the entrance of the second subject, but this time the consequence is that no second subject follows at all at this point. Instead, Mozart harks back to material which has already been presented, and elaborates motifs from the five 'blocks'. With this material, in a veritable 'intermediate group', he creates a new harmonic situation—in the 'Prague', a cadence on to the dominant—after which the second subject is allowed to follow.

The elements of this formal principle are already present under a different rubric in the early G minor Symphony, K. 183, where the characteristic contrasting blocks adorn the path leading to the dominant half close followed by the return to the motivic material of the opening—but it takes Mozart to the same harmonic goal as first time round, and he needs a new, motivically 'free', formal element to get to a position in which the second subject can enter. There, it appears to be the reaction to problems peculiar to a minor tonality. By contrast, in the 'Prague', this principle is vigorously promoted, and despite the persistence of the element of motivic contrast it provides a sound basis for a much more spacious symphonic structure— more spacious than was possible in the 'Paris', for example, where the contrasting motivic elements were over-extended.

The continuation turns once again to a principle employed in the orchestral introductions of arias and concertos, and in the early symphonies: the quiet second subject opens out into a closing group which consists of several subdivisions and leads to the cadence several times. In the symphony, by a particularly happy inspiration, Mozart brings back all the motifs with which he made his way from the end of the 'first subject' to the first dominant half close. This means that the two harmonically significant processes of the exposition are equipped with the same material— nothing unusual in works of that time.[8]

---

[8] Cf. bs. 121 and 55, 125 and 66, 136 and 63. See Küster, *Formale Aspekte*, 60, for a discussion of similar techniques in concerto movements (e.g. K. 467, 491, and 622—passages dating from 1785–7).

After the development, the recapitulation of a movement in sonata form is supposed to return to the music of the exposition but to assert harmonic stability by remaining in the tonic, thus creating the perennial problem of avoiding the modulation that took place in the exposition. Here Mozart produces an unusual solution, which, once again, has forerunners in some of his earlier works. In the D major Flute Quartet composed in Mannheim, for example, he brought back the motivic material of the first modulating group from the exposition, not in the recapitulation, but earlier, in the development. That kept the recapitulation free of the modulation, but allowed the motivic material to be heard a second time in the latter part of the movement. He does not do exactly the same thing in the 'Prague' Symphony: he does not detach a discrete segment of the exposition and put it in an unexpected place, but we do suddenly encounter, in the development section, music taken from the middle of the exposition's first-subject group. Mozart allows the complete half-close construction to follow and even runs on into the intermediate group, but after a short time he abandons that as abruptly as he inserted the material from the exposition in the first place: in the sixth bar of the elaboration of the opening idea an A enters in the bass and persists for thirteen bars like a technical fault before becoming the pedal-point on the dominant of D major, and the suspense that has built up is not relaxed until the recapitulation begins in earnest. Once again the modulating material from the exposition which would have to be modified in an orthodox recapitulation, in order not to damage the harmonic structure, lies in the sections inserted here so unexpectedly. Then, in the recapitulation, Mozart once again skips all the exposition material that has already featured in the development.

If Mozart's conquest of Prague began with *Figaro*, composed for Vienna, he consolidated it with this symphony (and clinched it with *Don Giovanni*). Yet it is obvious that the 'Prague' was originally composed for Vienna, too—which is rather odd, because, unlike the traditional Viennese symphony, it lacks a minuet and trio: in fact, the 'Prague' is the only three-movement symphony Mozart wrote for Vienna. Were there special circumstances in which such a 'short' work could be performed—as the first item in a concert, perhaps? At the very start of Mozart's Vienna period, on 3 April 1781 (when he was still on the staff of the Archbishop of Salzburg), one of his symphonies was performed at the beginning of a concert, and it is thought to have been the one in C major, K. 338, the last in three movements before the 'Prague'. It was nearly two years later, on 4 January 1783, that Mozart wrote to ask his father to send him the scores of four symphonies, including K. 182—another in only three movements (see above, Chapter 6). It looks, therefore, as if Mozart was able to play three-movement symphonies in Vienna without feeling obliged to compose minuets specially for that audience. Was it necessarily the case, then, that this new three-movement symphony was meant for Prague in the first place? After all, the last symphony Mozart had composed before it—the four-movement 'Linz'—was commissioned by the very man who played an important role in bringing him to Prague: Johann Joseph Anton Count Thun.

Mozart would have had every opportunity to perform (and indeed compose) the 'Prague' as a 'Vienna'. The work he finished on the feast of St Nicholas 1786 was a milestone in his development as a symphonist, and musically, despite the 'missing' minuet, fully the equal of the three late 'great' works. But he could not have foreseen that it would preside over the next stage of his career under the name of Prague.

29

Twice Three is Five, and Other Experiments: Piano Quartets and String Quintets, 1785–1787

Mozart's *œuvre* is not dominated by any genre or genres in particular, and there is no one type of work above all others that we associate with him in the way that we do Schubert and the Lied, or Wagner and opera. There were years at a stretch in which Mozart wrote no operas. The great period of keyboard concertos occupied only three of his ten years in Vienna. Its sudden end has been connected with the fact that all at once, after a gap of four years, Mozart had the opportunity to write not just one but two operas: *Der Schauspieldirektor* and *Figaro*. The symphony is also 'missing' during the concerto-writing period. Clearly Mozart's concentration on particular genres led for the time being to a block where others were concerned; then after a certain amount of time some of those others suddenly usurped the central position in his interest, but elements of what the composer had learnt in his most recent works were handed on to the new compositions in other genres.

All the above applies to the string quartets and quintets: neither of them can be called the one predominant medium among Mozart's chamber music for strings, and he concentrated on them in separate periods, several years apart. Here again, interest in the one type seems to have prevented him from working on the other, yet, here again, there was some cross-fertilization.

Mozart's earliest experiments with four- and five-part chamber music for strings belong on the fringes of the divertimento. Apart from the String Quartet, K. 80, composed in Lodi in 1770, there were the three Quartetti-Divertimenti, K. 136–8 (early 1772), which are for strings in four parts (but probably meant to have more than one player to a part). These were followed at relatively short intervals by two groups, each of six quartets: K. 155–60 (1772–3) and K. 168–73 (Vienna, 1773). Then all at once the first quintet came on the scene: K. 174 in B flat major was finished in Salzburg late in 1773, and with it one era ended. It was nearly ten years before the next string quartet was composed. That was K. 387 in G major, the first of the 'Haydn' Quartets, another set of six, which took two years to complete (with the 'Dissonance', 14 January 1785). This time two more years went by before Mozart turned to the quintet again, and in the interval, exceptionally, he wrote one isolated quartet, the 'Hoffmeister', K. 499, dated August 1786. The next phase of quintet-writing came in the early summer of 1787, with the two works in C major and G minor (K. 515 and 516), and the arrangement of the 'Nacht Musique', K. 388, originally composed for wind octet in 1782 (the string quintet version is K. 406/K⁶ 516b¹). After another gap, the three 'Prussian' Quartets (K. 575, 589, 590) were composed in 1789–90, and like the 1773 quartets these were followed closely by a quintet: K. 593, in D major, 1790. The E flat major Quintet, K. 614, dated April 1791, leaves the impression that Mozart may not yet have begun to think of writing more quartets when he died.

In fact, it is reasonable to suppose that Mozart always wanted to try out what he had discovered in each of his groups of quartets in five-part writing as well, especially in view of the timing of the first and the two last quintets.² The case of the middle group, the quintets of 1787, is somewhat different. Since the stage of development reached in the 'Dissonance' Quartet, certain fundamental creative circumstances had changed in Mozart's work: the predominant activity of 1784 and 1785, the composition of keyboard concertos, initially involved new orientations (not in matters of form alone: his only two concertos in the minor mode date from this period), but that interest suddenly waned in the course of 1786. Opera composition came back on stream at the end of 1785, and in January 1787 Mozart journeyed to Prague with his first new symphony for years. Moreover, this was only one segment of the soil out of which the quintet compositions of 1787 grew, a soil not directly nourished by the composition of quartets at all; in fact, the quintets had a much broader base among the chamber music as a whole than the 'quartet theory' allows for.

In October 1785, nine months after the composition of the 'Dissonance' Quartet, Mozart finished the Piano Quartet in G minor, K. 478, his very first work for that medium. As indicated, there are a number of signs that he was not concerned here with chamber-music techniques alone but also benefited from the experience of writing his keyboard concertos, where

---

¹ On the dating of K⁶ 516b, see A. Tyson, 'Proposed New Dates for Many Works and Fragments Written by Mozart from March 1781 to December 1791', in C. Eisen (ed.), *Mozart Studies* (Oxford, 1991), 213–26, esp. 223.

² Rosen, *Classical Style*, 264–6.

the soloist is pitted against a relatively large body of strings. The effort to assimilate a different area of experience might explain why it took such a relatively long time to finish this first piano quartet; another forerunner is the Quintet for Piano and Wind, K. 452, composed early in 1784. The G minor Piano Quartet set Mozart on a path which remained an enticing prospect although other tasks took priority for the time being (more keyboard concertos and the two operas). However, in the first week in June 1786, exactly five weeks after the première of *Figaro*, he wrote a second piano quartet (K. 493, in E flat major). Then, before another five weeks had elapsed, he composed the Piano Trio in G major, K. 496 (his first work in the medium since the Divertimento, K. 254, of 1776); another piano trio followed in the November, but before it there came the 'Kegelstatt' Trio, K. 498, finished on 5 August, and the 'Hoffmeister' Quartet, K. 499, finished exactly two weeks later.

The dates allow hardly any room for doubt about how to interpret all this. Yes, the operas led to major changes in Mozart's output, but that is not the sole reason why the series of keyboard concertos came to a halt (that Viennese concert-goers had grown tired of Mozart is not the reason, either). Rather, this is yet another example of a genre having served its turn and retreated for a time to the background of his interest. That is how it was with the end of the great symphony-writing period in 1774, with the farewell to full-scale concertos for the violin in 1775, with the provisional abandonment of fugue at the end of 1783 (so far as surviving compositions allow us to judge); and that too is how the alternation between string quartets and quintets came about. There are perhaps already signs that the composition of keyboard concertos was losing its appeal for Mozart at the turn of the year 1785–6: for example, the fact that he made his last experiment with recapitulation in first-movement concerto form, in the E flat major Concerto, K. 482, and did not set himself any comparably ambitious goals in any of the later concertos. These appear to have been composed under intense pressure: he turned to old sketches for the A major Concerto, K. 488, the C major, K. 503, and the B flat major, K. 595, and in the case of the 'Coronation' Concerto, K. 537, he did not even have time to write out the solo part in full in the autograph score. Only the C minor Concerto, K. 491, may have offered him a special challenge, by the fact that it was in the minor.

To that extent there are also internal reasons within his keyboard concerto output that might have made Mozart decide to seek fresh woods and pastures new. Additionally, and in addition to the return to the opera-house, it looks as if experimentation with chamber-music techniques pushed concerto-composition into the background, especially, to begin with, chamber music with keyboard. It is probably no coincidence that in the Quintet, K. 452, the forerunner of the 1786 chamber works, the piano appears in the company of wind instruments, not strings. Here the bass function falls to the bassoon, an instrument which Mozart had long credited with the agility that he asked of the cello only from the later 'Haydn' Quartets onwards. The agile cello is, however, a *sine qua non* in the new forms of chamber music for strings and keyboard. The step which Mozart took in the later 'Haydn' Quartets led to its ultimate consequence, therefore, in the 'String Quintet', K. 406, his arrangement of the 'Nacht Musique', K. 388: the bassoon part was given to the cello.

The Piano Quartet in G minor, K. 478, represents an earlier stage on that journey, the first in some respects since the exploration of new possibilities in the 'Haydn' Quartets. The concerto techniques adhering to the piano–strings relationship make it possible for Mozart to take what he had learnt about chamber-music techniques in writing the 'Haydn' Quartets and develop it along new lines. In the second Piano Quartet (E flat major, K. 493) these techniques still owe much to concertante style, as is shown in the development of the first movement: a theme from the exposition (the 'sujet libre' from the modulation) is elaborated in a manner akin to sonata form; after the development has opened in a thoroughly concerto-like manner, this theme lies almost exclusively in the strings, for the piano takes no part in its elaboration (apart from the opening and a brief unison passage) but instead develops its own completely independent and purely virtuosic figuration. This antithesis of virtuosity (for the 'soloist') and thematic working (for the 'orchestra') is entirely typical of Mozart's concerto movements.[3] For that reason the next step, Mozart's true 'conquest' of the piano trio, also seems to be a further scaling-down of concerto techniques to the chamber-music context rather than any direct borrowing from violin-sonata style.[4]

In his further progress along the path on which he had started two and a half years earlier with the Piano and Wind Quintet and continued with the first 'genuine' piano quartet, Mozart spent the summer and autumn of 1786 surveying the possibilities. One of the works of that period was a string quartet pure and simple, and even the orchestral compositions can probably be said to have contributed new ideas, the 'Prague' as a sym-

---

[3] Küster, *Formale Aspekte*, 142.
[4] K. Marguerre, 'Mozarts Klaviertrios', *MJb* 1960–1, 182–94.

phony, and the C major Concerto, K. 503, as a work using traditional concertante forms. One last step led to the string quintets; with that the survey was completed, and of all the genres Mozart had experimented with, only the piano trio retained its attraction for him. In the next few years, until the string quartet re-entered the field with the 'Prussian' set, the alternatives were, on the one hand, the numerically smallest possible medium with keyboard but going beyond the character of the violin sonata, and, on the other hand, a string-only medium exceeding the four-part limit: thus, in both cases, the criteria for concertante style were met. What were the advantages of writing for string quintet, and were they so decisive that categorization in these terms can really be sustained?[5]

Mozart's quintets always have the same combination of two violins and two violas performing on the bass platform provided by a cello. So far as that goes, the first intimation of the musical possibilities of this structure is already present in the first of his quintets, K. 174, where the two violins and the two violas form clear pairs, sometimes modified in the course of events to the extent that new pairs form, of violin and viola; the cello is excluded from these pairings and is employed as bass by all the various pairs. It is another instance recalling the baroque trio sonata, except for the doubling of the number of melody instruments from two to four, and for the bass's loss of its thorough-bass function (expounded in chords on a keyboard instrument). The process demonstrates the significance groups of three can have in the quintet and this is in fact one of the string quintet's fundamental advantages over the quartet.

The emancipation of the cello from a purely bass function in the later 'Haydn' Quartets had two consequences for Mozart's chamber music for strings: not only does the music now provide a platform for another virtuoso, but also, when an important solo falls to the cello, the remaining instruments have to take the role of accompanists. The way the latter affects the formation of trios within a quintet is illustrated in the opening bars of the first of the 1787 quintets (C major, K. 515), where the solo function alternates between cello and first violin, while the second violin and the two violas form an accompanimental trio.

This goes even further at the start of the G minor Quintet, K. 516. It begins with a 'trio', made up of the two violins and the first viola. After eight bars the opening music is repeated (with a slightly different ending) but this time it is heard an octave lower on the two violas, and the cello,

<hr />

[5] On the quintet medium in general, see T. Sieber, *Das klassische Streichquintett* (Berne and Munich, 1983).

with the violas playing the music originally given to the violins, and the cello that of the viola. Nothing of that kind happened in the early B flat major Quintet; there, even when the violas relieved the violins in the upper parts, the third voice was always the cello (except in two places in the Adagio, when the bass line goes to the second viola). The way the first viola functions as the bass in the opening bars in K. 516, when it has hitherto been either the leader of the pair of violas or the partner of the first violin, is radically new compared to the earlier quintet, and the novelty can only be explained by the fact that the former hierarchies have been put into question by the emancipation of the cello in chamber music (although even now it still performs its traditional bass function).

Thus the appearance that a string quintet may consist of two string trios is present even in the first work Mozart wrote for the medium, but there it is better understood as a relic of an enriched trio-sonata praxis. The situation is totally different in the G minor Quintet, K. 516. The antithesis of a high and a low trio, set out in its opening bars, would make no such impression in a string quartet, even, because there both groups would necessarily include a violin: the sound-character of two 'trios' would be differentiated only by the constitution of the bass register (viola with two violins in one case, cello with violin and viola in the other).

In a quintet constituted as 'twice three', on the other hand, one of the five players always has to assume a dual role, as the cellist once did, and at the start of the G minor Quintet this is the fate of the first viola. It begins as a high bass, then switches to the leading role, so that it performs an axial function in the texture here. Six-part writing for five instruments can conceivably take a different form, however, as turns out midway through the finale of the work (bars 192 ff.). Here too a high trio and a low one confront each other, but this time the cello takes the melody from the first violin, and the second viola draws on the part of the second violin. In these circumstances, the axial character of the first viola is rather special, because all it does in the context of the low trio is develop the material that it already had when it belonged to the high one, while the other components of the texture appear mirrored around its 'bass' part.

With these limitless possibilities for reconstructing the textures, Mozart's quintet style in 1787 draws close to one species of concertante music, namely the chamber concerto, in which each part is taken by a soloist, without any orchestral accompaniment (the sixth 'Brandenburg' Concerto, for example). Regarding the string quintets as a special form of the chamber concerto, and the piano trios and quartets as special forms—'for the chamber'—of the piano concerto, offers an additional explanation of the direction in which Mozart's new ideas about concerto form took him after the period of concentration on the piano concerto was over. He had his eye not only on opera but also on the possibility of uniting his manifold discoveries in concerto techniques with his advances in the field of chamber music—the violin sonata as well as the string quartet. Another tradition which contributed to Mozart's quintets can be seen in the order of the movements in the G minor Quintet: having the minuet in second place is a symptom of influence by the divertimento. The choice of tonality in the finale, on the other hand, reflects an advance made in the concertante music: as in the D minor Piano Concerto, and above all the G minor Piano Quintet, here too the music switches to the major. The divertimento appears to leave a particularly strong mark on the C minor Quintet, K. 406, the string-quintet arrangement of the 'Nacht Musique', K. 388, which Mozart made at much the same time as composing K. 515 and K. 516, but it was already implicit in the title of the original scoring for wind octet.

Mozart offered the three quintets (the two new works and the arrangement) for sale by subscription, in manuscript copies, in April 1788, approximately a year after their composition. The venture seems to have failed, however, because he advertised the subscription for a second time in the *Wiener Zeitung* two months later, and then one of them (K. 515) was issued in print by Artaria in the following year. In 1789 Mozart went to Berlin, whence he returned with a renewed interest in composing quartets, which gave birth to the three 'Prussian' works. The techniques of writing chamber music for strings which he had evolved in the quintets of 1787 must have been in the forefront of his mind in these new works, and at least in the matter of grouping the voices he reached a conclusion that was not perhaps foreseeable from the quintets: the last of the 'Prussian' Quartets illustrates how 'five-part' (or even, to some extent, 'six-part') writing can be achieved with only four instruments. We shall return to the 'Prussian' Quartets in a later chapter, but now is the appropriate moment to discuss this culminating stage in the evolution of what is strictly speaking a typical quintet technique. The slow second movement of the last 'Prussian' Quartet begins decorously enough in four parts, in a characteristic quaver rhythm. Subsequently the four-part chordal texture is relaxed, and the music modulates out of the home key. In bar 63, however, the home key suddenly returns, bringing with it the quaver rhythm of the movement's opening. Exactly the same notes are played as at the start, but by means of double-stopping the first violin now also plays the notes that were earlier played by the viola, thus leaving the viola at liberty to do something else (it interjects short dotted figures into the texture). By this relatively simple tactic the music is now in five parts—but Mozart has not finished yet. Eight bars later (see Ex. 29.1) the quaver theme appears yet again, played only by the second violin and the viola. The cello develops a new, independent part, derived from the earlier viola figure, while the first violin rests. In the next bar the first violin takes over the cello figuration, but the cello, instead of resting, joins the two other instruments in the material from the opening bars. The outcome in this case does not actually amount

Ex. 29.1. String Quartet in F major, K. 590, 2nd movement, bars 71–4. Violin 2 and viola play the theme from the start of the movement (with cello in bars 72 and 74). A free accompanimental figure alternates between violin 1 and cello.

to setting up two pairs of trios, as at the beginning of the G minor String Quintet, but the four-instrument basis has been developed to form new structures that go back to quintet technique. The cello is not only the first violin's partner in a framing function, fitting round a three-part inner texture (as at the start of the C major String Quintet, K. 515), but also its part is as ambivalent as that of the first viola in the opening bars of the G minor Quintet, for it switches to and fro between the functions of melody and bass, from one bar to the next. The three-part writing for the inner voices here is by no means an exciting expansion of technical possibilities: on the other hand the two distinct parts given to the cello appear to be the fruit of the cogitations which stamp Mozart's 1787 quintets on the basis of the chamber works from the 1786 exploration. There Mozart worked out a textural structure which at first sight seems realizable only in quintets[6]— yet, when pushed, it is capable of transference to the quartet medium, in works in which the emancipation of the cello enables it to reach a new pinnacle.

[6] On the question of chordal structure, see M. Flothuis, *Mozart, Streichquintett g-Moll, KV 516* (Munich, 1987), 6.

30

The Limits of Music: *Ein musikalischer Spass*, K. 522

In June 1787 Mozart was in mourning for his father, who had died on 28 May, and the most important composition on which he was engaged at the time was *Don Giovanni*. Yet during that summer he also finished two works which come under the heading of divertimentos and to which he gave individual titles when entering them in his catalogue of works: *Ein musikalischer Spass* (dated 14 June) and *Eine kleine Nachtmusik* (10 August). Repeatedly, these four facts have been considered in relation to each other, sometimes all at once, sometimes only two or three of them. Horst Seeger, in his book on Mozart published in the bicentenary year 1956, commented on the two divertimentos: 'We have in the antithesis the complete profession of Mozart's artistic faith!'[1] Wolfgang Hildesheimer, in his much discussed book, originally published in 1977, interpreted the connection differently:

The autograph manuscript [of *Ein musikalischer Spass*] was completed two weeks after the news of his father's death . . . Naturally we connot say whether the inspiration for a musical joke after his father's death was a coincidence or not. It does seem certain that the death of Leopold Mozart, for years such a dominant figure in his son's life, must have released some unconscious response, and it also seems probable that it was a feeling of liberation. Can this have been conscious? Might he have expressed it? It is possible that *Ein musikalischer Spass* was self-therapy, either to conquer his grief or else to laugh off his guilt feelings at his lack of sympathy. We cannot plumb the depths or shallows of Mozart's inner motivations. What occurred to Mozart when his father died? Apparently the ludicrous incompetence of his colleagues and pupils. Absurd, but not unthinkable. It is more probable, however, that nothing conscious occurred to him at all on his father's death, but all the more occurred to him for *Don Giovanni*, instead.

He must have been following some inner need when writing the *Spass*, for he cannot have had a commission for it . . . It is improbable that the *Spass* was ever performed during Mozart's time. It was simply something for his own enjoyment.[2]

[1] H. Seeger, *W. A. Mozart (1756–1791)* (Leipzig, 1956), 136.
[2] W. Hildesheimer, *Mozart* (Frankfurt am Main, 1977); tr. M. Faber (London, 1983), 208–9.

The word 'improbable' applies more aptly to those two statements. First, it is altogether doubtful that Mozart saw any particular connection between the two divertimentos, or wanted others to see one, as Seeger does; it is equally doubtful that a 'complete profession of artistic faith' can be drawn from merely two works composed in a context like that. Second, that *Ein musikalischer Spass* was performed in Mozart's lifetime is far from 'improbable', because some of the instrumental parts for it survive in Mozart's own hand. If it was 'something for his own enjoyment' and not performed it would have survived only in an autograph score, exactly as it was composed. Third, thanks to Alan Tyson's work on the paper-types of Mozart's manuscripts, published more recently than Hildesheimer's book, we now know that the first movement of *Ein musikalischer Spass* was composed at least eighteen months earlier than the rest of the work, and possibly as much as three years. Furthermore, we know that movement was performed when it was new, because parts for the first violin and bass have survived, written on a paper which is found otherwise only in connection with work which can be dated between 1784 and the end of 1785 (the remaining first-movement parts, on paper Mozart used between 1784 and the end of 1786, were probably written out in association with the same event).[3] The first movement, then, has no connection whatever with Leopold Mozart's death, but the addition of three more movements at the time when Mozart was composing *Don Giovanni* could have been the outcome of affectionate recollection of Leopold Mozart, whether as father or as teacher, as Eric Blom conjectured.[4] In its four-movement form, too, the work was probably performed at the time of completion; at all events, there is a new second-violin part of 1787, which comprises a revision of its first-movement music, and the second and third movements in the first-violin part are written in the remaining space at the end of the earlier first-movement part. All the other instrumental parts for the second, third, and fourth movements are missing—but in view of the survival of the two violin parts it is safe to assume that they did once exist. Something else that is missing is a full score of the first movement in its original form (1784/5); this might be the score which belonged to Franz Schubert, who gave it to his friend Anselm Hüttenbrenner. Thus the primary sources alone present an exceptionally colourful picture of the history of *Ein musikalischer Spass*, a composition which has survived complete, notwithstanding the loss of several of the original manuscripts.

[3] Tyson, *Mozart*, 239–42. [4] Blom, *Mozart*, 213.

In particular, the question as to why Mozart wrote the second-violin part out a second time is answered by the realization that the two copies have nothing to do with providing multiple copies for a performance by an orchestra but reflect two different historical 'layers' in the work. This reinforces the view that it was composed as a genuine sextet (not a piece for orchestra): the vignette on the title-page of the first printing (Pl. 9) illustrates that view, and so too does Mozart's specification in his catalogue. He wrote: '2 violini, viola, 2 corni, e Basso', that is, using singular forms for both viola and bass. It is true that traditionally 'basso' was also used as a collective term for a bass contingent of more than one instrument, and also that Mozart did not necessarily mean a single player to the part when he wrote 'viola'. Nevertheless, in this case, his terms can be taken literally, not least because it was the usual practice at that date to have just one

PL. 9. *Ein musikalischer Spass.* Vignette on the title-page of the earliest edition (Offenbach: Johann André, 1802 or later), showing a hopeful band of hopeless players.

player to each part (the 'bass' being the sole exception in the sense that it might be played by more than one instrument).[5]

All the same, the title-page vignette is misleading. The players who gave the earliest performances under Mozart's direction, at least, were certainly not the rustic amateurs the engraving represents. And as for the music itself, does it really reproduce the style of a village band?

That question has been hotly debated by Mozartians. The alternative title 'Dorfmusikanten-Sextett' (Sextet for Village Band) is apocryphal, unlike *Ein musikalischer Spass*. Hermann Abert wrote:

For all the technical aberrations, this has nothing to do with mocking a village band, in the manner, say, of the Scherzo of Beethoven's Pastoral Symphony. The famous wrong notes of the wind and string players are not the joke itself, but merely incidental to the work's humour. The real subject of the parody is the fictive composer of the music: that he finds 'interpreters' worthy of him is the crowning touch, but the true hero is always the composer alone.[6]

'Wrong notes', so far as the horns are concerned, refers above all to the 'mistake' in the second movement, the Minuet. But in order to understand it we must take contemporary performance skills into account and distinguish between the hypothetical village band who may or may not have been the target of Mozart's humour, and the actual players who first performed for him. Playing 'wrong' at that point took considerable skill in Mozart's time, because the notes required were accessible on contemporary horns only to players who were masters of the technique of hand-stopping; if, instead of being played as written, the notes are played unstopped, the passage sounds only half as wrong (but then the composed 'deficiencies' of the accompanying ensemble come into the reckoning). No doubt Mozart wanted to create the effect of imperfect stopping, but in this particular instance the horns are in greater danger of playing other notes (i.e. the 'correct' ones) by mistake, than of playing the notated 'wrong' ones on purpose.

The first violin, too, needs to have perfect technique at his command at the end of his solo cadenza in the third movement. A player who wants to make the leap to the 'wrong' d'''' convincing must first have been one hundred per cent correct in hitting the preceding wrong notes, in spite of the (for Mozart's time) fairly high register. Furthermore the violinist had to

---

[5] See J. Webster, 'Towards a History of Viennese Chamber Music in the Classical Period', *Journal of the American Musicological Society*, 27 (1974), 212–47.

[6] Abert, *Mozart*, ii. 327.

attack the passage from the second position, because the infelicities reckon with a botched move to the fourth position, and that in turn explains why the player inadvertently lands on the ninth position instead of the eighth.

Clearly, the parts for the two horns and the first violin, at least, are written for first-class players—but new problems arise from that. It was still usual in the eighteenth century for instrumental parts to be handwritten (printed ones were only gradually coming in, thanks to simplified production methods and diminishing costs), and consequently players always had to reckon with copyists' errors. Good players, at least, would recognize them at a glance and automatically correct them. In the case of this particular work, therefore, Mozart had to impress upon the players the importance of resisting their better judgement and playing exactly the notes that they had in front of them (perhaps that was the reason why he copied the parts himself, to avoid the risk of a well-meaning copyist making 'corrections' in his turn).

The same unconditional obedience to the composer's wishes is needed with regard to the dynamic markings, which are responsible for intermittent misplaced accents (for example, *f* in bar 2 of the third movement), and it is even more necessary in the matter of ornamentation, which is sometimes added without any consideration of what is going on at the same time in the other parts (to take another example from the third movement: bar 58, where the first violin's chord of C major collides with the second violin's F major arpeggio). This is scarcely the style of a village band, but it does call to mind the description that the writer and composer Christian Friedrich Daniel Schubart devoted to an entire orchestra in his *Ideen zu einer Ästhetik der Tonkunst* (published posthumously in 1806):

The orchestra at the court of Württemberg consisted of the world's leading virtuosos—and that was what was wrong with it. Each player formed his own circle and could not endure to conform to a system. Therefore ornaments were often played loud and clear when they had no business in the ensemble. An orchestra manned with virtuosos is like a world of kings without dominions.[7]

These 'errors' of ornamentation apply not only to ornaments as such but also to comparable enrichments of the notated melodic material—to details, that is, of the articulation of individual parts. Frequently these fail to cohere because they contain structures involving passing notes or suspensions in small note-values which are fundamentally at odds with each other. In the coda of the first movement, for example, the two lower strings play scales

---

[7] C. F. D. Schubart, *Ideen zu einer Ästhetik der Tonkunst*, ed. J. Mainka (Leipzig, 1977), 139.

up and down in quavers, paying no heed to the fact that what they are doing is completely incompatible with the more complex harmonic structures in the two violins' parts; at the same time the two horns are supposed to be following the violins, except that now and then they are given an alternative route, because not all the notes the violins can reach are accessible to them, and here again the second-violin part, in particular, does not accord with the 'diversion' given to the second horn. There is another example in the first-movement recapitulation, where the second violin and the viola assert their accompanimental part in penetrating octaves, and elbow the theme itself out of the foreground. In the revised version of the second-violin part Mozart repeatedly makes the instrument diverge from the viola for isolated single notes; inevitably, the two players cannot help but be convinced that something in each of their parts is not 'in tune' with the other's part.

Passages like that are clearly meant to give even the players a bit of a shock, and make them ask themselves if their virtuosity isn't being taken for a ride. The audience, at the same time, must be wondering if all these incorrect ornaments, suspensions, and passing-notes are part of an improvisation that has gone horribly wrong—for such is the normal reason for that kind of 'augmentation' of the music as written. But improvisation in turn belongs to the virtuoso's frame of reference. In this light, the questions of the interpretation of *Ein musikalischer Spass* seem to relate far less to village bands and their shortcomings than to contemporary virtuosos, who also had their weak spots: hand-stopping for horn-players, extreme registers for violinists, and improvisation for all of them—after all, the actual interpreters had to be in the position to reproduce convincingly the errors attributed to them by the composer. It is open to doubt if they themselves felt completely secure from such accidents in their normal working lives: the shock they would get from their individual blunders may well have stimulated Mozart's ingenuity. *Ein musikalischer Spass* called for virtuosos to perform it, and confronted them with fictive, but highly ingenious, professional cock-ups—and it was intended, moreover, to amuse an audience. At least at the level of interpretation (in the sense both of performance and of reception), therefore, the work would strike the target groups of a specific class of players and a specific audience as exactly what its title calls it: 'A Musical Joke'—nothing less, and nothing more, either. But how does it look from a composer's standpoint?

Hermann Abert believes, as cited above, that Mozart was parodying a fictive composer, and Wolfgang Hildesheimer enlarges on that opinion:

The wonderfully feigned lack of imagination is aimed at inferior quality, and does not attempt grotesque humour. In fact, Mozart's tartget was a synthesis of his colleagues. The fashionable composers of the time (Gyrowetz and Duschek), his uninspiring pupils (Süssmayr and Hummel), all are victims of this merciless 'joke'; but their 'intellects' are parodied and thus transformed into intellect. The synthetic composer taken to task is probably a general representative of the non-Mozart and non-Haydn music of the time—second-rate, superficial, stubbornly and enduringly devoid of any significant idea.[8]

Hildesheimer's attacks on Mozart's contemporaries and pupils must be let pass as his personal way of looking at things, but it is not altogether clear who first conjured up this phantom of the fictive composer. Mozart, at all events, never admitted having any such person in mind, and the spurious title 'Sextet for Village Band' could not have been bestowed on the work before the nineteenth century, when improvements in horn and violin technique made it increasingly difficult to understand the errors composed into the score. Mozart's intentions at the level of interpretation do not stop at the level of composition, nor, indeed, at elementary questions such as the flouting of the ban on consecutive fifths and octaves, or disobedience of the command to make intelligent use of the available aural space. Mozart doubles individual parts without taking texture into account (the intrusiveness of an accompanimental part, as at the beginning of the first-movement recapitulation, is a case in point), and in a similar spirit he involves the first violin and the 'basso' in a melodic confrontation, in the middle of the Trio, regardless of the fact that their parts lie three octaves apart—or four, if 'basso' is interpreted as a double bass, or a group including a double bass, playing an octave lower than notated; yet at that distance there can be no sense of consonance or otherwise. Another elementary matter: from time to time Mozart follows a dominant harmony with a subdominant harmony instead of the orthodox tonic, which means that the leading-note effect of the dominant is left hanging in the air. And it is not surprising, in the context of the 'musical joke', to find that Mozart returns to the thoughts on the scherzo which engaged him in the 'Haydn' Quartets. In the Minuet, the Trio starts in a wholly inappropriate, rhythmically inept manner, which is along the same lines as the dynamic 'wrong-footing' that goes on in the early stages of the Minuet in the G major Quartet, K. 387 (see Ex. 22.1, on p. 192). Possibly the 'fictive composer' had difficulties with standardized types of movement, but it is scarcely conceivable that he

[8] Hildesheimer, *Mozart*, 208.

did not notice such an elementary technical blunder at all—and it is even more unlikely if he was one of the people on Hildesheimer's list. Rather, it looks as if at this point *Ein musikalischer Spass* is taking a development that had already worked itself out in Mozart's own compositions one stage further: Mozart had already pushed minuet form to the very limits, and here it goes over the edge. It follows that the conventions of movement typology are also abandoned, along with the laws of harmony and part-writing, and everything else in the composer's rulebook.

But that is not all. The two occasions in the finale when the music simply free-wheels for bars on end (bars 108–42, 330–64) might come under Hildesheimer's rubric of 'feigned lack of imagination', but only to the superficial glance. It is far more likely that this is nonsense 'composed out', just as it is at a similar spot in the middle of the movement, where Mozart takes a routine cadence—a scalar figure descending a sixth—twists and turns it hither and thither, but cannot get it to do what a routine cadence is supposed to do, namely, close (bars 168–206). What did he really want it for?

It is what he has used earlier, in bar 10 of the finale, to finish off the theme that 'goes wrong': this is in F major for four bars, and is then repeated a third lower, reaching D minor by sheer 'clumsiness'. The scalar routine cadence retrieves the situation by allowing F major to return without any form of mediation. The meaning of all this is revealed eight bars later when Mozart modulates from F major to A flat major by means of an exotic-sounding harmonic construction, and the 'clumsy' theme returns in A flat major; but as its second half is a third lower than its first once again we arrive at the tonic, F. True, it is F minor this time, but the routine cadence serves to restore the major character, and the circle of nonsense is completed. The feat repeats itself: shortly before the end of the movement the horns state the theme in a completely orthodox form (bar 429: the strings follow suit eight bars later). Alas, all is not well that ends well, because the last sounds emitted by the viola (E flat major), the horns (F major), the first violin (G major), the second (A flat major), and the bass (B flat major) clash appallingly. But Mozart isn't trying to emulate Shakespeare, he's cracking 'a musical joke', and so the world is in perfectly good order in those final bars, even if on completely unmusical terms: the five different keys in which the piece ends have not been chosen arbitrarily, but are 'in tune' with each other, forming triads on the first five notes of the E flat major scale.

It is extremely unlikely that Abert's 'fictive composer' would have been in the position to give this last movement the shape that Mozart gave it. He would not have been able to legitimize the 'clumsy' theme retro-actively, as it were, and he would not have found the way to reintroduce it in its 'correct' shape at the end via the horns. The inner logic with which Mozart handles both these aspects would take the edge off a parody, whereas it does not detract from 'a musical joke'. The fact that the parody hypothesis becomes particularly doubtful in the closing bars is only natural.

This standpoint also makes sense of what happens in the third move-ment. Hermann Abert wrote: 'The third movement is dedicated to the first violin's skill in cantilena; what a shame that, at the very start, he hits $f\sharp''$ instead of $f\natural''$.'[9] The movement is in C major, and so it is necessary to stay in that key for a while at the beginning to establish it. The erroneous $f\sharp$ tilts the tonality from C major towards G major on only the second note, and this is undoubtedly one of the 'mistakes' arising from the first violin's attempt to give the movement an improvisational character; but the passage would sound at least as wrong without the 'wrong note' as it does with it, because Mozart gives the accompaniment wrong notes to play as well (which leads to the second violin and the bass playing consecutive fifths, just to make matters worse). The proper tonal relationships are restored 'clumsily' (bar 4); apart from an attempt at ornamentation by the first violin, which again goes adrift, relative order reigns—for as much as two bars, when coherence appears to be lost for good. Eventually the 'wrong' opening theme returns (bar 24), but somewhat differently this time. First time around, Mozart took a simple formula of melodic construction and started the second half of the theme off by repeating the first half a second lower, but arrived back in the tonic by the end. Now, from the new start in bar 24, it is all repeated a second lower, and even the cock-eyed accompaniment is repeated exactly. By this means Mozart sets the scene for a minor section in which the harmony completely ignores anything before or after it, and any sense of tempo is distorted by the abandonment of concepts of accented and unaccented beats. Time and again a new cadence is prepared, only to be diverted at the last minute to produce a false close; this becomes so confusing that the execution of the only genuine cadence (bar 35: D minor) sinks without trace in the musical torrent. All at once, however, the theme is back, but this time it too is in the minor. All is

---

[9] Abert, *Mozart*, ii. 328.

sweetness and light: no more incorrect passing-notes, no more consecutive fifths (because the accompaniment has been completely overhauled), no ambiguous harmonies; even the incoherent bars of melody are smoothed over for a while. As in the last movement, here too the theme is suddenly put to rights in a completely unpredictable and idiosyncratic way. After that section in the minor with its perpetual failures to arrive at a cadence, it would have shown a 'lack of imagination' to have the theme re-enter in the major; the minor mode works like a gauze behind which Mozart can cunningly convey what the theme ought to sound like. At the same time he admits that at the beginning of the movement he manufactured incoherence by 'losing' two bars, which he inserts now (bars 43–4). Would the 'fictive composer' have been capable of all that?

At the end of the solo cadenza, in which Mozart puts the first violin in such an awkward predicament *vis-à-vis* the listener, there is a little joke which he had played before, in 1779, in the Sinfonia Concertante, K. 364: the caricature of a vocal cadenza from an aria (cf. Ex. 13.1, on p. 113). The range between the highest and the lowest notes is three and a half octaves here (as there) and, in addition to the fact that the highest note is 'wrong' (because of the preceding error in changing position), Mozart distorts the lowest by making it pizzicato. That would have been impossible in the serious context of the double concerto—and how much less permissible in the ironically regarded offering of the 'fictive composer'.

It turns out, after all, that the first movement is the one with the fewest of these esoterica; perhaps Mozart was more interested in mocking a hypothetical composer in 1784/5 than he was by mid-1787. By the third movement at the latest, and probably also in the Trio section in the second, other aspects have pushed to the forefront, and he is firing off at any number of targets: the cock-up that appears to be beyond redemption, the disorientation of the sight-reading player (or listener), the limitations of treatises of composition. A bungling incompetent might have brought off some of these tricks, involuntarily, but the critical thing is that Mozart is able to resolve the blunders constructively and build them into a balanced composition which, however, he erects against the grain of the musical norms of his time. It looks, therefore, as if Mozart was not only reflecting here on musical shortcomings he encountered every day but also experimenting with skills his art left unused, with good reason: normally he never needed to accomplish anything like the gradual legitimation of matter which he had earlier bungled in the way he does here in the third and fourth movements. So the object of the exercise is not first and foremost to deride other composers of Mozart's acquaintance (perhaps them least of all) but to poke fun at their interpreters; above all it is a study of musical impossibilities—just 'a musical joke'. And he went further than he had thought conceivable in 1781, when he was composing *Die Entführung* and believed that 'music, however horrifying the situation, must never offend the ear but continue to please, consequently it must always remain music': then he had looked for more subtle ways of representing Osmin's rage; now, by contrast, the offence to the ear was part of the pleasure.

Ein musikalischer Spass thus bears witness in a negative kind of way to what the stage of his art that Mozart had reached by then looked like. He had started his career as a wunderkind, and in the early 1770s had started to shake off that description and evolve a personal style as a composer. His visits to Italy had released new powers in him, resulting in greater concentration on vocal music, enhancement of his technical inventiveness (as exhibited in the later Salzburg symphonies), and the composition of concertos. When he went looking for a job in 1777–8 he had still not rid himself of the child-prodigy image, but his youth now caused scepticism rather than astonishment. There is no longer any sign of that particular problem from 1779 onwards and as a composer, too, Mozart can probably be said to have triumphed over his past by then. The music he wrote during his last years in Salzburg, 1779–81, demonstrated—probably quite consciously—that he was more than a merely local, provincial composer. Another phase—the fourth—began with the move to Vienna: in the new environment, and building on the late Salzburg compositions, he developed a style with which he surpassed not merely the local standards but also those of the age as a whole. He reflected on his art; he questioned basic preconceptions and in doing so discovered new possibilities for music. It can perhaps be seen happening already in innovations like the individualization of the stock characters of Singspiel in *Die Entführung*, the forte second subject of the 'Linz' Symphony, or the chromaticism in the middle movement of the 'Strinasacchi' Sonata. But in 1784–5, in bringing wholly new dimensions to the concerto, and in exploring new techniques in chamber music, Mozart went beyond the accepted contemporary limits laid down in the musical rulebook, not in details alone but comprehensively. This advance in his maturity is mirrored in the difference between what he said about his Osmin and the *Musikalischer Spass* of six years later. Mozart had reached what in the event was his 'late' style, at the age of 30—which is a preposterous statement in itself. The thought of what might have happened if he had lived to 60 takes the breath away.

31

A Romance and its Context: *Eine kleine Nachtmusik,*
K. 525

In his monograph on Mozart (1945), Alfred Einstein refers to *Eine kleine Nachtmusik* as 'one of Mozart's best-known works', then adds: 'The truth is that it is one of the most enigmatic'.[1] The enigmas have still not been solved. We still do not know the reason for its composition, although its title and Mozart's date for it provide clues: if it was finished on 10 August 1787, it could well have been performed one evening that summer, in the open air, as a serenade or 'night music'. It is also probable that it was meant for orchestra: Mozart specified 'Bassi' for the lowest part in the ensemble, as compared to 'Basso' in *Ein musikalischer Spass* (although, admittedly, he also writes 'viola' not 'viole'). What is not at all clear, however, is the work's content. In his own catalogue Mozart described it as 'A little night music, consisting of an Allegro, Minuet and Trio.—Romance. Minuet and Trio, and finale'. Like the 'Haffner' Symphony, which has lost the minuet and trio which it must originally have had between the first and slow movements, so too *Eine kleine Nachtmusik* lost the first of its minuets somewhere in its history. This is confirmed by the numbering of the leaves of the autograph: Mozart numbered them up to eight, but there is no '3', and the gap comes between the end of the first movement and the beginning of what is now the 'second' movement.

It is not very probable that leaf no. 3 was rudely torn from the autograph;[2] it is more likely that Mozart was not careful enough about keeping the sections of his work together. Each of the first two surviving movements fills a folio sheet, folded once to form two leaves (four sides); these could have been stitched together. However, the third and fourth movements of the four-movement work that we know are written on three single leaves; in the final movement, Mozart numbers the sides, in addition to the leaf, as an extra safeguard of the order. It looks, therefore,

---

[1] Einstein, *Mozart*, 206.
[2] See E. F. Schmid, NMA, IV/12, vi, Kritischer Bericht, p. f/15.

as if the missing minuet and trio was also written on a single leaf which simply became separated from the little stack of single and double leaves making up the autograph. The Romance, which generations of hearers have experienced as a 'normal' slow second movement, was thus conceived by Mozart as a genuine middle movement, framed immediately between two minuet and trio movements, and further by the two outermost, fast movements. The only surviving minuet begins in that lumbering, two-part staccato (two-part, because the violins are playing in octaves, as are the violas and bass), from which the rhythmic staccato impulse persists even underneath the flowing arch-shapes of the trio. There is no way of knowing what Mozart did to counterbalance that in the first minuet and trio. The opening Allegro is laid out in a concise sonata form; the finale, with its busy accompanimental motif, which is nevertheless capable of coming to an abrupt stop at will, is a rondo. These movements bear out the serenade's claim to be 'little', and the instrumentation throughout can also be so described, for only the early divertimentos of around 1772–3 (K. 136–8, for example) come so close to the string quartet.

The Romance, however, begs to be regarded in a different light, on formal grounds, and its none too common title is also interesting. The 'romance' is a vocal genre in origin, with Spanish and French roots, and it is therefore somewhat unexpected in an instrumental work. It is true that the French composer François-Joseph Gossec called the middle movement of one of his symphonies a 'romance' as early as the mid-1770s, but it was some while before the term was used by a German composer—and it first happened in works directed at the French market (for example, in the third of Haydn's 'Paris' symphonies, No. 85, 'La Reine').

Mozart's only vocal romance does actually acknowledge the original mixture of textual and musical elements: it is the number in *Die Entführung* with which Pedrillo gives the two women the signal for flight ('In Mohrenland gefangen war . . .'). As a strophic song it has nothing in common formally with Mozart's instrumental romances, which have a different structural scheme. That scheme, however, is already present in its essential elements in what was probably Mozart's earliest romance, the fifth movement of his Gran Partita for wind and bass, K. 361. He used the title again in the fifth of the Vienna serenades, K⁶ 439*b*, and in connection with middle movements in two of the horn concertos, K. 447 and 495, and two piano concertos, K. 466 and 537.

The distinctive characteristics of Mozart's romances are most plainly set out in those of the D minor Piano Concerto and *Eine kleine Nachtmusik*.

These are slow movements in a rondo-like form. Their individual sections are always repeated shortly after being played for the first time; in the concerto this can mean that the soloist plays the section first and the orchestra takes it up for the repeat. Both romances begin with the statement of an eight-bar theme, divisible into two approximately equal halves; the first half leads to a half close, the second to a full close (so the structure can be expressed as AA^1). The repetition of the theme is followed by a new eight-bar structure, of which, however, only the first four bars are really new, because the second four repeat the music from the second half of the first eight-bar entity; thus, ignoring the repeats, the structure can be expressed as AA^{1}BA^1; in the concerto a short coda is added to this opening complex.

Up to this point the music has been in the tonic, but now the dominant comes into the picture, followed after a certain time—in accordance with the norms of rondo form—by the return to the tonic, to allow the 'theme' to re-enter. This is one of the 'little' features of the serenade, comprising only eighteen bars where the soloist in the concerto has twenty-eight bars in which to spread himself (repeats included). The theme re-enters in its original, eight-bar form (AA^1); in the concerto the soloist's statement is once more repeated by the tutti. Then the major-mode world is invaded by a section in the minor (sixteen bars long in the serenade, but fifty-nine in the concerto), before the theme returns, this time without repeats and in the form AA^{1}BA^1. Even the tutti repetition in the concerto is reduced to the minimum here; there is a closing coda in both movements.

Thus the romances of the D minor Concerto and *Eine kleine Nachtmusik* resemble each other not only in the succession of the individual thematic blocks but also even in the structure and preparation of the thematic foundations on which the form is laid out in the different dimensions of these two particular works. How do they compare with Mozart's other instrumental romances?

The one in the Gran Partita also has a first large-scale complex in the major and a middle section in the minor, but it does not have the separate dominant section between the two, and furthermore the middle and outer sections are in different tempos and rhythms: a 2/4 allegretto is framed by the two appearances of a 3/4 adagio. That contrast of tempo is also characteristic of the romances in the serenade and the concerto, except that in each of them it is composed out: in *Eine kleine Nachtmusik* it happens when the basic rhythm intensifies from the leisurely start to the pulsating accompanimental semiquavers of the minor section. As for the Romance in the D minor Concerto, Leopold Mozart described it eloquently in a letter to his daughter: 'The adagio is a romance, the tempo is taken as fast as the players can manage to bring out the fast [semiquaver] triplets, which begin at once on page 3 of the Romance, and they must work at it to ensure that the theme does not sound dull' (5 January 1786).

The Romance in the fifth of the K^6 439*b* serenades consists formally of only the introductory section of the other romances, and the one in Horn Concerto, K. 495, can be said to finish before it reaches the section in the minor. The Romance in the Horn Concerto, K. 447 (composed at around the same time as *Eine kleine Nachtmusik*), conforms most closely to the pattern described above, although it does not have a distinct minor section with the intensification of the rhythm—but here perhaps Mozart, as in other aspects of his horn concertos, was being merciful to the soloist. There remains the middle movement of the 'Coronation' Concerto, K. 537: the title 'romance' is found only on a sketch for a melody from which the composer developed the typically expansive, introductory tonic section. But the finished movement goes its own way: there is an extensive middle section touching on the dominant and minor, which has no truck with rondo form (and does not use the same means to distinguish itself as the middle section of the Gran Partita's Romance, either). Mozart did not give the movement any title in its finished form: did it take a different direction from one that would have allowed him to call it a romance?

It can be said, then, that the Romance in *Eine kleine Nachtmusik* is as well made, down into the smallest details, as anyone would expect a piece of music by Mozart to be at this date: a banal enough conclusion. But the very act of comparing the serenade with its 'contemporaries' draws attention to a detail of the Romance which should not be overlooked: it too harbours a 'musical joke'. To effect the transition from the first episode (in the dominant) back to the theme, Mozart employs means that would undoubtedly be regarded as 'composed free-wheeling' if they were found in the *Musikalischer Spass*, completed only a few weeks earlier. A completely inconsequential, routine cadence of the first violin is detached from its context; the second violin repeats it parrot-fashion, then it is played in octaves by both violins—and those octaves are handed on down, via second violin and viola, to viola and bass. The two violins pick it up again, to expound it in fugato-like imitation, in which the bass too finally joins; then at last the theme is reached. The fugato serves the move back to the tonic, so it is not completely unmotivated, but the preceding toing and froing with the routine cadence borders on what Mozart does in the finale of *Ein musikalischer Spass* with different material (performed in horrendous thirds and leaving no chance of overlooking the comic intention). At the time when Mozart was composing *Don Giovanni*, one scene of which exploits the friction caused by three incompatible dance bands playing side by side, that sort of thing was clearly part of his 'normal' artistic practice.

32

Leporello's Mortal Peril: *Don Giovanni*, K. 527

The commission for an opera which Mozart negotiated with the impresario Pasquale Bondini in the spring of 1787 took the composer back to Prague in the following autumn. He had still not finished the opera, *Don Giovanni*, when he set out from Vienna on 1 October, but the première took place exactly four weeks later, on 29 October—the ink, allegedly, was scarcely dry on the orchestral parts for the overture. It had been hoped that the première would be given in celebration of a one-day visit by Archduchess Maria Theresia and Prince Anton Clemens of Saxony; but the royal couple had passed through Prague two weeks earlier and had had to be content with *Figaro*.

Like *Figaro*, the new opera was a collaboration between Mozart and Lorenzo Da Ponte.[1] The *Don Giovanni* the pair conceived was a 'dramma giocoso', that is, an *opera buffa*, which still remained within the tradition of the Don Juan story. In musico-dramatic terms, the action would dominate every section of the work, and that, for a start, ruled out the virtuoso arias typical of *opera seria*. Apart from that, one must always expect the unexpected, and the emphasis on the action is the reason why so much takes place in ensembles of various forms. In accordance with tradition, the action hots up at the end of each of the two acts, where the music proceeds uninterrupted by any passages of secco recitative and one 'number' succeeds another, with a natural tendency for the formal complexity and the numbers of people involved to increase. (Two acts are the norm: in this respect the four-act *Figaro* can be viewed as a two-act work in disguise.) The finale of the last act must also deliver a 'lieto fine'—a happy end. Such an ending is going to be a close-run thing in a treatment of the Don Juan material, but the opera's subtitle, *Il dissoluto punito* (The Libertine Punished) gives a clue as to what to expect: Don Giovanni will pay for all the upheaval and distress he caused during his path through life by going to

---

[1] On the opera as a whole, see Kunze, *Mozarts Opern*, 319–431, and Rushton, *Don Giovanni*.

hell, which counts as a happy outcome, especially as it restores the moral order.

Don Giovanni's path through life: strictly speaking, Mozart and Da Ponte show their audience only the last day of it. There is no shortage of hints about that: at the end of the great sextet, quite early in the second act, the singers exclaim 'Che giornata, o stelle, è questa! Che impensata novità!' ('What a day, O heavens! What a strange, unheard-of thing!') This comes in its due place in an extensive network of detailed stage directions provided by Da Ponte. It is night when the curtain rises on the first act and the scene outside the house of the Commendatore, in which he is killed by the 'libertine' he has caught in the act of seducing his daughter, Donna Anna. It is still night when Don Giovanni and his servant, Leporello, meet Donna Elvira in the street, searching for the 'barbaro', the brute who abandoned her—none other than Don Giovanni, of course. It gives him a shock when he recognizes her, and he leaves Leporello to make sure, by means of the 'Catalogue' aria, that she understands that she is neither the first nor the last to be so treated by him. Immediately after that the two men fall in with a party of peasants celebrating a wedding, and Don Giovanni entices the bride, Zerlina, away from her new husband, Masetto, in order to carry her off to his mansion. In the nick of time (naturally— this is *opera buffa* after all) he is thwarted by the arrival, first, of Donna Elvira who rescues Zerlina from her fate (for the time being), and then of Donna Anna and her betrothed, Don Ottavio. Don Giovanni succeeds in making his escape just in time to prevent Donna Anna from identifying him as her father's murderer. On reaching his house, Don Giovanni decides (in 'Fin ch'han dal vino', the so-called 'Champagne' aria) to throw a big party, in order to bring the social barriers tumbling down: this desire (reinforced later by his famous exclamation 'Viva la libertà!') will prove fatal for him, the aristocrat, which only goes to show that *Don Giovanni* is anything but an expression of pre-revolutionary ideas—quite the reverse.

That the events from the first attempt to seduce Zerlina until now take scarcely less time in the opera than they would do in real life is confirmed by Leporello's grumbles just before Don Giovanni's aria: he has brought Zerlina's wedding party to the house and put himself to a lot of trouble to keep them in a good mood. Don Giovanni is well satisfied and the party, at which Elvira, Anna, and Ottavio also turn up, begins. It must now be midday or thereabouts. Don Giovanni tries to resume his unfinished business with Zerlina, but she lets out a scream which alerts the entire company of guests to what is going on; to begin with he tries to shift all the blame on to Leporello, but when all his excuses fail he escapes through the crowd and the first act ends.

The next scene to take place at night for certain is the one in the graveyard: before Leporello arrives to meet his master there, Don Giovanni looks at his watch and announces that it is not yet two in the morning. Don Giovanni's account of a new adventure—following his unsuccessful serenading of Donna Elvira's maid, for which he sent his servant away at the beginning of the second act—is interrupted by the voice of the Commendatore. The fact that he has already been buried and a statue erected to his memory is the only improbable feature of the opera's twenty-four-hour span, but no *opera buffa* worthy of the name was ever halted by little things like that. The statue prophesies to the 'libertine' that he will cease to laugh before dawn breaks. Now we know that Don Giovanni will not survive the late supper to which he invites the statue.

But we should take a closer look at what happens between the time when Don Giovanni and Leporello separate just after the beginning of Act II and their rendezvous in the graveyard. Before they part, Leporello tries to give notice after the débâcle at the party, but is mollified by a retrospective payment of danger money. That clears the decks for the next adventure: Don Giovannni's courtship of Donna Elvira's maid. Made wary by the failure of his experiment with the classless society in the previous act, he decides to observe class distinctions this time and makes Leporello change hat and cloak with him. Leporello, in his master's clothes, then has to play the part of the remorseful rake to deceive Donna Elvira; fooled by the disguise, she is drawn out of the house and leaves the stage on the arm of the man she thinks is Don Giovanni. That leaves the coast clear for the real Don Giovanni—in his servant's clothes—to serenade Elvira's maid (see Pl. 10). He has scarcely finished, however, when he is surprised by Masetto, at the head of a band of armed peasants, looking for Don Giovanni to bump him off. The disguise fools them too: Don Giovanni sends the group of peasants off searching in all directions until Masetto is left alone with him; Masetto hands over his weapons to show his new 'ally' their quality—which gives Don Giovanni the chance to give him a good hiding.

Was the audience alert enough in the first moments after the interval not merely to notice the exchange of clothes but to impress it upon its mind? (The disguises form the basis of a relatively inconsequential scene of mistaken identity, another stock feature of *opera buffa*.) Is it aware that Leporello is roaming the streets in his master's cloak and hat, while Don

Don Giovanni.

Rappres.^t dal Signor Bassi.

PL. 10. Mozart's first Don Giovanni, Luigi Bassi, serenading Donna Elvira's maid. Engraving by Medardus Thoenert. At this point in the opera it is Leporello who is wearing the plumed hat and stylish coat.

Giovanni gives a horde of bloodthirsty peasants an exact description of 'his master'? Does it bear all this in mind until after the aria in which Zerlina comforts the beaten Masetto with talk of the beating of her heart? The circumstances favour some things happening unnoticed, others being noticed only fleetingly and then forgotten; but at least Da Ponte and Mozart put themselves in the shoes of the people on the stage, among whom only Don Giovanni and Leporello know of the disguises adopted by themselves, and even they may not be able to foresee all the consequences at the outset. Thus the situation is able to escalate, every ounce of inflammable material in the scene weighs double—Mozart and Da Ponte exaggerate things as they can be exaggerated only in opera. In nine short bars of recitative Donna Elvira and Leporello are suddenly encountered again, in the dark entrance hall of Donna Anna's house. Under the protection of the darkness there, Leporello tries to shake off his companion; the music with which Donna Elvira leaves the recitative mode marks the start of the sextet. Suddenly Donna Anna and Don Ottavio enter; Leporello almost succeeds in making his getaway unnoticed, but as he slips out of the hall he runs straight into Zerlina and the limping Masetto.

Da Ponte's text for the sextet is constructed relatively innocently. It begins like any conventional duet or larger ensemble: each character on the stage in turn delivers a closed, rounded portion of text (for example, a stanza), in a following section they conjoin in dialogue, and finally they all sing at once. The duet for Zerlina and Don Giovanni in the first act is constructed in exactly that manner:

DON GIOVANNI. Là ci darem la mano,
                  là mi dirai di sì.
                  Vedi, non è lontano,
                  partiam, ben mio, da qui.

(There we will take hands, there you will say yes. Look, it's not far, let us go, my dear.)

ZERLINA. Vorrei, e non vorrei,
            mi trema un poco il cor;
            felice, è ver, sarei,
            ma può burlarmi ancor.

(I want to, and yet I don't, my heart trembles a little; it's true, I would be happy, but perhaps he's laughing at me.)

(*Both, alternately*) G. Vieni, mio bel diletto!
                        Z. Mi fà pietà Masetto.

G. Io cangierò tua sorte!

Z. Presto non son più forte.

(Come, my treasure!—I feel sorry for Masetto.—I will change your destiny!—My strength has almost gone.)

> (*Both, together*) Andiam, andiam, mio bene
> a ristorar le pene
> d'un innocente amor.

(Let's go, let's go, my darling, and assuage the pangs of an innocent love.)

The structure illustrates a quasi-dialectical approach: the first singer's 'thesis' is followed by the second singer's 'antithesis'; the alternation of thesis and antithesis intensifies before the 'synthesis' is finally reached. However, in the duet for Don Giovanni and Zerlina (in which they run through the text twice altogether) only the text is actually so constructed, not the music. Zerlina sings her stanza to the same melody that Don Giovanni has just sung, and one might deduce from that that, in Mozart's opinion, she has already ceased to resist.

The sextet in Act II begins with a stanza from Elvira, followed by one (musically wholly different) from Leporello; immediately thereafter Don Ottavio and Donna Anna enter and join in with one stanza each. Da Ponte concludes this stage by bringing Elvira and Leporello together, as they seek to leave the scene in a shared stanza (Elvira looking for Leporello, Leporello looking for a way of escape). But their flight is prevented by Zerlina and Masetto; in the next stanza the first half is delivered by one couple, Zerlina and Masetto, and the second half by another, Donna Anna and Don Ottavio, after which the two couples conjoin for another half-stanza in four parts, in typical ensemble style. Only then are first Elvira and then Leporello fully integrated into the sextet. Da Ponte's verses are thus dramatically logical but the structure does not go beyond a conventional succession of mini-duets.

Mozart ventures further. He tears Da Ponte's neat patchwork up into little scraps, and makes them as self-sufficient as he can. First, Elvira's and Leporello's feeling their way in the dark becomes a 'number' in its own right, in a typical, shadowy E flat major. Ottavio's entrance in a brightly lit, imposing D major, which seizes the attention with an unexpected blast of trumpets, could not be in bolder contrast—but with the tearfulness of Donna Anna's stanza Mozart unobtrusively leads the way back to the sphere of Elvira and Leporello (not, admittedly, to E flat major but to its relative, C minor). No sooner has he reached this goal than the next 'number' ensues, the entrance of Zerlina and Masetto. Once again, Leporello's abandonment of his disguise branches off from that to form an integrated structure in its own right, only to launch the sextet's powerful concluding section in which all the characters pour out their indignation at Don Giovanni's latest outrage.

Every stage in the action follows swiftly on the one before; Da Ponte's text may still be wholly a sextet, but Mozart transcends that framework by the means with which he takes advantage of the situation musically. Fragmenting the sextet gives it a form which, strictly speaking, should be found only in an act-finale: individual numbers—predominantly small ensembles—are linked together in a kind of chain.[2] True, Da Ponte's text sets certain limitations on the procedure, but some of these numbers (especially at the beginning and end of the sextet) begin in such a way as to make Mozart's intentions sufficiently clear. A peerless dramatist, he sets out to deceive the spectators, and puts both them and himself in the position of the people on stage. Donna Elvira, Donna Anna, Zerlina, Don Ottavio, and Masetto cannot know that the man with Elvira is not Don Giovanni. The real Don Giovanni would have little chance of escaping if he was discovered in the entrance hall of Donna Anna's house: Don Ottavio is about to strike the man dead when Leporello saves himself by identifying himself. If the hat and cloak described in such detail to the avenging peasants by Don Giovanni a little earlier did indeed conceal Don Giovanni himself the consummation promised by the opera's title would take place at once, the libertine would be punished, and the opera would come to an end—after a final ensemble to round things off, like the one sung when the end does eventually come.

Mozart mirrors all of that in his pseudo-finale. It is much shorter than a real one: at 277 bars it is much less than half the length of either of the real ones in this opera (653 and 871 bars respectively). The success of his deception is illustrated by the conclusion drawn by Edward J. Dent, who wrote:

The situation is most amusing, but totally unnecessary to the drama, unless it is to lead up to Ottavio's . . . determination to inform the police. But there is one reason of indisputable cogency for the presence of all these characters on the stage together—they are there to sing a sextet built up on the conventional scheme of the operatic finale. If the evidence is hardly proof of Don Giovanni's crime, it is irrefutable proof that this was intended to be the end of an act, for at no other point

---

[2] Osthoff, 'Opera buffa', 724.

could such a movement possibly be introduced; and if it is not to end an act there is no conceivable reason for introducing it, or its characters, at all. Nothing but a curtain can follow it. Leporello's explanatory aria is an anticlimax, and any way it tells us nothing that we do not know already. Ottavio's aria, lovely as it is, is a still worse anticlimax, and dramatically impossible . . . [3]

But if one of the two, librettist or composer, did indeed regard the situation as a potential finale, it was not Da Ponte—who wrote a 'normal' sextet—but Mozart. Of course angry tirades rain down upon (the absent) Don Giovanni in this pseudo-finale, and at disproportionate length, for this last stanza occupies more than half the total number of bars in the sextet. That the reproaches directed at Leporello as Giovanni's accomplice are in secco recitative is purely a formal matter, and that his aria in reply to them may strike listeners as an anticlimax was probably fully intended by Mozart. The noose tightens, but round the wrong neck, and the dramatic energy of the scene necessarily expires in a lot of huffing and puffing.

This is the first example of a pseudo-finale in Mozart's *œuvre*; there is another in *Così fan tutte*, but there it is set up by the structure of the text and the drift of the action. The situation in the *Don Giovanni* sextet, moreover, has no precedent in any of the earlier dramatic versions of the Don Juan material. Da Ponte followed closely Giovanni Bertati's libretto for an opera composed only a few months earlier, *Don Giovanni o sia Il convitato di pietra* by Giuseppe Gazzaniga (first performance 5 February 1787 in Venice), but that 'omits' a long stretch of the material we know from Mozart's opera, from the end of the scene in Act I where Don Giovanni entices Zerlina away from Masetto to the start of the scene in the church-yard in Act II.[4] Even so, Da Ponte did not invent all of that material: Don Giovanni's serenade and the scene where he beats up the peasant bride-groom were to be found in a play of about 1770 by Francesco Cerlone, but in very different contexts (and the peasants have different names). Cerlone put the serenade in the middle of the second of his three acts, and used it to grant Don Giovanni access to Donna Anna's rooms; the Commendatore is killed only then. Da Ponte separated these two elements and gave them new functions, with the serenade addressed to Donna Elvira's maid, and (as in Bertati's version) the murder of Donna Anna's father providing the starting-point of the entire drama. Again, in Cerlone's version, the beating-

---

[3] Dent, *Mozart's Operas*, 168–9.
[4] On the relationship of Da Ponte's version to those by Bertati and Cerlone, see S. Kunze, *Don Giovanni vor Mozart: Die Tradition der Don-Giovanni-Opern im italienischen Buffa-Theater des 18. Jahrhunderts* (Munich, 1972), 59–71; 158–87.

up comes at the end of the second act, after Don Giovanni has enticed the Zerlina figure away from her wedding breakfast, but Da Ponte divided the material and had the beating happen only some time after the wedding scene.

By means of this redistribution Da Ponte considerably strengthened and tightened the structure of the drama. The opera starts with an outrage, and thereafter the 'Anna plot' is one of the main struts of the action. The 'Zerlina plot' develops only gradually, by contrast, and does not begin with a comparable outrage, which it would do if Masetto had been beaten in Act I. The structure is rounded off by the 'Elvira plot', which is more peripheral in that it offers neither the outrage of the Anna plot nor the gradual development of the Zerlina plot, but it still adds to the sum total of Giovanni's offences. With Donna Anna, the nobleman's daughter, and Zerlina, the peasant girl, Don Giovanni is shown to range to both extremes of the social scale, and his downfall lies in the fact that the two extremes meet: in the first-act finale, in the Act II sextet, and after his descent to hell, at the very end of the opera (but not at the actual moment of his descent to hell: the happy ending lies in the knowledge that the libertine has been punished). Don Giovanni is opposed by a front made up of social extremes: the cry of 'Viva la libertà' with which, at the beginning of the Act I finale, he hopes to bring down the social barriers between himself and Zerlina is his own death sentence: it is in everybody's interests to see the libertine punished.

Don Giovanni's flirtation with the classless society trips him up in front of a large number of his own guests at the end of Act I; he goes down to hell in privacy. Mozart draws the distinction between the two by his contrasting use of on-stage music. The impossibility of linking the sphere of the aristocrats with that of the peasants is the principle which generates the music played at Don Giovanni's party in Act I. Donna Anna and Don Ottavio open the dance, and Mozart writes for them a courtly minuet (3/4), appropriate to their social standing. A second stage band strikes up a contredanse (2/4), in which Don Giovanni partners Zerlina. The crotchet is the same in these two dances, but they are differently accentuated, so that a strong beat is shared only at every second bar of the minuet and every third of the contredanse. Finally a third orchestra plays a rustic allemande (3/8) for Leporello and Masetto: this is so fast that each bar takes no longer than a crotchet of the other two. But again it does not conform to either of them, because each bar of the allemande is divided into three beats, while in the others each crotchet is divided into two quavers.

The maximum of composed chaos in the finale of Act I is contrasted with the perfect order of the 'Tafelmusik' in that of Act II. There Mozart gives the wind band an operatic medley to play: first a number from *Una cosa rara* by Vicente Martín y Soler (it was first performed in 1786, the same year as *Figaro*, and the libretto was by Da Ponte), then one from Giuseppe Sarti's *Fra i due litiganti il terzo gode* (1782), and finally one from his and Da Ponte's own *Le nozze di Figaro*, the smash hit of the previous season in Prague. The Martín piece is in D major, the Sarti in F major, and the Mozart in B flat major. 'Non più andrai' in B flat major: that should make the audience sit up, because it is in C major in its original context. The transposition is anything but accidental, however, because the tonalities of D, F, and B flat have played a crucial role in *Don Giovanni* since the beginning of Act I. Leporello's opening number is in F major, Donna Anna and Don Giovanni enter in B flat major, and the duel is fought in D minor. The opening phase of the finale of Act I follows a similar progression: Don Giovanni encounters Zerlina and Masetto in his garden: F major. Enter Donna Elvira, Donna Anna, and Don Ottavio: D minor. Having been invited to the party, they gather their strength for what lies ahead: B flat major. But the finale begins in C major, which conveys no threat (and even allows the hope that it will end similarly). Catastrophe does not strike until the finale of the second act, and Mozart sounds the tonal warnings clearly, not in the supper-music alone. Donna Elvira enters,

PL. 11. The Commendatore's statue seizing Don Giovanni. Vignette on the title-page of the first edition of the full score (1801).

the musicians leave hastily—but the music is still in B flat major, the key of the *Figaro* excerpt. Donna Elvira leaves, but meets the statue outside, and we hear her scream; Leporello is sent to the door, returns shaking with fear, and tells his master what he has seen: F major. Then Don Giovanni himself opens the door to his guest, and the preliminaries to his damnation run their course in D minor.

The operatic numbers Mozart chose to quote in this scene did not have to be in the keys he needed for the overall tonal plan of his opera: he transposed them according to his need. But there were other, musical reasons for choosing the ones he did. The first piece is in 6/8, which could be said to double the 3/8 of the allemande in the first finale; the second is in 3/4 like the minuet there, and 'Non più andrai' is alla breve, with two beats to the bar, like the contredanse which Don Giovanni himself dances there. The complicated blend of duple and triple metres from the Act I finale is thus reproduced, and Don Giovanni can be seen to be caught not only in a structure of tonalities but also in one of metres, from neither of which he can escape. The very Tafelmusik to which he eats his supper expresses perfect order.

The chaos and the order of the on-stage musics in the two finales are dependent on the total co-operation of librettist and composer. Don Giovanni sets out the programme of the musical mixture at his Act I party in his aria 'Fin ch'han d'al vino': let minuet, follia, and allemande be danced side by side without order ('Senza alcun ordine la danza sia, chi il minuetto, chi la follia, chi l'alemanna farai ballar'). But those three dances, though different in style, are all in triple metres: perfect chaos comes only with the addition of the duple metre of the contredanse. In the supper scene in Act II, however, Don Giovanni and Leporello comment on the music while the wind band is playing, so the text and the music must fit each other unconditionally, and must moreover spring naturally from the context.

Mozart has been hailed as a 'master of the finale',[5] and what he said in letters to his father at the time when he was working on *Die Entführung* illustrates the attention he paid to the finale as a musical form even then. In *Figaro*, too, he devoted special care to the way the act-finales were built up, and the construction of the tonal relationships between the separate stages in the action of each one in turn. At the same time, one of the most detailed contemporary accounts of what an operatic finale demands is to be

---

[5] A. Greither, *Die sieben großen Opern Mozarts: Versuche über das Verhältnis der Texte zur Musik*, 3rd edn. (Heidelberg, 1977), 60.

found in the memoirs of Lorenzo Da Ponte. Can it be said that two artists, equally gifted in the construction of effective finales, found each other? It is impossible not to attribute the greater initiative to Mozart, for in his case a line of development can be traced back unbroken to 1781 and the last-minute prevention of the sacrifice of Idamantes in *Idomeneo*. The fabrication of a pseudo-finale from a conventional sextet is another indication. In that scene, incidentally, Mozart made it clear where he drew the line between appearances and the relentless realism of his music: the sextet in the entrance hall of Donna Anna's mansion is in E flat major, a tonality which has no connection with Don Giovanni's fate. Leporello is in no danger at all.

33

A Summer in Alsergrund: The Last Three Symphonies

It is obvious that in the first half of 1788 Mozart was looking for new ways of stabilizing his position. He had broken new ground artistically in the preceding two years and, rather as at the stage when he had left the status of 'child prodigy' behind him but the world about him had been slow to notice it, so now he had to find some way of improving the external circumstances in which he worked so that they matched up to his inner advancement. One important step in the right direction had been taken in December 1787 when he was made a Composer to the Imperial and Royal Chamber (with the less than princely annual salary of 800 gulden), and another followed in May 1788, with the production in Vienna of the opera he had composed for Prague, *Don Giovanni*. The former ended his search for a court appointment, and the latter represented the first occasion on which the Vienna Opera had accepted a work which Mozart had composed for another city—a feat he had failed to accomplish with *Idomeneo*. (In theory it might have been possible with *La finta giardiniera*, at least: two productions of the work are recorded as having been given in Frankfurt and one in Mainz during Mozart's time in Vienna.[1]) While breaching the operatic barrier signified a temporary advantage, yielding about the same amount of money as he would have earned from a small concert given at his own risk (the Vienna *Don Giovanni* brought in 225 gulden, considerably less than he sometimes made from a concert), a post at court, as a recurrent source of income, also eased his longer-term financial position.

It would seem that Mozart had been looking for some such security for quite a while, perhaps under the influence of Haydn, whose comments, as quoted by Niemetschek (see above, p. 190), support this assumption. Obviously Mozart did not want any serious restraints placed on the freedom he had enjoyed for several years, and there is no indication that he made any real effort to obtain a post as a Kapellmeister, with all the duties which it would entail. The obligations that went with the post he did

[1] R. Angermüller, *Mozart: Die Opern von der Uraufführung bis heute* (Frankfurt am Main, 1988), 63.

obtain presumably corresponded exactly to what he was prepared to do: in return for his 800 gulden he was required to provide the dance music for the masked balls held during the Vienna carnival. During the summer of 1786 he had angled for an appointment at the court of Donaueschingen, which would presumably have involved him in about the same amount of work (and which he would have been able to do 'from home'—that is, from Vienna). He had written to Sebastian Winter, who was the Mozarts' manservant on their first journey to Paris, and had been in the service of Prince von Fürstenberg ever since:

Since His Serene Highness has an orchestra, His Highness could enjoy the sole ownership of pieces which I would write for his court alone, which would be very agreeable, in my humble opinion. If HSH would do me the honour of ordering from me a certain number of symphonies, quartets, concertos for various instruments, or other pieces according to his wishes, throughout the year, and would pay me an agreed annual sum for them, HSH would be served faster and better, and I would work with more peace of mind because the work would be assured. (8 August 1786)

Some 'assured' work which would allow him to 'work with more peace of mind' was obviously Mozart's goal—as long as it was linked with an appropriate financial reward, enough to assure him of a living. In that respect his Vienna court appointment must have been somewhat unsatisfying, because one predecessor—Gluck—had earned 2,000 gulden in the same position. Gluck, however, had been more famous than Mozart could claim to be, for he had changed the whole face of opera with the works he had written for the German capitals, for Italy, and, above all, for Paris. Mozart admitted his disappointment in a letter to his sister: 'In answer to your question about my appointment, the Emperor has taken me into his household . . . that is, has given me a formal posting; but at only 800 florins for the time being'; but he could console himself with the knowledge that 'no one else in the household earns so much' and he also appeared to nourish the hope of a rise in the future (2 August 1788).

Mozart had moved into new lodgings in Vienna only in the previous December, but a consequence of his financial position was the decision to move again, to the suburb of Alsergrund, lying to the north-west of the city. He wrote to Michael Puchberg, a fellow Freemason:

As I shall have less interruption from visitors I shall have more time for work—and when I have to go into the city on business, which will be seldom in any case, any fiacre will take me for 10 kreuzer. Furthermore, the lodgings are cheaper and will be pleasanter in the spring, summer, and autumn, because I also have a garden. (Probably 16 June 1788; see Pl. 12.)

Puchberg, born in 1741, had joined a cloth company in Vienna at about the age of 27, and eventually became its managing director. Mozart started to entrust his financial affairs to him in 1787, if not earlier, when Puchberg took delivery of the 1,000 gulden that Mozart inherited on the death of his father (he was in Prague for the première of *Don Giovanni* at the date when the money was due to arrive in Vienna). In the spring of 1788 Puchberg took charge of the sale of copies (handwritten, not printed) of the string

PL. 12. A bird's-eye view including no. 135 (now no. 16) Währingerstrasse, Alsergrund: Mozart's suburban lodgings in the summer of 1788. (From *Vogelschau der Stadt Wien* by Joseph Daniel Huber, published *c*.1770.)

quintets, K. 406, 515, and 516: he issued subscription vouchers and would have arranged for deliveries in due course. Unfortunately the number of subscribers was lower than expected, which led Mozart to place a second advertisement in the *Wiener Zeitung* on 25 June 1788, announcing the postponement of publication from 1 July to 1 January 1789. The composer also looked further afield, and he told Puchberg, in the letter quoted above: 'You need not worry about the subscription; I'm going to put the date back by several months; I hope to find more admirers abroad than here.' In fact, another advertisement was placed in the June issue of the Weimar paper *Journal des Luxus und der Moden*.

Mozart hoped that the move to Alsergrund would give him more time to work. Indeed, he reported in another letter to Puchberg: 'I've done more work in the ten days that I've been living here than I managed to do in two months in the other place' (27 June 1788). In respect of what he actually composed that is certainly true, but his real wishes were for something similar to what he had outlined in his application to Donaueschingen two years earlier: an official contract would let him 'work with more peace of mind because the work would be assured'. All the appearances are that Mozart was pessimistic about any improvement in his standard of living, in spite of his court appointment—perhaps because the salary was less than he had hoped. He still lived from hand to mouth; the change in his position as from the previous December may have made it clear that there were no further openings for him, if he wanted to go on in his present life-style; in other words, there was no prospect of his achieving any greater professional or, more concretely, financial security in the long term. This was the background to the candid letter he wrote to his brother mason, Michael Puchberg, probably on 16 June 1788, which has already been quoted above, but which now follows in full.

Honourable Brother in the Order,
Dearest, best of friends!

The conviction that you are my true friend, and that you know me to be an honest man, encourages me to open my heart to you and make you the following request. Since I am frank by nature, I will go straight to the point without mincing words.

If you could find the love and friendship for me to help me for one or two years with one or two thousand gulden, at an appropriate rate of interest, it would be like helping me to buy a field and a plough at one and the same time! You will agree, I know, that it is hard, nay, impossible to live when a man has only irregular sums of money coming in! When a man does not have a certain, basic amount of capital, at least, it is impossible ever to get straight. A man can do nothing if he has nothing to start with. If you do me this act of friendship, I shall be able firstly, having something in hand, to meet necessary expenses when they fall due, and therefore more easily than I do now, when I have to defer payment and then often have to hand over the whole of the sum I have just earned at the most inconvenient moment. Secondly, I shall be able to work with less on my mind and a lighter heart, and therefore I shall earn more. As to security, I don't believe that you will have any doubts! You know more or less how I stand, and are familiar with my principles! You need not worry about the subscription; I'm going to put the date back by several months; I hope to find more admirers abroad than here.

Now I have bared my whole heart to you in a matter which is very important to me—acted, that is, as a true Brother, but it is only to a true Brother that one can pour out everything. Now I look forward to your answer, or, rather, to a favourable answer, and I don't know—I believe you are a man like myself who, if he possibly can, will certainly help his friend, if he is a real friend—his brother, if he is a true Brother. But if perhaps you cannot spare such a large sum all at once, I beg you at least to lend me a few hundred gulden by tomorrow, because my landlord in the Landstrasse [the district where the Mozarts had lived up to December 1787] made such a fuss that I had to pay him on the spot to avoid unpleasantness, which threw me into great disorder! We are sleeping for the first time tonight in our new quarters, where we shall stay winter and summer. I think it will make no difference, essentially, and may even be better. I don't have much to do in the city as it is, and as I shall have less interruption from visitors I shall have more time for work—and when I have to go into the city on business, which will be seldom in any case, any fiacre will take me for 10 kreuzer. Furthermore, the lodgings are cheaper and will be pleasanter in the spring, summer, and autumn, because I also have a garden. The address is Währingerstrasse, at the sign of the Three Stars, No. 135.

Please take my letter as a true sign of my complete trust in you, and may you ever remain my friend and Brother, as I shall be yours till death.

Your true, most sincere friend and Brother
W. A. Mozart

PS When shall we next make a little music at your house?
I have written a new trio!

Mozart's hope was to gain a creative breathing-space in which to do something on his own terms, without needing to take the public into account. 'A man can do nothing if he has nothing to start with': the importunities of his former landlord had shown that he had only enough money for immediate needs, and none to allow him to make plans for the longer term. The wish to have 'something in hand' is central to the understanding of Mozart's situation. Either Puchberg did not understand the purpose of the request, or he could not 'spare such a large sum all at once': at all events, he sent only 200 gulden. When Beethoven was 38, some of his friends drew up an agreement to free him of financial worries by paying him an annual income from their own pockets; Mozart, at 32, was unable to raise even a one-off payment to serve the same end. It is remotely possible that both Mozart and Puchberg understood the expression 'a few hundred' ('ein paar Hundert') as 'a couple of hundred' ('ein Paar hundert'), so that 200 gulden met Mozart's most immediate needs, but the loan was not followed by any larger sum. Mozart applied to Puchberg twice more, exerting greater pressure on his 'Brother'; he perhaps had some concrete reason to foresee a gradual worsening in his situation when he prophesied: 'If you do not help me, most worthy Brother, in the situation I am now in, I shall lose my honour and my credit, which is the one thing I wish to preserve' (27 June 1788). But Puchberg did not come up with any more money, and Mozart had another go, probably in July:

Dearest friend and Brother in the Order.

By taking great care and pains I have got my affairs to the state where all I need is an advance on these two pawn-tickets. I beg this favour from you, by our friendship, but it must be at once. Forgive my importunity, but you know my position. Oh, if only you'd done what I asked you to do! If you would do it even now, everything would go swimmingly.

Ever yours, Mozart

Compared to what he had asked earlier, Mozart must have needed a relatively small sum if he offered two pawn-tickets as security, perhaps just enough to cover the rent. It is likely therefore that in referring here to his 'position' Mozart did not mean a precarious financial one but his professional situation, and was reminding Puchberg that a loan now (of the 'one or two thousand gulden' he had asked for earlier) would be nothing more than an advance on future profits. Puchberg was not to be drawn, however—although the artistic product of those first ten days in Alsergrund gives a concrete example of the vistas that could have opened for Mozart if he had been given the economic backing he asked for.

This reading of Mozart's financial position in the summer of 1788, that is, at the beginning of the notorious series of begging letters to Michael Puchberg, depends on a reinterpretation of one of the letters. The letter in question is undated but has customarily been placed in June 1788, before the one written on the day the Mozarts moved to Alsergrund. In it Mozart asks for 100 gulden, although he still owes Puchberg 8 ducats (36 gulden); he promises to pay back the 136 gulden 'next week (when my concerts in the Casino start)', because 'I must necessarily have the subscription money in my hands by then'. The subscription referred to is commonly identified as the one for the sale of copies of the string quintets, but that can hardly be the case, because it was not Mozart but Puchberg who collected the money for that subscription—and for Puchberg first to hand over the total to Mozart and then to receive it back from him in settlement of a debt does not make sense. Mozart's reference to his 'concerts in the Casino' (note the plural) raises another question: the Casino was used for concerts in the winter season, and it is doubtful if he would have attracted an audience there for at least two, perhaps more, in midsummer (when concerts were given in the Augarten). It is much more probable that Mozart would have arranged to give such concerts in Advent or Lent (as he did in Lent 1784, for example).[2] True, the possibility of a summer series of subscription concerts arose again in 1789, but no venue was mentioned, and in 1790 Mozart told Puchberg that he was thinking of giving some in his own home. In view of the uncertainty about dates, and especially the objections to associating the reference to 'subscription money' with the sale of the string quintets, we ought to take the probabilities as a starting-point and try to assign the letter to a date in the winter when concerts were much more frequent.[3] It makes better sense to assume that at some stage Mozart had managed to pay back all but 36 gulden of the money he had borrowed from Puchberg, but the situation had deteriorated again, and he had arranged to give a series of subscription concerts to keep the wolf from the door. Since there is no evidence that Mozart borrowed money from Puchberg before June 1788, the undated letter is likely to have been written in the winter of 1788–9, and followed by settlement of the debt in full. We shall return to the story in due course, to see how it developed later, but for now we can assume that by about the turn of the year 1788–9 Mozart had managed to repay the 200 gulden lent him by Puchberg in the previous June.

During the first two months in Alsergrund, apart from smaller vocal and instrumental compositions, Mozart finished two works for beginnners (the Sonata Facile, K. 545, and the Violin Sonata, K. 547), the two piano trios, K. 542 and 548, and—most importantly—the three 'great' and 'last'

---

[2] Einstein, for one, took it for granted that Mozart gave his concerts in winter (see *Mozart*, 234).

[3] Braunbehrens also doubts the customary dating of the letter (see *Mozart in Vienna*, 324).

symhonies (K. 543 in E flat major, K. 550 in G minor, and K. 551 in C major, the 'Jupiter'). The trios were published by Artaria in November 1788, with the B flat major Trio of 1786 to make a third,[4] while Hoffmeister brought out the Adagio and Fugue for strings, K. 546, of which the Adagio was a new piece, composed as an introduction to Mozart's arrangement of his keyboard fugue, K. 426. Another work to be published was the song 'Beim Auszug in das Feld', K. 552, which appeared in a weekly magazine devoted to furnishing 'agreeable and instructive activities for children in their leisure hours'. Was Mozart looking to branch out as a pedagogue with the two sonatas for beginners? An advertisement he placed in the *Wiener Zeitung* of 16 July, offering a 'Singing Tutor for the Soprano voice', is another hint that he was thinking along those lines. At the same time it can scarcely be coincidence that suddenly, upon the publication of the three keyboard trios (fruits of his experiments in the field of chamber music), nothing more was heard of the attempt to market manuscript copies of those other experimental chamber works, the string quintets, until, with equal suddenness, the first of them was also published by Artaria in the following spring (between January and May).[5] Did Mozart and Artaria perhaps plan to present the public with his new musical ideas across a broad front, even including the three symphonies? These could certainly have been written for Artaria, who had published Haydn's six 'Paris' symphonies in two groups of three in 1787, and symphonies by Michael Haydn and Franz Anton Rosetti, also in threes, the year before that; the series suddenly broke off, however, and resumed only in 1791 with three works by Dittersdorf. Maybe the financial backing Mozart tried to get from Michael Puchberg was intended to service an ambitious joint venture with Artaria—who was then unable to sustain it, perhaps because of the recession following Joseph II's ill-starred war against the Turks, of which the only success was the hard-fought recovery of Belgrade. In that case, Artaria might have offered to publish the quintets in compensation. There is another factor to support the supposition that the symphonies were connected with some such plan: the first three of Haydn's 'Paris' symphonies (Nos. 82–4), which Artaria published six months before Mozart wrote his three great works, are in C major, G minor, and E flat major—the same keys as Mozart's.

[4] A. Weinmann, *Vollständiges Verlagsverzeichnis Artaria & Comp.*, 3rd edn. (Vienna, 1985), No. 204.

[5] Haberkamp, *Erstdrucke*, i. 282.

We must start from the premiss that Mozart's activities as a composer had specific causes. If he did not write the three last symphonies for publication, it might have been for performance instead; but that is not very likely in the summer of 1788. The line of occasions on which they might have been performed begins with the winter concert season, and stretches on to the spring of 1791, a period which includes Mozart's journey to Frankfurt for the coronation of Leopold II in 1790. But in the previous seven years in Vienna Mozart had written just two symphonies (the 'Linz' and the 'Prague', to which can be added the 'Haffner', which started life as a serenade): the fact that he suddenly sat down and wrote three in eight weeks, without any discernible prospect of a performance, strengthens the likelihood that there was another incentive. Even the supposition that Mozart retreated to Alsergrund to compose in peace and quiet is not enough in itself: Mozart was a man and a musician of the eighteenth century, not a 'Romantic' bent on composing purely according to his own inclinations. Doing that would not have helped him in the position he described in his letters to Puchberg, and only work targeted to specific purposes could do anything to change the position. Mozart must have intended from the first to compose music which would enhance his reputation through the medium of print, but his intentions were frustrated, not by Puchberg alone but perhaps also by a publisher, possibly Artaria— both, after all, were businessmen put in the same boat by the country's politico-economic situation.

These three symphonies by Mozart, like the nine by Beethoven, have acquired a stamp of singularity and individuality, which goes back to the nineteenth century, but the context uniting them is purely circumstantial, and they do not make a cycle in any formal sense like, for example, Haydn's three early symphonies, 'Le matin', 'Le midi', and 'Le soir'. And yet, bearing in mind that Mozart may have written them for publication, it is conceivable that there might be connections on a plane similar to those that can be seen to exist between the six 'Haydn' Quartets. If any can be found, then it would mean, on the one hand, that in their range and variety the three might be considered a kind of symphonic 'testament'; on the other hand, in some respects it ought to be possible to perceive similar premisses behind them, similar questions being asked by the composer— even in matters of detail—and comparable solutions being found. We should examine, above all, questions of form, orchestration, tonality, and tempo—but in order to do so we must first look for the similarities, or complementarities, between the E flat major Symphony (the only one of the three to have a slow introduction), the G minor Symphony (the only one in a minor key), and the 'Jupiter' (with its famous closing fugue).

The slow introduction of the E flat major Symphony gets the first movement off to an unusual start: because the introduction gathers weight and captures the audience's attention in its own particular way, the Allegro begins by relieving tension. The change of mood is also linked to a change of metre, from 4/4 to 3/4 (in Mozart's other two symphonies with slow introductions, the 'Linz' and the 'Prague', the time signature does not change at this point). The piano theme in triple time which enters after the common-time slow introduction thus already gives a special momentum to the first movement of the E flat major Symphony.

The G minor Symphony, K. 550, shows a different but no less original approach to the question of the symphony, while its minor tonality demands a special harmonic disposition: in the latter respect Mozart follows essentially the path which had served him well fourteen years earlier in the other G minor Symphony, K. 183. There, however, he began forte and in triple time, and here he begins piano and in common time; on the other hand this symphony does not have the slow introduction of the E flat major Symphony, and so the Allegro seems to appear from nowhere: an effect enhanced by the fact that the first sound heard, for almost a bar, is the pulsating quaver rhythm of the violas before the violins enter with 'the tune'. The piano theme of the G minor Symphony therefore has a quite different quality from the piano theme of the E flat major Symphony, with its weighty introduction, and the minor tonality means that the movement develops along different lines as well.

The 'Jupiter' Symphony, again, has its own way of beginning, with a theme which emerges forte out of the unison of the whole orchestra. The exposition also continues differently from the other two works, although it resembles the 'Prague' Symphony in that, after the first imperfect cadence on to the dominant and a fermata, Mozart returns to the opening theme and elaborates it as a means of preparing the new tonal and thematic situation. At the same stage in the E flat major Symphony, he develops a forte motif from the 'intermediate group', while in the G minor Symphony, which proceeds from essentially the same premisses as the 'Jupiter', these processes are affected by the minor tonality. Thus three kinds of symphonic process are 'expounded' in these expositions, and might claim to be in some sense a compendium, at least in regard to Mozart's own output.

The orchestration of the three symphonies also has a compendious aspect. All three call for strings with flutes, bassoons, and horns. The C major also has oboes, trumpets, and drums, in addition, and the E flat major has clarinets, trumpets, and drums. The G minor, in its original version, has only oboes in addition to the core contingent, and in the absence of the special colouring the other two symphonies gain from the trumpets, the blend of the woodwind gives it a peculiar intimacy. Mozart eventually went a step further, and the later version of the G minor Symphony, while still without trumpets and drums, has clarinets as well as oboes, whereas the other two have only the one or the other. That, admittedly, was an idea that came to the composer later than the summer of 1788, but the possibility that he acted on it in order that the three works should not only represent three different symphonic timbral spectra but also be explicitly comparable in that respect cannot be ruled out.

In spite of that particular difference there are strikingly close textural and motivic affinities between the works—even in a place where one would least expect it at first glance, that is, between the 3/4 Allegro of the E flat major Symphony and the 4/4 Allegro of the G minor Symphony. The exposition of a symphony in a major key modulates to the dominant, a fifth upwards, but one in a minor key modulates to the tonic's relative major, a third upwards; in these two symphonies, therefore, the modulation leads to the same key: B flat major. This was no surprise to Mozart, of course, and in both symphonies he developed the exposition's epilogue (the last section immediately before the repeat or the development) in a similar fashion and from similar motivic material—in 3/4 in one case and in 4/4 in the other. In both cases there is first a descending phrase for the violins alone, which is deceptively similar in its details in the two works. In the following bar the violins are joined by the remaining strings and all the wind in unison, and then the phrase is repeated an octave lower (there is a slight variation at the end in K. 550) (see Ex. 33.1*a* and *c*). There is again great similarity between the two works in the preparation of the cadence. It happens on a foundation of the play with tonalities which is conducted with impeccable musical logic; the similarities are so close, within so small a space (notwithstanding the differences in the metres), that it is virtually impossible to call them accidental (see Ex. 33.1*b* and *d*).

In the development section, on the other hand, the first movement of the G minor Symphony goes its own way, being the only one of the three works to enter the 'sharp' realm, and that so insistently that the listener risks losing all sense of tonal orientation. It takes only a few steps to leave

Ex. 33.1.

(a) Symphony in E flat major, K. 543, 1st movement, bars 135–7.

(b) K. 543, 1st movement, bars 141–2.

(c) Symphony in G minor, K. 550, 1st movement, bars 88–91.

(d) K. 550, 1st movement, bars 98–100.

the key in which the exposition ended, B flat major (two flats, like G minor itself), and reach F sharp minor (three sharps). The return journey, the semitone step to G minor, goes via the scenic route and occupies the whole of the rest of the development. The other two symphonies take advantage of a different tonal relationship: if C major is converted into C minor, it acquires E flat major as relative. To that extent there is a remarkable similarity in the ways the developments of the E flat major Symphony (in A flat major) and of the C major Symphony (in E flat major) begin, as regards both mood and the manipulation of motivic material. In both works Mozart returns to cantabile themes which he first introduced only just before the end of the expositions, after the entrances of the second subjects, where both were 'superfluous' by the rules of conventional sonata form. In the E flat major Symphony the theme in question constitutes an appendix to the second-subject group (which is identifiable by an underlying bagpipe drone), while in the C major Symphony the concluding group suddenly breaks off to admit the theme, which here is a literal quotation from the rondo-refrain of the bass aria 'Un bacio di mano', K. 541, which Mozart had composed a few weeks earlier, in May 1788. In both symphonies it looks suspiciously as if he introduced these themes solely for the sake of starting the developments with them; at all events he again responds to similar questions in the two works with similarly tailored solutions.

It has already been shown, in the cases of the string quartets and of the A major Concerto, K. 488, that Mozart liked to relate the tempos and metres of the separate movements in his works. The inner movements of the three last symphonies were also subjected to an overall concept—but evidently only after the composer had abandoned the idea for the opening movements. The 'Jupiter' Symphony begins with an Allegro in 4/4, the Allegro main section of the E flat major Symphony is in 3/4; thus the even number of beats to a bar in the first case, and the uneven number in the second case, constitute a crucial difference between them. Mozart's original conception of the first movement of the G minor Symphony might, moreover, have yielded a mediating stage between them, for he seems to have entertained the idea of writing it in a 'compound' metre, namely 6/8, which divides into twice three quavers, that is, an even number times an uneven number. The evidence for this is a sketch, with this symphony's unmistakable opening theme rendered in 6/8, on a sheet of paper on which Mozart sketched a number of potentially symphonic ideas following the composition of the G minor Quintet in the previous year (one of the sketches is for the 'Coronation' Concerto, K. 537, which was finished in February 1788). He may then have decided to change the metre to alla breve (giving an even number of beats in the bar) for dynamic considerations: the sketch in 6/8 does not include the opening bar for the violas which ensures the sense of the music appearing from nowhere, but starts with a 'normal' up-beat. The sketch also shows, incidentally, how directly the symphonies of the summer of 1788 evolved out of the work Mozart had been doing in the preceding months.

Were such considerations behind the treatment of metrical differentiation in the first movements? It recurs, at all events, in the second movements. All three are marked 'andante', but while the direction is unqualified in the G minor Symphony, 'con moto' is added in the E flat major, and 'cantabile' in the C major. The E flat major switches from triple to duple metre for this movement, the 'Jupiter' from quadruple to triple, so that the distinction found in the opening movements is still upheld. The G minor, in its second movement, does now occupy the middle ground with a 6/8 signature, so the metrical spectrum is 'complete' in the same sense that it is in the Tafelmusik in Act II of *Don Giovanni*.

Comparable relationships pertain in the third movements, too, which are all minuets and trios. Let us examine just one: the instrumentation of the trios. Originally the word 'trio' referred to its being a movement in three-part harmony, most notably in the case of the sections scored for three soloists, usually wind, inserted in French operatic music of the Baroque period (perhaps the best-known example is a 'French overture' by Bach, the C major Orchestral Suite, with the passages for two oboes and a bassoon inserted in the introductory movement and the Bourrée). By Mozart's time all that was left of the original 'trio' character in the trio section of a minuet movement was the principle of reducing the scoring and a tendency to favour the wind, and this is the background to the role played by the wind in the trios of the three late symphonies. In the Trio of the E flat major Symphony it is the wind instruments that present the theme, while the strings at first provide only a basic accompaniment. After the double bar, however, the roles are exchanged, and the strings take over the elaboration of the melody while the winds fall silent until the melody returns in its original form—at which point the original scoring is also reinstated. The Trio of the G minor Symphony (in G major, the only one of the three trios to be in a 'sharp' key) differs in that the three-stage alternation happens before the double bar is reached, and (what else?) in the inverse order, with 'strings' passages framing a middle 'wind' passage. It is impossible to categorize the section following the double bar at all clearly: the bass strings and the woodwind interact in it. The opening section of the Trio returns in anything but a schematic fashion, because the horns, who have taken no part in the proceedings until now, intervene in the original strings–winds–strings alternation in the most positive and determinative way (to be set aside only in the final bars). The relationships of the E flat major Trio are thus transmuted here from large-scale to small-scale and further transformed by a surprise at the end—there can scarcely be any doubt that Mozart intended it as a surprise.

Surprise is elevated to a principle in the Trio of the 'Jupiter': wind instruments make an entrance on their own before the Minuet has fully run its course—too early, that is (and initially as a 'traditional' trio at that, with two oboes and a bassoon, joined by a flute after four bars). The Trio proper then begins with what sounds like a closing cadence, executed by the same three woodwind and a horn. The cadence seems to be an echo of the close of the Minuet tutti, but listeners who follow the second section of the Minuet attentively, including the repeat as written, will realize that the 'echo' occurs only after the repeat—in other words, it is not the end of the Minuet but the start of the Trio. Winds and strings are not separated in this Trio with the same distinctness as in those of the other two symphonies: it could hardly happen after the anticipation of a wind-only Trio in the last stages of the Minuet. The principle of marking a tripartite division in the instrumentation is observed, however, in that the central part of the Trio is for tutti, and the opening and close are, up to a point, soloistic. By slipping a passage for wind alone into the Minuet of the 'Jupiter', Mozart turns one of the typical elements of a trio on its head; the Trio, when it follows, is also irregular in thematic terms. Yet even in these circumstances, the solo–tutti–solo alternation is a means by which Mozart holds fast to the precedent he set in the Trio of the E flat major Symphony and elaborated in that of the G minor.

The minor-key central section of the Trio of the 'Jupiter' Symphony contains, in an idiosyncratic minor guise, the four-note motif which underlies the main subject of the last movement. Mozart had used the motif before this, in his very first symphony (K. 16, composed in London in 1764), and other composers were also familiar with it in forms similar to the one it has in Mozart's hands; its source is the *Gradus ad Parnassum*, the bible of contrapuntal theory, written by Johann Jakob Fux and published in 1725. It cropped up again in one of Mozart's middle-order symphonies (K. 319), in the Credo of the Mass, K. 192, and in the Sanctus of the 'Credo' Mass, K. 257. There is something striking about the appearance of these four notes in the early symphony, too, where they are presented in a context which closely resembles the beginning of the Andante of the G minor Symphony, K. 550; if the consecutive string entries are heard as a melodic succession, it turns out to be exactly the theme of the 'Jupiter' finale (viola $e\flat'$, violin II f', violin I $a\flat'$, resolving on to g').[6] The G minor Symphony itself also contains something corresponding to the adoption of the theme from the Minuet for the finale: the rapidly ascending opening of the theme of the minor-key finale is heard in the

[6] M. Flothuis, 'Eine zweite "Jupiter-Sinfonie"?', *Mitteilungen des ISM*, 31 (1983), 18–20.

major in the Trio, in the flute melody in the separate wind segment (thus inverting the tonal relationships of the 'Jupiter' Symphony). But this is another instance where two's company: the third symphony, the E flat major, does not offer a comparable thematic connection between its Minuet and finale.

The sense of finality is particularly strong in the finale of the 'Jupiter'. Mozart presents separate thematic phrases in the manner of a fugato, but, unlike the normal practice in other fugal finales of the time (for example, the last movement of the first of Mozart's own 'Haydn' Quartets, K. 387), it is not these phrases which are developed fugally but the openings of the intermediate and concluding groups. But these considerations still do not betray how the movement (and the work) will end, which is in the combination of five themes in a single fugal complex, or 'double counterpoint with five subjects', or 'five-part counterpoint' (which means that the themes can be moved freely within the texture without giving rise to such technical solecisms as consecutive fifths). All the themes but one have already been introduced when the movement's closing fugue begins; its exposition is constructed in more or less the same way as that of the first, starting with a concise, block-like presentation of the theme, followed by a transition to an interrupted cadence on the dominant, then the true modulation on to the dominant (ushered in with a 'fugal' elaboration of the main subject), a second-subject segment, and a concluding group. The material Mozart takes into his closing fugue is (1) the four-note first subject, (2) the motif which was used to prepare the transition to the first imperfect cadence, (3) the modulation motif from the thematic elaboration, (4) the second subject, and (5) the second subject's countersubject which is not, at first, concentrated on a single part (see Ex. 33.2). For more than thirty bars, the coda contains nothing but these five themes in constant movement between the orchestral parts.

The symphony probably has this coda to thank for its nickname of 'Jupiter'. It is said to go back to the London-based German impresario Johann Peter Salomon, but since the same nickname, with the same pedigree, has also been attached to Haydn's Symphony No. 90 (another work in C major), and since it is not known which of the two was given the name first, it cannot be ruled out that it was given to Mozart's by mistake (the earliest known instance is 1822).

There is something else to note about this coda: the 'Jupiter' is the only one of these three late symphonies to have a proper one. Together with the slow introduction to the E flat major Symphony (again, the only one

Ex. 33.2. 'Jupiter' Symphony in C major, K. 551, 4th movement, bars 388–92. Violin 1: the modulation motif (3); violin 2: the second subject's countersubject (5); viola: material used to prepare for the first imperfect cadence (2); cello: second subject (4); bass: first subject (1). (Numbers in parentheses refer to the listing in the text.)

of its kind in the group), it forms a kind of frame around the three works, with the one in the middle (the only one in a minor key) having neither introduction nor coda.

In view of the evidence that Mozart discarded drafts for a movement in one of these three symphonies purely because it was in the 'wrong' metre, we have to concede the possibility that he conceived three interrelating sequences of symphonic movements according to compatible principles. Virtually nothing is accidental in the work of a composer such as Mozart was in his thirty-third year; at most, chance was responsible for phenomena which were the common property of the age, but not in the least for things which were exceptional then and at any time. This is yet another facet of the limitless mastery, the complete individualization of compositional techniques, which make posterity think of these symphonies as a 'testament'— when they cannot really be more than the outcome of the normal demands Mozart was making of himself at the time of writing.

Things did not work out for Mozart in the summer of 1788. His pleas to Puchberg failed to get the answer he really wanted, and the spell of creativity stopped the day after he finished the 'Jupiter' Symphony. On 11 August he entered the song 'Beim Auszug in das Feld', K. 552, in his catalogue, which was followed (after the canons to which the next chapter is devoted) at relatively large intervals by a divertimento for string trio (K. 563) at the end of September, and another piano trio (K. 564) at the end of October. Early in 1789 he gave up the lodgings in Alsergrund and moved back into the city.

34

Vienna, 2 September 1788: 'Bona nox' and Nine Other Canons, K. 553–62

In September 1788 Mozart could look back on more than four and a half years of what had become an institution in his life, namely the thematic catalogue in his own handwriting, whose title-page he had inscribed 'Catalogue of All my Works from the Month of February 1784 to the Month of ____ 1 ____'—but what date it might have reached was never filled in. The catalogue might be said to have revived a family tradition, inaugurated by his father in 1768 when he compiled his painstaking 'Catalogue of Everything which this 12-year-old Boy has Composed since his Seventh Year, and which can be Inspected in the Original Manuscripts', in order to rebut the doubts then circulating in Vienna as to the child's abilities. Unfortunately there is a fifteen-year gap between the two catalogues, and the idea of a 'tradition' further suffers from the fact that Leopold Mozart's was a list of works already composed and included only their titles, whereas in his own Mozart entered the pieces at or soon after the time of completion and included their opening bars.

There are sometimes striking differences, however, between the scores themselves and the incipits quoted in the catalogue, even in the headings giving performance directions. For example, the soprano aria 'Fra l'oscure ombre funeste' in the oratorio *Davide penitente*, which Mozart recycled from his C minor Mass, is marked 'andante' in the score but 'larghetto' in the catalogue. In other words, Mozart was not concerned with making an exact, archival record, but wrote much of his catalogue from memory— almost as if rewriting those few opening bars. The incipits are always on the right-hand page, the date, the title, and other information on the left. The catalogue tells us, for instance, that the orchestra for the F major Concerto, K. 459, should include trumpets and drums, but no parts for them are to be found either in the score or anywhere else. The names of people for whom particular works were intended are given, for example, 'Non temer, amato bene', K. 505, is described as 'Scena con Rondò mit klavier Solo. für Mad:^selle^ storace und mich'. Nancy Storace had been the first Susanna in *Figaro*. The titles *Eine kleine Nachtmusik* and *Ein musikalischer Spass* would not have been handed down to posterity if they had not been written in the catalogue—and there are other pieces whose very existence is known only from entries there, such as Two Contredanses, K. 565.

There are some limits to the catalogue's reliability. Above all, the dates cited are those on which the works in question were finished, which can give a misleading impression; for example, the very first entry is dated 9 February 1784, but that does not mean that the work in question, the E flat major Piano Concerto, K. 449, was composed from start to finish in a few days or weeks before that date—indeed, parts of it were written as much as fifteen months earlier.[1] Also Mozart sometimes got behind with the entries—the summer of 1785 was a particularly bad time, what with the preparations for the première of *Figaro*—or he might simply forget to enter a work at all: the Horn Concerto, K. 447 (*c.*1787), is a case in point.[2]

All the above should make it clear that when he entered no fewer than ten canons under the date 2 September 1788 it does not necessarily mean that he had devoted that entire day, from dawn till dusk, to the composition of canons, only that he decided to bring the catalogue up to date with a series of canons composed (maybe) recently. (See Pl. 13.) Two of the canons are in three parts (K. 559 and 562), the other eight in four, and most of them are on extremely brief texts:

K. 553   'Alleluia, amen.'
K. 554   'Ave Maria.'
K. 555   'Lacrimoso son io, perduto ho l'idol mio.'
K. 556   'Grechtelt's enk, wir gehn im Prater . . .'
K. 557   'Nascoso è il mio sol, e sol qui resto,
          piangete voi il mio duol, ch'io moro presto.'
K. 558   'Gehn wir im Prater, gehn wir in d'Hetz,
          gehn wir zum Kasperl . . .'
K. 559   'Difficile lectu mihi mars et jonicu.'
K. 560*b* 'O du eselhafter Martin . . .'
          (or: 'O du eselhafter Peierl . . .', K. 560*a*)
K. 561   'Bona nox! bist a rechta Ox . . .'
K. 562   'Caro bell'idol mio, non ti scordar a me,
          tengo sempre desio d'esser vicino a te.'

---

[1] Tyson, *Mozart*, 153.   [2] Ibid. 247.

Pl. 13. A recto side from Mozart's autograph thematic catalogue, showing the incipits of the symphonies in G minor, K. 550, and C major, K. 551, the song 'Beim Auszug in das Feld', K. 552, and eight four-part canons, K. 553–8, 560, and 561.

Apart from the fact that they are all canons, the pieces are a fairly heterogeneous bunch. The state of the autographs is enough in itself to illustrate their chequered histories. The majority of them were originally written down on one sheet of paper, but it was one of those manuscripts which were later cut up. The job was done neatly enough, as far as possible without slicing through any pen-strokes—so that it is still possible to reconstruct how the three strips of paper, now in the possession of three

separate owners, originally fitted together. When complete, this sheet bore
K. 553–8 and K. 561, 'Bona nox'. K. 559 and 560 are thought to have
been composed somewhat earlier than the rest, and K. 559, like the one
remaining canon, K. 562, is in three parts. So the seven written on the one
sheet were all for four voices and it is likely that they were composed
within a short time of each other; when Mozart made the entry in his
catalogue he bulked it out with three works in the same genre which he
wrote down elsewhere.

In other respects, K. 555, 557, and 562 form a group on their own.[3]
Their Italian texts had already been set as canons by Antonio Caldara
(1670–1736), who lived in Vienna for many years as deputy Kapellmeister
at the imperial court, and these versions were known to the Mozart family:
there is a copy of them on a sheet headed 'Canoni di Caldara' in Leopold
Mozart's handwriting,[4] and in places Mozart's melodies are not all that
dissimilar. The melodies demonstrate above all that Mozart was after
something more than merely keeping his hand in at counterpoint: only
listen to the melting A major of 'Caro bell'idol mio' ('My beloved,
beautiful, adored one, do not forget me, I shall always long to be close to
you'), which suddenly sounds fearful at 'non ti scordar a me'; to the
anguish of the wide-reaching melodic arc of 'Lacrimoso son io' ('I am full
of tears, for I have lost my beloved'); to the chromatic, F minor lament of
'Nascoso è il mio sol' ('My sun is hidden, and I wait here alone; weep for
my sorrows, may I die soon').

K. 553 and 554, on religious texts, form another group. The 'Alleluia'
attaches itself to a tradition, for the melody with which it begins is
extremely close to the plainsong 'Alleluia' for Easter Saturday. There is
something unexplained in the history of the 'Ave Maria', which is to be
found carved in stone at Kloster Bernried on Lake Starnberg, to the south
of Munich; the suggestion that Mozart composed the canon there has been
disproved.

There is no real distinction to be made between the 'Latin' and
macaronic texts of K. 559 and 561 on the one hand and the remaining
three canons in German on the other: all five texts are basically nonsense,
and all may well be by Mozart himself. K. 556 and 558 are about visits to
the Prater, which had been open to the public since 1766; the latter
includes references to two of the entertainments to be seen there. 'Kasperl',
created only in 1781 by the actor Johann Laroche, was the hero of a series

---

[3] See A. Dunning in NMA III/10, pp. xii–xv.   [4] Plath, 'Beiträge I', 111.

of farces, a sly servant who was rapidly replacing the traditional Hanswurst in the affections of the Viennese public; the 'Hetz', or 'fun house', which burnt down in 1796, was still commemorated in a doggerel about Viennese life as late as 1812.[5]

According to anecdote, K. 559 and 560*a* (K. 560*b* is a later version) belong together. 'Difficile lectu' is not as Latin as it looks: Mozart exploited the idiosyncratic pronunciation of the tenor Johann Nepomuk Peyerl to produce a ribald result in performance. 'O du eselhafter Peierl' ('O Peyerl, you donkey') is written on the back of the same sheet, allegedly so that it could be sung immediately afterwards. The German text of the second canon takes up the 'Latin' of the first, and 'lectu mihi mars' is converted into 'o leck mich doch geschwind im Arsch' ('Lick my bum, quick'). The significance of 'jonicu' only emerges in singing, when uninterrupted repetitions seem to produce 'cujoni' ('scoundrel').

Peyerl is known to have been working in Vienna in 1785–7, so the pair of canons presumably date from that period. Entering them in his catalogue in September 1788, however, Mozart gave the first line of the second as 'O du eselhafter Martin': the target of this version was apparently Philipp Jakob Martin, a concert promoter, for, probably later still, Mozart substituted 'Jacob' for 'Martin' in the first line; 'Lipperl' (= Philipp) comes later in both these versions.[6]

'Bona nox' is probably the best-known of these canons; like most of the others, posterity handed it down with some well-meant alterations to the text, in order to purge it of 'offensive' expressions. The original text is as follows:

Bona nox!	
bist a rechta Ox;	('you're a right ox')
bona notte,	
liebe Lotte;	('dear Lottie')
bonne nuit,	
pfui, pfui;	('wee-wee')
good night,	
heut müßma noch weit;	('we've a long road tonight')
gute Nacht, gute Nacht,	('Good night, good night')

[5] C. Osborne, *Schubert and his Vienna* (London, 1985), 79; K. Pfannhauser, 'Epilegomena Mozartiana', *MJb* 1971–2, 268–312, esp. 282.

[6] My thanks to the editors-in-chief of the Neue Mozart-Ausgabe, Salzburg, for enabling me to study the canons on microfilm. (The Köchel numbers 560*a* and *b*, assigned by the NMA editors, supersede K[6] 559*a* and K. 560.)

scheiß ins Bett, daß' kracht;	('shake the bed with a shite')
schlaf fei g'sund	('sleep well, sleep tight')
und reck' den Arsch zum Mund	('give your arse a big bite')

Thus the text is made up of the words 'good night' in all the languages Mozart knew: ecclesiastical Latin, Italian, French, and English, interspersed with lines in German to make rhyming couplets, and ending with the German 'Gute Nacht' and a litany of other rhymes familiar to the Mozarts (and many of their fellow-countrymen, no doubt). They even turn up in a letter from Mozart's mother to her husband (26 September 1777).

The various expurgated versions of these canons may be prudish, but they are not squeamish in their manhandling of the originals. The pinnacle of daintiness was probably reached with 'Difficile lectu', of which Fritz Jöde (1887–1970), a leading music educationist, made a Christmas canon: 'Heut ist ein Kindelein geborn, von einer Jungfrau auserkorn' ('Today is born a holy child, of a mother meek and mild').

With the nonsense canons, in particular, Mozart's chief interest probably lay in the texts themselves, so that setting them to music was just an addition to his enjoyment (like the fun he had with the Peyerl canon). With the rest, other aspects appear to have carried more weight: the chromaticism of 'Lacrimoso son io' and 'Nascoso è il mio sol', for example, presented a special technical challenge in canons. In 'Ave Maria', all four parts start directly one after the other on the same note, so that the four entries add up to one long-drawn-out note on the 'A' of 'Ave'—rather like the effect created with the high notes of the two soprano soloists in the 'Domine Deus' of the C minor Mass. Again, however, 'Caro bell'idol mio' stands out: it is the only one in which an aspect of the text, the anxious 'non ti scordar a me', is brought out in the setting. The other canons either stick in a single basic emotion, or the music skates over developments expressed in the words. The lines are therefore unusually long (eleven bars) in 'Caro bell'idol mio'; in the other canons, typically only six bars long with all the lines sung simultaneously, there is simply not enough time for any change of mood.

The surviving drafts of 'Alleluia' and 'Nascoso è il mio sol' show that Mozart actually composed the canons as pieces in three or four parts. Writing the parts one above the other saved space, but also ensured that the harmonies worked, although the singers are of course intended to enter one line at a time, in the usual way. There is another reason to be glad of the chance that allowed these two drafts to survive, for it makes it possible to date them. Both are written on paper of the same type as the sheet on which Mozart wrote down the fair copies of seven canons, including them.[7] This makes it likely, at least, that these two date from the late summer of 1788—whereas the two Peyerl canons had already been in existence for some time by then.

[7] Tyson, *Mozart*, 134.

35

Cello Cantilenas and their Reasons: The 'Prussian' Quartets

On 8 April 1789 Mozart found himself on the road from Vienna to Prague for the third time, this time in the company of Prince Karl von Lichnowsky, Beethoven's future patron. On this occasion he spent only seven and a half hours in the Bohemian capital, for his journey took him on to the Saxon court in Dresden, to Leipzig, to the Prussian capital, Berlin, and the King of Prussia's residence in Potsdam, before he set off homewards again via Dresden and Prague, reaching Vienna on 4 June; in order to pay Leipzig a second visit he interrupted his stay at the Prussian court at the beginning of May. Any attempt to reconstruct the journey in more detail than this comes up against the same difficulty as the one that faces us when we ask exactly why he undertook it at all: the fact that no continuous series of letters survives from those weeks on the road. There cannot be any real doubt that Mozart was looking for work, though not necessarily at the Prussian court, for in Prague itself he used his brief stay to revive acquaintanceships, such as that with Domenico Guardasoni, who had succeeded Pasquale Bondini in the management of the National Theatre, and 'all but promised me 200 ducats for the opera and 50 ducats travelling expenses next autumn' (to Constanze Mozart, 10 April 1789). By 'next autumn' Mozart meant the autumn of next year, 1790, and 'all but' meant, of course, that no promise had actually been given. In fact it was 1791 when Prague next hosted the première of an opera by Mozart, which was *La clemenza di Tito*. Nothing more—not even the subject—is known about the project Mozart and Guardasoni discussed on Good Friday 1789.

But Mozart was going on to Berlin in any case, and an old friend from his stay in Mannheim in 1777–8, the oboist Friedrich Ramm, had come to Prague from there to pass on information about the Prussian court, although it is hard to interpret in the almost telegraphic form in which Mozart passed it on to his wife in this same letter:

Something else: Ramm left here for home only a week ago. He came from Berlin and said that the King had often and urgently asked if I was definitely coming and as I still didn't come he said I'm afraid he's not coming. Ramm became thoroughly alarmed, tried to assure him of the opposite. To judge by this my affairs shouldn't do badly.

Six weeks later he wrote from Berlin, 'in a hostelry in the Tiergarten', to sum up the outcome of his journey:

My dearest little wife,
. . . You must look forward to seeing me again more for my own sake than for the money. 100 friedrichs d'or are not 900 florins but only 700, or so I've been told here. Secondly, Lichnowsky left me because he was in a hurry, and consequently I had to pay for my own keep (in Potsdam—an expensive place). Thirdly, I had to lend [him] 100 florins, because he was running low—I couldn't very well refuse, you know why. Fourthly, the concert in Leipzig fell out badly, as I always said it would, so I had the journey of thirty-two miles there and back for almost nothing; that was all Lichnowsky's fault, because he would not leave me in peace, I had to go back to Leipzig—but—I'll tell you all about it when I see you. Here, firstly, a concert would be more trouble than it's worth, and secondly, the King doesn't approve. You must be content, as I am, with this: that I am lucky enough to find favour with the King. What I've just written is strictly between ourselves. (23 May 1789)

The first thing one wants to know is the significance of the '100 friedrichs d'or', and the question takes us straight to the heart of the problems surrounding this whole journey: every question produces, not an answer, but a further question. Firstly, Mozart must have done something to earn a sum as large as that. It is the sort of amount that would have been appropriate payment for a project such as the one on which he made a start that summer: six string quartets for King Friedrich Wilhelm II, and six keyboard sonatas for his daughter Princess Friederike (letter to Michael Puchberg, 14 July 1789). (As a comparison, Mozart had been paid 450 gulden for *Don Giovanni* in Prague.) Another possibility is that both Mozart and the King expected the money to be the first of a series of annual payments; perhaps the intention was that the King would give Mozart a titular court appointment, at a salary similar to that paid him by the Emperor in Vienna, in return for services comparable to those he had offered to the court at Donaueschingen. But when was the payment made to Mozart, and when did he first meet the King?

Mozart's letter from the Tiergarten refers to a comment his wife must have made about one of his earlier letters. Since he had arrived in Berlin only four days earlier, on 19 May, it must have been during his stay in Potsdam, before he went back to Leipzig, that the King had said something that opened the new prospects for him; the four days between 19 and 23 May were not enough for letters to have travelled from Berlin to Vienna and back. But it had not been easy to arrange to see the King. His first approach is documented in the 'Kabinettsvortrag' of 26 April: the regular schedule of submissions presented to the King through his private office. On that occasion Mozart was instructed to apply in the first instance to the Superintendent of Music of the Royal Chamber, Jean-Pierre Duport—in other words, he was made to go through the proper channels. Three days later, in Potsdam, he noted in his thematic catalogue that he had composed 'six variations for keyboard solo, on a minuet by Duport' (in fact, he wrote nine altogether, K. 573).

Mozart's entry in the Prussian 'Kabinettsvortrag' reads as follows: 'One Mozart by name (on entry described himself as a Kapellmeister from Vienna) states that Prince Lichnowsky brought him here in his company, that he wishes to lay his talents at Your Majesty's feet, and awaits the command whether he might hope that Your Majesty would receive him.' This sheds some light on Mozart's journey: the fact that he was 'in Prince Lichnowsky's company' explains the curious toing and froing of the next few weeks. The three days they had spent in Leipzig on the way from Dresden to Potsdam had been too short a time to do more than make provisional arrangements for a concert. Since Mozart was tied to Lichnowsky's plans, he had to postpone the concert until Lichnowsky's return journey—and hope that he would have accomplished what he wanted to do in Berlin and Potsdam by then. Mozart complains that Lichnowsky nagged him into returning to Leipzig; evidently he did not complete his business in Potsdam in time, and so he had to go back to Leipzig and then return to the Prussian court. (The round journey of thirty-two German miles was about 145 English miles.) The second stay in Leipzig began on 8 May, so Mozart must have left Potsdam on 6 May. He wrote to his wife the day before that: the letter is lost, but must have contained a report on his prospects, and he must also have been given 100 friedrichs d'or by then, or he would not have been able to tell her about it in a way that made her look forward to seeing it so greatly. She wrote to him on 13 May—another lost letter, which reached him on 20 May; it could have contained her comments on his prospects. It looks very possible, therefore, that Mozart was received by Friedrich Wilhelm II at some time between his presenting himself at the private office on 26 April and his departure for Leipzig on 6 May.

But Nissen, in his biography of Mozart, refers to his arrival in Berlin on 19 May as being 'for the second and last time'.[1] When had Mozart first been in Berlin? The only possible time lies between 30 April and 2 May, when Lichnowsky is known to have been in the city. So when had Lichnowsky left Mozart 'because he was in a hurry, and consequently I had to pay for my own keep (in Potsdam—an expensive place)'? Does Nissen perhaps use 'Berlin' loosely for 'the Prussian court', thus including Potsdam? Then it could be the case that Lichnowsky went to Berlin and Mozart stayed in Potsdam to pursue his own business. In fact, the dates can be fixed more precisely than that.

There is no record of anything Mozart did in Potsdam—or Berlin— during those three days. His last recorded action in Potsdam before 30 April was to enter the Duport Variations in his thematic catalogue on 29 April, and the next was to write to his wife on 5 May. He must almost certainly have met the King in the interval and received the 100 friedrichs d'or at his hands, for whatever service he had rendered. It could have been given him in the course of a 'normal' general audience (such things did happen when he met other princes), it could even have been occasioned by the Duport Variations (the subject of which turned out to be an astute choice); at all events, Mozart was able to congratulate himself 'that I am lucky enough to find favour with the King'. It demonstrates that he must have been very quick to gain the King's favour (even when sent through the proper channels); it also indicates that he is not at all likely to have attacked Duport (a hypothesis that has bobbed up from time to time since 1856), because that would have delayed rather than hastened the process.[2] Nevertheless, he had little time for anything else, and as Lichnowsky, after his brief visit to Berlin, was urging departure ('he would not leave me in peace, I had to go back to Leipzig'), Mozart had to postpone other activities, including a concert at court, until he had been to Leipzig and back.

Mozart's stay in Berlin from 19 May onwards was not without significant incident, if Nissen can be believed:

As the news that Mozart was there spread through Berlin, he was made extremely welcome everywhere, but especially by Friedrich Wilhelm II. Not only was the King well known to hold music in high esteem, and to pay good money for it, but

---

[1] Nissen, *Biographie*, 533.

[2] See Abert, *Mozart*, ii. 521, on the article in the *Neue Berliner musikalische Zeitung* (1856), 35.

he was also an amateur with genuinely good taste, if he could not quite be called a connoisseur. For as long as his stay in Berlin lasted, Mozart had to improvise for him almost every day, and often also play quartets with members of the royal orchestra in the King's room. Once when he was alone with the King, His Majesty asked him what he thought of the Berlin orchestra, and Mozart, to whom nothing was more foreign than flattery, replied: 'It has the greatest collection of virtuosi in the world; and I have never heard quartet-playing of the like anywhere else; but when the gentlemen are all together, they could do better.' The King was pleased by his candour, and said with a smile, 'Stay here with me, and you could make them do better! I will offer you an annual salary of 3,000 thalers.' 'Should I leave my good Emperor altogether?' honest Mozart asked, and fell silent, moved and thoughtful. Consider, reader, that our good Mozart hesitated to abandon the Emperor who at that very date was allowing him to starve. The King, too, appeared moved, and after a pause he went on: 'Think about it. I will keep my word, even if it should be a year and a day before you come here.' The King later recounted this conversation to various people, including Mozart's wife, who travelled to Berlin after her husband's death, and was very handsomely supported by her late husband's patron.[3]

As we have already seen, there is evidence that contradicts the implication that Mozart's good relationship with Friedrich Wilhelm II dated only from his stay in Berlin in the second half of May. A question mark also hangs over the offer of a job: in retelling the tale, did the King perhaps quote a higher figure for the salary than he had actually offered to Mozart himself? What reason would Mozart have had to refuse it? Was he concerned about the state of musical life in Berlin—as illustrated by his discovery that, for example, the public were not interested in concerts and the King did not approve of them? He could earn the equivalent of a third of the sum quoted by Nissen from concerts alone in Vienna. Was there some other reason for him to be wary? Or did he not want to leave Vienna? Had he hoped that the King of Prussia would give him a title and a salary in return for services he could render from the capital of Austria? Had such a thing been possible it would have carried some political ballast: Mozart already had an Austrian title, as a Composer to the Imperial and Royal Chamber; the rivalry between Prussia and Austria, which had reached its peak in the Seven Years War, continued to fester, until their joint interest in opposing the French Revolution led to the *rapprochement* expressed in the Declaration of Pillnitz in August 1791. Two years earlier than that, it would hardly have possible for Mozart to bear both a Prussian and an Austrian title

[3] Nissen, *Biographie*, 535–6.

simultaneously; Friedrich Wilhelm II ought to have seen that, too, and perhaps his offer actually took a more hypothetical form, on the lines of 'It would be very agreeable . . . in different circumstances . . . then you could accept the appointment without too much trouble . . .' Or was it only after Mozart's return to Vienna that pressure was put on him?

No sooner was Mozart back in Vienna than his wife fell ill, and he found himself therefore in some difficulty. A journey involving a considerable outlay had opened new prospects for him, but it looked as if political factors would prevent their realization. He had brought some money back with him: even if he had had to dip into the 100 friedrichs d'or, he must have made something from concerts in the last fortnight in Berlin;[4] but now he was faced with doctors' bills, and moreover he had to find 400 gulden by 2 August in order to repay a loan. The money had originally been lent him for four months by a brother Freemason, Franz Hofdemel, but he had sold the bill of exchange to a third party after only three months, which made Mozart's duty to repay all the more pressing. Coming in the middle of the summer, always a financially precarious season for him, the situation was dire. He may have been a bad manager, as his biographer Ignaz Ferdinand Arnold avowed in 1803, but if he decided to continue to finance himself by borrowing money from people like Michael Puchberg, when he had been offered a salary of 3,000 thalers, he must have had good reasons for it.

If he was unable to accept the offer of a post at the King of Prussia's court, he nevertheless took the matter of composing sonatas and quartets for him very seriously at first. In his hurry to get started on them, evidently, he bought Bohemian music paper while still on the homeward road, between 30 May, when he stopped in Dresden, and 2 June, when he reached Prague.[5] The paper in question was not at all suitable for quartets, having ten staves on a side. The paper Mozart normally bought in Vienna had twelve staves, enabling him to write three four-part systems on a side, whereas he could write only two on this paper, and was left with two blank staves. But he obviously regarded the quartets as too urgent to be put off; he may, in any case, have bought only a small amount of the paper, perhaps no more than the ten sheets he used in composing the D major Quartet, K. 575, and the first movement, and half of the second, of the B flat major Quartet, K. 589. He could have written that much by the time

---

[4] Braunbehrens surmises that Mozart could have taken more than 1,000 gulden home with him (*Mozart in Vienna*, 329).

[5] Tyson, *Mozart*, 36–47, esp. 43.

he reached Vienna on 4 June, and he probably went on with the work at that time (perhaps on the Bohemian paper, if any remained). He entered the D major Quartet in his thematic catalogue in June, and a first piano sonata (also in D major, K. 576) in July. To judge by the evidence of the handwriting and paper of the autographs, he composed more of the B flat major Quartet and the first two movements of a third quartet (F major, K. 590) in that same summer, but on Viennese paper with twelve staves. Then, however, he broke off the work, and did not finish those two quartets until the May and June of 1790. In that last phase he composed not only the last two movements of the F major Quartet but also the last two of the B flat major Quartet; the minuet of the latter was written out on paper of a type that he had already used in the previous summer, but as he wrote alternative drafts for the finales of both quartets (K⁶ 458a and b) in the following year, that minuet also belongs in the summer of 1790, and Mozart wrote it out on the remainder of a double sheet (binio) which he had already broached for the conclusion of the second movement. This stint of work on the quartets in the early summer of 1790 has the air of a special effort to finish something on which he had fallen behind schedule— especially as he also tried to increase the number of works in the set with a quartet in E minor (draft: K⁶ 417d).[6] Then, all of a sudden, he abandoned the whole project; from July 1790 onwards there is no sign that he did any more work on this particular set of quartets, or any other compositions in the same medium; similarly, the piano sonata he had composed in the previous summer is the last he ever wrote. What might the reason have been for that renewed exertion in the early summer of 1790? The only clue is found in Nissen's account of the conversation he had had with King Friedrich Wilhelm II, since when 'a year and a day' had passed. He wrote to Michael Puchberg: 'Now I'm forced to hand over my quartets (laborious task that they have been) for a derisory sum of money' (12 June 1790). Did Mozart's original intention of writing two sets each of six works conceal some kind of probationary employment—whose term had now expired? At all events he only completed a third quartet, so as to have at least the prospect of making money from publishing the three as a set. This had stylistic consequences.

The three 'Prussian' Quartets were not published until 28 December 1791, a few weeks after the composer's death. The advertisement in the *Wiener Zeitung* described them as 'three brand-new concertante quartets':

---

[6] On the sketches for K⁶ 417d, and K⁶ 458a and b, see Tyson, *Mozart*, 93, and Wolff, 'Creative Exuberance', 195.

'concertante' is correct above all because of the equality Mozart developed between the instruments, paying particular attention to the cello, which enabled him to build up the thematic structures in an unusual way. Friedrich Wilhelm II was himself a cellist; his teacher had been Duport, who had aroused his interest in the modern cello. Like Boccherini, who had been connected with the Prussian court since 1787, Duport belonged to the generation of early champions of a kind of sound which was inspired by the instruments of Antonio Stradivari. The Prussian royal family owned a Stradivari cello: Friedrich Wilhelm III, a pupil of Duport like his father before him, tried to sell it in London in 1806, but failed because he asked an extremely high price for it. It must have been a very good instrument, therefore, but all further trace of it was lost during the Napoleonic wars.[7] Obviously Mozart wished to pay tribute to the King's special preference, perhaps even his special strengths (but more likely those of Duport!) in these works, and it is also possible that the wish was combined with his reaction to a new ideal of cello sound which was only beginning to gain ground at that period. According to Nissen he told the King that he had never elsewhere heard quartet-playing like that he had encountered at the Prussian court: was Duport's conception of the sound a Stradivari cello could produce the immediate reason for the relationships in the 'Prussian' Quartets (as Regina Strinasacchi's playing may lie behind some of the details in the Violin Sonata, K. 454)?

By the summer of 1790 Mozart stopped mentioning the possibility of dedicating the quartets to the King of Prussia, even when he entered the B flat major and F major quartets in his thematic catalogue, whereas on entering the D major Quartet there in the previous summer he had written: 'A quartet for 2 violins, viola, and violoncello, for His Majesty the King of Prussia'. Evidently he was no longer obliged to bear in mind the King's special preference for the cello when he was finishing the two later quartets.[8] In the minuets, the treatment of the cello is already more 'normal', although their general premisses are recognizably those of the one in the D major Quartet (where the Trio, however, is a horse of a totally different colour). The change is clearest in the finales, where there is no trace of the cello cantilenas which distinguish all the other movements. In the 6/8 finale of the B flat major Quartet, in any case, the more succinct phrase-structures run counter to that kind of melodic flowering; in the F

---

[7] W. H. Hill, A. F. Hill, and A. E. Hill, *Antonio Stradivari* (London, 1902; repr. Great Missenden 1980), 126.

[8] Tyson, *Mozart*, 43–4.

major finale, although the cello is asked, as in the movements composed earlier, to travel to its highest register (reaching *c″*) it is only as the bass line in a context where the other instruments are also very high. Great demands continue to be made of the cellist, but he will look in vain for the 'principal' roles given him in the earlier movements, and in that respect these two quartets are back in the paths already trodden in the later 'Haydn' Quartets and the 'Hoffmeister'.

Yet assigning the cello a role as a principal voice is precisely the outstanding thing that Mozart does in this group of works, with immense consequences for the texture of the string-quartet medium, and he does it in spades. Even where a movement already seems to be dominated by surprises from the cello, Mozart finds the means to screw the excitement to an even higher pitch, as for example in the trio of the D major Quartet (see Ex. 35.1). The section begins with the two violins playing together in octaves, effectively extending the up-beat over two bars; the beat itself remains indeterminate because Mozart extends the first slur over the barline, thus robbing the first beat of the first full bar of its accent. Viola and cello enter in the third bar, the viola on the same note as the second violin, the cello (sounding an octave lower than notated) on the *g′* of the first violin. The second violin then falls silent, the first violin and the viola play on in approximately the same register, but the cello has a cantilena which takes it way above them: at the first note of bar 5 it is an octave higher than the first violin. The first six bars are repeated, approximately, from bar 7 onwards, only this time the cello line is a continuation of what it played before (like a consequent clause following an antecedent). The programme outlined by these twelve bars remains the composer's secret for the time being. The 'up-beat' formula vanishes as the music continues, and one cello phrase follows another directly; for eight bars the cello is accompanied by first violin and viola alone, then the first violin yields its staccato quaver movement to the second violin, thus obtaining the freedom to add a new accompanying voice to the texture in a higher register. This is not actually the point at which the cello loses the position of being the highest voice in the ensemble, for the first violin's succession of quavers has ventured closer and closer into the regions of the cello's cantilenas and has already occasionally reached a higher pitch. However, it is only after the four-part texture has been in play for eight bars that the unbelievable happens: the music of the twelve opening bars returns but it is the cello which unexpectedly voices the up-beat formula, and the second violin which takes over what was originally the cello's first cantilena; at the

Ex. 35.1. String Quartet in D major, K. 575, 3rd movement, Trio, bars 1–12.

'repeat' the viola gets the up-beat formula, while the first violin and viola play the cello's second cantilena (in octaves)—and the cello turns its attention to the accompanimental quavers. Thus, the cello phrases of the middle section would have been perfectly appropriate to a cello solo, and the first violin's accompanimental line, even though it ventures a little high, would not have destroyed that impression. The final bars, however, demonstrate that Mozart had no intention of turning his string quartet into a cello solo, and meant the solo, with its limited duration, to be understood as an organic part of his quartet style. The listener who believes that the music is firmly in the hands of the 'soloist' will be, not disappointed, but literally better advised.

There is every sign that the movement had the desired effect. Just as Mozart took a piece by J. C. Bach as his inspiration in an aria he composed 'as an exercise' in 1778, so, it appears, Beethoven took this very movement as the launching-pad for the Trio in his Piano Trio. Op. 1 No. 3. Of course Beethoven did not attempt to reproduce Mozart's work in his own piece, any more than Mozart did Bach's in his aria, but selected individual aspects of it to reshape in accordance with his own personal style; in any case the underlying conditions of a piano trio are different from those obtaining in a quartet of four instruments of similar construction. Beethoven extends the 'consequent clause' of Mozart's opening theme from four bars to six, and he does without a cantilena middle section. On the other hand he has a metrically indeterminate up-beat formula (on the piano), followed by an antecedent clause (cello)—the basic melodic structure of which is similar to Mozart's, a repetition of the up-beat formula, and that 'extended' consequent on the cello. The middle section of Beethoven's movement is dominated by elaboration of the piano's up-beat formula instead of cantilenas, and that is the essential difference between the two pieces. The 'elaboration' prepares for the return of the up-beat formula in the final section, where it is once more given to the piano. Distributing the four musical elements of the movement's opening across the entire texture, as Mozart does with his four string parts, would probably not have worked in the piano-trio medium (in which the piano would have had to take on two of the elements). Yet Beethoven's movement, like Mozart's, ends with the consequent melody played in octaves (cello with violin). The initial premisses of Beethoven's piano-trio texture were, therefore, different from those of Mozart's 'cello-heavy' string quartet, but he was obviously so fascinated by certain isolable elements that he integrated them into his own work.

Beethoven's Piano Trios, Op. 1, appeared in print in 1795, four years after Mozart's quartets, but he may have begun work on them as early as 1791–2. He arrived in Vienna in 1792, and it may have been there that he became acquainted with the D major Quartet of Mozart which appears to lie behind the Trio movement of his Op. 1 No. 3—the dates fit, at least. There is also one circumstance in particular that may have spurred Beethoven to transfer the techniques he discovered in Mozart's quartet to his own piano trio, and that was the publication, in September 1792, of the arrangements of the 'Prussian' Quartets for piano trio by Mozart's pupil Joseph Freystädtler. The arrangement of the D major Quartet is disappointing at first glance: it lacks the Minuet and Trio altogether, leaving a work in three movements, like Mozart's original piano trios.[9] But—who knows?—that could have been the very thing which prompted Beethoven's experiment.

A spotlight also falls on Karl von Lichnowsky at this point. Once Mozart's pupil, and the man who took him to Prussia, it was to Lichnowsky that Beethoven dedicated his Op. 1 trios. When Beethoven left Bonn, Count Waldstein had expressed the wish that he would received Mozart's guardian spirit from the hands of Haydn, but perhaps Lichnowsky's hands also played a part. There again, Beethoven could have found the 'Prussian' Quartets for himself, by some other means.

[9] My thanks to the library of the Musikwissenschaftliches Institut of the University of Leipzig, and to the Music Department of the Austrian National Library in Vienna.

36

Anton Stadler's Clarinet: The Clarinet Quintet, K. 581, and the Clarinet Concerto, K. 622

Clarinets were clearly not among the instruments that Mozart normally reckoned to use when composing orchestral or chamber music in the early part of his career. They were not at his disposal within the narrower context of the court orchestra in Salzburg, but only when players were hired from the band of the principate's regular troops; this appears to have had an effect on the use he was able to make of them—in terms both of genres and of their technical role, for he employed them primarily as harmony instruments, like the oboe and horn, not as melody instruments.[1] It is easy, therefore, to understand his delight when he first encountered them in ensemble music in Mannheim and discovered their obbligato potential. 'Ah, if only we had clarinets [in Salzburg]! You wouldn't believe the wonderful effect a symphony makes with flutes, oboes and clarinets', he wrote to his father during his stop in Mannheim on the way home from Paris (3 December 1778).

In Vienna he made the acquaintance of the clarinettist Anton Stadler who (like his younger brother Johann Nepomuk Stadler) was a member, first, of the imperial wind band and, later, of the court orchestra also. They must have met by 23 March 1784 at the latest, for on that day Stadler took part in the performance of, 'among other well-chosen pieces, a grand wind composition of a quite unusual kind by Herr Mozart'. An account of the concert was published a few months later which allows the work to be identified as the Gran Partita, or Wind Serenade, K. 361 (although that is in seven movements and the witness talks of only four).[2]

Thereafter Mozart and Stadler often worked together, including occasions when they provided music for meetings of Masonic lodges, for Stadler too was a Freemason. They also met at the Jacquins, as the history of the 'Kegelstatt' Trio reveals. The friendship gained a new dimension,

---

[1] D. Blazin, 'The Two Versions of Mozart's Divertimento, K. 113', *Music and Letters*, 73 (1992), 32–47.

[2] See Deutsch, *MDB*, under 23 Mar. 1784 and the start of 1785.

however, from an invention of Stadler's, the earliest explicit report of which is to be found in an article on the Stadler brothers, in a music dictionary published in 1792: 'The elder . . . according to recent information from Vienna, from the year 1790, has extended the lower range of his instrument by a major third; so that instead of E being the lowest note, as it is otherwise, he can produce D♯, D, C♯, and C, with unusual ease.'[3]

Stadler's invention forms one in a whole series of experimental versions of instruments produced during the eighteenth and nineteenth centuries, from the 'giraffe' piano—an upright grand—to the keyed bugle. Like many of the others it did not enjoy a long career. The bass clarinet of the modern orchestra, developed by Adolphe Sax in 1838, before he invented the saxophone, is quite distinct from the instrument invented by Stadler, which was also called bass clarinet; in order to avoid confusion, therefore, Stadler's instrument is commonly referred to nowadays as the basset clarinet; no example of it survives.

We owe the term 'basset clarinet' to the Czech musicologist Jiří Kratochvíl, who made (or co-ordinated) many discoveries about Mozart's late works for clarinet.[4] He demonstrated that not only the Clarinet Quintet, K. 581, and the Clarinet Concerto, K. 622, were written for Stadler's new instrument, but also the clarinet obbligato for the aria 'Parto, ma tu ben mio' in *La clemenza di Tito*. This was particularly difficult to establish in the case of the quintet and the concerto, because Mozart's autographs do not survive in either case. What has been possible to prove is that both works were later adapted to make them playable by standard instruments of the time, by means of rewriting all the passages which lay too low for them but were within the range of Stadler's extended instrument. In the absence of the autographs, reconstructing the original versions from the adaptations demanded musical sensibility as well as the capacity for a wellnigh forensic attention to detail, but eventually the places where persons unknown must have altered both works at some date after Mozart's death were ferreted out.

Let us turn to the question of when Stadler invented his instrument. Mozart is no direct help to us in the matter, for he did not call it by a

---

[3] E. L. Gerber, *Historisch-Biographisches Lexicon der Tonkünstler* (Leipzig, 1790–2), ii, col. 556.

[4] J. Kratochvíl, 'Betrachtungen über die Urfassung des Konzerts für Klarinette und des Quintetts für Klarinette und Streicher von W. A. Mozart', in *Internationale Konferenz über das Leben und Werk W. A. Mozarts (Prag 1956)* (Prague, 1958), 262–71. See also A. Hacker, 'Mozart and the Basset Clarinet', *Musical Times*, 110 (1969), 359–62; G. Croll and K. Birsak, 'Anton Stadlers "Bassettklarinette" und das "Stadler-Quintett" KV 581', *Österreichische Musikzeitschrift*, 24 (1969), 3–11.

distinct name, and does not appear to have known the expression 'bass clarinet'. He used the Italian word 'clarinetto' in the entry for the quintet in his thematic catalogue and in the instrumental specifications for the aria in *Tito*; and he used the German form ('Clarinette') in regard to the concerto in the catalogue. Thus he made no attempt to distinguish it from the 'Clarinett' of the 'Kegelstatt' Trio, although he can hardly have written that for any but the standard instrument of the day. In any case, the trio survives in autograph, so it can be seen that it was not adapted as the quintet and the concerto were (it was rewritten for violin, in place of the clarinet, but that is a separate matter). The trio was finished in August 1786, the quintet in September 1789, and we can assume that the clarinet parts in both works were written for Stadler; can we assume, therefore, that the invention of the new instrument dates from some point during that three-year interval?

In fact, a look at the early history of the Clarinet Concerto enables us go a bit further than that.[5] A draft for its first movement survives, which differs in two striking and material details from the final version: the concerto is in A major, the draft in G major, and while the concerto is for 'Clarinette', as mentioned above, the sketch specifies the solo instrument as 'Corno di Basseto', that is, the basset horn. The basset horn was Anton Stadler's second instrument and Mozart wrote obbligatos for it in another aria in *Tito* and in the Requiem. A remark in a letter from the time when Mozart was finishing the concerto establishes that he wrote it for Stadler (7 October 1791). To judge by the handwriting and the paper, the sketch could date from 1787 or later (though not earlier),[6] but why would Mozart have started a basset horn concerto for Stadler at that date, only to set it aside and finish it later as a concerto for basset clarinet? (There is no serious reason to doubt that the work was intended for Stadler from the first.) Did Stadler perhaps ask for a concerto for his other instrument, the basset horn, at around the time of the 'Kegelstatt' Trio? Was Mozart so busy with *Don Giovanni* in the following months that he was overtaken by Stadler's progress on his invention? Did Mozart set the concerto sketch aside in order to work on the quintet instead—and return to it after Stadler's success in *Tito*, in Prague in the autumn of 1791? According to that scenario the Clarinet Quintet was his first work for the new instrument, and the date of composition would have followed hard upon its perfecting.

[5] E. Hess, 'Die ursprüngliche Gestalt des Klarinettenkonzerts KV 622', *MJb* 1967, 18–30.
[6] Tyson, *Mozart*, 35.

And from that it would follow that the draft of a G major concerto for the basset horn predates the quintet.

The Clarinet Quintet has several features that are also encountered in the 'Prussian' Quartets. As the cello, in the first of those, is slow to reveal the kind of prominent role it is going to play, so here, too, the clarinet has only 'unimportant' material to play for a surprisingly long time: figuration which bridges the gaps between string phrases, and the second, 'consequent' part of the first-subject group. The second subject is presented by the first violin alone, to begin with, but then the clarinet takes it over and simultaneously the mood changes to the minor mode. The clarinet is therefore late in claiming a role which allows it to take any decisive part in the action.

With the sudden vault into the minor and the resultant darkening of the A major atmosphere, Mozart has really done no more than he did once before, in the fifth 'Haydn' Quartet (K. 464, also A major). He demonstrates, that is, that the direct path is not necessarily the best, and that the longer route, notwithstanding the sudden darkening, contains an enriched range of colours and other purely musical attractions. Of course the clarinet (whether basset or standard) permits such coloristic enrichment to take a particularly intense form. It can be seen, in the first movement of the Clarinet Concerto in particular, that temporary darkening can lead to completely new consequences for the overall design of individual formal sections; the more or less exactly contemporary opening movements of the two last keyboard concertos (the 'Coronation', K. 537, in D major and the B flat major, K. 595) do not contain anything that is truly comparable.[7]

In another respect, the opening movements of the Clarinet Quintet and the concerto are as different from each other as they could conceivably be. This is not merely a matter of differences between the genres, which give the concerto an extended orchestral introduction of which there is no equivalent in the quintet; it affects in particular the way the 'solo' instrument is treated, as has already been suggested. The second violin and viola, in particular, do not play as central a part in the thematic action in the quintet as they do in the 'Prussian' Quartets (and the cello, too, features only selectively in this regard), which could have meant that the clarinet would take a more obviously starring role; in fact, however, it shares the limelight with the first violin, in a decidedly chamber-musical spirit. It

---

[7] Küster, *Formale Aspekte*, 173. On the dating of K. 595, see Tyson, *Mozart*, 156.

retreats well into the background during the development section of the first movement, moreover; Mozart allows the strings a display of virtuosic semiquaver figuration, descending into the depths several times, while the clarinet performs a genuinely accompanimental part with a quaver motion that creates an impression almost of a composer at a loss for anything better to do—in a concerto the soloist would certainly have staked a claim to a larger share of any virtuosic display that was going. It is another of the steps in the direction of true chamber music which Mozart took in compositions of the period of *Figaro* and later; the clarinet, in this quintet, has far less of the character of a concerto soloist about it than falls, for example, to the piano in the E flat major Quartet, K. 493.

The atmosphere of their slow movements is something in which the quintet and concerto draw especially near to each other. Both are in the subdominant, D major, both are in 3/4 time, the clarinet has similar soloistic parts in both, and above all the violins have the same rocking quaver motion in both. The presence of the orchestra in the concerto again makes a difference, of course; the reciprocal play as the orchestra repeats separate thematic phrases from the clarinet's music in its own independent terms, has a different quality from the 'soloistic' writing in the context of the chamber piece, in which all the instruments share, especially the first violin. There is nothing of the concerto's slow movement in the G major sketch for basset horn, so it was presumably not started until 1791. The inner affinity between the quintet and the concerto demonstrates how much Mozart associated this atmosphere with the clarinet, and how much he had come to regard it, apparently, as typical of the instrument.

After the second movements the two works go separate ways. The concerto ends with a virtuoso rondo, characteristic of the concerto genus. The quintet, equally characteristically, has a minuet and trio and signs off with a fast finale—a theme and variations in this case. They share one fundamental quality with Mozart's other 'late' works and that is the individualization of tradition. It is no surprise to find that the composer serves up some surprises in the quintet's minuet, a form familiar as breathing to him since childhood. The most obvious are in the first of the two trios, a minor section scored for the strings alone (the other is in the major and the clarinet is included). In a typical minuet the music would have proceeded in regular, clearly punctuated four-bar periods, and arrived eventually, after eight bars for example, at a double barline from which a repeat of the minuet could be launched. In a minor-mode trio, moreover, a change of key to the relative major could also be expected in mid-movement, in this case from A minor to C major. Here, however, Mozart jerks the regular periodic structure right off its hinges in the seventh bar and mercilessly crushes any hint of major modality. The goal of C major is reached in the end, but it happens abruptly and unexpectedly, in the fifteenth of the sixteen opening bars. Once again, Mozart takes his hearers on a detour and makes the conventional course of events (the sequence of tonalities) an unsettling experience.

There are more surprises in the variation movement. Mozart's concern here is not only to illuminate a theme from different angles but also to establish an inner kinship between the variations, so that the later ones are inconceivable without the prior passage of the earlier ones. For this reason the initial 'theme' is only a stump of what is actually subjected to the variation process. The two violins begin alone, with music that might sooner have been composed for a pair of horns. The two lower strings add their voices only occasionally, and the clarinet is confined to brief, cadential interjections. It follows that the main task of the first variation is to integrate the clarinet into the proceedings; for the rest, however, exactly the same music is heard here (except in the middle section) as in the theme, with no variation in the order of the notes. In the second variation, viola and cello are at last involved from the start—but the clarinet completely disappears from the scene. The new, expanded function of the lower strings leads to a new harmonic progression: the premisses of the 'theme' which is supposed to delineate the framework within which the variations unfold are laid aside and a new framework is set out. Again in the third variation the clarinet does not play from the first, and the instrumentation is as it is in the second variation; but completely different tonal relationships now obtain, within the framework of normal variation techniques, for we have reached the 'minore', the conventional move into the minor mode. This brings with it a textural impoverishment, for only tonic and dominant are involved now. All the other harmonic degrees have been eliminated step by step, as we can see, looking back at the previous variation. The theme and its recurrence with the addition of the clarinet (the first variation), contain the three cadential degrees—tonic, subdominant, and dominant—and also the minor degrees, II and VI. In the second variation the minor degrees are replaced by the subdominant and the tonic, and finally in the third the subdominant is also dropped. Thus the 'minore' is a kind of stump of the theme, harmonically speaking, from which not only the ghosts of earlier and later variations can be derived, but also the ghost of the theme itself. Meanwhile the question of the instrumentation continues to roll: the principal voice in the 'minore' is the viola, whose first chance to play more than an accompanying role arrived only in the previous variation. The next variation (the fourth, 'maggiore') restores the horn-like theme to the two violins, in conjunction with a free clarinet part, similar to the situation in the first variation, but with the viola and cello accompanying from the start—which is more like the second variation. The fourth variation is the only one begun by all five instruments—but the clarinet is missing for the first time in the cadence at the end of the first half, whereas until this juncture the cadences have seemed to be the clarinet's domain. This variation ends unexpectedly with four freely transitional bars until, with a fifth, the conventional change of tempo—to adagio—is reached. Once again the four strings begin without the clarinet. As the instrumentation of the fourth variation seems to be like a development of that of the first, so here the part-writing relates to that of the second—and the first violin even starts with a variant of the theme there. The clarinet also absents itself this time from the closing cadence of the entire variation; another five transitional bars lead to the allegro conclusion, which lets go of the theme shortly after it starts, forgetting all about its musical structures and remembering only its spirit.

Mozart's variation technique here constitutes a logically constructed development of harmonic and instrumental features, and it is no longer confined to the limits allowed by a 'dual framework' as in the opening movement of his A major Sonata, K. 331 (see above, pp. 170–1). The harmonic 'framework', traditionally assured by the invariance of the inter-relationship of two musical parts, is subjected here to a development process: that is, the variation process affects more than the 'theme', and with that, Mozart leaves traditional variation procedures behind. (He had already moved in that direction in the 'Duport' Variations, K. 573, which had opened doors for him in Berlin for a while: the introduction of the relative minor in the cadential sections of the second variation, for example, shows the application of new harmonic procedures.) We see him questioning fundamental parameters of the theme, and retaining only its most general musical outline. Anarchy threatens, but new parameters emerge in the time the cycle of variations takes to run its course. Perhaps Mozart thinks it better, for now, to frame new laws from the sum of what has issued so far, rather than to return to the cycle's beginning with each new variation.

37

'The demeaning of women'? The Design of *Così fan tutte*, K. 588

Così fan tutte is undoubtedly the one opera of Mozart's Vienna period with which posterity had difficulties—and still does to this day. The sheer number of times it has been refashioned is one indicator of that fact; in the course of a statistical study of some twenty leading German opera-houses it was found listed under more than thirty different titles, which cloak some wildly varying versions of the original work. The objections have tended to concentrate on the time-scale and the characters' responses to dramatic developments, but the bottom line is the verdict passed on the work in 1891, in Wilhelmine Berlin: 'We cannot endure the demeaning of women on the stage'. Another constant is the perceived contradiction between the libretto, which is judged to be offensive, vulgar, and lascivious, and 'Mozart's divine music'.[1] In some respects, understanding of the work has been served by the effort to draw as close as possible again to the original, but some problems persist and the search for greater clarification must go on.

Così fan tutte was commissioned for Joseph II's 'National Theatre' (sited in the old Burgtheater) following the enthusiastic reception of *Figaro* when it was revived in Vienna in 1788. It was the third time that Mozart and Lorenzo Da Ponte sat down to create an opera together. By that stage general dramatic concepts must have been worked out and agreed between them, and they will have gone to work as a seasoned team. The première took place on 26 January 1790.

The dramatic substance of the opera consists of a bet and its uncomfortable consequences: Ferrando (tenor) and Guilelmo (baritone; 'Guglielmo' in modern editions, but the name is spelt 'Guilelmo' by Mozart in long

---

[1] S. Vill (ed.), *Così fan tutte: Beiträge zur Wirkungsgeschichte von Mozarts Oper* (Bayreuth, 1978); see in particular: S. Vill, 'Aufführungsstatistik 1790–1974', 283–7; K. Hortschansky, 'Gegen Unwahrscheinlichkeit und Frivolität: Die Bearbeitungen im 19. Jahrhundert', 54–66 (56 for the Berlin verdict); L. Finscher, in discussion, on p. 64.

stretches of the autograph, and in the first printing of the libretto[2]) sing the praises of their respective fiancées—two sisters, Dorabella and Fiordiligi—with such inordinate rapture that the 'old philosopher' Don Alfonso becomes suspicious, and tempts the two lovers to test the young women's fidelity for a wager. Ferrando and Guilelmo tell the ladies that they have been ordered to the front and take their leave; in no time at all they return in disguise and each proceeds to woo the other's betrothed. Don Alfonso wins the bet.

One of the objections to the opera is that the failure of Fiordiligi and Dorabella to recognize their fiancés in disguise is absurd, especially as it is only a few hours (a few minutes, in the theatre) since they last saw them. The shortness of the time was not a problem to Mozart and Da Ponte: quite the contrary, they make a particular point of it, and the entire action is supposed to take place within one twenty-four-hour period—just as with *Figaro* (*La Folle Journée* in Beaumarchais's original title) and *Don Giovanni* (see above, Chapter 32). These works, like *La clemenza di Tito* which drew on a much older libretto, observe the 'unity of time' asked for by Corneille in his *Discours sur la tragédie* (1660) and condemned by Lessing in his *Hamburgische Dramaturgie* (1767), but in *Così fan tutte* Mozart and Da Ponte actually focus on the restriction of the time-scale. Immediately after the plot has started to run its course, Fiordiligi cries out that she will not admit any other men into her house 'on this day, after this tragic event' (I. ii); and later, one reason for Ferrando's indignation at Dorabella's succumbing to Guilelmo's wooing is that she has forgotten about himself 'in un giorno, in poch'ore' ('in a single day, in just a few hours'; II. viii). It is clear, however, that the composer and the librettist both foresaw the question mark that would be placed on the women's failure to recognize their lovers. To make it more plausible they inserted a scene in which the two men are first of all presented in their disguises to the sisters' maid, Despina. She does not recognize either of them, and the impossibility of penetrating the disguises is thereby established as a foundation for the later development of the plot. Those whose doubts are not answered by that must accept the scene as offering a premiss on which to base the rest (as if Mozart and Da Ponte are saying; 'Let's suppose, for the sake of argument, that the disguise—or the deception—of the two male actors is so good that recognition is one hundred per cent ruled out . . .').

---

[2] Tyson, *Mozart*, 185.

Other aspects of the intrigue are dealt with just as briskly, above all the question of the relationships between the original couples before the unhappy wager was made. In the first scene, from the first trio to the second recitative, Ferrando and Guilelmo reiterate those virtues of their betrotheds which they esteem particularly highly, but we do not directly experience the love of Ferrando and his Dorabella, or of Guilelmo and his Fiordiligi. The 'love-duets' that we hear first are duos about love sung by people of the same sex: after Ferrando and Guilelmo's praise of their (absent) ladies, there is a corresponding duet in which Fiordiligi and Dorabella sing about them. Later love-duets are all sung by the 'wrong' couples in the course of the second act, so that the men's 'victories' over the women's constancy carry dramatic and musical conviction as we witness them with our own eyes and ears. Stefan Kunze has pointed out that the 'wrong' couples go together better than the 'right' ones in purely musical terms. According to the classical typology of roles in an *opera buffa*, the rank of 'first pair of lovers'—comparable to Donna Anna and Don Ottavio in *Don Giovanni*, for example—belongs more plausibly to Fiordiligi and the tenor Ferrando than to Fiordiligi and the baritone Guilelmo; he is more aptly partnered by Dorabella, whose part lies lower than her sister's.[3] This is unlikely to be either accident or error. Alan Tyson discovered that the original numbering of the pages shows that Mozart composed all the ensembles in the first act before he wrote a single aria or recitative. In its earliest state the autograph reveals that until shortly before the finale of this act the 'first' soprano was called Dorabella and the 'second' Fiordiligi. Later Mozart simply swapped the names round and created the cast as we know it today.[4] The critical fact, however, is that there is one place where the original names were not changed: at the start of the first scene, before the wager has been made, Ferrando already sings 'La mia Dorabella . . .' and Guilelmo 'La mia Fiordiligi . . .'.[5] This means that in the original cast the tenor Ferrando and the first soprano (only later Fiordiligi) would have made a 'right' couple, and the baritone Guilelmo would have had to try to win the first soprano for himself in the course of the action. In that situation the opera would have conformed to the conventional ideas of casting of the day—but it would not have been musically satisfactory. The explanation for the alteration would therefore

---

[3] Kunze, *Mozarts Opern*, 475.   [4] Tyson, *Mozart*, 184–5.
[5] My thanks to the editors-in-chief of the Neue Mozart-Ausgabe in Salzburg for enabling me to confirm this from microfilms.

appear to be that Mozart came to realize only when he was already writing the music that musical fundamentals were at risk: if the only love-duets were sung by the 'wrong' couples, then it must be the 'wrong' couples who were united by the demands of music and the classical typology of the roles, and not the 'right' ones, otherwise the music would go badly wrong in the duets. Ferrando therefore gained the first soprano as his partner in the duets, and she, dramatically, had to be the original beloved of Guilelmo, but could have the name of Fiordiligi transferred to her. In Dorabella's case the solution was reversed.

Questions such as those we have already looked at are overshadowed by the essentials of the dramatic action itself; indeed, the action is capable of overturning the expected answers to these questions, as the matter of 'right' and 'wrong' couples illustrates. What did Mozart choose to emphasize as the essentials of Da Ponte's libretto?

He divided the opera into five parts, signalling the end of each by the use of a stereotyped, unambiguously 'concluding' formula, which is heard for the first time at the end of the overture. The formula consists of a circling around the tonic, followed by a rest, and then by three chords which confirm the tonic. (See Ex. 37.1.) It is the kind of device a composer might have used unthinkingly, as a matter of routine, but Mozart appears to have used it here with a conscious intention. There were plenty of other formulaic cadences with which to finish off numbers and scenes within the parts (including weaker variants of the one described), and they have the effect of allowing the principal one to stand out boldly in its concluding and articulating function. After the overture it is next heard at the end of scene i, where Mozart actually added an orchestral postlude[6]— which gave him the opportunity to end with it. This is the scene in which Ferrando and Guilelmo accept Don Alfonso's wager and discuss spending the 100 zecchini they are confident of winning on 'una bella serenata' in honour of their lady-loves. The key is the same as at the end of the overture, C major, denoting that the situation is still what it was there. To some extent the scene can be regarded as an introduction, perhaps comparable to the 'Prologue in Heaven' in Goethe's *Faust*, in so far as the action is set up in it, but does not actually start moving.

The second point in Act I at which the 'concluding' formula is heard is at the end of the sextet. By now the audience has made the acquaintance of the three female characters of the opera and witnessed the lovers' leave-

---

[6] Tyson, *Mozart*, 187.

Ex. 37.1. *Così fan tutte.*

(a) End of the Overture, bars 257–61.

(b) End of the trio, No. 3, bars 74–6.

(c) End of the sextet, No. 13, bars 216–19.

(d) End of Act I, bars 693–7.

(e) End of Fiordiligi's aria, No. 25, bars 125–7.

(f) End of Act II, bars 667–71.

taking. It has also heard Dorabella's despairing aria 'Smanie implacabili' ('Merciless longing'), as well as the aria 'In uomini, in soldati' ('Among men, among soldiers') in which Despina advises the sisters not to take love so seriously, and gives a clue as to her likely reaction when the two 'strangers' arrive. In the sextet itself the two men, in their exotic disguise, are introduced to Fiordiligi and Dorabella, make their first advances, and are repulsed indignantly. Does that mean that they have already won the bet? They are perfectly sure that they will, and express their delight that their beloveds have resisted so stoutly. Don Alfonso has his suspicions about the delight, however; he succeeds in disrupting the 'concluding' effect of the formula, and forces the action to move straight on into the next passage of recitative by claiming the 'Albanians' as old friends.

The dramatic position of this sextet is comparable in some respects to that of the sextet in *Don Giovanni*; consisting of three fast numbers in a row, it is another 'pseudo-finale'.[7] Only Don Alfonso's admission of defeat is still needed to signal the end of the opera, and again Mozart uses the device of constructing the situation like a finale in order to heighten the tension. But the concluding cadence comes too soon, Don Alfonso asserts his doubts, and the action continues. Only after Fiordiligi's aria declaring her rock-like constancy ('Come scoglio', No. 14) and Guilelmo's first solo sortie ('Non siate ritrosi', No. 15) are he and Ferrando able to give vent to their joy (No. 16, Trio, 'E voi ridete'—'Are you laughing?'). By now the situation when the 'concluding' formula was in view has been left well behind, and the trio ends with a suspiciously fleet succession of triplet quavers—like the trio in scene i and Despina's first aria. This formula, too, has significance: it crops up again in the second act, in Dorabella's aria 'È amore un ladroncello' ('Cupid is a thief'), which follows her abandonment of her love for Ferrando, and at an early stage in the finale, when Don Alfonso and Despina crow over the success of their 'comedy'. All five numbers are revealed to be over-hasty and ill-judged—and the joy of Ferrando and Guilelmo after the Act I sextet is also of short duration. Obviously adding this thread to the fabric of the work was a relatively late idea—apart from the opening trio all these numbers belong to the same late stage of composition.[8]

The third part of the opera runs to the end of Act I, where the formula from the end of the overture is heard once more. The finale, only two numbers after 'E voi ridete', contains Ferrando and Guilelmo's second joint assault on the ladies, employing sterner means. They claim to have taken poison, are cured with the aid of magnetism by a 'doctor' (Despina in disguise), and ask for kisses to assist their recovery. Once again Fiordiligi

---

[7] Tyson, *Mozart*, 188–9, contemplates the possibility that 'it could once have been intended as the Act I finale in a three-act opera'.

[8] Cf. remarks by Tyson, ibid. 182, 188, 195.

and Dorabella remain constant and the situation remains the same, to all appearances, as it was at the end of the sextet. But the appearances are becoming deceptive. Previously the concluding formula has been heard only in C major, so its transposition a whole tone higher to D major now has to be understood as a heightening of tension. The dramatic temperature is rising. Words like 'foco' ('anger') and 'amor' ('love') appear in the text, in the last lines of the act, but while Ferrando and Guilelmo merely express the fear that the former might be converted into the latter, Despina and Don Alfonso predict that it will be.

New dramatic initiatives are introduced in the second act of *Così fan tutte*, as they are after the midpoint of *Figaro*. Ferrando and Guilelmo have clearly recognized that their fiancées' fidelity is an impregnable fortress, so long as they go on laying siege to it as a combined force. They therefore separate in Act II and try their 'luck' singly.

The fourth stage in the action to end with the recurrence of the concluding formula goes up to Fiordiligi's great rondo-aria 'Per pietà, ben mio, perdona' ('Forgive me, beloved'), in which she appeals to the absent Guilelmo to pardon her paying any attention at all to the sufferings of the supposed stranger (Ferrando). The situation now is even more expectant than it was at the end of Act I: consequently Fiordiligi's aria is in E major, that is, another whole tone higher than the D major of the act-finale. But E major is the fatal key in which, in the 'introduction' in Act I, Don Alfonso compared women's constancy to the phoenix of Arabia—fabled but never seen, and it is also the key in which Fiordiligi, Dorabella, and Don Alfonso wished the 'departing' soldiers a prosperous voyage.[9] In purely musical terms the action is coming full circle: Don Alfonso may be on the point of being proved correct, or the 'prosperous voyage' may be about to reach its destination. But Ferrando, who overhears Fiordiligi's aria, concludes from it that he and his friend have won the bet: 'Amico, abbiamo vinto', he says to Guilelmo. In the mean time, however, Guilelmo has succeeded in his courtship of Dorabella. So three things have happened in this first part of Act II: Ferrando and Guilelmo have separated, Dorabella has surrendered, Fiordiligi has resisted. Guilelmo regards his conquest of Dorabella as proof that his Fiordiligi is the better of the two sisters. This assertion provokes Ferrando to launch into his cavatina 'Tradito, schernito' ('Betrayed, taunted'), but his fury drives him on to pursue his wooing of Fiordiligi, in which he is eventually successful. This

[9] Kunze, *Mozarts Opern*, 511.

is one of the strands in the action during the fifth part of the opera, but not the only one, for the concluding formula is not heard again until the end of the act, when peace is restored (the circling round the tonic is there—as in Fiordiligi's aria—minimally varied).

This division of the work serves a different principle from any idea of demeaning women. If that was really Mozart's aim, giving prominence to Fiordiligi's aria by making it one of the structural pivots would be the last thing he would want to do: he would be more likely to single out the love-duets between the 'wrong' couples instead. The positioning of that concluding cadence at the end of 'Per pietà', of all places, suggests completely different intentions, which are reinforced by the means Mozart and Da Ponte have Ferrando and Guilelmo use in the furtherance of their ends. Against this background, there can be no question of 'the demeaning of women'.

Guilelmo wants to give Dorabella a trinket in the shape of a heart as a token of his love. At first she holds back, but he insists: 'Son tutto vostro!' ('I am all yours!') and: 'Cedete, o cara!' ('Yield, beloved!') She replies: 'Mi fate morir', literally 'you make me die', that is, 'it would kill me'. Guilelmo is not at all perturbed by the thought that this matter is one of literally life-and-death importance to her, and he answers that in that case they will die together. It is enough to break her resistance, but Guilelmo finds time for the aside: 'Infelice Ferrando!' ('Poor old Ferrando!')

Dorabella's surrender makes Fiordiligi's position worse in every respect. Not only does it remove Ferrando's inhibitions in respect of winning her, but also Dorabella tells her about it and advises her, seconded by Despina, to follow her example. Fiordiligi rejects the advice, and forms the plan of putting on men's clothing and following her beloved Guilelmo to the wars. In a musical number that begins as an aria 'Fra gli amplessi' ('In his embrace'), as she starts her preparations, she is surprised by Ferrando who turns the aria into a duet. She is caught completely off her guard, and in the state of high excitement in which she is already she can no longer find the strength to offer further resistance. It was already there in Da Ponte's text, but Mozart's music expresses it too.

The sight of a male character breaking down the resistance of a female one has been seen in an earlier opera by Mozart: in Don Giovanni's first attempt to seduce Zerlina ('Là ci darem la mano').[10] There, the text followed a standard duet pattern: Don Giovanni's thesis is at first countered

---

[10] This comparison has already been made by Kunze, *Mozarts Opern*, 468.

by Zerlina's antithesis, and before her resistance can be broken (leading to the goal of a true duet) the alternation of thesis and antithesis has to intensify. Compared to the text of the duet between Ferrando and Fiordiligi, the dialogue of Don Giovanni and Zerlina is a model of roguish innocence. Da Ponte provided thirty-four lines of verse (or thirty-five, if the last two are divided according to the internal rhyme; see below). The first fourteen of these nod in the direction of sonnet form in their rhyme-structure, in that two strophes of four lines each are followed by two of

FIORDILIGI.	Fra gli amplessi in pochi istanti	In a few moments I shall be in the arms
	Giungerò del fido sposo;	of my faithful bridegroom;
	Sconosciuta a lui davanti	unknown to him in these clothes,
	In quest' abito verrò.	I shall stand before him.
	Oh, che gioia il suo bel core	Oh, what joy his good heart
	Proverà nel ravvisarmi!	will feel at seeing me again!
FERRANDO.	Ed intanto di dolore	And meanwhile I, poor wretch,
	Meschinello io mi morrò.	will die of sorrow.
FIORDILIGI.	Cosa veggio? Son tradita!	What do I see? I am betrayed!
	Deh, partite!	Begone!
FERRANDO.	Ah no, mia vita!	Ah no, my life!
	Con quel ferro di tua mano	With that sword in your hand
	Questo cor tu ferirai,	pierce this heart!
	E se forza, oh Dio, non hai,	And if, oh God, you have not the strength,
	Io la man ti reggerò.	I will guide your hand!
FIORDILIGI.	Taci, ahimè! Son abbastanza	Hush, alas! I am sufficiently
	Tormentata ed infelice!	tormented and unhappy!
(*with Ferrando*)	Ah, che omai la mia [sua] costanza	Ah! Already my [her] constancy
	A quei sguardi, a quel che dice	begins to crumble at these looks,
	Incomincia a vacillar!	at these words!
FIORDILIGI.	Sorgi, sorgi!	Stand up, stand up!
FERRANDO.	Invan lo credi.	In vain you hope for that.
FIORDILIGI.	Per pietà, da me che chiedi?	In pity's name, what do you want of me?
FERRANDO.	Il tuo cor o la mia morte.	Your heart or my death.
FIORDILIGI.	Ah, non son, non son più forte!	Ah no, my strength has almost gone!
FERRANDO.	Cedi, cara!	Yield, beloved!
FIORDILIGI.	Dei, consiglio!	Gods, advise me!
FERRANDO.	Volgi a me pietoso il ciglio.	Heaven look mercifully upon me.
	In me sol trovar tu puoi	In me alone you will find a husband,
	Sposo, amante e più, se vuoi.	a lover, and even more, if you will.
	Idol mio, più non tardar.	My adored one, tarry no longer.
FIORDILIGI.	Giusto ciel! Crudel, hai vinto,	Righteous heaven! Cruel man, you have won me!
	Fa di me quel che ti par.	Do with me what you will.
(*with Ferrando*)	Abbracciamci, o caro bene,	Let us embrace, my beloved,
	E un conforto a tante pene	It will be a comfort after such torments
	Sia languir di dolce affetto,	to swoon with sweet emotions
	Di diletto sospirar.	to sigh with joy.

three lines (rhyming abab, cdcd, eef, ggf). Fiordiligi begins—aria-like—with the first strophe and then also the second before Ferrando interrupts her in the middle of it. This is contrary to the rules not only of polite behaviour but of duet form too: the illusion that Fiordiligi is singing an aria is enhanced by the fact that her opening strophe is not answered by a complementary strophe from Ferrando, that is, Da Ponte does not construct the duet in the normal way. Mozart goes further; he has Fiordiligi begin 'adagio' and increases the tempo to 'con più moto' at the start of her second strophe, thereby creating the impression of a slow introduction preceding a moderately fast number. Ferrando's interruption is therefore a shock for the audience as well as for Fiordiligi—especially as it is accompanied by a simultaneous modulation from a radiant A major to A minor.

In spite of his ill-bred incursion Fiordiligi is still capable of exercising some control, and for two bars of recitative she forces Ferrando to hold his tongue and banishes his minor modality from the music. She cannot re-establish her initial A major, but at least manages to substitute C major. There is further disruption of formal conventions in Ferrando's appropriation of four and a half out of the six remaining lines of the 'sonnet', instead of taking a gentlemanly share of three. He makes matters worse by using the lines to challenge Fiordiligi to stab him with the sword which she intended to buckle on as part of her disguise as a soldier-boy, and even volunteers to guide her hand. Mozart's attitude to this situation is revealed by a detail in the notation which is hidden from the listener: in spite of the imperious change to C major he retains the A major key signature with three sharps, as if Fiordiligi might still have the strength to regain the opening key—and he only abandons it after Ferrando's completion of the 'sonnet'.

Order has been seriously disrupted. The next fourteen lines do not resemble a sonnet in any way, but are made up of three strophes of four lines each, with an extra, fifth line attached to the first and third strophes. Now, the key of C major has been fully established with Fiordiligi's words 'ahimè! Son abbastanze tormentata ed infelice'. A strophe in pure C major ensues, which is sometimes cut in performance because it is conveniently in the same key at the end as at the beginning. But without this intermediate stage, in which the situation between Fiordiligi and Ferrando is more or less evenly balanced, the following stage is scarcely comprehensible. Fiordiligi's 'Sorgi, sorgi' prepares the transition back to the minor, that is, to Ferrando's sphere: we have reached the peripeteia, the change of fortune. The words with which Ferrando begins the duet's penultimate strophe, 'Cedi, o cara', are almost the same as those with which Guilelmo urged Dorabella to yield to him, 'Cedete, o cara', but instead of Guilelmo's single recitative statement Mozart allows Ferrando to utter his imperative no less than four times. This is the first time in the duet that a strophe is started by Ferrando and not Fiordiligi, and the first time that he sings half a line which Fiordiligi completes (with 'Dei, consiglio!'). She has still not surrendered, but her strength is ebbing fast. Now, in the middle of a strophe, Mozart once again has Ferrando turn the accustomed order topsy-turvy: he enters Fiordiligi's A major, chooses a new tempo and a new metre, and begins a new 'aria' of courtship, of almost unimaginable seductive power. The fact that with the first line of it he not only provides the rhyme to Fiordiligi's 'Dei, consiglio' but also invokes divine assistance in his turn can only be interpreted as pure cynicism, attributed to his character by Da Ponte. Ignoring the disruption of the rhyme-structure the librettist gives Ferrando four lines, a strophe in quantity but nothing else—another element which goes against due order.

Da Ponte provided two more lines for Fiordiligi to sing solo. To emphasize the straits in which she now finds herself, Mozart divided the first into three segments, separating 'Giusto ciel!' from 'crudel', and isolating 'hai vinto' from that; furthermore he scattered the three exclamations through the last part of Ferrando's strophe. He gave Ferrando's last words, which are interrupted by that 'hai vinto', an accompanying oboe line; tenor and instrumentalist have the same notes at first. Then the oboe detaches itself and stands alone uttering a merciless e''—Fiordiligi could be said to have a free choice of when to surrender to it, but that she must do so at some point is now beyond question: 'Fa di me quel che ti par'.

Even more clearly than in Dorabella's case, this is not the surrender the pseudo-lover was asking for. At the start of the duet Ferrando offers Fiordiligi the choice between stabbing him or loving him, but the former possibility, her last remaining refuge, vanishes, at the very latest, at the moment when he embarks his A major 'aria'. He leaves her no choice, the position is tantamount to rape—at least so far as Da Ponte was concerned. It was nothing to do with him whether the love-duet with which the scene finishes was convincing or not: that was Mozart's business.

Mozart did not mitigate in any way the desperate position to which Ferrando drives Fiordiligi, but he paid attention to Ferrando's state of mind as well. Already in the first bar, before the tenor interrupts the soprano's aria, the orchestra plays a figure which bears a noticeably strong resem-

Ex. 37.2. *Così fan tutte.*
(a) String motifs at the start of Ferrando's aria, No. 17, and of the duet for Fiordiligi and Ferrando, No. 29.
(b) Phrases sung by Ferrando in the trio, No. 3 (bars 6–8), and in the duet, No. 29 (bars 28–30).

blance to the orchestral prelude to the aria in Act I ('Un'aura amorosa') in which we heard Ferrando luxuriating in the thought of his Dorabella's constancy—in A major, to boot (see Ex. 37.2*a*). Then, he sings the first line after he has turned Fiordiligi's aria into a duet ('con quel ferro di tua mano') to exactly the same C major melody as he sang at the end of Act I, scene i, for the line 'far io voglio alla mia dea' ('I will serenade my adored one'; see Ex. 37.2*b*). Both these dreams have been superseded in the mean time; quotation is an important element in *Così fan tutte*, and these two instances in particular paint Ferrando's complete disillusionment. The picture receives its finishing touch with his cry 'il tuo cor o la mia morte'; after Dorabella and Guilelmo's duet this does indeed appear to be his only choice. It is what empowers him to sing of his love to Fiordiligi, who is betrothed to Guilelmo, with such irresistible sincerity, and it is on that basis alone that Fiordiligi's surrender and the love-duet carry musical conviction. The relative ease with which Dorabella yields earlier to Guilelmo is not a reflection on any of the characters but the outcome of the dramatic situation. After the change of course to which the first act-finale drove the two men, the resistance of one of the two sisters has to crumble. Clearly, it cannot be that of the prima donna, because 'demeaning women' is not the end in view. The design of the two seduction scenes as one finely graded cumulative succession is simply an expression of Mozart and Da Ponte's dramatic instinct.

The finale of Act II includes the 'marriage' of the wrong couples (with Despina disguised as a lawyer), the 'return' of Ferrando and Guilelmo, and the revealing of the bet. The three men are obviously completely unprepared for the horror that overcomes the sisters—and Despina too—and they observe: 'Son mezzo matte' ('They're half mad'). Da Ponte and Mozart then deliver the *lieto fine*, the happy ending essential to a *buffa* opera: the six characters join together to affirm that happiness is the ability to meet the vicissitudes of life with a certain serene detachment. The finale ends with the formula from the overture: all has turned out well in the end, the 'right' couples, Fiordiligi and Guilelmo, and Dorabella and Ferrando, are reunited; the fact that the opera ends as it began, in C major, is only fitting, formally and dramatically.

The *lieto fine* is thus comparable to that of *Don Giovanni*: here, as there, tension is maintained up to the very last minute, and the chain of events with some intensely dramatic elements, bordering at times on tragedy, continues until immediately before the end. To that extent the finales of both operas present us with a heap of broken pieces. In *Don Giovanni*, after the protagonist has been dragged down to hell, all the others must admit the truth about themselves and the past; in *Così fan tutte*, the mutual trust between all the characters has been very severely shaken. The only happy thing about either of these endings is the consoling thought that a strong moral can be drawn, and the praise of serene detachment in *Così fan tutte* is comparable to the recognition in *Don Giovanni* that the evil-doer always comes to a bad end ('Questo è il fin di chi fa mal').

Constructing finales (and teasing audiences with pseudo-finales) and achieving the happy ending at the very last minute seem to constitute the common denominator, the principle that Da Ponte and Mozart gradually worked out as the broad basis for a successful operatic plot. The indications are that it did not begin to take shape until they were already at work on

Don Giovanni, and was developed further in *Così fan tutte*; it is not to be found in *Figaro*. Perhaps the difficulty with *Così* is that, almost as soon as Mozart died, posterity lost the sense of the tragedy inherent in the work—a tragedy often revealed in the poetico-musical structures.

Yet there are other difficulties, within the work itself. The title comes from the libretto (it is also found in the libretto of *Figaro*[11]). The words are uttered by Don Alfonso not long before the finale of Act II, and Ferrando and Guilelmo repeat them in agreement: 'That's how they all behave'—referring expressly to women, because otherwise it would have to be 'Così fan tutti'. But the act of promoting the words to be the opera's title wrenched them from their context, and they cannot be regarded as containing the work's moral message in its entirety, because the lessons of the finale are yet to come. The title is therefore not the best aid to understanding the work, indeed, it is something of a hindrance—albeit one that Mozart himself, presumably, erected in the first place. Don Alfonso's words come in one of the last passages of the opera to be composed, and Da Ponte only ever calls it by its subtitle, 'La scola degli amanti', that is, 'the school for lovers' (presumably male and female this time).[12] If listeners imagine that the message of the work is complete when those words are spoken they will fail to pay the proper attention to the shocks administered to the cast in the finale, because it is only with them that the lovers complete the education of the subtitle. The lesson the opera has to teach is not over until the eyes of Ferrando and Guilelmo are opened and the closing ensemble is sung. It touches only tangentially the opinion Don Alfonso expressed in the introduction, that women's constancy is as rare as the phoenix; the question of guilt is not raised among the four lovers. Don Alfonso is the only person to be accused of any wrongdoing, and that by Fiordiligi and Dorabella; 'Ecco là il barbaro che c'ingannò' ('There is the villain who deceived us all'). Before Ferrando and Guilelmo add anything to that, Don Alfonso reveals his true purpose—which was to teach the two men a lesson. Their promise never to put their beloveds' fidelity on trial again indicates that they now understand how inhumanly they behaved in having agreed at the start not to betray themselves to the women by either word or gesture, and to obey Don Alfonso unconditionally (Guilelmo: 'tuttissimo'). They kept their word and surrendered their true identities: this is expounded both in the words of the libretto and especially in the beauty of the music with which each lover courts the other's beloved,

[11] Kunze, *Mozarts Opern*, 442.   [12] Tyson, *Mozart*, 197.

above all in the love-duets of the 'wrong' couples (though they are 'right' according to the conventions of casting *opera buffa*). In view of the consistency with which Ferrando and Guilelmo keep up their unnatural self-control, the women's (late) surrender is not so much a question of character but, if anything, one of time and physical strength.

38

An *Opera Seria* for the 1790s: *La clemenza di Tito*, K. 621

The first performance of *Così fan tutte* was given in Vienna on 26 January 1790. The next première of an opera by Mozart took place in Prague on 6 September 1791, and the work was *La clemenza di Tito*. The twenty-months gap between the two premières was about six months shorter than the interval between *Don Giovanni* and *Così*, and only a little longer than that between *Figaro* and *Don Giovanni*. To that extent, therefore, *Tito* belongs in the sequence of the great operas of Mozart's Viennese period, but it differs from its three *buffa* predecessors in being an *opera seria*. Furthermore, the interval since *Così* had been of a different character from those between the earlier operas. After the première, it was given only nine more performances in the following few weeks: Emperor Joseph II died on 20 February and all forms of public entertainment were cancelled as a mark of official court mourning. This appears to have made Mozart's shaky financial position even worse: the frequency of letters begging Michael Puchberg for help certainly increased. The money he received from Puchberg between December 1789 and June 1790 alone, in nine separate instalments, amounts to more than 800 gulden. We can assume that he paid back some of those loans individually, as his letters regularly affirm that he will, with reference to concrete prospects that will enable him to do so; but it is reasonably certain that he had no reserves of his own at all.

There was an obvious change in Mozart's circumstances during the summer of 1791. He began his collaboration with Emanuel Schikaneder on *Die Zauberflöte*. Franz, Count von Walsegg-Stuppach sent his ominous 'grey messenger' to commission the Requiem—possibly on the recommendation of Michael Puchberg. And on 8 July the Bohemian Estates directed the Prague impresario Domenico Guardasoni to commission a 'cellebre maestro' to compose an opera for performance on the occasion of the coronation of Leopold II as King of Bohemia. (Mozart had travelled to Frankfurt am Main in the autumn of the previous year for Leopold's coronation as Holy Roman Emperor.) The subject favoured in Prague was 'the clemency of Titus', for which a libretto already existed, by Pietro

Metastasio, the poet who had presided over the last great flowering of *opera seria*.[1] His 'Titus' libretto was by then 57 years old, and had first been set in 1734 by Antonio Caldara, then vice-Kapellmeister at the Viennese court. It made the ideal basis for an opera to be played on a great royal occasion, especially a coronation, for it both praised a prince and celebrated the virtues which subjects hope to find in a ruler.

Titus is merciful. His fundamental principle is to rule benevolently, for, as he says: 'Del più sublime soglio l'unico frutto è questo; tutto tormento è il resto, e tutto è servitù' ('This is the only profit of the loftiest throne; all else is anguish and servitude'). His benevolence does not falter even when Servilia, the woman he has chosen as his bride, refuses the chance of becoming empress on the grounds that she has long since given her heart to Annius. He does experience a crisis of conscience when his friend Sextus leads a conspiracy against him, is arrested, and asks to be put to death quickly; but even here clemency prevails and Titus pardons him. Another conflict arises when Vitellia, who was prompted by jealousy to incite Sextus to conspiracy, but has subsequently been selected by Titus to be his empress instead of Servilia, confesses to being behind the plot. Still Titus remains true to himself: 'Sia nota a Roma, ch'io son lo stesso' ('Let it be known in Rome that I am what I was before'). Operas carry moral messages (as we have already seen in the cases of *Don Giovanni* and *Così fan tutte*), and in *Tito* the message is pointedly addressed to the ruler himself. That the medium chosen for the message is an opera is not so surprising: it is a relic, to some extent, of the privilege once enjoyed by a Court Fool.

Looked at closely, Metastasio's text was too out of date to meet the expectations of audiences in the 1790s. It needed some adaptation before it could serve for a 'true opera', 'una vera opera' as Mozart described the outcome in his thematic catalogue, where he also recorded that the revision was the work of Caterino Mazzolà. Mazzolà was poet to the court theatre in Dresden, but was briefly employed at the Viennese court in the early summer of 1791. It is doubtful if Mozart's remark signified merely an extraordinary satisfaction with Mazzolà's work: Mazzolà's position was comparable to some extent to Da Ponte's when he adapted *Figaro* from another writer's stage play, and Mozart never mentioned Da Ponte's name in his catalogue. Perhaps Mozart wanted to emphasize the premisses on which he was prepared to undertake the setting of this old-fashioned, if celebrated, operatic treatment,[2] given that, in view of Leopold II's vacillat-

---

[1] Eisen, *Mozart Documents*, 67.   [2] Lühning, *Titus-Vertonungen*, 83.

ing policy with regard to opera, he was not in a position to refuse the commission. But the adjective 'true' cannot be dismissed lightly: within limits which they both acknowledged, Mazzolà's refurbishment was acceptable to the composer.

Mozart and Mazzolà were obvious choices for Guardasoni. He had known Mozart personally for some time and his opera company had been enormously successful in Prague with operas by Mozart. It has been conjectured that when Mozart called on Guardasoni in spring 1789 on his way to Prussia, and discussed an opera to be commissioned for 1790, they might have settled on Titus as the subject even then, but it is not really very likely that they would have considered an old libretto like Metastasio's *Tito* for their next joint venture, when they had had such good success with two comedies. But even in the special circumstances in which *La clemenza di Tito* was commissioned, Mozart was a first-class choice for Guardasoni, Prague audiences, and the Bohemian Estates, if a 'cellebre maestro' was what they wanted; at all events, the published libretto affirms that the music was 'dal celebre Sig. Wolfgango Amadeo Mozart'. As for Mazzolà, Guardasoni had already staged several operas with librettos by him, in addition to which he happened to be in Vienna at the time when the work on *Tito* had to be done—which was convenient if Mozart was to be the composer.[3] When Guardasoni set off from Prague for Italy to place suitable singers under contract, two days after receiving the commission of the Bohemian Estates, he must have regarded it as a fortunate coincidence that his journey took him via Vienna where he could entrust the opera to two seasoned operatic professionals whom he already knew.

Helga Lühning, who has made an intensive study of *La clemenza di Tito*—both of the genesis of Mozart's opera and of other settings of Metastasio's libretto—has argued that Guardasoni might have approached only Mazzolà to begin with, because Mozart was not told exactly who the singers would be until some time later. Alan Tyson has shown, however, on the basis of his study of the paper-types of Mozart's autographs, that the composer began with the ensembles, which he could write for types of voices (soprano, tenor, etc.) without needing to take the particular qualities of individual singers into account.[4] Thus Lühning's thesis is countered by an equally strong likelihood that Guardasoni engaged Mozart as well as Mazzolà while passing through Vienna. He had, after all, undertaken to find a celebrated composer, and such a one would surely be capable of

---

[3] Lühning, 'Zur Entstehungsgeschichte', 315–16.
[4] Ibid. 315–16; Tyson, *Mozart*, 48–60, esp. 54–5.

making something of even a mediocre libretto; moreover the composer would be able to steer the librettist in directions that would suit his own personal stylistic predilections. It is also possible, indeed, that it was Mozart, with Guardasoni's agreement, who first approached Mazzolà. Mazzolà had been Da Ponte's 'tutor' in dramaturgy; Da Ponte had left Vienna in March 1791 because he could not come to a satisfactory arrangement with the new Emperor. One party at court, at least, had it in mind to make Mazzolà Da Ponte's successor as court poet. Mozart may well have come into contact with him shortly after the writer reached Vienna, and before the question of collaboration ever arose.

The accumulated information on this matter contains one anomaly. Undoubtedly Mozart was a 'cellebre maestro' in the eyes of Prague, but the specification could also, and perhaps more suitably, be applied to a composer who ranked higher in the court hierarchy, Antonio Salieri for instance. In fact, there is a letter which Salieri wrote to Prince Anton Esterházy in late August 1791, saying that he had turned down the commission to compose the opera for the Bohemian coronation with a light heart, although Guardasoni had been very insistent, using financial persuasion as well as paying him repeated visits.[5] Officially, therefore, Mozart was Guardasoni's second choice; even so, the designation 'cellebre maestro' does not need to be regarded merely as an attempted justification, for it did represent the Prague view of things. At all events, work on *Tito* must have begun before July was out, with Mazzolà and Mozart coming to an agreement on the goals they would pursue in their joint project.

Mozart does not appear to have been the only person who found Metastasio's text unusable when it was looked at closely. We have no means of knowing whether Mazzolà was fired by conviction in his labour of revision or simply produced what he was being paid for, but the commission from the Bohemian Estates allowed for alterations to the libretto. Guardasoni undertook to procure a new opera either on a completely new libretto (for which two drafts were produced) or one composed on the same subject as Metastasio's *Tito* ('. . . mi obligo di procurar un Opera nuovamente composta sul Suggetto del Tito di Metastasio'). The only specifications were that the subject should be Titus, and that it should conform to the Metastasian viewpoint; one thing *not* required, however, was that the original libretto should be set without alteration.

---

[5] Cf. [Anon.] 'The Acta Musicalia [of the Esterházy Archive, nos. 101–52]', *Haydn Studies*, 15 (1984), 93–180, esp. 153–6.

What was it in the original libretto that did not conform to Mozart's idea of a 'true opera' for the 1790s? The comparison with Mazzolà's version provides an answer. It is also interesting to see how Mozart went to work on an *opera seria*, after having spent the previous ten years establishing himself as an all-time master of *opera buffa*. One of his great strengths in that field was his skill in constructing act-finales, but the 'chain' structure called for in a *buffa* finale is alien to *seria* forms, and relies on ensembles in situations of a kind that were not to be reconciled with *seria* conventions unless some adjustments were made. Did Mazzolà's revision take any steps towards *buffa* structures, and if so how were the character-istics of *opera seria* preserved? Finally—risking what is, strictly speaking, an impermissible comparison between the music of an *opera seria* and an *opera buffa*—what were the problems of writing ensembles in *La clemenza di Tito*, when the issue is viewed with the Da Ponte operas in mind?

Metastasio's *Tito* was permeated with the fundamental constituents of the ideal of *opera seria* which he had formulated by the 1730s. It would be unjust to expect anything else, and the observation is not a qualitative judgement. *Opera seria* was regarded as a form of the spoken theatre with music added; Metastasio was thought of as a poet, not 'simply' a librettist.[6] There is no place in the spoken theatre for the ensemble, with two (let alone more) voices speaking at once, or even for the 'dialectical' duet in which the action advances rapidly in the exchange of thesis and antithesis, ending in synthesis (as in the duet of Zerlina and Don Giovanni). *Opera seria* knew just two musical forms: secco recitative and the set-piece aria. The first advanced the action, the latter allowed the music to unfold and hence show off the vocal virtuosity of a soloist. It was therefore singers' theatre to an exceptionally high degree. The virtuosity of the arias is the product of a dramatic framework shaped by the relative expansiveness of the recitatives, and it also expected a creative contribution from the singers themselves, who improvised ornamentation of the vocal line in the score according to their individual technical abilities and tastes. The attraction of a *seria* opera lay in the virtuosity, above all the unpredictability of the ornamentation, and that attraction was diminished as soon as a second or third singer was admitted to make the aria a duet or trio. When the musical attraction of the show-piece aria was sacrificed to the demands of the drama, therefore, it detracted from the fundamental conditions of the *seria* genre—and had an effect on the arias themselves, not just the ensembles.

---

[6] Osthoff, 'Opera buffa', 680; Lühning, *Titus-Vertonungen*, 2.

The whole *seria* edifice was in danger of collapse by the last decades of the eighteenth century; several aspects of the old festive opera for the big court occasion in the Metastasian style had been watered down, and a 'true opera' needed some other foundation.

Mazzolà certainly took some steps to move the dramatic emphasis away from the recitatives and towards the arias. The result was not only a closer integration of the arias into the action but also the creation of opportunities for dramatic ensembles, such as the finale of Act I, which in Mazzolà's two-act version includes the conflagration of the Capitol, instigated by Sextus (in Metastasio's version it happens in the second of three acts). Mazzolà's inroads into the original text penetrate to the very foundations of the work's conception. They include the reworking of Metastasio's recitatives to provide for closed musical forms and the writing of completely new passages; in both cases the purpose was to allow for more ensembles. In addition, some arias were cut. Where Metastasio's version consists of twenty-five arias and four choruses, Mazzolà's has eleven arias, three duets and three trios, one quintet and one sextet, and five choruses.

Nevertheless, the ensembles in *Tito* have a different function from the duets and trios of Mozart's *buffa* operas. In the latter they often serve particularly exciting dramatic ends, providing the basis of the pseudo-finales, or mapping situations of great psychological complexity, like the duet for Fiordiligi and Ferrando in Act II of *Così fan tutte*. That kind of deepening and broadening of dramatic elements is much more tentative in *Tito*, and found only in the act-finales. To some extent, the finale of Act I employs techniques Mozart developed in the Da Ponte operas, but more often than not it is the recitative techniques which are new, and the whole finale is only a fraction of the length of a typical *buffa* finale. At the textual level we are back to a relatively simple succession of duet-particles.

The other ensemble numbers fit into the generic mould of *opera seria*—although their very presence there is an assault on it. Some can be termed 'exit ensembles', by analogy with exit arias, for like them they merely use a musically closed form to confirm the dramatic situation already reached in the recitative. Such is the case in the very first number in the opera, a duet in which Vitellia incites Sextus to assist her plot against Titus—which she has already done in the preceding recitative. Sextus begins the duet with 'Come ti piace imponi' ('Command what you will'), but he has in any case ended the recitative by asking her to forgive him for not acceding to her wishes immediately and unconditionally—'Perdonami, ti credo, io m'ingannai' ('Forgive me, I believe you, I was wrong'). That has already restored their good relations, and harmony prevails in the duet. True, they do not actually leave the stage after this 'exit' duet, but it is tantamount to an exit in that it sets the seal on the situation established in the recitative. The textual structure is the same as that of the *Don Giovanni* duet 'Là ci darem la mano': a strophe for him, a strophe for her, one in which they sing alternately, and one in which they finally sing together. The difference in the dramatic potential of the two duets is undeniable, and it reveals the boundaries that were still drawn typologically between the *buffa* and *seria* genres.

Tito has examples of another situation in which an ensemble is adapted to *seria* conventions, when the action being carried onwards in recitative reaches a climax and suddenly freezes. At such a moment, there would be an aria in traditional *seria*: but coming at a moment of high tension, an ensemble, quite as much as an aria, stops the action in its tracks. The moment of decision in the drama for which the recitative was pressing with increasing urgency is postponed, while the ensemble presents with even greater clarity the positions the characters have already reached or revealed, and exploits the resulting configuration for purely musical purposes. The outstanding example is the Trio, No. 18 ('Quello di Tito è il volto'—'This is the true face of Titus'), in which Sextus is brought before the Emperor and Publius, the prefect of the Praetorian Guard, as a prisoner. Sextus expects to be sentenced to death, Titus is horrified by Sextus' crime, and Publius is trying to measure the conflict waged by mercy and duty in the Emperor's conscience. The three elements are quite separate; in the first part of the trio each character sings his portion of the text 'a parte', or aside—as if no one overheard it. Mozart hated this particular stylistic convention, as he told his father while he was writing *Idomeneo*: 'These things are perfectly natural in dialogue—a person quickly says a few words aside—but in an aria, where the words must be repeated, the effect is appalling' (8 November 1780). Nothing could be further from 'a few words aside' at this point in *Tito*; the musical situation of the trio is too exposed, in the nature of things, while the dramatic situation only magnifies the exposure.

Mazzolà provides an elegant solution to the problem, which moreover is exactly in line with the direction Mozart had been taking in the past few years. The convention of speaking aside is not accepted unquestioningly but held up to the light and a justification is found for it on dramatic grounds. After the three characters have sung their opening strophes aside, to distinct and independent accompaniments, Mazzolà goes to the very brink of the possible, and places words in Titus' mouth which the Emperor speaks directly to Sextus and which could serve to tear the configuration of the characters apart: 'Avvicinati!' ('Draw nearer!')—'Non odi?' ('Don't you hear me?'). The actual words come straight out of Metastasio, where, being an element in the action, they are in the recitative, as one would expect in a *seria* opera. But Mazzolà uses them in a context which he expected (rightly) to be composed as a closed musical form with full accompaniment. The initiative he has Titus take here (Titus, who never acts but only reacts throughout the entire work!) leads *seria* technique to the very limits of what it can do. If Sextus directly answered the Emperor and replied to his words with words of his own, the configuration of the characters established in the preceding recitative would instantaneously fall apart, and an element in the action would invade the ensemble. It falls to Sextus to safeguard the limits of *seria*. His reaction is to freeze: 'O voce che piombami sul core' ('O voice which falls like lead upon my heart'). With that the positions of the characters are maintained during the concluding allegro, in which Titus and Publius come together with the same words, but Sextus continues to embody a separate aspect of the action. But at that moment when Mazzolà leads *opera seria* to its utmost limits he uses the precise words to characterize the situation—not the dramatic situation alone but the formal one too, in which the *seria* ensemble is the only possible resort: 'Non odi?'

All the appearances indicate that Mozart composed only the numbers and the accompanied recitatives. As for the secco recitative: 'much to be regretted—[it] is all in a pupil's hand', as Niemetschek remarked in 1798.[7] The pupil in question has not been identified with complete certainty; the name of Franz Xaver Süssmayr is often put forward, but it is not clear why, in that case, Niemetschek does not give it, although Süssmayr stayed with him in 1794 when one of his operas was having its first performance in Prague.[8] But Niemetschek's opinion of the recitatives is not undeservedly harsh. Mazzolà's success in reducing the sprawl of Metastasio's recitatives is undermined (even when full allowance has been made for the historical context) by the laboured techniques employed in their settings.[9] The 'pupil' had evidently been taught that separate passages of recitative must begin with a sixth chord (with a third in the bass to enable resolution on

---

[7] Niemetschek, *Life of Mozart*, 82.

[8] Lühning, 'Zur Entstehungsgeschichte', 302.

[9] Even the comparison with the much more expansive recitative phrase structures in Mozart's previous *opera seria, Il re pastore* (1775), is illuminating.

Ex. 38.1. *La clemenza di Tito*, recitative before the duet, No. 1. Cadences in bars 7–9 and 83–4.

to the tonic); consequently, every time the end of one such passage coincides with the start of a new one (new, because of an initiative in the text), there is a stereotyped interrupted cadence, and these recur countless times in the course of the opera. All too often the impression is created that a full cadence is on the verge of being reached but fails to be for reasons of convention. (See Ex. 38.1.)

Mozart's comment that Mazzolà's adaptation of Metastasio's libretto had turned it into a 'true opera' naturally does not extend to the musical realization of the recitatives. Nevertheless, as was said above, his judgement leaves no room for doubt that he approved of the outcome—even though it could not hope to measure up to the specifications of a *buffa* libretto of the calibre of Da Ponte's librettos for Mozart. The composer certainly did not expect it to, and it would be pointless to imagine that he did, because the generic boundaries were clearly marked. Mozart's goal was an *opera seria* within the framework of his own conception of that genre and the *données* of his time. That much is made plain, not only by the dramatic construction of the ensembles but also by the music, which, even in the arias, follows different paths from those traced in a comedy as recent as *Così fan tutte.*

Niemetschek was not alone in his censure of the recitatives. Karl, Count von Zinzendorf (1739–1813) was an Austrian civil servant who kept a diary, the sixty volumes of which include much detailed comment on musical events. He found *La clemenza di Tito* 'the most tedious spectacle' ('le plus ennuyeux spectacle'), but that can hardly refer to that part of the evening's entertainment for which Mozart himself was responsible. All the same, Mozart and Mazzolà did have difficulties in winning over the general public to their advanced style of *opera seria*. Empress Marie-Louise, a princess of Naples by birth, is said to have described *Tito* as 'a German dog's breakfast' ('una porcheria tedesca'). That goes much further than either Niemetschek's or Zinzendorf's remarks. The Empress appears to have been an attentive observer of operatic life in Vienna, too, without ever being aroused to much enthusiasm for any of the performances she saw.[10] Perhaps, having grown up in a centre of operatic tradition, she found it impossible to like the independent growths that sprouted in 'Italian' opera north of the Alps, least of all such excrescences as Mozart's very individual style. In the case of *Don Giovanni*, given 'by highest request' in Prague four days before the première of *Tito*, the difficulties may have stayed within manageable limits;[11] but the resistance to Mozart's ideas of what constituted a 'true opera', when extended to the realm of *opera seria*, was only to be expected.

---

[10] Abert, *Mozart*, ii. 565.   [11] Landon, *1791*, 111.

39

Machinery, Symbolism, Music: *Die Zauberflöte*, K. 620

When Mozart began *Die Zauberflöte* in May 1791, he entered composi-tional *terra incognita*. He had written all his previous operas, Singspiele, and serenatas for theatres answerable to representatives of the *ancien régime*: great princes like the Archbishop of Salzburg and the Elector of Bavaria, and the Emperor himself and other members of the house of Habsburg in Vienna, Prague, and Milan. Even the two early works, *Apollo et Hyacinthus* and *Bastien und Bastienne*, were created ultimately under those same auspices, for the former was composed for Salzburg University and the latter was 'composed at Emperor Joseph's command', as Leopold Mozart records, even if it was first performed in Dr Mesmer's garden. Never before had Mozart written for a theatre of the kind found at that date in Vienna's suburbs, which served a wider and quite different public from the one that went to the Court Opera.

His contact with this new world came about through Emanuel Schikaneder, a friend of Mozart's since 1780 when he had visited Salzburg as a member of a touring theatre company. Schikaneder, who was to write the libretto of *Die Zauberflöte* and play Papageno in its first production, had taken on the management of the Theater auf der Wieden in 1789. Constanze Mozart told her second husband, Mozart's biographer Georg Nikolaus Nissen, that Schikaneder needed Mozart's music to settle his own debts, but that is extremely unlikely.

Controversial as Nissen's account of the genesis of *Die Zauberflöte* is, there is no harm in quoting the words he put in Schikaneder's mouth, outlining what was required of the composer as he tackled a commission unlike any he had ever faced before. 'Write me an opera wholly to the taste of today's Viennese public; you can still give the connoisseurs and your own reputation their due as well, but put the ordinary people of all ranks first. I will see to the text, sets, and so on, everything as people want it nowadays.'[1] If those were the conditions Mozart did not have much say

---

[1] Nissen, *Biographie*, 548–9.

in the text, but he and Schikaneder will have discussed and agreed on their aims.

It is quite clear that Freemasonry was an important common denominator in the ideas both men brought to the work.[2] The path followed by the youth Tamino and the trials he has to undergo, from the moment when he seeks entrance to the temples of Wisdom, Reason, and Nature, in his hunt for the 'wicked' Sarastro, in the finale of Act I, up to the finale of Act II, when he and Pamina enter the temple together, are comparable to the process of admission of a seeker into the circle of initiates. The ideas and imagery of Freemasonry permeate many details of the opera: the Queen who sends the stranger Tamino off to rescue her abducted daughter Pamina is described as 'star-flaming' ('sternflammend'), which is not just a colourful attribute appropriate for a 'Queen of the Night' but also endows her with a central Masonic symbol, the flaming star (reproduced on the title-page of the first edition of the libretto). There is the significance of the number three: not only three temples, but also three ladies attending the Queen, and three genies given by her to accompany the travellers, Tamino and Papageno, on their way. 'Three-ness' permeates the music too, most obviously in the celebrated 'threefold chord' for wind at the end of the Priests' March with which Act II opens. The repetitions of the chord in the threefold rhythmic pattern mean that it is actually played nine times altogether. A simple threefold playing of the chord would have been enough for 'authentic' Masonic atmosphere, but Mozart chose to intensify, or potentiate, the number by squaring it. Sarastro's aria 'O Isis und Osiris', which follows the march, borrows another Masonic feature, for the repetition of the last line of each four-line stanza by the chorus of Priests to the same music alludes to the 'responsory' element of the original Masonic ritual.

In spite of this, *Die Zauberflöte* is not really an opera 'about' Freemasonry. It would not have been very sensible to produce one in the climate of 1791, when the order was coming under a great deal of suspicion, and it would scarcely have been 'wholly to the taste of today's Viennese public', or at any rate that section of it which patronized Schikaneder's theatre. Freemasonry may have provided a framework on which to hang the opera's plot, but the librettist followed many other leads in the construction of a theatrically effective action. According to Nissen, Schikaneder undertook to provide the sets—the 'decorations' which could

---

[2] P. Nettl, *W. A. Mozart* (Frankfurt am Main, 1955), 150–4.

make a crucial contribution to the piece's success. Elaborate visual effects, virtuosic use of props and stage machinery, were essential elements in the Viennese suburban theatres if the public was to be satisfied. Mozart's remark about his mother-in-law, the day before he took her to see *Die Zauberflöte*, would certainly apply to the majority of the regular audiences at Schikaneder's theatre: 'It's probably true to say that your Mama will see the opera but she won't hear it' (to Constanze Mozart, 8–9 October 1791).

Schikaneder made generous use of the kind of stage machinery which was common in the period: claps of genuine theatrical thunder when the star-flaming Queen makes her entrance, and again when the child of nature, Papageno, breaks the Masonic command of silence imposed at the start of the trials. During the trials by fire and water, the fire, at least, belongs to the essential repertory of effects regularly seen in any theatrical 'spectacle' worthy of the name. The appearance of wild animals on the stage belongs in the same category. On this occasion, however, the roles of the beasties attracted by Tamino's flute-playing were taken by children: according to the playwright Franz Grillparzer in his autobiography (1836), his mother's maid had played a monkey. This must have made it a lot easier to ensure their rapid exit into the wings when Tamino stops playing. And the earthquake which swallows Papageno when he tries to clasp his Papagena the first time she presents herself to him as a pretty young girl (he has only seen her as an old crone hitherto) is another 'routine' contrivance.

The entrances of the Three Boys called for something a bit more out of the ordinary. They are assigned to guide Tamino and Papageno on their journey and, as the Three Ladies sing, will 'hover about you on your way'. Sure enough, on their second entrance a stage-direction has it that 'The Three Boys enter in a flying machine bedecked with roses'; on their third 'The Three Boys descend in their machine'. There can be no doubt that Schikaneder was reacting to the excitement aroused in Vienna by the recent successful launch of a hot-air balloon. Eight years after the Montgolfiers had made the very first such ascents, the people of Vienna had flocked to the Prater to see one, on 9 March and 29 May 1791, but had gone home disappointed each time. Mozart's wife spent part of that summer at the spa of Baden near Vienna, and he wrote to her there: 'At this very moment Blanchard is either about to rise—or make fools of the Viennese for the third time!' (6 July 1791). The next day he wrote: 'I didn't go to see the balloon, because I have the use of my imagination, and also I believed that nothing would happen again this time. But now the Viennese are celebrating! All their grumbles have been forgotten and replaced by hymns of praise' (7 July). Schikaneder could, therefore, have hatched the idea of flying boys as early as March, pinning his hopes on the balloonist, François Blanchard; once the successful ascent had been made, after four months of public impatience, he could incorporate the idea in his theatrical enterprise with confidence.

Another event that summer caused Schikaneder a much worse headache, or so we often read. He is supposed to have been forced to make radical changes to his plans for *Die Zauberflöte* when the work was well under way, because of an opera which opened in a rival suburban theatre, the Theater in der Leopoldstadt, in June 1791. This was *Kaspar der Fagottist und die Zauberzither* (Kaspar the Bassoonist and the Magic Zither), which also exploited the affair of the hot-air balloon,[3] 'The original idea of *Die Zauberflöte*, then,' as Edward J. Dent wrote, 'was to be more or less as follows: the hero makes the acquaintance of the fairy queen, who gives him a portrait of her daughter and sends him to rescue her from captivity in the castle of the wicked magician, which he will do by the help of the magic flute.'[4]

Certainly, it is possible that, if the original conception of *Die Zauberflöte* was along those lines, it might have had to be altered, but there is no proof that it was like that, and it is actually rather unlikely. The first contrary witness is Mozart himself, and what he said in a letter to his wife: 'To cheer myself up, I went to the Kasperl theatre, to see the new opera *The Bassoonist*, which has made such a stir—but it's nothing' (12 June 1791). He had had a bad day, as he had been telling her, and he would undoubtedly have been doubly annoyed by something that threw an obstacle in the path of his own work, but he could not see what the attraction of *Kaspar der Fagottist* was, and he had only gone to the Theater in der Leopoldstadt to find out.

Furthermore, the 'break' in *Die Zauberflöte* becomes all the harder to fathom, the more closely one examines the details in its first act (which was not reworked, according to the change-of-plan hypothesis) to discover their relevance for the way the drama develops in the second act. The structure of the relationships within the dramatis personae is extremely complex, and that is probably a fundamental reason for the misunderstandings about the course followed by the plot. The audience takes note of the Masonic elements, and the 'Egyptian' elements, and follows the love-story of Tamino and Pamina: problems arise only when one enquires just when

---

[3] Branscombe, *Die Zauberflöte*, 30.   [4] Dent, *Mozart's Operas*, 218–19.

the Queen of the Night ceases to be Dent's 'fairy queen' and becomes the 'villainess', and equally when and how Tamino, who was sent on his journey by her, detaches himself from her sphere.

Apart from the inconsistencies, there are points of contact in this area of the work with things that were current in the operatic world in 1791. Although the connections are not immediately obvious, they shed some light on where the roots of the *Zauberflöte* problems lie. Caterino Mazzolà, the librettist of *La clemenza di Tito*, had written an opera, *Osiride*, for Dresden in 1781 (music by Johann Gottlieb Naumann), which also brought together ancient Egyptian religious beliefs with Freemasonry and the testing of a pair of young lovers. Mozart's *Tito* itself contains parallels to the benevolent ruler (Titus / Sarastro), the female plotter (Vitellia / the Queen of the Night), and the young man she sends into action (Sextus / Tamino),[5] Let us, however, deny ourselves an examination of whether or not Mazzolà's Egyptian libretto had any influence on *Die Zauberflöte*: the relationships that develop during the course of the opera between Sarastro, the Queen of the Night, and Tamino are completely different from those between Titus and the lovers, Vitellia and Sextus.

More than half the first act is spent in the realm of the Queen of the Night, and the sole dramatic purpose of this section of the opera is to get Tamino started on his journey to rescue Pamina. That object is achieved with the first of the Queen of the Night's great arias, 'O zittre nicht, mein lieber Sohn . . . Zum Leiden bin ich auserkoren' ('O tremble not, my dear son . . . Suffering has chosen me for its own'). After that, the quintet which takes us up to the first change of scene consists, so to speak, of the departure formalities. Tamino's rapturous falling in love with Pamina at the first sight of her portrait is the necessary precondition of the Queen's aria, for it makes it clear what must happen next: he must be taken across a dramatic threshold beyond which his journey to Pamina can begin. Only the Queen of the Night can do that, and although she and Tamino are not a 'pair' (as Vitellia and Sextus are), a common interest for the purposes of the plot must be established between them. Tamino's quest for Pamina would be inconceivable without a positive encounter between him and her mother. The fact that she later turns out to be one of the unenlightened makes no difference whatever—only it must remain hidden from Tamino and the audience alike for an inordinately long time.

The Three Ladies take responsibility for setting up the meeting between Tamino and the Queen, and for arranging his journey thereafter. For the rest of the drama, however, they delegate the function of watching over the prince to the Three Boys—and with that, strictly speaking, the conflict between good and evil is already engaged. The boys are the second group of three actors in the drama who appear as the hero's potential guides. Unlike the number nine, which can be understood as the potentiation of the 'divine' three, a more dangerous, ambiguous role is assigned to the number six. Two times three means a polarization of three, giving it two different character traits, two extremes. Two times three can be rendered geometrically as two equilateral triangles interlaced in a stellate hexagram, with the apex of one triangle pointing upwards and the other downwards, which in turn may be interpreted as follows:

The triangle pointing upwards symbolizes the spiritual element, that which strives towards God, the good, the creative, and the triangle pointing downwards symbolizes the material element, the bad, that which inclines towards evil, the destructive;[6]

or as follows:

The hexagram is made by two regularly intersecting triangles, of which the one points upwards as a symbol of flaming fire, and the other downwards as a symbol of falling water. In this six-pointed star, known in the East as the Shield of David, two forces penetrate each other and unite: heavenly and earthly, male and female: an image of marriage! A sign of the godhead taking the world as bride.[7]

Correspondingly, in the opera the two groups of three also strive to separate from each other: the Three Boys (male) carry their mission right through to the end of the opera, by which time Tamino, at least, has reached his goal, that is, they go with him (who at a late stage has to undergo a 'sixfold' trial by fire and water) into Sarastro's realm of light, while the Three Ladies (female) remain in the darkness of the Queen of the Night. To that extent, by reason of their very symbolism, the Three Boys embody a central dramatic impulse, and do so from the first.

Next in Act I, in the time it takes to change the set, Papageno reaches Sarastro's realm, where he finds Pamina and even sings a duet with her, but when they try to escape they are caught by the Moor Monostatos. Finally

---

[6] F. K. Endres, *Mystik und Magie der Zahlen* (Zurich, 1951), 153.

[7] A. Rosenberg, 'Versuch einer Symbolik der Zahlen', *Offene Tore*, 13 (1969), 137–51, esp. 144.

we reach Sarastro himself and the environment in which he lives, and the preparations for testing Tamino and Papageno are put in hand.

Thus the first act does not fully clarify the configuration of the characters in what might be called the upper social bracket. The Queen of the Night, a coloratura soprano, has been presented as one extreme, and, as we might expect, the complementary extreme, Sarastro, is a basso profondo, Further than that, the symbolism of the two roles remains open: with his deep voice, Sarastro could stand for the downward-pointing triangle, but so could the Queen, as the representative of the female principle. It has also not been made explicit yet that the two groups of Three Ladies and Three Boys are drifting apart. On the other hand, the Tamino–Pamina aspect is gradually coming into focus: that the soprano and the tenor will find each other seems, by the end of the first act, to be only a question of time. Papageno's position is a complicating factor in the structure of relationships. We learn that he too will find a mate, but how and on what conditions remains a mystery for now. It is he the baritone, and not Tamino the tenor, who has a duet with the soprano Pamina in Act I; against the background of the questions asked in *Così fan tutte*, this is a 'wrong' couple, and that it comes to pass leads precisely to the 'grotesque' outcome that was pointedly avoided in *Così fan tutte*.

The 'introduction'—that is, the first scene—of *Così fan tutte* handles the business of exposition much more deftly than the whole first act of *Die Zauberflöte*. The structure of relationships is set out plainly there, with Ferrando and Guilelmo singing the praises of their lady-loves, and Don Alfonso listening to them; and the underlying programme with which the action will be concerned is forecast in Alfonso's scepticism and the resulting wager. Similarly in *Don Giovanni*: with the relationship of the protagonist and his servant, and the on-stage murder of the Commendatore, a programme is set up for the action and a 'classic' couple is presented in the persons of Donna Anna and Don Ottavio (and will be 'repeated' in the figures of Zerlina and Masetto; both pairs will be severely shaken up by Don Giovanni). *Die Zauberflöte* also has an Introduction (so designated), but it is a lot shorter and less eventful than those of the two earlier operas, and in comparison with them the whole of the scene set in the realm of the Queen of the Night, up to the first set-change, tends to be regarded as introductory. However, the Introduction in *Die Zauberflöte* consists only of Tamino's first entrance, pursued by a monstrous serpent, his falling in a faint, and his rescue by the Three Ladies; the three then fail to agree on which of them should be left alone with him while the others go to inform the Queen of the Night of his arrival, because they have all fallen in love with him. Undoubtedly, so highly coloured a scene serves to capture the audience's attention, but all it contributes to the drama is the precipitation of Tamino into the Queen of the Night's realm, which is nowhere near as crucial as the wager in *Così fan tutte* or the scene outside the Commendatore's house in *Don Giovanni*.

The difficulties with the structure of relationships in the first act do not, therefore, support the hypothesis of a change of plan by Schikaneder, but they do have to be ironed out. The plot requires from the first that Tamino (and Papageno, too, to a limited extent) must somehow be granted admission to Masonic ritual, and romantic interest is guaranteed, in advance, by Pamina's plight. This makes it necessary for the Queen of the Night to be presented sympathetically at first, or Tamino would never set foot over the threshold that takes him to rescue and Freemasonry. It is essential—especially viewed in retrospect, perhaps even logical. The Introduction as such does nothing to clarify the complexity of the structure of relationships, all it does is grab the audience's attention.

What part did Mozart's music play in this popular entertainment, with its machines and its freight of symbolism? How else did he enhance Schikaneder's theatrical and dramatic purposes, in addition to introducing Masonic elements into the music and placing the characters in effective vocal combinations?

The music associated with the individual characters in the drama is greatly influenced, of course, by the different types of voices cast to sing the roles. The extremes personified by the Queen of the Night and Sarastro are not exhausted by her being a high soprano and his being a low bass; the agility of her music also contrasts with the dignified, processional pacing of his. Both have two arias, the second of which is in each case taken at a quicker tempo than the first; the Queen's Act I aria, 'Zum Leiden bin ich auserkoren', begins with a slow (no specific marking) introduction and switches to an 'allegro moderato', while her Act II aria, 'Der Hölle Rache kocht in meinem Herzen', is a much faster 'allegro assai' from the first. Sarastro, on the other hand, takes his first aria, 'O Isis und Osiris', 'adagio', and he never gets faster than a 'larghetto' (in 'In diesen heil'gen Hallen') which is probably slower than the introduction of the Queen's first aria.

Die Zauberflöte seems, at first sight, to inhabit a world of Singspiel characters and conventions which has borrowed the Queen of the Night from *opera seria*. This was clearly to Mozart's taste: Konstanze, in the much earlier opera *Die Entführung*, already moved on much the same musical plane as the Queen of the Night. The Queen is, moreover, kept as far as possible apart from the Singspiel surroundings: in the first act she takes no part in any spoken dialogue, one of the technical characteristics of the genre; when she does descend to speech, in the second act, the content of what she says is charged with significance, but it is kept very brief. Sarastro's 'parallel' in *Die Entführung*, however, is Selim Pasha, who does not sing at all. How Mozart integrates the 'sage' into his music is quite astonishing: in terms of musical form, he makes Sarastro a typical Singspiel figure, limited to participation in spoken dialogue and to music in the simple song forms which marked out Singspiel as a genre from its beginnings. 'In diesen heil'gen Hallen' is a strophic song, extended slightly by textual repetition in its final section, and the modulations in the course of both stanzas of 'O Isis und Osiris' do not detract from its essentially song-like character.

These small extras are nevertheless crucial in differentiating Sarastro's 'songs' from Papageno's (in addition to the difference in tone). But Papageno's music, too, goes through a process of change, albeit on a quite different plane. His aria 'Der Vogelfänger bin ich ja' ('The birdcatcher, that's me'), at the start of the opera, in which he accompanies himself on his panpipes, remains a pure strophic song; on the other hand, 'Ein Mädchen oder Weibchen' ('A girl or a little wife is what I'd like') suddenly acquires a new accompaniment in its last stanza from the glockenspiel, Papageno's new instrument. The new environment in which he finds himself is having an effect on his Singspiel roots, and Reason is beginning to modify his 'child of nature' essence.

Lastly, a look at Tamino, Pamina, and Monostatos: Tamino's only genuine aria comes near the beginning of the work; the aria in which he alternates singing with playing the flute is only one section in the first finale. But his voice is a constant in the work, his presence is required in many of the ensembles, and thus he forms a point of crystallization for the perspective from which the course of events can be observed. Similarly Pamina: she too has aria-like sections to sing in the act-finales, and her only complete solo number is in the second act (which may complement the fact that Tamino's is in the first). Monostatos, who is placed on an equal footing with Papageno in their Act I duet (the *naïveté* shown by their both taking each other for the devil himself is one of their similarities), is a constant of a different sort from Tamino and Pamina: he does not even go through a learning process like Papageno's, and so it falls to him to sing the only 'pure' strophic song in the second act.

By such means Mozart made more of the developments which arise in the field of tension between the realms of night and sunlight. That Papageno's music takes on some of the attributes of a 'cultivated' man, thereby drawing away from that of Monostatos and closer to that of Sarastro, is entirely due to the composer. Sarastro's own departures from the 'pure' forms of strophic song are also motivated by Mozart's interpretation of the role: the music of all the other characters is consistent with what is already in the text.

There is a question to be asked about the instruments seen on the stage, which also touches Papageno and Tamino, as well as turning a spotlight on the opera's title. It has no connection with Freemasonry, and precious little to do with either the love-story of Tamino and Pamina, or the enmity between the Queen of the Night and Sarastro. Why, then, is the work called 'The Magic Flute'?

The instrument in question is given to Tamino by the Queen of the Night. Pamina tells him about its provenance just before they undergo the trials of fire and water:

> Es schnitt in einer Zauberstunde
> mein Vater sie aus tiefstem Grunde
> der tausendjähr'gen Eiche aus,
> bei Blitz und Donner, Sturm und Braus.
> Nun komm und spiel die Flöte an,
> sie leite uns auf grauser Bahn.

('In a magical hour, my father cut it from the deepest roots of the thousand-year-old oak tree, in the midst of thunder and lightning, storm and tempest. Come now, play the flute, and let it guide us on our dreadful path.')

The flute's magic power derives, therefore, from the circumstances in which it was made. Pamina is half-orphaned; when her father died he left everything to his wife and daughter, but he conferred command over the circle of the sun to Sarastro: we learn this from the talk between the Queen of the Night and Pamina before the Queen's second aria. (This is the only passage of spoken dialogue in which the Queen takes part, yet it is sometimes cut in performance.) Does the Queen perhaps underestimate the flute's power for good? Pamina too, who at least knows the flute's history well enough to be able to tell it, at first has no idea of its nature: when she turns to Tamino hoping to be reassured of his love, after her mother's 'revenge' aria, he does not speak to her, being under oath of silence, but plays the flute instead, which she interprets as rejection. It is only in her trio with Tamino and Sarastro, after being reconciled with both, that she appears to come to understand it. Tamino, at least, has a much earlier opportunity to discover the instrument's beneficent power, when his playing attracts an audience of wild animals.

In that scene, part of the first finale, Tamino suddenly discovers the power 'to lure the birds and pipe like them', as the birdcatcher Papageno boasts of himself and his panpipes in his entrance aria; the pipes are one of the tools of Papageno's trade. When the time comes for the birdcatcher to switch from the panpipes to his new instrument, the glockenspiel, it causes him some difficulty. At an early stage in their adventures, when he tries to run off with Pamina to find Tamino, he still plays the panpipes. Tamino hears him and declares: 'That's Papageno's tune!' He takes his magic flute and plays Papageno's 'call-sign', which is still the 'right' music to identify his companion and the world from which he has come. Papageno then finds that the panpipes are useless against Monostatos and the slaves who have joined the pursuit, but he has the presence of mind to play his glockenspiel, which puts all thought of pursuit out of their minds and sets them dancing instead. All the same, the glockenspiel has not yet implanted itself in Papageno's consciousness—or rather, he has not yet fully grasped that he has left his old identity behind and acquired a new one. That is why he tries to lure his Papagena in Act II, after their first encounter, with his panpipes, but their call, formerly 'Papageno's tune', has lost its power and she does not appear. He is on the point of hanging himself in despair when the Three Boys intervene and remind him of the glockenspiel, which has the desired effect in no time.

Papageno is the only character to be equipped with a musical instrument of his own at the start of the opera, but it proves to be inadequate not only musically but also in its power to work magic. It almost looks as if Tamino's highly specialized flute directly robs Papageno's 'natural' pipes of their power, perhaps at the very moment when they exchange 'Papageno's tune' during Papageno and Pamina's flight, for later the panpipes are only a relic of a time that cannot be recaptured. Papageno's glockenspiel therefore becomes a gauge of the magic power of Tamino's flute as well, and supports its universal efficacy—the protection it gives against the dangers of the trials, and its power to guide its owner to his goal. Once the property of the ruler of the realm of the sun, the flute is given by the Queen of the

Night to Tamino to help him find her daughter, but the other outcome of the gift is that he returns the instrument to its place of origin. Thus the flute, too, is one of the opera's constants, and perhaps it is the guarantee that the plot functions in the theatre (although its sound is heard scarcely more often than the singing of the minor character Monostatos).

In such matters the action and text of *Die Zauberflöte* are directly dependent on what the musical realization can do for them. It is hard to imagine that the flute would have been integrated so successfully into the course of the action without Mozart's intervention. The first Tamino, Benedikt Schak, could play the transverse flute as well as sing, but Schikaneder could not be expected to play the glockenspiel, which is a keyboard instrument. To sustain the illusion, Schikaneder (like other Papagenos ever since) was given a contraption on which to simulate playing, while the real instrument which gave forth the sound was placed in the wings, behind the flats at the side of the stage, and not in the orchestra pit, so that player and singer could see each other (see Pl. 14). Mozart watched most of the performance on 8 October 1791 from a box with friends,

only I went backstage for Papageno's aria with the glockenspiel, because I felt an urge to play it myself today, and I played a joke when Schikaneder had a rest, and I played an arpeggio. How he jumped—and then squinted sideways into the wings and saw me. When it came round the second time, I didn't do it. Then he stopped and refused to go on. I guessed what he was thinking and played another chord, whereupon he thumped his little peal of bells and said 'Shut up!' It made everyone laugh, and I do believe that it was the first time many people realized, thanks to this joke, that he wasn't playing the instrument himself.   (To Constanze Mozart, 8–9 October 1791)

Perhaps Mozart asked a bit too much of the normal audience at the Theater auf der Wieden in taking seriously Schikaneder's invitation to 'give the connoisseurs and your own reputation their due'. He certainly gave the opera a number of decidedly recherché musical features: maybe, in view of the symbolism and deployment of elaborate stage machinery, he didn't want to be outshone by Schikaneder in the matter of bold experimentation. So he had the two men in armour who guard the entrance to the trials by fire and water sing their 'adagio' air to the melody of a Protestant hymn, a setting of Psalm 12 in Martin Luther's metrical version. Listeners who can carry the 'original' text in their head will find it an apt comment on the stern warning sung on stage, especially the fifth verse of the hymn.

PL. 14. Interior of the Theater auf der Wieden, showing the scenery flats at the side of the stage, and the boxes praised by Mozart. (From the *Almanach für Theaterfreunde*, 1791.)

(It corresponds to verse 7 in the English psalter: 'The words of the Lord are pure words: even as the silver, which from the earth is tried, and purified seven times in the fire'.)[8] And the melody Papageno hums at the beginning of the quintet in Act I (when his mouth is closed by a padlock) bears an uncommonly close resemblance to an old-fashioned chaconne bass;

---

[8] R. Hammerstein, 'Der Gesang der geharnischten Männer: Eine Studie zu Mozarts Bachbild', *Archiv für Musikwissenschaft*, 13 (1956), 1–24, esp. 9.

Tamino comments on his 'talking of punishment, for he has lost his speech'. Of course, when singing the stereotypical bass to an old-fashioned dance form, Papageno is saying precisely nothing—and it is interesting that it is the very tune that Mozart is supposed to have hummed while playing billiards in Prague in 1791 (see Chapter 27). The bass accompanying the duet for Papageno and Papagena ('Pa-pa-pa . . .') is in very much the same historical style, and it is actually treated like a chaconne bass to begin with, coming round three times one after another without a break and without change. The accompanying stage-direction is: 'Both have some comic mime to the ritornello', that is, Papageno and Papagena are supposed to perform a dance to the recurring dance-bass. Finally, the fast section of the overture is fugal, with a subject taken from a keyboard sonata which Muzio Clementi is supposed to have improvised in 1781 in the course of competing with Mozart.

This historicism will have gone over the heads of those who, like Constanze Mozart's mother, saw rather than heard *Die Zauberflöte*. The consideration did not worry Mozart when he wrote the music, and he was not too seriously annoyed by the shortage of true hearers at the performances (especially as the work was a runaway success). The tone of a comment he made in the letter of 8–9 October to his wife, immediately after the story of his trick with the glockenspiel, reassures us on that point: 'By the way, you can't imagine how charming the music sounds from a box near the orchestra—much better than from the gallery: you must try it as soon as you come home.'

40

Süssmayr in the Spring of 1792: The Requiem in D minor, K. 626

Mozart died at one o'clock in the morning of Tuesday 5 December 1791, having taken to his bed two weeks earlier. What illness he suffered from, in an acute form from about 20 November onwards, will probably never be fully explained, partly because medical terminology was much vaguer in the late eighteenth century than it is nowadays, so that filtering one particular illness from the range of possibilities is virtually out of the question, but also because the symptoms available for diagnosis at this distance in time have been handed down, for the most part, in the reports of people who were not physicians (Constanze Mozart, for example) or did not actually treat the patient themselves (like Dr Eduard Vincent Guldener von Lobes, who wrote about the case in 1824 on the basis of what he remembered from discussions with Mozart's doctor at the time). Furthermore, it is even possible that the allegedly fatal illness was not the actual cause of death.

The view of the last few weeks of Mozart's life has been obscured by two things which concern him directly and a third of more general relevance. First, the two matters of directly 'Mozartian' interest: Antonio Salieri's death in 1825, in the Vienna General Hospital, was accompanied by rumours that, in the senile ramblings of his last days, he had confessed to having murdered Mozart by poisoning him. Also in 1825, Gottfried Weber published an article questioning for the first time how much of his Requiem Mozart had actually composed at the time of his death (it was no secret that he had left it unfinished). The two matters have loomed large in writing about Mozart ever since, the more so because of a tendency to connect them: the fact that the composer died while working on a Requiem exerts a strong fascination. At this distance in time we need to bear in mind that none of the eyewitness accounts of Mozart's illness, work on the Requiem, and death can claim credence in every respect, whether they were written down immediately or at various later dates. We have to assume that the longer the interval of time that passed before individual accounts were committed to paper, the less we can rely on them in matters of detail; on top of that we have to allow for the likelihood that often later interpretations by others will have intruded themselves on genuine memories, so that things heard and read will have further weakened recollections which were already fading. The third contentious matter is this: Mozart was bled during his last illness, but bleeding was a highly controversial treatment by the late eighteenth century; the controversy reached its peak with the accusations made by Samuel Hahnemann, celebrated as the founder of homoeopathy, against the doctors of Leopold II, after the Emperor's death on 1 March 1792.[1]

One thing of which we can be certain is that the late autumn of 1791 was exceedingly unpleasant in Vienna. In late October incessant rain, lasting for days on end, was suddenly succeeded by heavy falls of snow. These extreme conditions had moderated a little by mid-November, but in the second half of the month the föhn started blowing, bringing sirocco conditions in its wake.[2] Against that background it is scarcely possible to determine whether Mozart contracted a streptococcal infection in mid-November, which led to the simultaneous outbreak of several latent diseases, such as chronic renal failure (as Peter J. Davies concluded), or whether föhn and sirocco combined to strike him down with rheumatic fever, as the delayed outcome of earlier illnesses (a theory first formulated by Carl Bär in 1966), in which case the brief periods of remission could have coincided with brief improvements in the weather (unlike Davies, Bär rules out any renal disorder).[3] Both hypotheses rest on the assumption that Mozart's constitution had deteriorated over a period of years, and that he had suffered several latent illnesses without any symptoms having manifested themselves. We can form a general idea of how the symptoms of his 'fatal' illness appeared to onlookers: 'acute feverishness with swollen extremities, paralysis following severe pain, rash, vomiting (?), intermittent sweating (?), headaches'.[4] This list is summed up in the diagnosis of 'heated miliary fever' given in the St Stephen's Cathedral register of deaths. It is virtually impossible to judge how much worse such symptoms would have been made by blood-letting in Mozart's specific case;[5] equally, we must

---

[1] R. Fuhrmann, '"Frieselfieber und Aderlaß" im Spiegel der medizinischen Literatur zur Zeit Mozarts', *Mitteilungen der ISM*, 37 (1989), 83–136, esp. 126–7.

[2] Landon, *1791*, 159. C. Bär, *Krankheit–Tod–Begräbnis*, 2nd edn. (Salzburg, 1972), 102–5.

[3] P. J. Davies, 'Mozart's Illnesses and Death', *Musical Times*, 125 (1984), 437–42 and 554–61, esp. 561. Bär, *Krarkheit*, 88–118.

[4] Ibid. 40. [5] Fuhrmann, '"Frieselfieber . . ."', 130–1.

pass over the question of whether the omission of any mention of Mozart's case from the 'bleeding' controversy can be regarded as an admission of guilt on the part of the doctors who treated him, or had other, more innocent reasons.

Death put an end to work which may already have been halted by illness. The examples of his handwriting from the last weeks give no sign of deteriorating health—when we could expect to see the effects of increasing paralysis, if not simply of working in bed. It is therefore extremely unlikely that any of the pages of the Requiem written down by Mozart himself date from after the day when he retired to bed (which may have been 20 November). Up until then, and throughout 1791, he had taken on an enormous workload. He had composed two operas virtually simultaneously, and taken part in preparations for their performance right up to the first nights of both; the premières of *La clemenza di Tito* and *Die Zauberflöte* were only twenty-four days apart, and he had made the none too easy journey from Prague to Vienna during the interval. He had also worked on three concertos: the B flat major Piano Concerto was finished on 5 January and the A major Clarinet Concerto probably in October, both on the basis of earlier drafts, and the Horn Concerto, K. 412, had been written from scratch;[6] the last year in which he had composed a comparable amount of work in the concerto genre had been five years earlier. Other compositions had included the usual series of dances for balls at the imperial court during carnival (a particularly long season in 1791), the E flat major String Quintet, K. 614, pieces for the blind glass harmonica player Mariane Kirchgessner, who visited Vienna on her first major tour, his *Ave verum corpus* for the Corpus Christi day procession in Baden near Vienna, and, finally, the 'Little' Masonic Cantata, the last work he entered in his thematic catalogue, on 15 November, and the first performance of which he himself conducted on 17 November.[7]

On top of that great burden of work, Mozart may also have had new financial problems: on 12 November 1791 the Lower Austrian Provincial Tribunal confirmed a claim of 1,435 gulden, 32 kreuzer against Mozart on the part of Karl von Lichnowsky. How the case arose is a complete mystery, primarily because this not inconsiderable sum is mentioned nowhere else but in the tribunal's records, not even in the list of debts in the register of Mozart's estate. One explanation could be that Lichnowsky took on debts that Mozart owed to a third person, and intended to recover them

[6] Tyson, *Mozart*, 35, 156, 246–61.
[7] *Das Wiener Blättchen*, 26 Nov. 1791; cf. Eisen, *Mozart Documents*, 71.

through the courts, but wrote them off and cancelled proceedings when the composer died. Two of his brothers-in-law seem to have had a lot to do with Mozart at that particular time: Franz Joseph, Count Thun as a brother Freemason (where the connection could have been the 'Little' Masonic Cantata), and—and more particularly—Andrey Kyrillovich Razumovsky, who tried, in the autumn of 1791, to arrange a concert tour to St Petersburg for Mozart; it may have been with that in prospect that Mozart bought a guidebook published by a brother Mason in 1789, covering 'all the states of the Austrian monarchy, as well as the route to Petersburg via Poland'.[8] For the time being, at least, this evidently complex affair remains a mystery—apart from the record in the archives of the Lower Austrian court itself.[9]

As well as the possibility of a Russian tour, other professional prospects had opened up for Mozart. On 9 May he had been appointed to the unpaid post of deputy Kapellmeister at St Stephen's, with the assurance that he would succeed to the Kapellmeistership itself in due course (the incumbent, Johann Leopold Hofmann, was already in poor health, but did not die until 17 March 1793). That prospect has a biographical significance that can hardly be overestimated. It was almost exactly ten years since Mozart had bade farewell to full-time, salaried employment; his more recent efforts to obtain an appointment at Donaueschingen on terms he could fulfil without leaving Vienna, his duties as a court composer in Vienna, and perhaps his fishing expedition to Prussia, too, were all connected with the endeavour to maintain a predominantly freelance status (although he had already come round to contemplating some restriction on it in 1790). He evidently had other irons in the fire in the summer of 1791: 'a couple of Englishmen' came to see him at the end of June, but his letters to his wife do not explain whether that had anything to do with his old plans to visit England again. Apropos of the hot-air balloon ascent on 6 July he wrote that it was 'very inconvenient for me—it's preventing me from concluding my business'—but again he said nothing more, not even who was involved. Perhaps it had some connection with a project he had mentioned in equally vague terms some days earlier to Michael Puchberg: 'If you can assist me with something, my dearest Brother . . . I shall be

[8] U. Konrad and M. Staehelin, *Allzeit ein Buch: Die Bibliothek Wolfgang Amadeus Mozarts* (Wolfenbüttel and Weinheim, 1991), 50–1.

[9] W. Brauneis, '". . . wegen schuldigen 1435f 32xr": Neuer Archivfund zur Finanzmisere Mozarts im November 1791', *Mitteilungen der ISM*, 39 (1991), 159–63. The idea that Lichnowsky might have taken on some of Mozart's debts to a third party originated with Maynard Solomon, and was passed on to me by Bruce Cooper Clarke.

greatly obliged to you. It will be only for a few days and then you will receive 2,000 florins [gulden] in my name—from which you can deduct repayment' (25 June 1791). Niemetschek also mentions, in connection with Mozart's position at the time of his appointment as deputy Kapellmeister at St Stephen's, that 'he also received, almost simultaneously, commissions from Hungary and Amsterdam for works to be delivered at regular intervals'.[10]

Once the performances of *Die Zauberflöte* were under way, early in October 1791, Mozart had to catch up on work he had set aside. The Clarinet Concerto remained to finish, the D major Horn Concerto had perhaps already been started, and he had a commission to write a requiem; we do not know when he was asked to write the 'Little' Masonic Cantata. All this, if not more, had piled up over the previous months, but Mozart was hard at work reducing the pile by the beginning of October by the latest. Niemetschek has him say these words to his wife at some point during his last few weeks of life: 'I feel definitely . . . that I will not last much longer'.[11] With the amount and variety of things he had to do, and especially as a reaction after having got them done, over a period of months during which he had been worried all the time about his wife, who had had to take the cure at Baden in June and July (immediately before the birth of their son Franz Xaver Wolfgang) and again in October, perhaps he was exhausted and even depressed; but nothing in his work, or in the letters he wrote to Constanze in October, betrays any sign of a belief that he could not 'last much longer'. The only document that might be taken to provide evidence of such an emotion is extremely dubious; a letter allegedly addressed to Da Ponte in September 1791, it survives only in suspect sources and is regarded overwhelmingly as not genuine. It is by no means certain, therefore, that Mozart had any serious premonitions of death before November 1791 (although, according to Peter J. Davies, they are not uncommon in connection with chronic uraemic disease[12]).

Two among Mozart's compositions of 1791 form part of the central core of his *œuvre* on which his reputation has rested since his death: *Die Zauberflöte* and the Requiem. The fits of depression mentioned by eyewitnesses may have increased under the workload; the possibility that the text and significance of the requiem mass affected him more deeply in a debilitated psychological condition than it would have done in a state of continuing euphoria cannot be ruled out. But every attempt to go further

[10] Niemetschek, *Life of Mozart*, 45.   [11] Ibid. 43.
[12] Davies, 'Mozart's Illnesses', 554.

than that is hampered by the significance which is attached to the Requiem 'fragment' and the history of its writing. To that extent the frontier between momentary acute depression and a premonition of impending death is as hazy for an onlooker as the differentiation of plain truth from embroidery in the first- and second-hand accounts of those last weeks and days.

The Requiem is known to have been commissioned by Franz, Count von Walsegg-Stuppach, who had lost his wife on 14 February 1791 and wished to have a major setting of the requiem mass to perform in her memory. The commission is believed to have reached Mozart during the summer of 1791, when work on *Die Zauberflöte* was in full flood. The relative timing of the commission for *La clemenza di Tito* and the Requiem is uncertain, but the upshot was that he found himself with three large-scale works to write in a short space of time. The deadline for *Tito* was the closest, so it did not really matter that *Die Zauberflöte* was still unfinished when Mozart set off for Prague for the coronation opera's première. *Die Zauberflöte* had to be finished next, however (the last numbers were the Priests' March and the overture, composed on 28 September), and the Requiem had to wait until after that. And after other things too: Constanze Mozart had left home for her second visit to Baden when her husband wrote to her on 7 October that he had orchestrated 'almost the whole of Stadler's rondo'—the last movement of the Clarinet Concerto, that is. He seems to have expected Stadler back in Vienna shortly after mid-October. The last performance of *Tito* had taken place in Prague on 30 September, the day of *Die Zauberflöte*'s première, and Stadler stayed in Prague to give a concert on 16 October. Perhaps Mozart wanted to have the concerto ready for him on his return to Vienna. He must have looked forward to being able to concentrate on the Requiem after that—but it was delayed yet again by the composition of the 'Little' Masonic Cantata, which he finished on 15 November, just in time for the dedication of the new temple of the 'New-Crowned Hope' lodge.

Whenever it was started, it looks as if the work on the Requiem did not go ahead continuously; moreover, rather as when he wrote his operas, Mozart composed the movements in an order different from that in which they were due to be heard in performance.

The sung sections of the Mass for the Dead customarily comprise texts with very distinct liturgical functions. In addition to the Ordinary of the mass—that is, movements which form part of every mass (Kyrie, Sanctus, Benedictus, Agnus Dei, but not Gloria or Credo)—they include the

Proper: the movements peculiar to the liturgy of the mass for the repose of the souls of the dead. There have been minor changes over the centuries, but the Proper for a requiem mass is essentially standardized. Thus Mozart's Requiem contains not only the four sections of the Ordinary listed above but also the Introit 'Requiem aeternam', the Sequence 'Dies irae', the Offertory 'Domine Jesu Christe' with the inserted versus 'Hostias', and the Communion 'Lux aeterna'. The Sequence is long, with nineteen three-line stanzas, and it would have been permissible to set the Gradual, which begins with the same words as the Introit, and the Tract 'Absolve Domine' in its place, but the Sequence offered the composer better opportunities for musical development on a larger scale (it may or may not have been stipulated by Count Walsegg).

Mozart composed the Introit and the Kyrie fugue in full (though there is one problematic detail in the latter in the autograph). The score of the Sequence breaks off after running through the text of the eighteenth stanza just once—or, from Mozart's point of view, half-way through the 'Lacrimosa', the last of the six movements into which he divided the long text. The Offertory that follows was composed in full, but, like the completed movements of the Sequence, not fully orchestrated. Not a single bar in Mozart's hand has survived for the Sanctus, Benedictus, or Agnus Dei. We will return later to the question of whether or not those sections contain anything worked out from material conceived by Mozart for use expressly in them. The Communion, finally, is a reprise of the Introit and Kyrie, minus the first eighteen bars.

A purely external examination of the autograph indicates that there were two distinct phases of working. To begin with Mozart used a paper on which not only the staves had been printed but also vertical lines joining them at either end. On this he wrote down the Introit, the Kyrie (except the last seven bars), and the Sequence as far as the orchestral introduction of the 'Recordare'. The end of the Kyrie, the remainder of the Sequence (that is, the rest of the 'Recordare', the 'Confutatis', and the 'Lacrimosa'), and the Offertory are on a paper on which only the staves were printed: Mozart had to draw the braces at the left-hand end himself in order to join them together in systems.

Leopold Nowak drew the following conclusion about the work's genesis: 'This difference in the appearance of the score's pages betrays . . . the first interruption in composing the Requiem: Mozart had to go to Prague. If that was so, and there can scarcely be any doubt about it, then by 25 August he had written, more or less, the Introit, the Kyrie, and the first half of the Sequence'.[13] But this view has been overtaken quite unexpectedly by new discoveries.

First of all, a clear line between a first and a second phase of work is not so easily drawn. It is almost certain that the 'Rex tremendae majestatis' and the opening of the 'Recordare', which comes immediately after it, were not written until after Mozart's return from Prague, and after the première of *Die Zauberflöte*, indeed. The evidence for this is a sheet of paper on which Mozart wrote down sketches for the opera's overture and the Priests' March—that is, two numbers which he did not write until he was back in Vienna. Other sketches on the sheet include one for 'Rex tremendae', which is fundamentally different from the final version of the movement, and five bars of music in F major and 4/4 time, of which the most distinctive feature is descending scales. These scalar figures, recast in 3/4 time, are found in the Requiem towards the end of the instrumental introduction to the 'Recordare', the only movement in F major. It cannot be ruled out, therefore, that this sketch is a preliminary study for the 'Recordare' (the change of tempo calls to mind the case of the 4/4 opening motif of the G minor Symphony, K. 550, which probably began as a 6/8 figure). Finally, this same sheet of sketches also has one in D minor for the beginning of a fugue on 'Amen'. If this too was meant for the Requiem, it must have been for the ending of the 'Lacrimosa', which Mozart was unable to complete; the posthumous 'Amen' consists of two chords sung by the chorus in four parts.

The sketches for *Die Zauberflöte* enable us to date the whole sheet: the one for the overture is not just a random jotting of a theme, but five bars of a minor-mode elaboration of the main subject. In other words, it is not something which Mozart wrote down as an *aide-mémoire*, perhaps in mid-August 1791, so as to have it to hand when he returned to the opera in mid-September. He cannot have written it out until the very end of September, a flash of inspiration in the middle of working on the theme which had been conceived long before (the fact that he did not use the minor version in the end is of no consequence). The Requiem sketches are a different matter, and can be acknowledged as 'genuine' first drafts of themes: one for the major part of the musical development of the 'Rex tremendae' (bars 7 ff., following the first 'majestatis'), and the other for the 'consequent' phase in the introduction of the 'Recordare', an instrumental figure which recurs repeatedly with an articulating function between the

[13] In NMA I/1/2, vol. i, p. x.

sections of the text. Once again, the music of these sketches differs from that of the final version, but they have a quite different quality from the elaboration, in the middle of working on a piece of music, of a theme that Mozart had already settled on. He must therefore have written down these sketches—including the three for the Requiem—only after his return from Prague, and it follows that the movements which the sketches predated had not already been composed by the end of August.

An indication of when Mozart began work on the Requiem is offered by study of the papers he used. It transpires that he did not use the paper with vertical lines printed at the ends of the staves until after his return from Prague. Those parts of *Die Zauberflöte* that remained to be composed were written on it, as was, later, the 'Little' Masonic Cantata.[14] This supports a conclusion that the Requiem was started when Niemetschek, writing in 1798, said it was: Mozart set out for Prague with the intention that 'it would be the first task on his return', and when he was back in Vienna 'he at once started on his Requiem Mass and worked at it with great energy and interest; but his indisposition increased visibly and made him depressed. His wife realised it with misgivings.'[15]

We should nevertheless be cautious about accepting Niemetschek's account as gospel. He lived in Prague, and therefore he did not witness anything Mozart did after leaving for Vienna; his information about the composer's state of health while he worked on the Requiem can only have come from Constanze Mozart—but she did not rejoin her husband in Vienna until 17 October. He, however, wrote to her in Baden the day after telling her about his progress with the last movement of the Clarinet Concerto: 'This morning I was writing so busily that I didn't notice the time until half past one' (8 October 1791). Is that a reference to his first sustained session of work on the Requiem?[16] The only debatable point is what section he chose to start with: it cannot be ruled out that he composed not only the Introit and Kyrie but also the opening movements of the Sequence—because otherwise there would have been a surprisingly large interval between the *Zauberflöte* sketches and the three Requiem sketches found on the same sheet of paper.

Niemetschek goes on to the occasion, mentioned above, when Mozart first told his wife of his premonition of death. She had taken him for a

---

[14] Observation by Alan Tyson, quoted Maunder, *Mozart's Requiem*, 206, n. 17.

[15] Niemetschek, *Life of Mozart*, 43.

[16] Landon concludes that it is, on the basis of calculations which he does not set out in detail (*1791*, 149).

drive in the Prater, and 'they were sitting by themselves'. According to Carl Bär's meteorological research, the only days on which they could conceivably have sat out in the Prater would have been 20 and 21 October.[17] Niemetschek continues: 'As she felt that he was on the verge of a serious illness, and that the Requiem was getting on his over-sensitive nerves, she called in the doctor, and took the score of the composition away from him.'[18] Once again, Niemetschek does not give any dates but tells us only that Mozart composed the 'Little' Masonic Cantata before insisting on returning to the Requiem; from that account, the only period in which the later phase of work can be fitted is the few days from 15 to 20 November.

In sum, Mozart's first chance to devote himself exclusively to the Requiem came during the few days between the start on the composition (perhaps on 8 October) and Constanze Mozart's return from Baden: he left Vienna to fetch her home on 16 October. Scarcely another week can have passed before his health was the reason for a second interruption. After he had finished the 'Little' Masonic Cantata, there remained, again, less than a week of work. The sheer amount of the work that he finished (at least in draft) illustrates how little rest he allowed himself: he tackled all the work that came his way with the same, undoubtedly consuming intensity as the operas he had composed during the summer months. Was it simply exhaustion that made him tell his wife that day in the Prater that he felt he would not last much longer?

It is not easy to decide where the finished sections of the Requiem go within this tight framework. It appears that Mozart was able to write the Introit, Kyrie, and Offertory without interruption, although he did not orchestrate the Offertory; only the Sequence is broken off unfinished. We can perhaps infer from this that he had finished a continuous succession of movements in a first phase before setting off for Baden to fetch Constanze; but there should be two later phases characterized by interruption: the first on account of Constanze's concern, the second because his illness entered an acute stage. Does it help to look again at the different papers he used? From them it appears that a first phase (disregarding any interruption for his wife's return from Baden) could have reached from the Introit to the 'Recordare'; the break there could have been the outcome of Constanze's fear that the work was damaging his health. This hypothesis would also take account of the surviving sketches. It must remain open, however,

---

[17] Bär, *Krankheit*, 101.   [18] Niemetschek, *Life of Mozart*, 43.

PL. 15. First page of the 'Lacrimosa' from Mozart's autograph of the Requiem, with Joseph Eybler's annotation (top right). A clear illustration of Mozart's procedure of writing the string parts only in the introduction, followed by the chorus and bass only.

whether the composition of the Offertory or the second phase of work on the Sequence, up to midway through the 'Lacrimosa', immediately preceded the onset of serious illness. Joseph Eybler's famous annotation on the first page of the 'Lacrimosa' score, 'Last manuscript of Mozart', does not signify anything in this respect (see Pl. 15). There is no reason for thinking Eybler referred to that one page, for it is the first of a new gathering, with the Offertory on later pages, and the remark must apply, as Christoph Wolff has argued,[19] not merely to the eight bars of the 'Lacrimosa' on the first side alone but also to the completed sketches of the 'Domine Jesu' and 'Hostias'.

The intensity of Mozart's work on the Requiem is everywhere in evidence—not only in his involvement in the apocalyptic content of the text but also in the music's 'absolute' aspects. There are two fugues in the

[19] Wolff, *Mozart's Requiem*, 29–30.

sections he completed: the Kyrie double fugue, and the fugue on 'Quam olim Abrahae promisisti' which ends the Offertory. There are other places where the vocal writing concentrates and condenses in four-part fugato textures: there it tends towards the complexity of the Kyrie double fugue rather than to the economy of 'Quam olim Abrahae', and it always reflects a response by Mozart to characteristics of the text. Rather as he sets up the two textual elements ('Kyrie eleison' and 'Christe eleison') in confrontation in the two subjects of the Kyrie fugue, so he develops a double fugue at the end of the Introit from the 'Requiem aeternam' theme and a new theme ('Dona eis requiem'). The confrontation of 'rex tremendae majestatis' and 'qui salvandos salvas gratias' in the third movement of the Sequence, following the introductory bars, also verges on this double-fugue character: while the first line of the stanza passes to and fro between the sopranos and altos, the second line, to a completely different melody, is doing the same among the tenors and basses; then the pairs of voices exchange texts (there is no sign of this development in the sketch for this movement). If we compare the musical design of the Requiem in these points with the C minor Mass of eight years earlier we can appreciate the extent of the concentration, not only in the interrelations in the part-writing but also in, for example, the breath-taking concision of a fifty-two-bar Kyrie fugue.

The character of interrelation and concentration is also revealed in the thematic material in individual places, an early example being the first soprano solo entry in the Introit ('Te decet hymnus Deus in Sion'), for which Mozart selects the melody of the Magnificat in the 'tonus peregrinus'; this produces a heightened double significance in the text-music relationship, similar to the song of the Armed Men in *Die Zauberflöte*. Links are also created between one movement and another. The series of notes which unfolds in the first orchestral bars of the Introit, and then becomes the melody of the choral tutti, provides the bass line of the 'Dies irae' (interestingly, it owes much to Handel's *Funeral Anthem for Queen Caroline* of 1737[20]). There are perhaps also abbreviated allusions to the soprano melody at 'Dies irae', above that bass, in the very similar opening melodies of later movements in the Sequence ('Tuba mirum': trombone, bass opening and tenor continuation; 'Confutatis maledictis'): more of that later. In the Offertory, the processes of working with similar thematic material and developing fugal passages from material imported

---

[20] Ibid. 74–8.

from elsewhere continue: the ascending triad with which the chorus begins the 'Domine Jesu' in a simple homophonous texture becomes the subject of a brief fugato in 'Sed signifer sanctus Michael', sung by the soloists.

Other aspects of the design of the movements show a similar process of concentration. In the 'Recordare', for example, where seven stanzas of the Sequence are set, Mozart uses an unexpected formal structure. The orchestral introduction, the first stanza, and a postlude form a block thirty-eight bars long. For the second stanza ('Quaerens me') he devises something new, but returns to the first music for the third stanza ('Juste judex'), without allowing it the same amount of space this time: he dispenses with the orchestral introduction, and with the separate alto and bass solos, so that the stanza is only exactly half as long (nineteen bars) as the first. Then there is more 'new' music ('Ingemisco'). The sixth and seventh stanzas ('Preces meae' and 'Inter oves') are joined together in one large concluding section; here Mozart inserts new material between elements already familiar from the first stanza, so that although the introduction is again omitted the total length is the same (thirty-eight bars) as the opening section of the movement. To some extent, therefore, individual motivic elements are repeated, ritornello-like, but instead of functioning as thematic 'resting-places' they are unstable and vulnerable: the expectation aroused when the repetitions become apparent remains disquietingly unfulfilled.

The 'Confutatis' is another example, with its initial A minor being seriously questioned in the concluding section ('Oro supplex'). At first it appears that the tonality is dropping by a semitone in each line of the second stanza: after a start in A minor, the first line ends in A flat minor, the second in G minor. Then Mozart speeds the process up and takes only the first 'Gere curam' to reach G flat minor; the conciliatory effect of the F major 'concluding' cadence, too, does not last longer than the time it takes to enter the D minor of the 'Lacrimosa'.

Mozart died without these ideas reaching their fulfilment in the relatively brief spaces of the remaining sections of the Requiem: the Sanctus and Benedictus, and Agnus Dei (the 'Lacrimosa' also had to be finished, and he might yet have written new music for the Communion). This artistic question was not the only problem which presented itself when day broke on 5 December 1791; Constanze Mozart found herself with a financial difficulty: the person who had commissioned the Requiem had made a down-payment, and she owed it to him to deliver the work. It had to be completed.

The earliest mention of plans to complete the Requiem is a statement by Joseph Eybler, dated 21 December 1791, acknowledging receipt of the manuscript from Mozart's widow and undertaking to complete the work by the middle of Lent. More than two weeks had already passed since Mozart's death, and ten days since Constanze Mozart had petitioned the Emperor for a pension. The score had not been left to gather dust during that interval, however, although the motive in the first instance was not the completion of the contract, which must have been as important to Constanze Mozart for purely financial reasons as her hopes of a pension. But first of all the Requiem was needed for a more concrete and immediate occasion: Mozart's funeral. The *Wiener Nachrichten* of 13 December 1791 carries a report of the ceremony organized by the 'honest and grateful directors of the Wieden Theatre for the great composer Mozart in St Michael's Church'. Music was performed at the service, and the report in another newspaper, *Der heimliche Botschafter* for 16 December, tells us what it was: 'One of his last works is said to have been a Mass for the Dead, which was performed at his funeral.'[21]

Naturally the whole Requiem was not ready for performance on 10 December 1791, but it is not hard to work out what could be done. Besides the Introit, which Mozart had completed, they probably sang the Kyrie fugue, which had not been orchestrated by him but needed relatively little work. As the autograph shows, two hands scored it on the basis of the choral parts, one inserting strings and woodwind, the other the brass parts. The latter hand is recognizably that of Franz Xaver Süssmayr; the other remained unidentified for a long time. One reason for this is that it is very like Mozart's own handwriting, and indeed it was long believed that he had written out the string and woodwind parts himself. The distinctive difference is that the unknown writer formed his natural signs quite differently from the way that Mozart did at the end of his life. He may have been Franz Joseph Freystädtler,[22] a pupil and friend of Mozart's, who rejoiced in nicknames such as 'horse's mouth' and 'porcupine' which Mozart celebrated in one of his canons (K. 232). So it is possible that Mozart's Introit was performed at his funeral along with his Kyrie, completed by Freystädtler and Süssmayr; those two movements then served as

[21] W. Brauneis, 'Unveröffentlichte Nachrichten zum Dezember 1791 aus einer Wiener Lokalzeitung', *Mitteilungen der ISM*, 39 (1991), 165–8.

[22] L. Nowak, 'Wer hat die Instrumentalstimmen in der Kyrie-Fuge des Requiems von W. A. Mozart geschrieben? Ein vorläufiger Bericht', *MJb* 1973–4, 191–201.

the foundations for the completion of the rest, but that task was not undertaken by Freystädtler. There is little point in speculating about the reasons why not, especially as it is not even certain whether he was responsible for the string and woodwind parts in the Kyrie or not.

Joseph Eybler, who was the first to try to finish the Requiem, had worked for Mozart at the time of the première of *Così fan tutte*, and kept up the contact during Mozart's illness, but he does not appear to have been as close to him, or as closely involved in the Requiem, as Süssmayr could claim to have been. Süssmayr's work for Mozart had also been primarily in the operatic field, and he continued to show an interest in it, but Eybler wanted no more of the theatre and took a post as choirmaster at the Carmelite church in Vienna in 1792. That may be why Constanze Mozart thought Eybler was the more suitable of the two to be asked to finish the Requiem; in any case Süssmayr may not have made very good progress as Mozart's 'pupil'. She may have had good reason to believe that the Requiem was in good hands with Eybler: only two years later Johann Georg Albrechtsberger, court organist and Beethoven's teacher, said of him that 'after Mozart he is now the greatest genius in music Vienna possesses'.

The only original contribution Eybler made to the Requiem consists of two bars of soprano melody, with which he had a shot at continuing the 'Lacrimosa'. He clearly decided that he did not want to go any further in Mozart's footsteps, or subordinate his own musical ideas to the ones he found in Mozart's score. When he wrote his two bars he was, at all events, as well acquainted with those strongly individualized notions as anyone could have been: his scoring of the sections of the Sequence which Mozart had only sketched leaves no doubt of that, for in some respects it displays more understanding and more intelligence than what was done by his successor Süssmayr. Eybler's own Requiem of 1802, in C minor, shows the signs of his study of Mozart's D minor work eleven years earlier, and may be a kind of artistic reaction to the tension he must have felt in front of Mozart's manuscript at the turn of the year 1791–2 when facing up to the differences between his own style and intentions which he could discern but was scarcely able to carry out to order.

No documentation comparable to Eybler's receipt survives in the name of Süssmayr or any other composer, but in 1800 Süssmayr wrote to the publishers Breitkopf & Härtel, with his version of what had happened.

The task of completing the work was . . . offered to several masters. Some were unable to undertake it because of pressure of work; others, however, did not wish to hazard their own talent at the side of Mozart's. Eventually the task came to me, because it was known that while Mozart yet lived I had often sung and played through with him the movements that were already composed; that he had frequently talked to me about the detailed working of the composition, and explained to me the how and the wherefore of his instrumentation. The most that I can wish is that I may have succeeded at least well enough for connoisseurs to be able to find here and there in it a few signs of his unforgettable teaching. (5 February 1800)

We do not know what other composers, besides Freystädtler (possibly) and Eybler, were approached and refused. Constanze Mozart, writing to Breitkopf & Härtel in 1799, had implied that Mozart began to talk to Süssmayr about how he wanted the work completed only 'when he saw his death was upon him', but to judge by Süssmayr's own account the instruction he received from his 'teacher' did not take the form of a methodical introduction to the theory of composition; rather, Mozart employed him as amanuensis, and talked through with him problems which happened to come up in the course of the work. To that extent, he would probably have gained better insights into the composition from the first than Constanze Mozart, for one.

Mozart may well have taken Süssmayr more intimately into his confidence about the Requiem than anyone else, and the latter obviously knew about one thing which lightened his task. In a 'defence of the authenticity of Mozart's Requiem' Abbé Stadler wrote in 1826: 'The widow told me that a few scraps of paper with music on them were found on Mozart's desk after his death, which she had given to Herr Süssmayr. What was on them, and what use Süssmayr made of them, she did not know.'[23] Clearly Eybler did not see these sketches—and the reason may have been that he did not know of their existence, whereas Stadler's account leaves open the possibility that Süssmayr asked for them. Constanze Mozart Nissen wrote to Stadler a year or so after his 'defence':

The one reproach that can be made against Mozart is that he was not very tidy with his papers, and sometimes mislaid something that he had started. Rather than spend a long time looking for it, he would write it again; thus it came about that a thing could be written twice ... Let us suppose that Süssmayr did in fact find some fragments by Mozart (for the Sanctus etc.), the Requiem would nevertheless still be Mozart's work. (31 May 1827).

[23] M. Stadler, *Vertheidigung der Echtheit des Mozartischen Requiem* (Vienna, 1826), 16.

Did Süssmayr know more about what Mozart left on his desk than his widow did? And did he know enough to bring a little order to the 'fragments'?

The only 'scrap of paper' having any connection with the Requiem that now survives is the page which has already been described, with sketches both for it and for *Die Zauberflöte* side by side on it. But it is daunting to think of the problems confronting Süssmayr when he sat down to finish the Requiem even if he did have Mozart's sketches to help him. Wolfgang Plath, who was the first to identify the Requiem sketches on that sheet of paper, has remarked:

> From a jumbled mass of sketches for *Die Zauberflöte, Tito,* and other works, hard enough to comprehend in themselves, and all the harder for having been scribbled in haste, he had to detect, identify, and decode just the sketches for the Requiem, which were certainly not helpfully captioned . . . It's a tragicomic picture, but only too probable: Süssmayr placed in the possession of Requiem sketches, but having no idea what to do with them, because he can neither recognize them nor read them![24]

It is one explanation of why tracts of Süssmayr's contributions to the Requiem appear to come straight out of the world of *Die Zauberflöte*— although an equally good reason for that could be the fact that Süssmayr was already working as Mozart's assistant while the opera was being composed.

Sketches worthy of serious consideration would have been of themes, like those on the surviving sheet. Any in which the composer elaborated material he had already invented, like the one for the *Zauberflöte* Overture on this sheet, would be more likely to have been written down at a relatively short interval before a section of the work was finished, so that Süssmayr would not have needed to elaborate on it—if he recognized it for what it was. But it has to be accepted that there was not any great quantity of such material at his disposal, both because Mozart could not have sketched very much else and because of what Süssmayr actually composed. Those sections of the work contain scarcely any themes that could genuinely have come from sketches drafted by Mozart; the best are at the beginning of the Sanctus and Benedictus, in the Agnus Dei, a fugue in the 'Hosanna', and some thematically independent sections in the Benedictus (soprano entry bar 7, orchestra bar 19—very *Zauberflöte*-ish, vocal parts bar

[24] 'Über Skizzen zu Mozarts "Requiem"', in *Bericht über den Internationalen Musik-wissenschaftlichen Kongreß Kassel 1962* (Kassel, 1963), 184–7.

23). Richard Maunder, who considers the question of the authenticity of those sections in his comprehensive study, suspects that material which originated with Mozart is found only in certain themes of the Benedictus and large parts of the Agnus Dei.[25] He bases his argument on a comparison of Mozart's 'normal' compositional techniques with those used in the posthumous parts of the Requiem. There is no guarantee that Süssmayr used sketch material in the places for which Mozart had intended it; that means, at the same time, that Süssmayr would almost necessarily have worked up one of Mozart's thematic sketches differently from the way his 'teacher' would have done.

Maunder is inclined to doubt that Süssmayr had any Mozartian material to use in the Sanctus; his chief evidence is what he argues is an erroneous use of D major at this point in the overall sequence of tonalities. That rests on his observation that each movement of the work is in a key which has two notes of its triad in common with the key of the previous movement (for example, the D minor of the 'Dies irae' and the B flat major of the 'Tuba mirum' share D and F).[26] However, such is not always the case: the Offertory begins in G minor, although it appears that the 'Lacrimosa' would have ended in D minor, and the 'Hostias' is in E flat major, following the 'Domine Jesu' which—for all it starts in G minor—ends in G major with C minor orientation. This means that the Sanctus, as written by Süssmayr, could have originated with material sketched by Mozart— although it remains open to question whether Mozart would have given the movement exactly the dimensions that Süssmayr did.

As Christoph Wolff has shown, basing his argument on the evidence of the surviving sketch-sheet, Mozart made other sketches for complex elements in the composition—above all, probably, for details of the four-part vocal writing, which naturally occupies the foreground in music as densely worked as this. Wolff finds a similar textural density in precisely the vocal writing in the sections of the Requiem which Süssmayr composed. It is not improbable, therefore, that this was the very element—the concrete starting-point of the composition process—for which Mozart had made relatively extensive and detailed sketches on which Süssmayr could call. However, it remains perfectly possible that he misunderstood parts of them or used them in the wrong contexts.[27]

The Sanctus begins with a reminiscence of the thematic material of the 'Dies irae', carrying on a melodic span which begins with the Introit and

[25] Maunder, *Mozart's Requiem*, 55, 72.   [26] Ibid. 38.
[27] Wolff, *Mozart's Requiem*, 32, 38.

Ex. 40.1. Requiem in D minor, K. 626. The 'Dies irae' theme, with its variant forms in soprano, (tenor) and bass shown by underlaid italic type.

arches across the Sequence in the major mode. Abbreviated (as it is also in the main theme of the 'Confutatis', for example), the 'Dies irae' theme is transposed into the major for the sopranos—and turns up again, in the minor, in the tenor line (continued in the soprano) of the Agnus Dei (which Maunder also attributes to Mozart), and coupled, each time, with reminiscences of the series of notes which formed the bass line of the 'Dies irae'. (See Ex. 40.1.)

There is yet another source which may constitute evidence that Süssmayr based the Sanctus on ideas he had directly from Mozart. Sophie Haibel, Constanze Mozart's sister, set down her own reminiscences of Mozart's illness in a letter to Nissen dated 7 April 1825. This account, written more than thirty years after the event, is one of those which may have been distorted by things the writer had learnt and heard during the interval, and we cannot place complete trust in the recollection of the exact chronological order of things (such as the events in the twenty-four hours before Mozart's death). Frau Haibel wrote: 'Sissmaier was there at M's bedside; and the Requiem lay on the coverlet, and Mozart was explaining to him how he thought he should finish it after his death.' Later that night, she remembered: 'The last thing he did was to try and mouth the sound of the timpani in his Requiem: I can hear it to this day.' We cannot really accept without reservation her claim that Mozart directly gave Süssmayr specific instructions on how to continue the Requiem; if it was so, Constanze Mozart's approaches to other composers are incomprehensible in her financial situation (even if, as she later said herself, she had a personal disagreement with Süssmayr at the time). It is perhaps more likely that

Sophie Haibel remembered some occasion when she witnessed the 'tuition' Mozart gave Süssmayr in the form it normally took, perhaps on a day when he was feeling less ill, and it only became 'explanation' of the kind she described when she tried to recall it later. Furthermore, the timpani theme was not necessarily 'the last thing' in the Requiem which Mozart developed, but at best the last sound Sophie Haibel heard from his lips (the sound of timpani may have been no more than her own interpretation of whatever it was she did hear). It is perfectly plausible, on the other hand, in the light of the musical content of the Requiem, that a timpani passage was one of the things which Süssmayr had from Mozart (and, too, if she heard it, that it could have made a lasting impression on his sister-in-law). Which timpani passage might Mozart have had on his mind in his dying moments, which could also have been something he had thought of earlier? The endings of the Introit and the Kyrie are the first that come to mind: with them, at all events, Mozart would have been quoting something that is there in his autograph, something he had already composed and scored, and to which, therefore, he could have referred Süssmayr during his illness. The only other prominent timpani solos are found in the opening bars of the Agnus Dei and, especially, those of the Sanctus, and Mozart could in fact have told Süssmayr how he intended to realize both of these passages, because they both allude to the 'Dies irae' theme. Might Mozart have 'explained' to Süssmayr how he himself intended to use the 'Dies irae' theme in the Sanctus and Agnus Dei—perhaps mentioning the timpani in particular? Such would have been consistent with Süssmayr's own account of the instruction he had from Mozart. Was there perhaps even a 'scrap of paper' on which Mozart had written down the metamorphosis of the beginning of the 'Dies irae', which Süssmayr wanted later to orientate himself by? Although, if there is a kernel of truth in Sophie Haibel's account, the possibility cannot be excluded that he could have relied on his memory alone.

Other evidence that Süssmayr had access to material drafted by Mozart has recently come to light from a completely separate direction: Alan Tyson has established that the Horn Concerto, K. 412, which Mozart started in 1791, was finished by Süssmayr on Good Friday, 6 April 1792.[28] To that extent, Constanze Mozart was seriously understating the case if she told Stadler that all she had given Süssmayr was 'a few scraps of paper with music on them', because they must have included the substantial fragment

[28] Tyson, *Mozart*, 246–61, esp. 253.

of the score of the Horn Concerto. There is reason to believe, moreover, that Süssmayr can have started work on the Horn Concerto only after he had finished the Requiem; at all events, the concerto demonstrates not only that Mozart left more than one unfinished work in draft score but also that here, too, Süssmayr did not always know what to do with his master's sketches. The Rondo-Finale which he composed contains a sudden and abrupt quotation of the Gregorian 'Lamentations' plainchant: this is the theme used by Michael Haydn in his C minor Requiem to set the words 'Te decet hymnus, Deus, in Sion'—for which Mozart, in his D minor Requiem, quotes from the Magnificat. Perhaps it was quite by chance that Mozart had in front of him a piece of paper on which he also sketched material for this horn concerto (or it may have been a horn part which he wrote out for Leutgeb, so that they could rehearse the work together) just when he had the idea of using the 'Lamentations' theme in the Requiem and wanted to write it down. Later Süssmayr found it there and incorporated it in the Rondo because he did not understand the circumstances of its being there.[29] Here too the conjecture is supported by the autograph score.

Posterity regards Mozart's Requiem from two angles at once: as a complete work, but one known to have been finished by someone else, and as a fragment nevertheless. It may help us to understand this 'schizophrenia' if we consider comparable instances in architectural history. We are not accustomed to listening to a piece of music in the way that we look at the unfinished west end of Strasbourg Cathedral with its one spire, asymmetrically placed and clearly intended to have a partner; on the other hand we do not think of Cologne Cathedral as a fragment, although it remained unfinished for centuries and its two spires were completed only in 1880. The latter, in particular, provides a parallel to the history of Mozart's Requiem, even if the time-scale is very different: when the west end of Cologne Cathedral was completed, it was done according to ancient plans, so that the building as it now is at least does not differ to any disconcerting extent from what was originally intended. The join between the 'original' and the 'completion' is much less easy to pinpoint in the case of the Requiem; given Süssmayr's position in the first months of 1792, we have to accept that the frontiers between what was composed by Mozart, what was done by Süssmayr on the basis of Mozartian material, and what was written new by Süssmayr are fluid. The mystery which grew up

---

[29] Wolff, *Mozart's Requiem*, 44–51.

around Mozart soon after his death suddenly created a new set of rules: in particular the pressure on Constanze Mozart to get the Requiem completed became increasingly misunderstood as appreciation of Mozart's complete *œuvre* grew; what the music of the Requiem did not make plain about its genesis, the increasingly taxed memories of the eyewitnesses had to supply as the years passed. Süssmayr told of how several composers refused to undertake to complete the work because they 'did not wish to hazard their own talent at the side of Mozart's'. Did he himself not consider the matter from that point of view—when he must have heard that they had given that excuse? In his coming to the rescue of Mozart and his widow at that juncture between Mozart's creative life and his posthumous reputation, there lies an explanation of the outsider's role which he has played for two centuries of fascination with Mozart's life and work.

Select Bibliography

Letters and Documents

Many of the extracts quoted in the present book are not included in the published English translations, and therefore all have been newly translated from the German editions listed below. Since these are ordered chronologically, no volume or page references have been given.

ANDERSON, EMILY (ed. and tr.), *The Letters of Mozart and his Family*, 3rd edn., rev. Stanley Sadie and Fiona Smart (London, 1985).

BAUER, WILHELM A., and DEUTSCH, OTTO ERICH (eds.), *Mozart: Briefe und Aufzeichnungen, Internationale Stiftung Mozarteum*, complete edn., annot. Joseph Heinz Eibl, 7 vols. (Kassel, 1962–75).

DEUTSCH, OTTO ERICH (ed.), *Mozart: Die Dokumente seines Lebens*, Neue Mozart-Ausgabe, X/34 (Kassel, 1961); Eng. edn., *Mozart: A Documentary Biography*, tr. Eric Blom, Peter Branscombe, Jeremy Noble (London, 1965).

EIBL, JOSEPH HEINZ, *Mozart: Die Dokumente seines Lebens: Addenda und Corrigenda*, Neue Mozart-Ausgabe, X/31, i (Kassel, 1978).

EISEN, CLIFF, *New Mozart Documents: A Supplement to O. E. Deutsch's Documentary Biography* (London, 1991).

ROSENTHAL, ALBI, and TYSON, ALAN (eds.), *Mozart's Thematic Catalogue (British Library, Stefan Zweig MS 63): A Facsimile* (London, 1990).

Reference Books

ANGERMÜLLER, RUDOLPH, and SCHNEIDER, OTTO, *Mozart-Bibliographie* ([i] Bis 1970 [= *Mozart-Jahrbuch* 1975], [ii] 1971–5, [iii] 1976–80, [iv] 1981–5, [v] 1986–91; Kassel, 1976–92)

EIBL, JOSEPH HEINZ, *Wolfgang Amadeus Mozart: Chronik eines Lebens*, 2nd edn. (Kassel and Munich, 1977).

HABERKAMP, GERTRAUT, *Die Erstdrucke der Werke von Wolfgang Amadeus Mozart*, 2 vols. (Tutzing, 1986).

KÖCHEL, LUDWIG RITTER VON, *Chronologisch-thematisches Verzeichnis sämtlicher Tonwerke Wolfgang Amadé Mozarts*, 6th edn., ed. Franz Giegling, Alexander Weinmann, Gerd Sievers (Wiesbaden, 1964).

LANDON, H. C. ROBBINS (ed.), *The Mozart Compendium: A Guide to Mozart's Life and Music* (London, 1990).

Books and Articles on Mozart's Life and Work

ABERT, HERMANN, *W. A. Mozart*, rev. and enl. 7th edn. of Otto Jahn, *Mozart*, 3 vols. (Leipzig, 1955–66).

ALLROGGEN, GERHARD, 'Mozarts erste Sinfonien', in J. Schläder and R. Quandt (eds.), *Festschrift Heinz Becker zum 60. Geburtstag* (Laaber, 1982), 392–404.

BAUMAN, THOMAS, *W. A. Mozart, Die Entführung aus dem Serail*, Cambridge Opera Handbooks (Cambridge, 1987).

BLOM, ERIC, *Mozart*, The Master Musicians (London, 1935; corr. repr. 1946).

BRANSCOMBE, PETER, *W. A. Mozart, Die Zauberflöte*, Cambridge Opera Handbooks (Cambridge, 1991).

BRAUNBEHRENS, VOLKMAR, *Mozart in Wien* (Munich and Vienna, 1986); Eng. edn., *Mozart in Vienna, 1781–1791*, tr. Timothy Bell (Oxford, 1989).

CARTER, TIM, *W. A. Mozart, Le nozze di Figaro*, Cambridge Opera Handbooks (Cambridge, 1987).

DENT, EDWARD J., *Mozart's Operas: A Critical Study*, 2nd edn. (London, 1947).

—— and ERICH VALENTIN, *Der früheste Mozart* (Munich, 1956).

EINSTEIN, ALFRED, *Mozart: His Character, his Work* (London, 1946).

FELLERER, KARL GUSTAV, *Die Kirchenmusik W. A. Mozarts* (Laaber, 1985).

HEARTZ, DANIEL, *Mozart's Operas*, ed., with contributing essays, by Thomas Bauman (Berkeley and Oxford, 1990).

KUNZE, STEFAN, *Mozarts Opern* (Stuttgart, 1984).

KÜSTER, KONRAD, *Formale Aspekte des ersten Allegros in Mozarts Konzerten* (Kassel, 1991).

LANDON, H. C. ROBBINS, *Mozart: The Golden Years, 1781–91* (London, 1989).

—— *1791: Mozart's Last Year* (London, 1988).

LÜHNING, HELGA, 'Zur Entstehungsgeschichte von Mozarts "Titus"', *Die Musikforschung*, 27 (1974), 300–18.

—— *Titus-Vertonungen im 18. Jahrhundert: Untersuchungen zur Tradition der opera seria von Hasse bis Mozart* (Laaber, 1983).

MAUNDER, RICHARD, *Mozart's Requiem: On Preparing a New Edition* (Oxford, 1988).

NIEMETSCHEK, FRANZ, *W. A. Mozart's Leben nach Originalquellen beschrieben*, fac. of the 1st edn. [Prague, 1798], ed. Ernst Rychnowsky (Prague, 1905); Eng. edn., *Life of Mozart*, tr. Helen Mautner (London, 1956).

NISSEN, GEORG NIKOLAUS, *Biographie W. A. Mozart's* (Leipzig, 1828; fac. repr. Hildesheim, 1972).

OSTHOFF, WOLFGANG, 'Die Opera buffa', in W. Arlt (ed.), *Gattungen der Musik in Einzeldarstellungen I: Gedenkschrift Leo Schrade* (Berne and Munich, 1973), 678–743.

PLATH, WOLFGANG, 'Beiträge zur Mozart-Autographie I: Die Handschrift Leopold Mozarts', *Mozart-Jahrbuch* 1960–1, 82–117.

——, 'Beiträge zur Mozart-Autographie II: Schriftchronologie 1770–1780', *Mozart-Jahrbuch* 1976–7, 131–73.

Rice, John A., *W. A. Mozart, La clemenza di Tito*, Cambridge Opera Handbooks (Cambridge, 1991).

Rosen, Charles, *The Classical Style: Haydn, Mozart, Beethoven* (New York, 1971).

Rushton, Julian, *W. A. Mozart, Don Giovanni*, Cambridge Opera Handbooks (Cambridge, 1981).

—— *W. A. Mozart, Idomeneo*, Cambridge Opera Handbooks (Cambridge, 1993).

Sadie, Stanley, *Mozart Symphonies* (London, 1986).

Schmid, Manfred Hermann, *Mozart und die Salzburger Tradition* (Tutzing, 1976).

Steptoe, Andrew, *The Mozart–Da Ponte Operas: The Cultural and Musical Background to 'Le nozze di Figaro', 'Don Giovanni', and 'Così fan tutte'* (Oxford, 1988).

Till, Nicholas, *Mozart and the Enlightenment: Truth, Virtue and Beauty in Mozart's Operas* (London, 1992).

Tyson, Alan, *Mozart: Studies of the Autograph Scores* (Cambridge, Mass., and London, 1987).

Wolff, Christoph, 'Creative Exuberance vs. Critical Choice: Thoughts on Mozart's Quartet Fragments', in C. Wolff (ed.), *The String Quartets of Haydn, Mozart and Beethoven: Studies of the Autograph Scores* (Cambridge, Mass., 1980), 191–210.

—— *Mozarts Requiem: Geschichte, Musik, Dokumente, Partitur des Fragments* (Kassel and Munich, 1991); Eng. edn., *Mozart's Requiem*, tr. Mary Whittall (Berkeley, 1994).

Wyzewa, Théodore de, and Georges de Saint-Foix, *Wolfgang Amédée Mozart: Sa vie musicale et son oeuvre*, 5 vols.: i/ii, 2nd edn. (Paris, 1936); iii–v (1936–46).

Zaslaw, Neal, *Mozart's Symphonies: Context, Performance Practice, Reception* (Oxford, 1989).

Index of Works by Mozart

General Index